FREE Test Taking Tips DVD Offer

To help us better serve you, we have developed a Test Taking Tips DVD that we would like to give you for FREE. **This DVD covers world-class test taking tips that you can use to be even more successful when you are taking your test.**

All that we ask is that you email us your feedback about your study guide. Please let us know what you thought about it – whether that is good, bad or indifferent.

To get your **FREE Test Taking Tips DVD**, email freedvd@studyguideteam.com with "FREE DVD" in the subject line and the following information in the body of the email:

  a. The title of your study guide.

  b. Your product rating on a scale of 1-5, with 5 being the highest rating.

  c. Your feedback about the study guide. What did you think of it?

  d. Your full name and shipping address to send your free DVD.

If you have any questions or concerns, please don't hesitate to contact us at freedvd@studyguideteam.com.

Thanks again!

TExES Core Subjects EC-6 291 Test Prep

TExES 291 Study Guide and Practice Test Questions
[2nd Edition]

TPB Publishing

Interested in buying more than 10 copies of our product? Contact us about bulk discounts:
bulkorders@studyguideteam.com

ISBN 13: 9781628458442
ISBN 10: 1628458445

Table of Contents

Quick Overview

As you draw closer to taking your exam, effective preparation becomes more and more important. Thankfully, you have this study guide to help you get ready. Use this guide to help keep your studying on track and refer to it often.

This study guide contains several key sections that will help you be successful on your exam. The guide contains tips for what you should do the night before and the day of the test. Also included are test-taking tips. Knowing the right information is not always enough. Many well-prepared test takers struggle with exams. These tips will help equip you to accurately read, assess, and answer test questions.

A large part of the guide is devoted to showing you what content to expect on the exam and to helping you better understand that content. In this guide are practice test questions so that you can see how well you have grasped the content. Then, answer explanations are provided so that you can understand why you missed certain questions.

Don't try to cram the night before you take your exam. This is not a wise strategy for a few reasons. First, your retention of the information will be low. Your time would be better used by reviewing information you already know rather than trying to learn a lot of new information. Second, you will likely become stressed as you try to gain a large amount of knowledge in a short amount of time. Third, you will be depriving yourself of sleep. So be sure to go to bed at a reasonable time the night before. Being well-rested helps you focus and remain calm.

Be sure to eat a substantial breakfast the morning of the exam. If you are taking the exam in the afternoon, be sure to have a good lunch as well. Being hungry is distracting and can make it difficult to focus. You have hopefully spent lots of time preparing for the exam. Don't let an empty stomach get in the way of success!

When travelling to the testing center, leave earlier than needed. That way, you have a buffer in case you experience any delays. This will help you remain calm and will keep you from missing your appointment time at the testing center.

Be sure to pace yourself during the exam. Don't try to rush through the exam. There is no need to risk performing poorly on the exam just so you can leave the testing center early. Allow yourself to use all of the allotted time if needed.

Remain positive while taking the exam even if you feel like you are performing poorly. Thinking about the content you should have mastered will not help you perform better on the exam.

Once the exam is complete, take some time to relax. Even if you feel that you need to take the exam again, you will be well served by some down time before you begin studying again. It's often easier to convince yourself to study if you know that it will come with a reward!

Test-Taking Strategies

1. Predicting the Answer

When you feel confident in your preparation for a multiple-choice test, try predicting the answer before reading the answer choices. This is especially useful on questions that test objective factual knowledge. By predicting the answer before reading the available choices, you eliminate the possibility that you will be distracted or led astray by an incorrect answer choice. You will feel more confident in your selection if you read the question, predict the answer, and then find your prediction among the answer choices. After using this strategy, be sure to still read all of the answer choices carefully and completely. If you feel unprepared, you should not attempt to predict the answers. This would be a waste of time and an opportunity for your mind to wander in the wrong direction.

2. Reading the Whole Question

Too often, test takers scan a multiple-choice question, recognize a few familiar words, and immediately jump to the answer choices. Test authors are aware of this common impatience, and they will sometimes prey upon it. For instance, a test author might subtly turn the question into a negative, or he or she might redirect the focus of the question right at the end. The only way to avoid falling into these traps is to read the entirety of the question carefully before reading the answer choices.

3. Looking for Wrong Answers

Long and complicated multiple-choice questions can be intimidating. One way to simplify a difficult multiple-choice question is to eliminate all of the answer choices that are clearly wrong. In most sets of answers, there will be at least one selection that can be dismissed right away. If the test is administered on paper, the test taker could draw a line through it to indicate that it may be ignored; otherwise, the test taker will have to perform this operation mentally or on scratch paper. In either case, once the obviously incorrect answers have been eliminated, the remaining choices may be considered. Sometimes identifying the clearly wrong answers will give the test taker some information about the correct answer. For instance, if one of the remaining answer choices is a direct opposite of one of the eliminated answer choices, it may well be the correct answer. The opposite of obviously wrong is obviously right! Of course, this is not always the case. Some answers are obviously incorrect simply because they are irrelevant to the question being asked. Still, identifying and eliminating some incorrect answer choices is a good way to simplify a multiple-choice question.

4. Don't Overanalyze

Anxious test takers often overanalyze questions. When you are nervous, your brain will often run wild, causing you to make associations and discover clues that don't actually exist. If you feel that this may be a problem for you, do whatever you can to slow down during the test. Try taking a deep breath or counting to ten. As you read and consider the question, restrict yourself to the particular words used by the author. Avoid thought tangents about what the author *really* meant, or what he or she was *trying* to say. The only things that matter on a multiple-choice test are the words that are actually in the question. You must avoid reading too much into a multiple-choice question, or supposing that the writer meant something other than what he or she wrote.

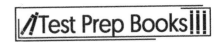

5. No Need for Panic

It is wise to learn as many strategies as possible before taking a multiple-choice test, but it is likely that you will come across a few questions for which you simply don't know the answer. In this situation, avoid panicking. Because most multiple-choice tests include dozens of questions, the relative value of a single wrong answer is small. As much as possible, you should compartmentalize each question on a multiple-choice test. In other words, you should not allow your feelings about one question to affect your success on the others. When you find a question that you either don't understand or don't know how to answer, just take a deep breath and do your best. Read the entire question slowly and carefully. Try rephrasing the question a couple of different ways. Then, read all of the answer choices carefully. After eliminating obviously wrong answers, make a selection and move on to the next question.

6. Confusing Answer Choices

When working on a difficult multiple-choice question, there may be a tendency to focus on the answer choices that are the easiest to understand. Many people, whether consciously or not, gravitate to the answer choices that require the least concentration, knowledge, and memory. This is a mistake. When you come across an answer choice that is confusing, you should give it extra attention. A question might be confusing because you do not know the subject matter to which it refers. If this is the case, don't eliminate the answer before you have affirmatively settled on another. When you come across an answer choice of this type, set it aside as you look at the remaining choices. If you can confidently assert that one of the other choices is correct, you can leave the confusing answer aside. Otherwise, you will need to take a moment to try to better understand the confusing answer choice. Rephrasing is one way to tease out the sense of a confusing answer choice.

7. Your First Instinct

Many people struggle with multiple-choice tests because they overthink the questions. If you have studied sufficiently for the test, you should be prepared to trust your first instinct once you have carefully and completely read the question and all of the answer choices. There is a great deal of research suggesting that the mind can come to the correct conclusion very quickly once it has obtained all of the relevant information. At times, it may seem to you as if your intuition is working faster even than your reasoning mind. This may in fact be true. The knowledge you obtain while studying may be retrieved from your subconscious before you have a chance to work out the associations that support it. Verify your instinct by working out the reasons that it should be trusted.

8. Key Words

Many test takers struggle with multiple-choice questions because they have poor reading comprehension skills. Quickly reading and understanding a multiple-choice question requires a mixture of skill and experience. To help with this, try jotting down a few key words and phrases on a piece of scrap paper. Doing this concentrates the process of reading and forces the mind to weigh the relative importance of the question's parts. In selecting words and phrases to write down, the test taker thinks about the question more deeply and carefully. This is especially true for multiple-choice questions that are preceded by a long prompt.

9. Subtle Negatives

One of the oldest tricks in the multiple-choice test writer's book is to subtly reverse the meaning of a question with a word like *not* or *except*. If you are not paying attention to each word in the question, you can easily be led astray by this trick. For instance, a common question format is, "Which of the following is...?" Obviously, if the question instead is, "Which of the following is not...?," then the answer will be quite different. Even worse, the test makers are aware of the potential for this mistake and will include one answer choice that would be correct if the question were not negated or reversed. A test taker who misses the reversal will find what he or she believes to be a correct answer and will be so confident that he or she will fail to reread the question and discover the original error. The only way to avoid this is to practice a wide variety of multiple-choice questions and to pay close attention to each and every word.

10. Reading Every Answer Choice

It may seem obvious, but you should always read every one of the answer choices! Too many test takers fall into the habit of scanning the question and assuming that they understand the question because they recognize a few key words. From there, they pick the first answer choice that answers the question they believe they have read. Test takers who read all of the answer choices might discover that one of the latter answer choices is actually *more* correct. Moreover, reading all of the answer choices can remind you of facts related to the question that can help you arrive at the correct answer. Sometimes, a misstatement or incorrect detail in one of the latter answer choices will trigger your memory of the subject and will enable you to find the right answer. Failing to read all of the answer choices is like not reading all of the items on a restaurant menu: you might miss out on the perfect choice.

11. Spot the Hedges

One of the keys to success on multiple-choice tests is paying close attention to every word. This is never truer than with words like almost, most, some, and sometimes. These words are called "hedges" because they indicate that a statement is not totally true or not true in every place and time. An absolute statement will contain no hedges, but in many subjects, the answers are not always straightforward or absolute. There are always exceptions to the rules in these subjects. For this reason, you should favor those multiple-choice questions that contain hedging language. The presence of qualifying words indicates that the author is taking special care with his or her words, which is certainly important when composing the right answer. After all, there are many ways to be wrong, but there is only one way to be right! For this reason, it is wise to avoid answers that are absolute when taking a multiple-choice test. An absolute answer is one that says things are either all one way or all another. They often include words like *every, always, best,* and *never.* If you are taking a multiple-choice test in a subject that doesn't lend itself to absolute answers, be on your guard if you see any of these words.

12. Long Answers

In many subject areas, the answers are not simple. As already mentioned, the right answer often requires hedges. Another common feature of the answers to a complex or subjective question are qualifying clauses, which are groups of words that subtly modify the meaning of the sentence. If the question or answer choice describes a rule to which there are exceptions or the subject matter is complicated, ambiguous, or confusing, the correct answer will require many words in order to be expressed clearly and accurately. In essence, you should not be deterred by answer choices that seem excessively long. Oftentimes, the author of the text will not be able to write the correct answer without

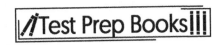

offering some qualifications and modifications. Your job is to read the answer choices thoroughly and completely and to select the one that most accurately and precisely answers the question.

13. Restating to Understand

Sometimes, a question on a multiple-choice test is difficult not because of what it asks but because of how it is written. If this is the case, restate the question or answer choice in different words. This process serves a couple of important purposes. First, it forces you to concentrate on the core of the question. In order to rephrase the question accurately, you have to understand it well. Rephrasing the question will concentrate your mind on the key words and ideas. Second, it will present the information to your mind in a fresh way. This process may trigger your memory and render some useful scrap of information picked up while studying.

14. True Statements

Sometimes an answer choice will be true in itself, but it does not answer the question. This is one of the main reasons why it is essential to read the question carefully and completely before proceeding to the answer choices. Too often, test takers skip ahead to the answer choices and look for true statements. Having found one of these, they are content to select it without reference to the question above. Obviously, this provides an easy way for test makers to play tricks. The savvy test taker will always read the entire question before turning to the answer choices. Then, having settled on a correct answer choice, he or she will refer to the original question and ensure that the selected answer is relevant. The mistake of choosing a correct-but-irrelevant answer choice is especially common on questions related to specific pieces of objective knowledge. A prepared test taker will have a wealth of factual knowledge at his or her disposal, and should not be careless in its application.

15. No Patterns

One of the more dangerous ideas that circulates about multiple-choice tests is that the correct answers tend to fall into patterns. These erroneous ideas range from a belief that B and C are the most common right answers, to the idea that an unprepared test-taker should answer "A-B-A-C-A-D-A-B-A." It cannot be emphasized enough that pattern-seeking of this type is exactly the WRONG way to approach a multiple-choice test. To begin with, it is highly unlikely that the test maker will plot the correct answers according to some predetermined pattern. The questions are scrambled and delivered in a random order. Furthermore, even if the test maker was following a pattern in the assignation of correct answers, there is no reason why the test taker would know which pattern he or she was using. Any attempt to discern a pattern in the answer choices is a waste of time and a distraction from the real work of taking the test. A test taker would be much better served by extra preparation before the test than by reliance on a pattern in the answers.

FREE DVD OFFER

Don't forget that doing well on your exam includes both understanding the test content and understanding how to use what you know to do well on the test. We offer a completely FREE Test Taking Tips DVD that covers world class test taking tips that you can use to be even more successful when you are taking your test.

All that we ask is that you email us your feedback about your study guide. To get your **FREE Test Taking Tips DVD**, email freedvd@studyguideteam.com with "FREE DVD" in the subject line and the following information in the body of the email:

- The title of your study guide.
- Your product rating on a scale of 1-5, with 5 being the highest rating.
- Your feedback about the study guide. What did you think of it?
- Your full name and shipping address to send your free DVD.

Introduction

Function of the Test

The Texas Examinations of Educator Standards (TExES) are a series of tests administered by the Educational Testing Service (ETS) and recognized by the Texas Education Agency (TEA). They measure the test taker's ability to meet the required educator standards necessary to obtain certification to teach in Texas public schools. The TExES Core Subjects EC-6 (test code 291) is specifically designed to evaluate the readiness of entry-level teachers in five core subject areas for grade school students up to grade six: English Language Arts and Reading (ELAR) & Science of Teaching Reading (STR); Mathematics; Social Studies; Science; and Fine Arts, Health, and Physical Education.

The exam is designed for first time teachers seeking initial certification in the state of Texas. Before registering for the test, prospective test takers should confer with their preparation program or prospective employer to determine whether this exam is appropriate for their certification needs.

According to the most recently reported statistics by ETS, almost 18,000 people took the TExES Core Subjects EC-6 Exam in 2015-16. Pass rates varied for each subject on the test; Fine Arts, Health, and Physical Education had the highest pass rate at 90%, while only 71% of test takers passed the Mathematics section.

Test Administration

Because this exam is designed for meeting Texas state certification standards, the majority of testing centers are located in Texas. However, testing centers can also be found throughout the United States and in Mexico and Puerto Rico. Refer to the TExES website for a full list of testing centers.

The TExES Core Subjects EC-6 tests are offered on a continuous basis throughout the year via a computer administered test (CAT) format. The complete test lasts for five hours and is offered in the morning and in the afternoon. For certification purposes, test takers must pass all five subjects; if they fail in any subject area, prospective educators can retake individual subject areas or the entire test after waiting a period of 45 days. Test takers have five attempts to pass the TExES Core Subjects EC-6 tests for certification; after the fifth attempt, any further scores will not be counted towards certification.

On the testing day, test takers will need to bring an admissions ticket (available via their ETS testing account) and two forms of photo ID. They are not permitted to bring any personal belongings or electronics to the testing area. However, testing accommodations are available for test takers with documented disabilities. Available accommodations include extended test time, access to food and beverages, and Braille format exams.

Test Format

The TExES Core Subjects EC-6 tests comprise five different areas of competency for incoming instructors. All exams take place on a computer and all question types are selected response (also referred to as multiple choice). The number of questions and time limits vary between subjects:

Test Name	Test Code	Number of Questions	Test Time
English Language Arts and Reading (ELAR) & Science of Teaching Reading (STR)	801	75	1 hour and 45 minutes
Mathematics	802	47	1 hour
Social Studies	803	41	35 minutes
Science	804	52	40 minutes
Fine Arts, Health, and Physical Education	805	52	40 minutes
TOTAL	**291**	**267**	**4 hours and 40 minutes**

The exam contents align with educator standards for the state of Texas, including both subject area content and pedagogical topics. A complete list of competencies covered in the exam can be found in the official TExES preparation manual.

Scoring

Each subject test is scored on a range of 100-300 with a minimum passing score of 240. An overall score for the combined TExES Core Subjects EC-6 tests is not reported because it is necessary to pass every individual subject test for certification purposes. Instead, overall test results are simply designated as "pass" or "not pass" depending on whether or not the test taker earned five scores at or over 240. Scores are available online through the test taker's ETS testing account 7 days after taking the exam.

Points are given for correct answers and no penalty is given for incorrect answers (in other words, there is no penalty for guessing on the exam).

Recent/Future Developments

The TExES Core Subjects EC-6 tests are the most up-to-date exams recognized by the TEA for certification. TExES exam policies were updated in 2015 to limit the number of exam attempts to five (including the first attempt and four retakes). For future test development purposes, additional questions may appear on the exam that do not count towards the test taker's score.

English Language Arts and Reading & the Science of Teaching Reading

Oral Language

Instructional Strategies for Oral Language, Listening and Speaking Skills, and Vocabularies

Oral Language

Oral or spoken language is also important when understanding a text. If proficient, a reader's speech will aid his or her ability to understand and comprehend words, sentences, paragraphs, and a variety of complex texts.

Listening Comprehension and Oral Language Activities

Oral language activities, such as purposeful read-alouds, allow students to focus on comprehension skills. Listening skills can promote and serve as a great foundation for comprehension skills. Understanding a text advances students' comprehension skills. When an instructor reads aloud, a student does not need to decode words for fluency. This allows students to listen and focus solely on the text for comprehension. Teacher read-alouds also provide students the opportunity to learn how to emphasize voice and tone while reading.

Building Oral Communication Skills

Oral language and presentation are also important in learning reading comprehension. Reviewing and identifying new and key vocabulary prior to reading the text helps students understand the text more efficiently. Once students are familiar with new vocabulary words, they will understand the paragraph with a new key word when approaching it, rather than reaching the word and skipping over the true meaning of the sentence or paragraph at large, or needing to stop and look up the word before continuing to read. This interrupts fluency as well as the understanding of text. Previewing text and skimming pictures for younger students, or reviewing bold subtitles for older students, can benefit students' comprehension by helping to gain an idea of what the text may be about before reading. There are different ways to find a text's purpose using auditory and speech skills, some of which include summarizing with a peer or paraphrasing the text.

When students are paired together or placed in small groups, they can share and discuss elements of texts. Literature circles are like book clubs. These circles allow students to speak freely, create their own discussions, and form questions about the text. Teachers can provide literature circle booklets, which may contain response or discussion questions to enhance conversation within the group.

Oral and Nonverbal Communication Skills in Various Settings

Early childhood educators are instrumental in developing effective communication skills in their students. Verbal and nonverbal communication skills are important in setting a positive, educational, supportive environment to optimize learning. They are equally important for students to master for use in their own daily lives. When communicating with others, students should be mindful to be fully attentive, make eye contact, and use encouraging facial expressions and body language to augment positive verbal feedback. Postures including hands on hips or crossed over the chest may appear standoffish, while smiling and nodding enhance the comfort and satisfaction of the other party. Active listening is the process of trying to understand the underlying meaning in someone else's words, which builds empathy and trust. Asking open-ended questions and repeating or rephrasing in a reflective or clarifying manner is a form of active listening that builds a positive, trusting relationship.

In tandem with different communication styles, educators and students alike should be aware of different learning styles. **Auditory learners** learn through hearing, so the educator can use verbal descriptions and instructions. **Visual learners** learn through observation, so the educator can use demonstrations, provide written and pictorial instructional content, and show videos. **Kinesthetic learners** learn through movement, involvement, and experience, so the educator can prepare lessons with hands-on learning, labs, or games with a physical component.

An important skill for children is the ability to communicate effectively with adults, and developing this comfort from a young age will be helpful throughout life. Educators can facilitate this through providing experiences where children need to talk to adults in the community. For example, educators may take the class on a field trip to the local community library, where students must ask the librarian for help locating certain health resources. Students might also prepare a health fair and invite parents, community members, and those from senior centers to come learn from posters, demonstrations, and presentations. Children can also work on developing communication skills using an array of technologies such as telephone, written word, email, and face-to-face communication.

Oral Language Structures

Oral language skills are important for students to have in order to thrive in an English-speaking environment. Beyond comprehending spoken English, understanding oral language structure helps students comprehend the context of what they are reading and how to respond appropriately. All languages utilize grammar, vocabulary, phonology, morphology, discourse, and pragmatics; these concepts combine to make words on a page actually form communication—the foundation of sentences.

As an instructor, it's important to be mindful of how comfortable the class is with oral language. Native speakers may be more proficient than those who are learning English as a second language; the latter may need more differentiated instruction to build their conceptual knowledge. No matter the range of student experiences, reading instructors should incorporate drills and lessons that frequently review oral language components throughout the course. This will ensure that core skills such as grammar and word formation remain fresh in students' minds as they continue to progress in reading proficiency. This can be done in a variety of ways and activities using both teacher-based and student-based grouping instruction.

Strategically, it's best to promote oral language by having students isolate and identify different aspects of sentences such as grammar and even vocabulary terms. Reviewing **phonology**, the sounds of English, and **morphology**, how words are formed, is also important. One way to review these aspects would be to present a sample of text and then have students deconstruct the sentences to identify these structures.

Discourse, which studies how language is used in communication, and **pragmatics**, which reflects the correct use of the language, can be reviewed through text examination and interactive activities. It's important to alter and differentiate instruction to review reading principles in different ways and expand critical-thinking skills. One method for reviewing discourse and pragmatics would be for the instructor to

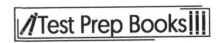

write or speak a sentence and then have the class discuss the discourse and pragmatics together. Students can also create the sentences themselves, demonstrating their ability to replicate correct language structure and recognize incorrect sentence components. When reviewing language structure, instructors should continue to assess how students are grasping the material and monitor progress. It's important to remember that reading improvements begin with a strong understanding of language fundamentals.

Learning of Standard American English by Speakers of Other Languages

Inevitably, all languages deviate from their standard format. In America, Standard American English has evolved into different forms (**dialects**) that are spoken across the country based on cultural influences and location. These dialects, while still considered English, are not Standard English. This is because some of the grammar, pronunciations, or general phonetics are inconsistent with the designated standard. Whether students are native English speakers or learning English as a second language, learning Standard English will give them a holistic understanding of American language conventions.

Students have likely encountered examples of American English deviation before, so the risk here is that they think slang or idiomatic choices reflect correct English usage. It's important to frequently review English language structure to ensure students know the proper pronunciations of words and how sentences fit together. However, this still doesn't eliminate confusion with hearing other English dialects; after all, these dialects are still English. One way to teach students Standard American English is to illustrate the difference between the standard and other dialects.

Citing specific examples of dialectic English that are incorrect from the standard is key. For example, Americans living in the South tend to use the word *y'all* to summarize the phrase *you all*. *Y'all* isn't recognized as part of Standard American English, so the correct version is *you all*. Distinctions such as this will help students visualize and hear proper English in use, which will help them recognize and use Standard English when reading and speaking.

In addition to reviewing proper word use and phonetics, training should also incorporate pronunciation. Writing and reading Standard English is very important, but students should also be knowledgeable of the incorrect and correct way to say the words they're reading. In addition to explaining pronunciation rules, instructors can periodically ask students to say and pronounce random words in a reading passage to test their skills. Again, showing students correct and incorrect pronunciations will build their familiarity with correct Standard English and help them distinguish wrong pronunciation tropes. Visualization activities and tools will also help. Flash cards with pronunciation guides for keywords are just one way to help students pronounce difficult vocabulary words.

Relationship Between Language Acquisition and Students with Disorders

The **Nativist theory of language development** holds that humans learn speech naturally as a result of inborn ability. According to the theory, children naturally have a language acquisition device that enables them to understand and eventually replicate the language. Children are naturally inclined to pick up language. However, this view can be seen as contrary to the **interactionist learning view**, which holds that children learn language as a result of their interaction with others. Therefore, the more children are exposed to language, the more they pick up vocabulary and can string together phrases. It's helpful and open-minded to consider that both ideas impact language learning.

An instructor can assess students to see if their issues are based on lack of instruction or erroneous exposure to language or if a student has a learning disorder that is inhibiting their ability to learn as fluidly as other students. There are several language-related disorders and delays that could be making reading difficult for students, so identifying these issues early is key.

Instructors must be patient and engaging to assess student performance and encourage them to not fear failure. Hearing how students respond to reading or actually speak will give indications of what issues are present. For example, students who face difficulties with written English by reversing words or letters and sometimes having trouble identifying rhyming words may have common **dyslexia**. Another common problem is difficulty recognizing letter sounds, which delays students' language progression. All of these issues may occur naturally, interrupting learning ability, but they can be treated through differentiated instruction.

The most effective way to remedy language issues is to identify specific areas of difficulties and provide supplemental instruction. This process is referred to as **articulation therapy**. The first step is isolation, to see if students can make key sounds or help them make the sounds needed for English. Instructors then work to improve the students' understanding of syllables, words, phrases, sentences, reading, and conversation. All of these areas build on each other. Improving English sound production will impact the understanding of syllables and words and therefore pave the way for reading and speaking proficiency.

Linguistic and Cultural Diversity

The classroom must be a place that emphasizes respect for all individuals as well as collaboration to achieve a successful learning environment. In addition to teaching reading skills, the instructor is expected to be a model of tolerance and inclusiveness for all students, thus encouraging them to be open-minded toward others. In the United States, it's likely that instructors will have students from a broad range of cultural and linguistic backgrounds. Obviously, these students must be made to feel welcome, and any linguistic difficulties they have should be treated as simply another step in the learning process, not a result of their background. Any difficulty is an opportunity for the whole class to learn and grow.

Encouraging polite and respectful behavior is key. An instructor doesn't necessarily need to explain polite behavior, but rather, should serve as a role model for the class. When addressing students' issues, the teacher should be sensitive to how they feel and be encouraging no matter their religious or ethnic background. It's also important to monitor how students act and respond to one another. Proper language and behavior should be enforced when necessary, and if there is ever anything rude or insensitive said or done, it must be addressed and corrected. Teachers should emphasize the idea that, while everyone is different, they are all equal. Therefore, students must be treated respectfully. Teachers should observe whether students are listening to other students and not being distracted or showing signs of disrespect. Tone and physical behavior must also be monitored; there's no excuse for rudeness. When disrespect occurs, steps should be taken to ensure it isn't repeated. It's important to remember that behaviors and lessons in early learners will inform how children grow and mature.

Reading and writing activities can also provide lessons in respect and collaboration. For instance, students can do group work on a text that discusses respectful behavior for reading practice, and also talk about the meaning of the written content. Other lessons can look at readings from different cultures to expand the students' appreciation and interest in diversity.

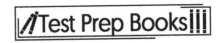

Phonological and Phonemic Awareness

Phonological Awareness vs. Phonemic Awareness

Phonological awareness is the recognition that oral language is made of smaller units, such as syllables and words. Phonemic awareness is a type of phonological awareness. Phonemic-aware students recognize specific units of spoken language called phonemes. Phonemes are unique and easily identifiable units of sound. Examples include /t/, /b/, /c/, etc. It is through phonemes that words are distinguished from one another.

Role of Phonological and Phonemic Awareness in Reading Development

Phonological and phonemic awareness do not require written language because phonemic awareness is based entirely upon speech. However, phonological and phonemic awareness are the prerequisites for literacy. Thus, experts recommend that all kindergarten students develop phonemic awareness as part of their reading preparation.

Once students are able to recognize phonemes of spoken language, phonics can be implemented in grades K-2. Phonics is the direct correspondence between and blending of letters and sounds. Unlike phonemic awareness, phonics requires the presence of print. Phonics often begins with the alphabetic principle, which teaches that letters or other characters represent sounds. Students must be able to identify letters, symbols, and individual sounds before they can blend multiple sounds into word parts and whole words. Thus, phoneme awareness and phonics predict outcomes in word consciousness, vocabulary, reading, and spelling development.

The Continuum of Research-Based, Systematic, Explicit Instruction

Instruction of phonological awareness includes detecting and identifying word boundaries, syllables, onset/rime, and rhyming words. Each of these skills is explained below.

- Word boundaries: Students must be able to identify how many letters are in a word and that spaces between words indicate where a word begins and ends.

- Syllables: A syllable is a unit of speech that contains a vowel sound. A syllable does not necessarily have to be surrounded by consonants. Therefore, every syllable has a rime. However, not every syllable has an onset.

- Onset: An onset is the beginning sound of any word. For example, /c/ is the onset in the word cat.

- Rime: The rime of a word is the sound that follows the word's onset. The /at/ is the rime in the word cat.

- Syllabification: Syllabification is the dividing of words into their component syllables. Syllabification should begin with single-syllable words and progress toward multi-syllable words.

- Rhyming words: Rhyming words are often almost identical except for their beginning letter(s). Therefore, rhyming is an effective strategy to implement during the analytic phase of phonics development.

Instruction of phonemic awareness includes recognizing, blending, segmenting, deleting, and substituting phonemes. These skills are explained below:

Phoneme Recognition

Phoneme recognition occurs when students recognize that words are made of separate sounds and they are able to distinguish the initial, middle, and final phonemes within words. Initial awareness of phonemes should be done in isolation and not within words. Then phoneme awareness can be achieved through shared readings that are supplemented with identification activities, such as the identification of rhyming words.

Blending

Sound blending is the ability to mix together two or more sounds or phonemes. For example, a consonant blend is a combination of two or more consonants into a single sound such as /ch/ or /sh/. Blending often begins when the teacher models the slow pronunciation of sound parts within a word. Students are to do likewise, with scaffolding provided by the teacher. Eventually, the pronunciation rate is increased, so that the full word is spoken as it would be in normal conversation.

Segmenting

Sound segmentation is the ability to identify the component phonemes in a word. Segmentation begins with simple, single-syllable words. For instance, a teacher might pronounce the word tub and see if students can identify the /t/, /u/, and /b/ sounds. The student must identify all three sounds in order for sound segmentation to be complete.

Deleting

Sound deletion is an oral activity in which one of the phonemes of a spoken word is removed. For example, a teacher may say a word aloud and then ask students to say the word without a specific sound (e.g., "What word would be formed if cat is said without the /c/ sound?"). With repetition, deletion activities can improve phoneme recognition.

Substituting

Like deletion, substitution takes place orally and is initiated through modeling. However, instead of deleting a phoneme or syllable, spoken words are manipulated via the substitution of phonemes for others (e.g., "What word would be formed if we change the /b/ in bun to /r/?").

Differentiating Instruction to Reach a Full Range of Learners

The following strategies can be used to develop phonological and phonemic awareness in students that struggle with reading, disabled learners, special-needs students, English language learners (ELLs), speakers of nonstandard English, and advanced learners:

- Differentiated instruction for struggling readers, disabled students, or students with special needs should include the re-teaching and/or emphasis of key skills, such as blending and segmenting. Such instruction should be supported through the employment of a variety of concrete examples that explain a concept or task. Teaching strategies of such concepts or tasks should utilize visual, kinesthetic, and tactile modalities, and ample practice time should be allotted.

- Instruction of phonological and phonemic awareness can also be differentiated for ELLs and speakers of nonstandard English. Most English phonemes are present in other languages.

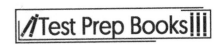

Therefore, teachers can capitalize on the transfer of relevant knowledge, skills, and phonemes from a student's primary language into the English language. In this way, extra attention and instructional emphasis can be applied toward phonemes and phoneme sequences that are nontransferable between the two languages.

- Advanced learners benefit from phonological and phonemic instruction with greater breadth and depth. Such instruction should occur at a faster pace and expand students' current skills.

Continual Assessment of Phonological and Phonemic Awareness Needs to Occur

Entry-level assessments, progress monitoring, and summative assessments need to be administered in order to determine students' phonological and phonemic awareness. Appropriate formal and informal assessments for such purposes include:

The Yopp-Singer Test of Phonemic Segmentation
This is an oral entry-level or summative assessment of phonemic awareness during which a teacher reads one of twenty-two words aloud at a time to a single student. The student is to break each word apart by stating the word's sounds in the order that the sounds are heard or said, and the teacher records the student's responses. Correctly segmented letter sounds are circled and incorrect responses are noted. If a student does well, then he or she is likely to do well in other phonemic areas. Upon poor student performance, the sound(s) with which a student struggles should be emphasized and/or retaught shortly after the time of the assessment.

After the Yopp-Singer Test, the blending of words, syllabification, and/or onset-rime identification should be assessed. The last set of phonological and phonemic skills to be assessed is composed of isolation, blending, deletion, and substitution.

Recognizing Rhyme Assessment
Word awareness, specifically awareness of onset-rime, can be assessed as a progress-monitoring activity. During this assessment, the teacher says two words. Students are to point their thumbs up if the words rhyme and down if the words do not rhyme. Immediate feedback and remediation are provided if the majority of the students respond incorrectly to a word pair.

Isolation or Matching Games
Games can be used to identify initial, medial, and final phonemes. During a phoneme-isolation activity, the teacher says one word at a time. The student is to tell the teacher the first, medial, or last sound of the word. During phoneme-matching activities, a teacher reads a group of words. The student is to say which two words from the group begin or end with the same sound. A similar activity can be completed to assess deletion and/or substitution (e.g., "What word would result if we replaced the /c/ of *cat* with an *h*?"). In this way, teachers can assess if remediation or extra instruction on initial, medial, or final phonemes is required, and lessons can be developed accordingly.

Phoneme Blending Assessment
In this assessment, a teacher says all the sounds within a word and a student listens to the teacher and is asked for the word that they hear when the sounds are put together quickly. This skill will be needed when students learn letter-sound pairs and decipher unknown words in their reading. Thus, mastery of this assessment can be used as an indicator to the teacher that the students are ready to learn higher-level phonological and/or phonemic tasks.

Please note that student results should be recorded, analyzed, and used to determine if students demonstrate mastery over the assessed skill and/or identify the needs of students. If mastery is not demonstrated, then the assessments should be used to determine exactly which letter-sound combinations or other phonemes need to be remediated. Any of the strategies earlier addressed (rhyming, blending, segmenting, deleting, substituting) can be used for such purposes.

Alphabetic Principle

Explicit, Research-Based Strategies for Print Awareness

Print awareness aids reading development, as it is the understanding that the printed word represents the ideas voiced in spoken language. Print awareness includes the understanding that:

- Words are made of letters; spaces appear between words and words make sentences.

- Print is organized in a particular way (e.g., read from left to right and top to bottom, read from front to back, etc.), so books must be tracked and held accordingly.

- There are different types of print for different purposes (magazines, billboards, essays, fiction, etc.).

Print awareness provides the foundation on which all other literacy skills are built. It is often the first stage of reading development. Without print awareness, a student is not likely to develop letter-sound correspondence, word reading skills, or reading comprehension skills. For this reason, a child's performance on tasks relevant to their print awareness is indicative of the child's future reading achievement.

The following strategies can be used to increase print awareness in students:

- *An adult reads aloud to students or during shared reading experiences.* In order to maximize print awareness within the student, the reader should point out the form, function, orientation, and sounds of letters and words.

- *Shared readings also build one-to-one correspondence.* One-to-one correspondence is the ability to match written letters or words to a spoken word when reading. This can be accomplished by pointing to words as they are read. This helps students make text-to-word connections. Pointing also aids directionality, or the ability to track the words that are being read.

- *Use the child's environment.* To reinforce print awareness, teachers can make a child aware of print in their environment, such as words on traffic signs. Teachers can reinforce this by labeling objects in the classroom.

- *Instruction of book organization can occur during read-alouds.* Students should be taught the proper orientation, tracking, and numbering conventions of books. For example, teachers can differentiate the title from the author's name on the front cover of a book.

- *Let students practice.* Allowing students to practice book-handling skills with wordless, predictable, or patterned text will help to instill print awareness.

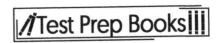

Strategies to Develop Letter Recognition

Among the skills that are used to determine reading readiness, letter identification is the strongest predictor. Letter recognition is the identification of each letter in the alphabet. Letter recognition does not include letter-sound correspondences; however, learning about and being able to recognize letters may increase student motivation to learn letter sounds. Also, the names of many letters are similar to their sounds, so letter recognition serves as a gateway for the letter-sound relationships that are needed for reading to occur. Similarly, the ability to differentiate between uppercase and lowercase letters is beneficial in determining where a sentence begins and ends.

To be fluent in letter identification, students should be able to identify letter names in and out of context with automaticity. In order to obtain such familiarity with the identification of letters, students need ample experience, acquaintance, and practice with letters. Explicit instruction in letter recognition, practice printing uppercase and lowercase letters of the alphabet, and consistent exposure to printed letters are essential in the instruction of letter recognition.

Research has revealed that the following sequencing guidelines are necessary to effectively promote letter naming and identification:

1. The initial stage includes visual discrimination of shapes and curved lines.

2. Once students are able to identify and discriminate shapes with ease, then letter formations can be introduced. During the introduction of letter shapes, two letters that share visual (p and q) or auditory (/a/ and /u/) similarities should never be presented in succinct order.

3. Next, uppercase letters are introduced. Uppercase letters are introduced before lowercase letters because they are easier to discriminate visually than lowercase letters. When letter formations are first presented to a student, their visual system analyzes the vertical, horizontal, and curved orientations of the letters. Therefore, teachers should use think-alouds when instructing how to write the shape of each letter. During think-alouds, teachers verbalize their own thought processes that occur when writing each part of a given letter. Students should be encouraged to do likewise when practicing printing the letters.

4. Once uppercase letters are mastered, lowercase letters can be introduced. High-frequency lowercase letters (a, e, t) are introduced prior to low-frequency lowercase letters (q, x, z).

5. Once the recognition of letters is mastered, students need ample time manipulating and utilizing the letters. This can be done through sorting, matching, comparing, and writing activities.

Using the Alphabetic Principle to Aid Reading Development

The alphabetic principle is the understanding of the names and sounds produced by letters, letter patterns, and symbols printed on a page. Through the alphabetic principle, students learn letter-sound correspondence, phonemic awareness, and the application of simple decoding skills such as the sounding out and blending of letter sounds. Since reading is essentially the blending together of multiple letter sounds, the alphabetic principle is crucial in reading development.

As with the instruction of letter recognition, research has revealed the following sequence to be effective in the teaching of the alphabetic principle:

- Letter-sound relationships need to be taught explicitly and in isolation. The rate at which new letter-sound correspondences can be presented will be unique to the student group. The order in which letters are presented should permit students to read words quickly. Therefore, letter-sound pairs that are used frequently should be presented before letter-sound pairs with lower utility. Similarly, it is suggested to first present consonant letter-sound pairs that can be pronounced in isolation without distortion (f, m, s, r). Instruction of letters that sound similar should not be presented in proximity.

- Once single-letter and sound combinations are mastered, consonant blends and clusters (br, ch, gr) can be presented.

How Writing Can Promote Letter Recognition and Alphabetic Principle

After the alphabetic principle and letter-sound combinations are mastered, students need daily opportunities to review and practice them. This can be done through the blending, reading, and writing of phonetically spelled words that are familiar in meaning. Daily journals or exit tickets are cognitive writing strategies used to help students practice and reflect on what they have learned. They can also help teachers assess what students have learned.

Developing Print Awareness, Letter Recognition, and the Alphabetic Principle

The following strategies to develop print awareness, letter recognition, and the alphabetic principle within students who struggle with reading, disabled and special-needs students, English Learners, speakers of nonstandard English, and advanced learners have been identified:

Streamlining the skills and concepts presented and reducing the pace of instruction is essential in the development of print awareness, letter recognition, and the alphabetic principle of struggling readers and students with disabilities or special needs. Assessments can be used to determine the letters and sounds with which each student struggles. These letters and sounds should be the focus of instruction. Key skills and concepts need to be supported with a variety of concrete examples and activities that utilize auditory, kinesthetic, and tactile modalities. Extended practice and re-teaching of concepts are beneficial.

When working with ELLs or speakers of nonstandard English, teachers should capitalize on the transfer of relevant print awareness, letter recognition, and alphabetic principle concepts from the students' primary languages to the English language. However, not all languages are alphabetic. Also, key features of alphabets vary, including letters, directionality, and phonetic regularity. Therefore, teachers may need to employ the direct and explicit strategies presented above with ELLs, regardless of age.

Instruction that occurs at a faster pace, with greater breadth and depth, will benefit the development of print awareness, letter recognition, and the alphabetic principle in advanced learners.

Continual Assessment of Print Awareness, Letter Recognition, and the Alphabetic Principle

Entry-level assessments, progress monitoring, and summative assessments need to be administered in order to determine student print awareness, letter recognition, and alphabetic principle knowledge to

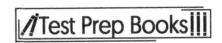

identify misconceptions that can be remediated in future lessons. Formal and informal assessment methods are as follows:

- Print awareness is easily assessed through observation. Teachers can give students a book and ask them to demonstrate their tracking and orientation knowledge. Similarly, teachers can ask students to identify parts of a book, such as its title or page numbers.

- The Concepts About Print (CAP) test assesses a student's print awareness. The CAP test is administered one-on-one, typically at the beginning and middle of a student's kindergarten year. During the CAP test, the teacher asks a student questions about a book's print. The teacher records the student's responses to the questions asked on a standardized rubric. This helps to identify specific areas of weakness for each student in terms of print awareness. These areas can then be reinforced and retaught in future lessons.

Planned Observations

"The Observation Survey" created by Marie Clay, can be beneficial in the assessment of a student's letter recognition and alphabetic principle knowledge. The Observation Survey includes six literacy tasks:

1. Letter Identification
2. Concepts About Print
3. Writing Vocabulary
4. Hearing and Recording Sounds in Words
5. Text Reading
6. Word Test

During such assessments, a student may be asked to identify a letter's name, its sound, rhyming pairs, isolated initial/final phonemes, blending of compound words/syllables, and word segments, or to add or delete phonemes in words. Similarly, teachers can say a letter and ask students to write that letter on a sheet of paper. The teacher records student responses. In this way, the teacher can identify the skills that have not yet been mastered by a single student, small group, or entire class. The teacher can then use any of the aforementioned strategies to reinforce those skills within individuals, small groups, or whole-class instruction.

Literacy Development

Foundations of Literacy and Reading Development and the Stages of Early Orthographic Development

Developing Language Literacy Skills

It is believed that literacy development is the most rapid between birth and 5 years of age. From birth until around 3 months, babies start to recognize the sounds of familiar voices. Between 3 months and 6 months, babies begin to study a speaker's mouth and listen much more closely to speech sounds. Between 9 months and 12 months, babies can generally recognize a growing number of commonly repeated words, can utter simple words, respond appropriately to simple requests, and begin to attempt to group sounds.

In the toddler years, children begin to rapidly strengthen their communication skills, connecting sounds to meanings and combining sounds to create coherent sentences. The opportunities for rich social interactions play a key role in this early literacy development and help children to understand cultural nuances, expected behavior, and effective communication skills. By age 3, most toddlers can understand many sentences and can begin to generalize by placing specific words into categories. In the preschool years, children begin to develop and strengthen their emergent literacy skills. It is at this stage that children will begin to sound out words, learn basic spelling patterns, especially with rhyming words, and start to develop their fine motor skills. Awareness of basic grammar also begins to emerge with oral attempts at past, present, and future verb tenses.

English Literacy Development
English language literacy can be categorized into four basic stages:

- Beginning
- Early Intermediate
- Intermediate
- Early Advanced

Beginning Literacy
This stage is commonly referred to as **receptive language development**. Educators can encourage this stage in literacy development by providing the student with many opportunities to interact on a social level with peers. Educators should also consider starting a personal dictionary, introducing word flashcards, and providing the student with opportunities to listen to a story read by another peer, or as a computer-based activity.

Early Intermediate Literacy
When a child begins to communicate to express a need or attempt to ask or respond to a question, the child is said to be at the early intermediate literacy stage. Educators should continue to build vocabulary knowledge and introduce activities that require the student to complete the endings of sentences, fill in the blanks, and describe the beginning or ending of familiar stories.

Intermediate Literacy
When a child begins to demonstrate comprehension of more complex vocabulary and abstract ideas, the child is advancing into the intermediate literacy stage. It is at this stage that children are able to challenge themselves to meet the classroom learning expectations and start to use their newly acquired literacy skills to read, write, listen, and speak. Educators may consider providing students with more advanced reading opportunities, such as partner-shared reading, silent reading, and choral reading.

Early Advanced Literacy
When a child is able to apply literacy skills to learn new information across many subjects, the child is progressing toward the early advanced literacy stage. The child can now tackle complex literacy tasks and confidently handle much more cognitively demanding material. To strengthen reading comprehension, educators should consider the introduction to word webs and semantic organizers. Book reports and class presentations, as well as continued opportunities to access a variety of reading material, will help to strengthen the child's newly acquired literacy skills.

Stages of Early Orthographic Development: Learning to Spell
Orthography is the representation of the sounds of a language by written or printed symbols. Learning to spell is a highly complex and cumulative process with each skill building on the previously mastered skill. This is considered **orthographic development**. It is imperative for educators to ensure that each skill is taught in sequential steps in order for children to develop spelling capabilities.

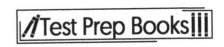

Emergent Spelling: Pre-Communicative Writing Stage

Children may be able to accurately identify various letters of the alphabet but will likely not be able to associate them to their corresponding sounds. Children may be able to string together letter-like forms or letters without a connection to specific **phonemes** (the smallest units of sound in a given language). Nearing the end of this phase, children progress from writing in all directions to writing in standard convention from left to right.

Letter Name-Alphabetic Stage

At this stage, children begin to understand unique letter-sound correspondence and can begin to differentiate between various consonant sounds. Children may even be able to connect two and three letters together in an attempt to spell a word, but the letters they use will generally only consist of consonants. Most show a clear preference for capital letters.

Within-Word Pattern Stage

With a strengthening ability to recognize and apply letter-sound correspondence, children in this spelling stage can use their understanding of phonics to attempt full words that incorporate vowels. With repeated and consistent exposure and practice, children start to focus on letter combinations, spelling patterns, consonant blends, and digraphs. In this stage, students are becoming aware of homophones and experiment with vowel sound combinations.

Syllables and Affixes Stage

Just as the name suggests, children at this stage are focused on syllables and combining them to form words. Children begin to develop a deeper understanding of the need for vowels to appear in each syllable, and words begin to readily resemble the proper conventions of English spelling to them.

Derivational Relations Stage

In this stage, students learn how spelling relates to meaning. Generalizations about spelling patterns and rules of spelling start to be more readily applied, which allows the child to attempt the spelling of unfamiliar words. Children begin learning about root words and consonant and vowel alterations. It is during this stage that children begin to accumulate a much greater vocabulary base.

Effective Teaching Strategies for Spelling

There are several effective strategies that educators can introduce to facilitate each developmental spelling stage. Strategies focused on alphabetic knowledge, including letter-sound games, are of primary importance in the beginning stages. As spelling skills strengthen, educators may choose to introduce word families, spelling patterns, and word structures. There is some controversy surrounding allowing children to use invented spelling in their writing. Research indicates that, provided there is spelling instruction taking place, allowing invented spelling supports growth in the areas of phonemic awareness, phonics, and general spelling skills.

Roles of Phonological Awareness, Phonics, and Word Recognition Skills in Literacy Development

It is imperative that educators understand the five basic components of reading education. If there is any deficit in any one of these following components, a child is likely to experience reading difficulty:

- Phonemic Awareness
- Phonics

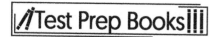

- Fluency
- Vocabulary
- Comprehension

Phonemic Awareness

A phoneme is the smallest unit of sound in a given language and is one aspect under the umbrella of skills associated with phonological awareness. A child demonstrates phonemic awareness when identifying rhymes, recognizing alliterations, and isolating specific sounds inside a word or a set of words. Children who demonstrate basic phonemic awareness will eventually also be able to independently and appropriately blend together a variety of phonemes.

Some classroom strategies to strengthen phonemic awareness may include:

- Introduction to nursery rhymes and word play
- Speech discrimination techniques to train the ear to hear more accurately
- Repeated instruction connecting sounds to letters and blending sounds
- Use of visual images coupled with corresponding sounds and words
- Teaching speech sounds through direct instruction
- Comparing known to unfamiliar words
- Practicing pronunciation of newly introduced letters, letter combinations, and words
- Practicing word decoding
- Differentiating similar sounding words

Phonological and Phonemic Awareness Instruction

Age-appropriate and developmentally appropriate instruction for phonological and phonemic awareness is key to helping children strengthen their reading and writing skills. Phonological and phonemic awareness, or PPA, instruction works to enhance correct speech, improve understanding and application of accurate letter-to-sound correspondence, and strengthen spelling skills. Since skill-building involving phonemes is not a natural process but needs to be taught, PPA instruction is especially important for children who have limited access and exposure to reading materials and who lack familial encouragement to read. Strategies that educators can implement include leading word and sound games, focusing on phoneme skill-building activities, and ensuring all activities focus on the fun, playful nature of words and sounds instead of rote memorization and drilling techniques.

Phonics

Phonics is the ability to apply letter-sound relationships and letter patterns in order to accurately pronounce written words. Children with strong phonics skills are able to recognize familiar written words with relative ease and quickly decipher or "decode" unfamiliar words. As one of the foundational skills for reading readiness, phonics essentially enables young readers to translate printed words into recognizable speech. If children lack proficiency in phonics, their ability to read fluently and to increase vocabulary will be limited, which consequently leads to reading comprehension difficulties.

Emergent readers benefit from explicit word decoding instruction that focuses on letter-sound relationships. This includes practicing sounding out words and identifying exceptions to the letter-sound relationships. A multi-sensory approach to word decoding instruction has also been found to be beneficial. By addressing a wide variety of learning styles and providing visual and hands-on instruction, educators help to bridge the gap between guided word decoding and it as an automatic process.

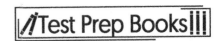

Role of Fluency in Supporting Comprehension

Fluency

When children are able to read fluently, they read with accuracy, a steady and consistent speed, and an appropriate expression. A fluent reader can seamlessly connect word recognition to comprehension, whether reading silently or aloud. In other words, reading fluency is an automatic recognition and accurate interpretation of text. Without the ability to read fluently, a child's reading comprehension will be limited. Each time a child has to interrupt his or her reading to decode an unfamiliar word, comprehension is impaired.

There are a number of factors that contribute to the success of reading fluency. It is important that students have many opportunities to read. Access to a variety of reading genres at appropriate reading levels and effective reading fluency instruction also play important roles in how successful children will become as fluent readers. The key is to have children repeat the same passage several times in order to become familiar with the words in the text and increase their overall speed and accuracy. Poems are an effective choice when teaching fluency, since they are usually concise and offer rhyming words in an entertaining, rhythmic pattern. Some other instructional strategies to consider include:

- Modeling reading fluency with expression
- Tape-assisted reading
- Echo reading
- Partner reading
- Small group and choral reading

Comprehension

Comprehension is defined as the level of understanding of content that a child demonstrates during and after the reading of a given text. Comprehension begins well before a child is able to read. Adults and educators can foster comprehension by reading aloud to children and helping them respond to the content and relate it to their prior knowledge. Throughout the reading process, the child asks and answers relevant questions confirming her or his comprehension and is able to successfully summarize the text upon completion.

Since reading comprehension encompasses several cognitive processes, including the awareness and understanding of phonemes, phonics, and the ability to construct meaning from text, educators should employ reading comprehension strategies prior to, during, and after reading. Reading comprehension is a lifelong process. As the genres of written text change and written language becomes more complex, it is essential that educators continually reinforce reading comprehension strategies throughout a student's educational career.

Some instructional strategies to consider are:

- Pre-teaching new vocabulary
- Monitoring for understanding
- Answering and generating questions
- Summarizing

Author's Purpose for Writing

When it comes to authors' writings, readers should always identify a position or stance. No matter how objective a piece may seem, assume the author has preconceived beliefs. Reduce the likelihood of accepting an invalid argument by looking for multiple articles on the topic, including those with varying opinions. If several opinions point in the same direction, and are backed by reputable peer-reviewed sources, it's more likely the author has a valid argument. Positions that run contrary to widely held beliefs and existing data should invite scrutiny. There are exceptions to the rule, so be a careful consumer of information.

Though themes, symbols, and motifs are buried deep within the text and can sometimes be difficult to infer, an author's purpose is usually obvious from the beginning. There are four purposes of writing: to inform, to persuade, to describe, and to entertain. Informative writings present facts in an accessible way. Persuasive writing appeals to emotions and logic to inspire the reader to adopt a specific stance. Be wary of this type of writing, as it often lacks objectivity. Descriptive writing is designed to paint a picture in the reader's mind, while writings that entertain are often narratives designed to engage and delight the reader.

The various writing styles are usually blended, with one purpose dominating the rest. For example, a persuasive piece might begin with a humorous tale to make readers more receptive to the persuasive message, or a recipe in a cookbook designed to inform might be preceded by an entertaining anecdote that makes the recipe more appealing.

Word Analysis and Identification Skills

Word Recognition Skills

As previously mentioned, instruction of phonological awareness includes detecting and identifying word boundaries, syllables, onset/rime, and rhyming words, and instruction of phonemic awareness includes recognizing, blending, segmenting, deleting, and substituting phonemes.

Phonics and Word Analysis

As mentioned, **phonics** is the study of sound-letter relationships in alphabetic writing systems, such as the English language, and it is paramount to a child's future ability to read and write. Phonics helps children recognize and identify letter symbols and translate these symbols into their corresponding sound units, phonemes. The study of phonics concerns itself with the **Alphabetic Principle**—the systematic relationships that exist between letters and sounds—as well as with **Phonemic Awareness**—the understanding that letters correspond with distinct sounds and that there are specific rules governing the placement of letters in the English language.

As children become more familiar with recognizing the names and shapes of each letter, called **graphemes**, they begin to verbally practice their corresponding sounds—the **phonemes**. Although this sounds straightforward, it can pose significant challenges to both the children and teachers.

For example, when children learn that the letter *y* is pronounced /wigh/, but that it can make other various sounds, including /ee/, /i/, and /igh/—depending on letter placement—it may take repeated practice in order for children to pronounce and read this one letter accurately. Some examples would be

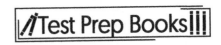

the words, *happy, gym,* and *cry.* Although each word contains the same vowel, *y,* the placement of the *y* in each word differs, which affects the letter's pronunciation.

For this reason, there is an ongoing debate in literacy circles regarding the appropriate instructional approach for teaching phonics. Should educators teach letter shapes with their corresponding names or letter shapes with their corresponding sound or sounds? Is it possible to combine instruction to include shapes, names, and sounds, or should each of these skills be taught in isolation with a cumulative approach—shape, sound/s, and name? Some experts believe that when children are introduced to letter names and shapes in isolation of their corresponding sounds, children can become quickly confused, which can delay reading acquisition. Therefore, the answer to what approach to take lies with a keen understanding of a student's background knowledge in English and each child's specific needs. In order to create effective phonics instruction and help students strengthen literacy development, it is strongly suggested that educators are sensitive and aware of these unique challenges to English language acquisition.

It is widely accepted that letter-sound relationships are best taught systematically, introducing one relationship at a time and gradually increasing in complexity. Effective instruction in the initial stages of phonics awareness involves explicit introduction of the most important and the most frequently used letter-sound relationships. For instance, short vowels should be introduced and practiced ahead of long vowels, and uppercase letters should be introduced ahead of lowercase as they occur the most often. Letters that frequently appear in simple words, such as /a/, /m/, and /t/ would be logical starting points.

The following guide offers an introduction of phonics instruction:

Introduction	Examples
Initial consonants	s, t, m, n, p
Short vowel and consonant	-it, -in, -at, -an
Consonant blends	-st, -bl, -dr
Digraphs	-th, -ph, -sh, -ch
Long vowels	ear, eat, oar, oat
Final (silent) e	site, mine, lane
Variant vowels and diphthongs	-au, -oo, -ow, -ou, -oi
Silent letters and inflectional endings	-kn, -gn, -wr, es, s

Effective phonics instruction begins with focusing on the overall literacy experiences of the students and connecting these experiences to further their literacy development. Best practices in teaching will work to establish a student's prior phonics knowledge, if there is any at all. Educators can differentiate their instruction based on their students' unique needs and background knowledge of phonics. Creating phonics activities that ensure students are actively engaged and motivated is key to overall success in literacy development.

Once children have mastered the relationship that exists between the names, shapes, sounds of letters, and letter combinations, educators may begin a more implicit instructional approach by incorporating the children's current phonics awareness with simple basal readers that focus on basic monosyllabic words. Grouping monosyllabic words according to their initial sounds continues to be an effective approach to instruction as the students advance in their understanding and application of phonics. When educators combine or further this practice with that of identifying the names of the initial letters in the words, children are likely to have more success with overall literacy development. A **word wall** with simple consonant-vowel-consonant words in alphabetical order acts as a visual reference to help strengthen a child's literacy development:

Word Wall

A	B	C
add	ball	car
age	bean	clean
ant	black	cub

At this stage, educators begin laying the foundation for reading readiness. Children begin listening to others read and start to recognize familiar sounds within the words being read. They independently practice sounding out words and will soon learn how to independently segment, blend, and manipulate the individual sounds in each newly acquired word.

When a child demonstrates phonological awareness and a clear understanding of how phonics works, they are ready to further their literacy development with **word analysis**. Word analysis is an effective study that helps students acquire new vocabulary. **Morphemes** are when words are broken down into their smallest units of meaning. Each morpheme within words carry specific meanings, therefore adding to children's understanding of entire words. When children begin to recognize key morphemes—especially prefixes and suffixes—they are beginning to demonstrate word analysis skills, which is a critical foundation in literacy development.

Word analysis helps children to read and comprehend complex reading materials, including informational texts. It is essential for vocabulary development. Word analysis skills also help children clarify the meaning of unknown words, figurative language, word relationships, and nuances in word meaning with the use of context clues.

Some effective instructional strategies to teach word analysis skills include Universal Design for Learning (UDL), studying words according to a subject theme, using diagrams and graphic organizers, and pre-teaching and reviewing new vocabulary on a regular basis. UDL involves the modeling of how to analyze new words by breaking them down into their individual morphemes and studying each morpheme separately. Once each morpheme in a given word has been identified and defined, students put the morphemes back together in order to understand the word in its entirety.

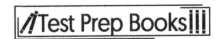

The following is a word analysis study of the word *astronaut*:

Word	Morpheme 1	Morpheme 2	Word Meaning
astronaut	astro—Greek origin, roughly translates to anything relating to the stars and outer space	naut—Greek origin, roughly translates to "sailor"	a sailor of outer space

Studying words according to a shared theme is another effective word analysis strategy. For instance, when studying mathematics, educators may focus on words that contain the same prefix, such as *kilometer*, *kilogram*, and *kilowatt*. Common suffixes in science include *microscope*, *telescope*, and *macroscope*.

Diagrams and graphic organizers provide students with visual clues to contrast and compare word meanings. From organizational charts and mind maps to Venn diagrams and more, visual aids help students readily see and analyze the similarities and differences in various word meanings.

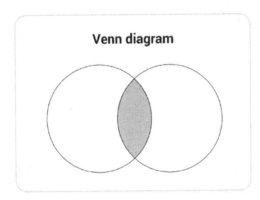

With the introduction to new topics of discussion or a new theme to any subject area, it is likely that there will also be an introduction to new, unfamiliar words. Both educators and students will benefit from a formal introduction to these new words prior to the lesson. Pre-teaching new vocabulary increases vocabulary acquisition and allows children to become comfortable and familiar with new terms ahead of the lesson. Pre-teaching new vocabulary has also been shown to reduce unnecessary stress and time that would otherwise be taken to stop lessons in order to explain unfamiliar words.

Letter-Sound Correspondences

When children begin to learn the various letter-sound correspondences, their phonemic awareness begins to overlap with their awareness of orthography and reading. One of the widely accepted strategies to employ when introducing children to letter-sound correspondences is to begin with those correspondences that occur the most frequently in simple English words. In an effort to help build confidence in young learners, educators are encouraged to introduce only a few letter-sound combinations at a time and provide ample opportunities for practice and review before introducing new combinations. Although there is no formally established order for the introduction of letter-sound correspondences, educators are encouraged to consider the following general guidelines, but they should also keep in mind the needs, experiences, and current literacy levels of the students. The following is intended as a general guide only:

1. a	6. n	11. g	16. l	21. x
2. m	7. c	12. h	17. e	22. v
3. t	8. d	13. i	18. r	23. y
4. p	9. u	14. f	19. w	24. z
5. o	10. s	15. b	20. k	25. j
				26. q

As a generally accepted rule, short vowels should be introduced ahead of long vowels, and uppercase letters should be mastered before the introduction of their lowercase counterparts.

Spelling conventions in the English language are primarily concerned with three areas: mechanics, usage, and sentence formation.

Distinguishing High-Frequency Sight Words from Decodable Words

Beginning readers enter primary school years with many challenges involving literacy development. Tackling the alphabetic principle and phonemic awareness helps children to recognize that specific sounds are usually comprised of specific letters, or a combination thereof, and that each letter or combination of letters carries a specific sound. However, these young readers are also faced with the challenge of sight word mastery. **Sight words** do not necessarily follow the alphabetic principle and appear quite often in primary reading material. Some sight words are decodable, but many are not, which requires the additional challenge of memorizing correct spelling. Some of these non-decodable sight words include words such as *who, the, he, does,* and so on. There are approximately one hundred sight words that appear throughout primary texts.

The goal for primary teachers is to help emergent readers to recognize these sight words automatically, in order to help strengthen reading fluency. One effective instructional approach is to provide children daily opportunities to practice sight words in meaningful contexts and to establish a clearly visible, large print word wall that children can freely access throughout the day. Dr. Edward William Dolch was a well-known and respected children's author and professor who, in the late 1940s, published a list of sight words he believed appeared most frequently in children's literature for grades kindergarten through second grade. Now known as the Dolch Word List, these sight words are still widely used in primary classrooms throughout the United States. Organized by grade and frequency, the Dolch Word List consists of 220 words in total, with the first one hundred known as the "Dolch 100 List." Dr. Edward Fry, a university professor, author, and expert in the field of reading, published another commonly used high-frequency word list approximately a decade later. Although similar in many ways to the Dolch List, the Fry Word List primarily focuses on sight words that appear most frequently in reading material for third to ninth grade. Other high-frequency word lists now exist, but the Dolch and Fry word lists are still widely used in today's elementary classrooms. The debate, however, is whether to teach high-frequency sight words in isolation or as part of the integrated phonics program.

Unlike many sight words, **decodable words** follow the rules of phonics and are spelled phonetically. They are spelled precisely the way they sound—as in words like *dad* and *sit*. When a child has mastered his or her phonics skills, these decodable words can also be easily mastered with continued opportunities to practice reading. Activities involving segmenting and blending decodable words also help to strengthen a child's decoding skills. Some educators will find that it is beneficial to integrate

lessons involving decodable words and high-frequency sight words, while others may see a need to keep these lessons separate until children have demonstrated mastery or near mastery of phonemic awareness. Some activities that encourage the memorization of sight words and strengthen decoding skills involve the use of flash cards, phonemic awareness games, air writing, and card games, such as *Bingo* and *Go Fish*.

Both Dolch and Fry word lists are organized according to frequency and grade level. It is widely accepted that educators follow a cumulative approach to reading instruction, introducing high-frequency sight words that are also phonetically decodable. Should words appear in the lesson that are not phonetically decodable, educators may wish to use this as an opportunity to evaluate the children's phonemic awareness skills and determine whether or not students are ready for lessons that integrate non-decodable sight words. For instance, an educator might challenge a student to study the parts of the non-decodable sight word by asking whether or not there are parts of the word that are phonetically decodable and parts that are not. This approach gives students the opportunity for guided word study and acts as a bridge between phonemic awareness skills and sight word memorization.

Determining what lists of words to introduce to students varies greatly and depends on an initial and ongoing spelling assessment of each child to determine his or her current spelling and reading levels. Effective instructional approaches also involve the intentional selection of words that demonstrate a specific spelling pattern, followed by multiple opportunities to read, spell, segment, and blend these word families. Students will benefit the greatest with ongoing formative and summative assessments of their decoding skills as well as their ability to apply their word knowledge to and memorize non-decodable sight words.

With the reinforcement of high-frequency word walls, daily opportunities to read, write, and engage in meaningful word games and activities, children will gradually begin to develop their reading and spelling skills and learn to become more fluent and capable readers.

Roots and Affixes

When students are invited to become word detectives, the study of root words and affixes is of prime importance. There are several instructional approaches to the study of root words and affixes, including a multi-sensory guided approach in which children can physically pull apart the affixes to be left with the root word and then manipulate the root word by playing with a variety of suffixes and prefixes. The following table begins with the original word containing both a prefix and suffix. The word is pulled apart into its individual components—root, prefix, and suffix. Then, it is given a new prefix and suffix to form a new word, carrying a completely new meaning:

Original Word	Root Word	Prefix	Suffix	New Prefix	New Suffix	New Word
inactive	act	in	ive	De	ate	deactivate
disbelieving	believe	dis	ing	Un	able	unbelievable
unbearable	bear	un	able	For	ing	forbearing

Effective instruction for root, prefix, and suffix study should involve the active exploration of words, with ample opportunity for children to read the words in meaningful context. Typically, a formal study of root words and affixes is introduced by the 4th grade, but it may be introduced earlier, depending on the students' understanding of basic phonics and spelling patterns. It is important for educators to keep in mind that new vocabulary terms, verb forms, plurals, and compound words may present a challenge for some students.

A formal study of root words, prefixes, and suffixes strengthens a child's knowledge of word meanings, expands vocabulary knowledge, and advances his or her understanding and application of various spelling patterns. Children will learn more about how affixes affect the spelling of the root word and can completely alter its meaning, which ultimately strengthens their ability to read, write, and spell accurately and effectively. As children become familiar with various affixes, they will begin to decipher the meaning of unfamiliar words that share the same affixes and roots.

Fluency Reading

Reading fluency has been traditionally defined as a student's ability to read accurately, quickly, and with appropriate expression. This definition only accounts for reading aloud, however, so it has been expanded to include silent reading. **Silent reading fluency** is the ability to read more than one word at a time without having to vocalize one's reading. If readers are able to derive the accurate meaning and message from a reading passage without involving too much labor of reading mechanics, they are said to be reading with fluency. Reading fluency is automatic, with less attention and effort spent on decoding, allowing the reader to concentrate fully on reading comprehension. When a reader reaches the fluency stage, reading becomes much more of an enjoyable activity.

Generally, fluent readers do not require the need to reread passages for understanding and have developed a fairly large inventory of sight-word vocabulary. Fluent readers are usually able to self-correct and employ a number of reading strategies. Signs that a child is having difficulty with reading fluency include reading slowly, focusing on only one word at a time, needing to reread the passage for understanding, and stopping often to decipher and decode unknown words. There are three main focus areas that relate to reading fluency: accuracy, rate, and prosody. When children read accurately with steady, consistent speed and appropriate expression, reading comprehension is likely to strengthen.

Areas of Fluency

Accuracy
Accuracy refers to the frequency of pronunciation errors a student might make when reading. When students make frequent pronunciation errors while reading, guess at the pronunciation of unknown words, or ignore words altogether, they are showing signs of **dysfluency**. Reading accurately requires the reader to read words correctly with minimal to no errors. When errors do occur, readers who read with accuracy are generally able to self-correct and continue reading without interrupting the flow of the reading.

Rate
Rate refers to a student's ability to recognize words automatically without having to spend any time on decoding them. This manifests in their ability to read texts at a steady and consistent rate. Both accurate reading and reading at a consistent rate greatly strengthen a reader's overall reading comprehension.

Prosody
Prosody refers to appropriate expression when reading—showing emotions, such as excitement, panic, or sorrow that accurately matches the intended emotions of the text. Readers may be able to read texts

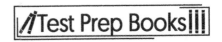

with accuracy and at a steady and consistent rate, but if they are unable to vocalize any expression in their reading or if the expression used does not match the intended expression of the text, their overall comprehension will be negatively affected. Readers who engage in an emotional or personal level with the text will experience greater reading comprehension and fluency.

Developing Fluency

In reading fluency, specific instructional strategies will help strengthen a student's ability to read text accurately, at a consistent rate, and with appropriate expression, and they will also help to strengthen reading comprehension. When students experience dysfluency in their reading, their overall comprehension will be negatively impacted. With an inability to make connections in their reading, children are unable to grasp the meaning in the text. When children are more focused on decoding individual words rather than on comprehending the text's message, much of their cognitive efforts are spent on deciphering the pronunciation of individual words, with little left to devote to comprehension of the text itself.

As children's reading fluency strengthens, they are able to interact on a much higher level with a variety of texts. It is important for educators to recognize that reading fluency acts as a bridge to reading comprehension and that time devoted to the individual components of reading fluency benefits a child's overall reading comprehension.

Reading Comprehension and Applications

Comprehension is defined as the level of understanding of content that a child demonstrates during and after the reading of a given text. Comprehension begins well before a child is able to read. Adults and educators can foster comprehension by reading aloud to children and helping them respond to the content and relate it to their prior knowledge. Throughout the reading process, the child asks and answers relevant questions confirming her or his comprehension and is able to successfully summarize the text upon completion.

Since reading comprehension encompasses several cognitive processes, including the awareness and understanding of phonemes, phonics, and the ability to construct meaning from text, educators should employ reading comprehension strategies prior to, during, and after reading. Reading comprehension is a lifelong process. As the genres of written text change and written language becomes more complex, it is essential that educators continually reinforce reading comprehension strategies throughout a student's educational career.

Some instructional strategies to consider are:

- Pre-teaching new vocabulary
- Monitoring for understanding
- Answering and generating questions
- Summarizing

How Word Analysis, Fluency, Vocabulary, and Academic Language Affect Comprehension

Word analysis is based on decoding words for fluency and then for meaning. Without word analysis, comprehension is extremely difficult to achieve. Vocabulary, word analysis, fluency and prior knowledge all support comprehension. Lack of fluent reading can impede a reader's ability to comprehend a piece of writing. In the primary grades, fluency and word recognition are taught first, followed by comprehension skills. A vast understanding of vocabulary is crucial to full comprehension. A reader who has a large, complex vocabulary will understand a text far more than one who lacks a vast vocabulary. Typically, the more students read over time, the more vocabulary they are able to understand using context clues; in turn, they obtain better comprehension skills and a deeper understanding of the text.

Oral or spoken language is also important when understanding a text. If proficient, a reader's speech will aid his or her ability to understand and comprehend words, sentences, paragraphs, and a variety of complex texts.

Characteristics of Specific Texts

Writing can be classified under four passage types: narrative, expository, descriptive (sometimes called technical), and persuasive. Though these types are not mutually exclusive, one form tends to dominate the rest. By recognizing the *type* of passage you're reading, you gain insight into *how* you should read. If you're reading a narrative, you can assume the author intends to entertain, which means you may skim the text without losing meaning. A technical document might require a close read, because skimming the passage might cause the reader to miss salient details.

1. **Narrative** writing, at its core, is the art of storytelling. For a narrative to exist, certain elements must be present. First, it must have characters While many characters are human, characters could be defined as anything that thinks, acts, and talks like a human. For example, many recent movies, such as *Lord of the Rings* and *The Chronicles of Narnia*, include animals, fantastical creatures, and even trees that behave like humans. Second, it must have a plot or sequence of events. Typically, those events follow a standard plot diagram, but recent trends start *in medias res* or in the middle (near the climax). In this instance, foreshadowing and flashbacks often fill in plot details. Finally, along with characters and a plot, there must also be conflict. Conflict is usually divided into two types: internal and external. Internal conflict indicates the character is in turmoil and is presented through the character's thoughts. External conflicts are visible. Types of external conflict include a person versus nature, another person, or society.

2. **Expository** writing is detached and to the point. Since expository writing is designed to instruct or inform, it usually involves directions and steps written in second person ("you" voice) and lacks any persuasive or narrative elements. Sequence words such as *first*, *second*, and *third*, or *in the first place*, *secondly*, and *lastly* are often given to add fluency and cohesion. Common examples of expository writing include instructor's lessons, cookbook recipes, and repair manuals.

3. Due to its empirical nature, **technical** writing is filled with steps, charts, graphs, data, and statistics. The goal of technical writing is to advance understanding in a field through the scientific method. Experts such as teachers, doctors, or mechanics use words unique to the profession in which they operate. These words, which often incorporate acronyms, are called *jargon*. Technical writing is a type of expository writing but is not meant to be understood by the general public. Instead, technical writers assume readers have received a formal education in a particular field of study and need no explanation as to what the jargon means. Imagine a doctor trying to understand a diagnostic reading for a car or a mechanic trying to interpret lab results. Only professionals with proper training will fully comprehend the text.

4. **Persuasive** writing is designed to change opinions and attitudes. The topic, stance, and arguments are found in the thesis, positioned near the end of the introduction. Later supporting paragraphs offer

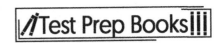

relevant quotations, paraphrases, and summaries from primary or secondary sources, which are then interpreted, analyzed, and evaluated. The goal of persuasive writers is not to stack quotes, but to develop original ideas by using sources as a starting point. Good persuasive writing makes powerful arguments with valid sources and thoughtful analysis. Poor persuasive writing is riddled with bias and logical fallacies. Sometimes logical and illogical arguments are sandwiched together in the same piece. Therefore, readers should display skepticism when reading persuasive arguments.

Main Idea and Supporting Details

Topic Versus the Main Idea

It is very important to know the difference between the topic and the main idea of the text. Even though these two are similar because they both present the central point of a text, they have distinctive differences. A **topic** is the subject of the text; it can usually be described in a one- to two-word phrase and appears in the simplest form. On the other hand, the **main idea** is more detailed and provides the author's central point of the text. It can be expressed through a complete sentence and is often found in the beginning, middle, or end of a paragraph. In most nonfiction books, the first sentence of the passage usually (but not always) states the main idea

Review the passage below to explore the topic versus the main idea:

Cheetahs

Cheetahs are one of the fastest mammals on the land, reaching up to 70 miles an hour over short distances. Even though cheetahs can run as fast as 70 miles an hour, they usually only have to run half that speed to catch up with their choice of prey. Cheetahs cannot maintain a fast pace over long periods of time because their bodies will overheat. After a chase, cheetahs need to rest for approximately 30 minutes prior to eating or returning to any other activity.

In the example above, the topic of the passage is "Cheetahs" simply because that is the subject of the text. The main idea of the text is "Cheetahs are one of the fastest mammals on the land but can only maintain a fast pace for shorter distances." While it covers the topic, it is more detailed and refers to the text in its entirety. The text continues to provide additional details called *supporting details,* which will be discussed in the next section.

Supporting Details

Supporting details help readers better develop and understand the main idea. **Supporting details** answer questions like *who, what, where, when, why,* and *how.* Different types of supporting details include examples, facts and statistics, anecdotes, and sensory details.

Persuasive and informative texts often use supporting details. In persuasive texts, authors attempt to make readers agree with their points of view, and supporting details are often used as "selling points." If authors make a statement, they need to support the statement with evidence in order to adequately persuade readers. Informative texts use supporting details such as examples and facts to inform readers. Review the previous "Cheetahs" passage to find examples of supporting details.

Cheetahs

Cheetahs are one of the fastest mammals on the land, reaching up to 70 miles an hour over short distances. Even though cheetahs can run as fast as 70 miles an hour, they

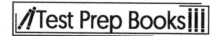

usually only have to run half that speed to catch up with their choice of prey. Cheetahs cannot maintain a fast pace over long periods of time because their bodies will overheat. After a chase, cheetahs need to rest for approximately 30 minutes prior to eating or returning to any other activity.

In the example, supporting details include:

- Cheetahs reach up to 70 miles per hour over short distances.
- They usually only have to run half that speed to catch up with their prey.
- Cheetahs will overheat if they exert a high speed over longer distances.
- Cheetahs need to rest for 30 minutes after a chase.

Look at the diagram below (applying the cheetah example) to help determine the hierarchy of topic, main idea, and supporting details.

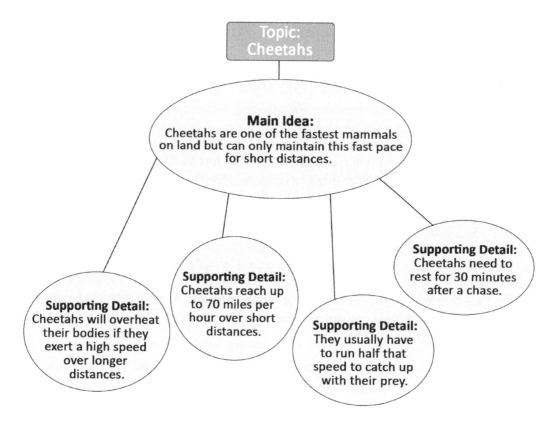

Point of View

Point of view is another important writing device to consider. In fiction writing, **point of view** refers to who tells the story or from whose perspective readers are observing as they read. In nonfiction writing, the **point of view** refers to whether the author refers to himself or herself, his or her readers, or chooses not to mention either.

Whether fiction or nonfiction, the author carefully considers the impact the perspective will have on the purpose and main point of the writing.

- **First-person** point of view: The story is told from the writer's perspective. In fiction, this would mean that the main character is also the narrator. First-person point of view is easily recognized by the use of personal pronouns such as *I, me, we, us, our, my*, and *myself*.

- **Third-person** point of view: In a more formal essay, this would be an appropriate perspective because the focus should be on the subject matter, not the writer or the reader. Third-person point of view is recognized by the use of the pronouns *he, she, they*, and *it*. In fiction writing, third person point of view has a few variations.

  o **Third-person limited** point of view refers to a story told by a narrator who has access to the thoughts and feelings of just one character.

  o In **third-person omniscient** point of view, the narrator has access to the thoughts and feelings of all the characters.

  o In **third-person objective** point of view, the narrator is like a fly on the wall and can see and hear what the characters do and say but does not have access to their thoughts and feelings.

- **Second-person** point of view: This point of view isn't commonly used in fiction or nonfiction writing because it directly addresses the reader using the pronouns *you, your*, and *yourself*. Second-person perspective is more appropriate in direct communication, such as business letters or emails.

Point of View	Pronouns used
First person	I, me, we, us, our, my, myself
Second person	You, your, yourself
Third person	He, she, it, they

Cause and Effect Relationships

When an author unfolds a cause and effect relationship within a given text, readers must work to uncover what has happened and why. Sometimes, the cause and effect relationships are melancholy, but they can also be positive. Before asking children to locate the cause and effect relationship within an informational text, it is first important to define the terms and then provide key examples with which the students can relate. For instance, a teacher might ask the children what happens after it rains. There will undoubtedly be a variety of responses, from *the ground becomes wet* to *the flowers grow*. From this simple exercise, educators can begin to model the relationship between the *cause*—why something happened—and the *effect*—what happened as a result.

Showing pictures, photographs, and other visual aids, and gradually encouraging children to use key graphic organizers will also help them solidify their understanding of cause and effect relationships. Teaching key vocabulary words that specifically relate to cause and effect are also effective instructional strategies. Educators should ensure that these vocabulary lists become incorporated into classroom word walls and personal dictionaries.

Moral Lessons and Themes

Topic, Main Idea, Supporting Details, and Themes

The **topic** of a text is the overall subject, and the **main idea** more specifically builds on that subject. Consider a paragraph that begins with the following: "The United States government is made of up three branches: executive, judicial, and legislative." If this sentence is divided into its essential components, there is the topic (United States Government) and the main idea (the three branches of government).

A main idea must be supported with details, which usually appear in the form of quotations, paraphrasing, or analysis. Authors should connect details and analysis to the main point. Readers should always be cautious when accepting the validity of an argument and look for logical fallacies, such as slippery slope, straw man, and begging the question. While arguments may seem sound, further analysis often reveals they are flawed. It's okay for a reader to disagree with an author.

It is important to remember that when most authors write, they want to make a point or send a message. This point or the message of a text is known as the **theme**. Authors may state themes explicitly, like in *Aesop's Fables*. More often, especially in modern literature, readers must infer the theme based on textual details. Usually after carefully reading and analyzing an entire text, the theme emerges. Typically, the longer the piece, the more numerous its themes, though often one theme dominates the rest, as evidenced by the author's purposeful revisiting of it throughout the passage.

Making Predictions

Predicting requires thinking ahead and, after reading, verifying whether predictions were correct. This method engages students with the text and gets them to pay attention to details that tell them whether their predictions might be coming true. The goal is to help students learn to base their predictions on clues from the text. They should not only state what they predict but also be able to comment on the specifics of the text that lead them to make those predictions.

Literal Reading Comprehension

The first level of reading comprehension is literal meaning. The word "literal" refers to an author's exact message or meaning. What is the author directly telling the reader? Literal comprehension is the direct meaning of the text, which may include setting, main idea, sequencing, elements of story, and cause/effect. Once word analysis is mastered, readers can begin to master literal reading comprehension. When a reader can decode, he or she can fluently read a text and understand its meaning. Readers use text evidence (facts, hints, and statistics, provided by the author to help support ideas or theories within texts) to further understand texts. When students identify text evidence, instructors are able to evaluate and assess whether students comprehend the questions being asked, and determine the students' ability to locate answers within a story. Citing evidence is extremely helpful during whole group discussions. Students can note the page, exact line, and paragraph where the answer was found. This literal understanding and response to questions helps struggling readers follow along, while aiding them in the learning process.

Inferential Reading Comprehension

The second level of reading comprehension is interpreting and forming the inferential meaning of texts. Inferential reading comprehension refers to "reading between the lines." "Reading between the lines" forces the reader to make generalizations from the text using text evidence. It is necessary for readers

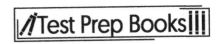

to have a complete understanding of the text in order to make inferences. A reader needs to understand the direct message, and then interpret the indirect meaning behind it. The response to questions may not be directly stated in the text; however, the answer must be figuratively inferred by perceiving the implied meaning. Inferencing may involve details from the story, sequencing, themes, drawing conclusions or making generalizations, and cause and effect relationships. As a reader's comprehension skills improve, his or her ability to form inferences also strengthens. Word analysis and direct literal comprehension must be mastered prior to young readers forming inferences; students may struggle to make inferences without prior mastery of these two skills.

Evaluating Reading Comprehension

The third level of reading comprehension is the ability to evaluate the text. Evaluating reading comprehension builds upon literal and inferential comprehension. Readers must be able to take the entire text and evaluate it for various criteria. A fluent reader may be able to recognize an author's bias once he or she forms and understands inferences. Bias is a personal opinion revealed throughout a text, based on comments or word choices. A reader must be able to evaluate unsupported assumptions, propaganda, and faulty reasoning in the text. Propaganda is meant to help or harm a particular group. An author's personal feeling(s) or bias may be decoded through small details and subtleties throughout the text. A reader should assess assumptions made by the author, and distinguish between fact and opinion. An author's opinions can lead to faulty reasoning. It is the reader's job to distinguish and separate the facts from the author's biases. Readers may also be asked to use evidence from the text to support their reaction to the text or towards characters. Evaluating themes is a difficult task and utilizes a reader's inferential understanding of a text to evaluate the overall purpose of the text. Use of language and the role of text structure and syntax play an important role in a reader's understanding of a text. The complexity of a text may impede a reader's understanding.

Reading to Learn

Text Structure

Depending on what the author is attempting to accomplish, certain formats or text structures work better than others. For example, a sequence structure might work for narration but not when identifying similarities and differences between dissimilar concepts. Similarly, a comparison-contrast structure is not useful for narration. It's the author's job to put the right information in the correct format.

Readers should be familiar with the five main literary structures:

1. **Sequence** structure (sometimes referred to as the order structure) is when the order of events proceeds in a predictable manner. In many cases, this means the text goes through the plot elements: exposition, rising action, climax, falling action, and resolution. Readers are introduced to characters, setting, and conflict in the exposition. In the rising action, there's an increase in tension and suspense. The climax is the height of tension and the point of no return. Tension decreases during the falling action. In the resolution, any conflicts presented in the exposition are solved, and the story concludes. An informative text that is structured sequentially will often go in order from one step to the next.

2. In the **problem-solution** structure, authors identify a potential problem and suggest a solution. This form of writing is usually divided into two paragraphs and can be found in informational texts.

For example, cell phone, cable, and satellite providers use this structure in manuals to help customers troubleshoot or identify problems with services or products.

3. When authors want to discuss similarities and differences between separate concepts, they arrange thoughts in a **comparison-contrast** paragraph structure. **Venn diagrams** are an effective graphic organizer for comparison-contrast structures because they feature two overlapping circles that can be used to organize and group similarities and differences. A comparison-contrast essay organizes one paragraph based on similarities and another based on differences. A comparison-contrast essay can also be arranged with the similarities and differences of individual traits addressed within individual paragraphs. Words such as *however*, *but*, and *nevertheless* help signal a contrast in ideas.

4. The **descriptive** writing structure is designed to appeal to one's senses. Much like an artist who constructs a painting, good descriptive writing builds an image in the reader's mind by appealing to the five senses: sight, hearing, taste, touch, and smell. However, overly descriptive writing can become tedious; sparse descriptions can make settings and characters seem flat. Good authors strike a balance by applying descriptions only to passages, characters, and settings that are integral to the plot.

5. Passages that use the **cause and effect** structure are simply asking *why* by demonstrating some type of connection between ideas. Words such as *if*, *since*, *because*, *then*, or *consequently* indicate relationship. By switching the order of a complex sentence, the writer can rearrange the emphasis on different clauses. Saying *If Sheryl is late, we'll miss the dance* is different from saying, *We'll miss the dance if Sheryl is late*. One emphasizes Sheryl's tardiness while the other emphasizes missing the dance. Paragraphs can also be arranged in a cause and effect format. Since the format—before and after—is sequential, it is useful when authors wish to discuss the impact of choices. Researchers often apply this paragraph structure to the scientific method.

Text Features

Text features are used to bring clarity or to affect the meaning of it. Sometimes a publication will follow a certain style guide/manual of style, which is a set of standards for how to write and format a publication. Some examples are APA, MLA, and the Chicago Manual of Style. If the publication is following one of those standards then the text features will be in accordance with that style guide.

Writers can come up with their own uses for text features based on what they feel is best. However, text features are generally used for a specific purpose. It's important to catch on to that purpose to maximize comprehension.

A clear layout is essential for good reader comprehension. Even with the use of many text features, the text needs to be laid out in a clear, consistent manner.

Bolding, Italics, and Underlining

Bolding, italics, and underlining are all used to make words stand out. **Bolded** words are often key concepts and can usually be found in summary statements at the end of chapters and in indexes. *Italics* can be used to identify words of another language or to add extra emphasis to a word or phrase. Writers will sometime place words in italics when the word is being referred to as the word itself. Quotation marks or italics can be used for this, as long as there is consistency. Italics are also used to represent a character's thoughts.

Entering Jessica's room, Jessica's mom stepped over a pile of laundry, a stack of magazines, and a pile of dishes. *My messy daughter*, she thought, shaking her head.

Text can be <u>underlined</u> for a number of reasons, but generally it's to indicate a key term or important point.

Color can also be a text feature, as different color text can be used to make certain parts stand out or to indicate that a new section is beginning. Even if something is in black & white, the text may be in different shades of grey.

Formatting
In addition, formatting—such as indentation or bullet points—helps to clearly present content. Content may also be left justified, centered, or right justified:

Left Justified

Centered

Right Justified

Text is often centered to stand out and catch the reader's eye.

Using Legends and Map Keys
Legends and map keys are placed on maps to identify what the symbols on the map represent. Generally, map symbols stand for things like railroads, national or state highways, and public parks. Legends and maps keys can generally be found in the bottom right corner of a map. They are necessary to avoid the needless repetition of the same information because of the large amounts of information condensed onto a map. In addition, there may be a compass rose that shows the directions of north, south, east, and west. Most maps are oriented such that the top of the map is north.

Maps also have scales, which are a type of legend or key that show relative distances between fixed points. If you were on a highway and nearly out of gas, a map's scale would help you determine if you could make it to the next town before running out of fuel.

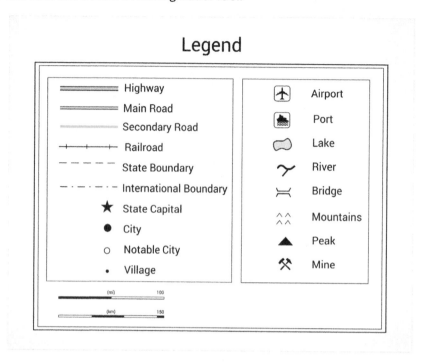

Analyzing Headings and Subheadings

Headings and subheadings are used in writing to organize discussions and allow the reader to find information quickly. Headings show a complete change in thought. Subheadings, which fall below headings, show different aspects of the same topic. For instance, if you saw the title *Government* and the heading *Forms of Government*, you might see the subheadings *Monarchy, Oligarchy, Democracy, Socialism,* and *Totalitarianism*.

Note the headings that got you to this point:

Reading

Key Ideas and Details

Using Text Features

Analyzing Headings and Subheadings

As well as providing organization and structure, headings and subheadings also put more white space on a page, which places less strain on the reader's eyes. It's a good idea to skim a document and get familiar with headings and subheadings. Write down the title, headings, and subheadings before you begin reading to provide structure to your notes and thoughts.

Instructional Strategies for Expository/Informational Texts

Structural Patterns of a Text

Teaching students text structure helps them to search for information when answering questions about the text. This again integrates reading and writing strategies when learning about comprehension. Text needs should be written in a logical way. Consistent and logical written thoughts aid in comprehension and help readers find information easier within the text, especially when trying to locate answers to comprehension questions. Students should recall that the broader meaning of text is located at the beginning of a story, and more specific details are provided throughout the text. Subtitles will help students locate information they are seeking.

Author's Point of View

It is important for readers to understand an author's purpose for writing a text. They need to identify the author's opinion in order to appropriately identify the facts that are being presented. Many standardized tests require students to identify an author's point of view and perspective and requires the use of inferential reading comprehension skills.

Generalizing the Knowledge Learned from Texts to Other Areas of Learning

Reading comprehension strategies are essential when studying other subject areas. Reading, writing, and language are built upon each other. In addition to these, social studies and the sciences are more complex disciplines that require basic knowledge of comprehension. Students who have mastered areas of reading, writing, and language will often perform better in other more difficult subject areas than those who have yet to obtain comprehension skills.

Identifying Similarities and Differences Between Texts

Oftentimes students need to compare and contrast different texts. As noted previously, Venn diagrams are a great way to compare and contrast texts. Venn diagrams allow students to relate information across a wide range of texts. This helps reading comprehension, as students need to utilize higher thinking skills and identify the relationships amongst more than one text.

Guided and Independent Reading

Independent reading strategies promote healthy reading for pleasure and enjoyment. Hopefully, these strategies promote a lifelong love of reading. Students should be given daily, independent reading time in the classroom. Teachers phrase this time as D.E.A.R. or "Drop Everything and Read" time. Typically, this time can be incorporated into a teacher's reading block. It is suggested that students have about 20 minutes of D.E.A.R. time daily. Students can read a book from home, the library, or one selected from the variety of books found within the classroom.

Teachers are required to have a classroom library. Some schools require a certain number of books or filled bookcases within a classroom. The library center should also contain more than just books. The classroom library should be an inviting environment for students. Small lamps make the area warmer—like home rather than school—and provide extra light for reading. Furniture—such as beanbag chairs, pillows, and small chairs—allow students to get comfortable, rather than reading at their desk. Not only is the environment important, but the reading center must also be an organized, designated space. If books are disorganized in the classroom library, students may be deterred from using the space appropriately, simply because they cannot find what they are looking for, or out of shear frustration. Organizing books by theme or genre helps students search for the books they desire. For students in younger grades, books should be grouped in plastic tubs using picture and word category labels like "animals" or "holidays." This organization method is especially helpful to those learning to read.

A listening center is also another helpful space in the classroom library. In the listening center, students listen to stories that are played through a sound device (like a CD or MP3 player) and follow along in the text. A teacher can switch the book out weekly to match a theme in the classroom, or can leave a "free choice bin" for students to choose what they would like to listen to. Again, listening to the story will encourage and emphasize reading strategies, such as voice and pacing.

Having a bookshelf with teacher or student text selections may encourage readers to select a good book quickly. Some students enjoy re-reading a book from a teacher read aloud; therefore, placing it in the "teacher pick" area may encourage developing readers to pick it up. Students also like to follow their classmates. Therefore, teachers should have a section where students can place a book that students can recommend to their friends. For older students, brief recommendation sheets can be filled out by the students. These sheets briefly list a few of a book's main themes so that potential readers can see if they are interested in reading the book. Reading from basal readers and school texts do not necessarily encourage reading for pleasure, as they are texts that are chosen by the school and instructor. For this reason, silent reading time is so important. Silent reading time gives students options and a chance to make their own choices. Students can choose the book and the appropriate reading pace when reading independently.

Generating Questions and Applying Knowledge to Text Topics

Questioning has immeasurable value in the reading process. Answering questions about a text gives purpose for reading to students and focuses them on reading to learn information. Similarly, generating questions about a text for others to answer enables a student to analyze what is important to learn in the text and glean summarizing skills. Keeping Bloom's Taxonomy in mind, teachers can scaffold students toward increased critical thinking capabilities.

Bloom's Taxonomy shows the hierarchy of learning progressing through the following stages:

- Remembering
- Understanding
- Applying
- Analyzing
- Evaluating
- Creating

Strategies that Facilitate Making Connections Across Multiple Texts

When analyzing two or more texts, there are several different aspects that need to be considered, particularly the styles (or the artful way in which the authors use diction to deliver a theme), points of view, and types of argument. In order to do so, one should compare and contrast the following elements between the texts:

- Style: narrative, persuasive, descriptive, informative, etc.
- Tone: sarcastic, angry, somber, humorous, etc.
- Sentence structure: simple (1 clause) compound (2 clauses), complex-compound (3 clauses)
- Punctuation choice: question marks, exclamation points, periods, dashes, etc.

- Point of view: first person, second person, third person
- Paragraph structure: long, short, both, differences between the two
- Organizational structure: compare/contrast, problem/solution, chronological, etc.

The following two passages concern the theme of death and are presented to demonstrate how to evaluate the above elements:

Passage I

Death occurs in several stages. The first stage is the pre-active stage, which occurs a few days to weeks before death, in which the desire to eat and drink decreases, and the person may feel restless, irritable, and anxious. The second stage is the active stage, where the skin begins to cool, breathing becomes difficult as the lungs become congested (known as the "death rattle"), and the person loses control of their bodily fluids.

Once death occurs, there are also two stages. The first is clinical death, when the heart stops pumping blood and breathing ceases. This stage lasts approximately 4-6 minutes, and during this time, it is possible for a victim to be resuscitated via CPR or a defibrillator. After 6 minutes however, the oxygen stores within the brain begin to deplete, and the victim enters biological death. This is the point of no return, as the cells of the brain and vital organs begin to die, a process that is irreversible.

Passage II

It was her sister Josephine who told her, in broken sentences; veiled hints that revealed in half concealing. Her husband's friend Richards was there, too, near her. It was he who had been in the newspaper office when intelligence of the railroad disaster was received, with Brently Mallard's name leading the list of "killed." He had only taken the time to assure himself of its truth by a second telegram, and had hastened to forestall any less careful, less tender friend in bearing the sad message.

She did not hear the story as many women have heard the same, with a paralyzed inability to accept its significance. She wept at once, with sudden, wild abandonment, in her sister's arms. When the storm of grief had spent itself she went away to her room alone. She would have no one follow her.

There stood, facing the open window, a comfortable, roomy armchair. Into this she sank, pressed down by a physical exhaustion that haunted her body and seemed to reach into her soul.

Excerpt from "The Story of an Hour" by Kate Chopin

Now, using the outline above, the similarities and differences between the two passages are considered:

1. **Style:** Passage I is an expository style, presenting purely factual evidence on death, completely devoid of emotion. Passage II is a narrative style, where the theme of death is presented to us by the reaction of the loved ones involved. This narrative style is full of emotional language and imagery.

2. **Tone:** Passage I has no emotionally-charged words of any kind, and seems to view death simply as a process that happens, neither welcoming nor fearing it. The tone in this passage, therefore, is neutral. Passage II does not have a neutral tone—it uses words like "disaster," "killed," "sad," "wept," "wild abandonment," and "physical exhaustion," implying an anxiety toward the theme of death.

3. **Sentence Structure:** Passage I contains many complex-compound sentences, which are used to accommodate lots of information. The structure of these sentences contributes to the overall informative nature of the selection. Passage II has several compound sentences and complex sentences on their own. It's also marked by the use of many commas in a single sentence, separating modifying words. Perhaps this variety is meant to match the sporadic emotion of the character's discovery of her husband's death.

4. **Punctuation Choice:** Passage I uses only commas and periods, which adds to the overall neutral tone of the selection. Passage II mostly uses commas and periods, and then one semicolon. Again, the excess of commas and semicolon in the first sentence may be said to mirror the character's anxiety.

5. **Point of View:** Passage I uses third-person point of view, as it avoids any first- or second-person pronouns. Passage II also uses third-person point of view, as the story is being told by a narrator about characters separate from the narrator.

6. **Paragraph Structure:** The first passage is told in an objective way, and each paragraph is focused on the topic brought up in the first sentence. The second passage has no specific topic per paragraph. It is organized in a sequential way, so the paragraphs flow into the next in a chronological order.

7. **Organizational Structure:** The structure of Passage I is told in a very objective, organized way. The first paragraph tells of the stages before death, and the second paragraph tells of the stages after death. The second passage is told in chronological order, as a sequence of events, like in a fictional story.

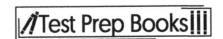

When analyzing the different structures, it may be helpful to make a table and use single words to compare and contrast the texts:

Elements	Passage I	Passage II
Style	Expository	Narrative
Tone	Neutral	Emotional
Sentence Structure	Long	Long/Sporadic
Punctuation Choice	.	. and ,
Point of View	Third	Third
Paragraph Structure	Focused	Sequential
Organizational Structure	Objective/Logical	Chronological

The main differences between the two selections are style, tone, and structure. Possibly the most noticeable difference is the style and tone, as one tone is more neutral, and the other tone is more emotional. This is due to the word choice used and how each passage treats the topic of death. These are only a handful of the endless possible interpretations the reader could make.

Summarizing and Paraphrasing

A summary is a shortened version of the original text, written by the reader in their own words. In order to effectively summarize a more complex text, it is necessary to fully understand the original source, and to highlight the major points covered. It may be helpful to outline the original text to get a big picture view of it, and to avoid getting bogged down in the minor details. For example, a summary wouldn't need to include a specific statistic from the original source unless it was the major focus of the piece. Also, it's important for readers to use their own words, but to retain the original meaning of the passage. The key to a good summary is to emphasize the main idea without changing the focus of the original information.

Paraphrasing calls for the reader to take a small part of the passage and list or describe its main points. Paraphrasing is more than rewording the original passage, though. Like summary, it should be written in the reader's own words, while still retaining the meaning of the original source. The main difference between summarizing and paraphrasing is the length of the original passage. A summary would be appropriate for a much larger piece, while paraphrase might focus on just a few lines of text. Effective paraphrasing will indicate an understanding of the original source, yet still help the reader expand on their interpretation. A paraphrase should neither add new information nor remove essential facts that will change the meaning of the source.

Facts and Opinions

It is important to distinguish between facts and opinions when reading a piece of writing. When an author presents **facts**, such as statistics or data, readers should be able to check those facts to verify that they are accurate. When authors share their own thoughts and feelings about a subject, they are expressing their **opinions**.

Authors often use words like *think, feel, believe,* or *in my opinion* when expressing an opinion, but these words won't always appear in an opinion piece, especially if it is formally written. An author's opinion may be backed up by facts, which gives it more credibility, but that opinion should not be taken as fact. A critical reader should be suspect of an author's opinion, especially if it is only supported by other opinions.

Fact	Opinion
There are nine innings in a game of baseball.	Baseball games run too long.
James Garfield was assassinated on July 2, 1881.	James Garfield was a good president.
McDonald's® has stores in 118 countries.	McDonald's® has the best hamburgers.

Critical readers examine the facts used to support an author's argument. They check the facts against other sources to be sure those facts are correct. They also check the validity of the sources used to be sure those sources are credible, academic, and/or peer-reviewed. When an author uses another person's opinion to support his or her argument, even if it is an expert's opinion, it is still only an opinion and should not be taken as fact. A strong argument uses valid, measurable facts to support ideas. Even then, the reader may disagree with the argument.

An authoritative argument may use the facts to sway the reader. In the example of global warming, many experts differ in their opinions of which alternative fuels can be used to aid in offsetting it. Because of this, a writer may choose to only use the information and experts' opinions that supports his or her viewpoint. For example, if the argument is that wind energy is the best solution, the author will use facts that support this idea. That same author may leave out relevant facts on solar energy. The way the author uses facts can influence the reader, so it's important to consider the facts being used, how those facts are being presented, and what information might be left out.

Authors can also demonstrate **bias** if they ignore an opposing viewpoint or present their side in an unbalanced way. A strong argument considers the opposition and finds a way to refute it. Critical readers should look for an unfair or one-sided presentation of the argument and be skeptical, as a bias may be present. Even if this bias is unintentional, if it exists in the writing, the reader should be wary of the validity of the argument.

Readers should also look for the use of stereotypes that refer to specific groups. **Stereotypes** are often negative connotations about a person or place and should always be avoided. When a critical reader finds stereotypes in a piece of writing, he or she should immediately be critical of the argument and consider the validity of anything the author presents. Stereotypes reveal a flaw in the writer's thinking and may suggest a lack of knowledge or understanding about the subject.

Counterarguments

If an author presents a differing opinion or a *counter-argument* in order to refute it, the reader should consider how and why this information is being presented. It is meant to strengthen the original argument and shouldn't be confused with the author's intended conclusion, but it should also be considered in the reader's final evaluation. On the contrary, sometimes authors will concede to an opposing argument by recognizing the validity the other side has to offer. A concession will allow

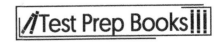

readers to see both sides of the argument in an unbiased light, thereby increasing the credibility of the author.

Authors can also reflect **bias** if they ignore an opposing viewpoint or present their side in an unbalanced way. A strong argument considers the opposition and finds a way to refute it. Critical readers should look for an unfair or one-sided presentation of the argument and be skeptical, as a bias may be present. Even if this bias is unintentional, if it exists in the writing, the reader should be wary of the validity of the argument.

Metacognitive Skills

Metacognitive strategies ask the student to decode text passages. In part, they require the student to preview text, be able to recognize unfamiliar words, then use context clues to define them for greater understanding. In addition, meta-cognitive strategies in the classroom employ skills such as being able to decode imagery, being able to predict, and being able to summarize. If a student can define unfamiliar vocabulary, make sense of an author's use of imagery, preview text prior to reading, predict outcomes during reading, and summarize the material, he or she is achieving effective reading comprehension. When approaching reading instruction, the teacher who encourages students to use phrases such as *I'm noticing*, *I'm thinking*, and *I'm wondering* is teaching a meta-cognitive type strategy.

Discovering Culture Through Reading

Regardless of culture, place, or time, certain themes are universal to the human condition. Because all humans experience certain feelings and engage in similar experiences—birth, death, marriage, friendship, finding meaning, etc.—certain themes span cultures. However, different cultures have different norms and general beliefs concerning these themes. For example, the theme of maturing and crossing from childhood to adulthood is a global theme; however, the literature from one culture might imply that this happens in someone's twenties, while another culture's literature might imply that it happens in the early teenage years.

It's important for the reader to be aware of these differences. Readers must avoid being **ethnocentric**, which means believing the aspects of one's own culture to be superior to those of other cultures.

Figurative Language

Figurative language is a specific style of speaking or writing that uses tools for a variety of effects. It entertains readers, ignites imagination, and promotes creativity. Instead of writing in realistic terms or literal terms, figurative language plays with words and prompts readers to infer the underlying meaning. There are seven types of figurative language:

Type	Definition	Example
Personification	Giving animate qualities to an inanimate object	The tree stood tall and still, staring up at the sky.
Simile	The comparison of two unlike things using connecting words	Your eyes are as blue as the ocean.
Metaphor	The comparison of two unlike things without the use of connecting words	She was in the twilight of her years.
Hyperbole	An over-exaggeration	I could eat a million of these cookies!
Alliteration	The patterned repetition of an initial consonant sound	The bunnies are bouncing in baskets.
Onomatopoeia	Words that are formed by using the very sound associated with the word itself	"Drip, drip, drip" went the kitchen faucet.
Idioms	Common sayings that carry a lesson or meaning that must be inferred	That math work was a piece of cake!

Interpretation

Since idioms and hyperboles are commonly used in everyday speech, educators may wish to introduce them early.

I'm so tired that I could sleep forever!—Hyperbole

He's not playing with a full deck!—Idiom

Other forms of figurative language can be found in poetry and in children's stories. As educators come across figurative speech, they can prompt children's critical thinking skills by asking what they think the author meant by those words or that particular sentence. Giving concrete examples of each style and challenging children to attempt writing their very own creative sentences will strengthen their understanding and application of figurative language.

Literary Genres

Fictional Prose

Fiction written in prose can be further broken down into **fiction genres**—types of fiction. Some of the more common genres of fiction are as follows:

- **Classical fiction**: a work of fiction considered timeless in its message or theme, remaining noteworthy and meaningful over decades or centuries—e.g., Charlotte Brontë's *Jane Eyre*, Mark Twain's *Adventures of Huckleberry Finn*

- **Fables**: short fiction that generally features animals, fantastic creatures, or other forces within nature that assume human-like characters and has a moral lesson for the reader—e.g., *Aesop's Fables*

- **Fairy tales**: children's stories with magical characters in imaginary, enchanted lands, usually depicting a struggle between good and evil, a sub-genre of folklore—e.g., Hans Christian Anderson's *The Little Mermaid*, *Cinderella* by the Brothers Grimm

- **Fantasy**: fiction with magic or supernatural elements that cannot occur in the real world, sometimes involving medieval elements in language, usually includes some form of sorcery or witchcraft and sometimes set on a different world—e.g., J.R.R. Tolkien's *The Hobbit*, J.K. Rowling's *Harry Potter and the Sorcerer's Stone*, George R.R. Martin's *A Game of Thrones*

- **Folklore**: types of fiction passed down from oral tradition, stories indigenous to a particular region or culture, with a local flavor in tone, designed to help humans cope with their condition in life and validate cultural traditions, beliefs, and customs—e.g., William Laughead's *Paul Bunyan and The Blue Ox*, the Buddhist story of "The Banyan Deer"

- **Mythology**: closely related to folklore but more widespread, features mystical, otherworldly characters and addresses the basic question of why and how humans exist, relies heavily on allegory and features gods or heroes captured in some sort of struggle—e.g., Greek myths, Genesis I and II in the Bible, Arthurian legends

- **Science fiction**: fiction that uses the principle of extrapolation—loosely defined as a form of prediction—to imagine future realities and problems of the human experience—e.g., Robert Heinlein's *Stranger in a Strange Land*, Ayn Rand's *Anthem*, Isaac Asimov's *I, Robot*, Philip K. Dick's *Do Androids Dream of Electric Sheep?*

- **Short stories**: short works of prose fiction with fully-developed themes and characters, focused on mood, generally developed with a single plot, with a short period of time for settings—e.g., Edgar Allan Poe's "Fall of the House of Usher," Shirley Jackson's "The Lottery," Isaac Bashevis Singer's "Gimpel the Fool"

Drama

Drama refers to a form of literature written for the purpose of performance for an audience. Like prose fiction, drama has several genres. The following are the most common ones:

- **Comedy**: a humorous play designed to amuse and entertain, often with an emphasis on the common person's experience, generally resolved in a positive way—e.g., Richard Sheridan's *School for Scandal*, Shakespeare's *Taming of the Shrew*, Neil Simon's *The Odd Couple*

- **History**: a play based on recorded history where the fate of a nation or kingdom is at the core of the conflict—e.g., Christopher Marlowe's *Edward II*, Shakespeare's *King Richard III*, Arthur Miller's *The Crucible*

- **Tragedy**: a serious play that often involves the downfall of the protagonist. In modern tragedies, the protagonist is not necessarily in a position of power or authority—e.g., Jean Racine's *Phèdre*, Arthur Miller's *Death of a Salesman*, John Steinbeck's *Of Mice and Men*

- **Melodrama**: a play that emphasizes heightened emotion and sensationalism, generally with stereotypical characters in exaggerated or realistic situations and with moral polarization—e.g., Jean-Jacques Rousseau's *Pygmalion*

- **Tragi-comedy**: a play that has elements of both tragedy—a character experiencing a tragic loss—and comedy—the resolution is often positive with no clear distinctive mood for either—e.g., Shakespeare's *The Merchant of Venice*, Anton Chekhov's *The Cherry Orchard*

Poetry

The genre of **poetry** refers to literary works that focus on the expression of feelings and ideas through the use of structure and linguistic rhythm to create a desired effect.

Different poetic structures and devices are used to create the various major forms of poetry. Some of the most common forms are discussed in the following chart.

Type	Poetic Structure	Example
Ballad	A poem or song passed down orally which tells a story and in English tradition usually uses an ABAB or ABCB rhyme scheme	William Butler Yeats' "The Ballad of Father O'Hart"
Epic	A long poem from ancient oral tradition which narrates the story of a legendary or heroic protagonist	Homer's *The Odyssey* Virgil's *The Aeneid*
Haiku	A Japanese poem of three unrhymed lines with five, seven, and five syllables (in English) with nature as a common subject matter	Matsuo Bashō "An old silent pond . . . A frog jumps into the pond, splash! Silence again."
Limerick	A five-line poem written in an AABBA rhyme scheme, with a witty focus	From Edward Lear's *Book of Nonsense*: "There was a Young Person of Smyrna Whose grandmother threatened to burn her . . ."
Ode	A formal lyric poem that addresses and praises a person, place, thing, or idea	Edna St. Vincent Millay's "Ode to Silence"
Sonnet	A fourteen-line poem written in iambic pentameter	Shakespeare's Sonnets 18 and 130

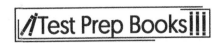

Literary Nonfiction

Nonfiction works are best characterized by their subject matter, which must be factual and real, describing true life experiences. There are several common types of literary non-fiction.

Biography

A **biography** is a work written about a real person (historical or currently living). It involves factual accounts of the person's life, often in a re-telling of those events based on available, researched factual information. The re-telling and dialogue, especially if related within quotes, must be accurate and reflect reliable sources. A biography reflects the time and place in which the person lived, with the goal of creating an understanding of the person and his/her human experience. Examples of well-known biographies include *The Life of Samuel Johnson* by James Boswell and *Steve Jobs* by Walter Isaacson.

Autobiography

An **autobiography** is a factual account of a person's life written by that person. It may contain some or all of the same elements as a biography, but the author is the subject matter. An autobiography will be told in first person narrative. Examples of well-known autobiographies in literature include *Night* by Elie Wiesel and *Margaret Thatcher: The Autobiography* by Margaret Thatcher.

Memoir

A **memoir** is a historical account of a person's life and experiences written by one who has personal, intimate knowledge of the information. The line between memoir, autobiography, and biography is often muddled, but generally speaking, a memoir covers a specific timeline of events as opposed to the other forms of nonfiction. A memoir is less all-encompassing. It is also less formal in tone and tends to focus on the emotional aspect of the presented timeline of events. Some examples of memoirs in literature include *Angela's Ashes* by Frank McCourt and *All Creatures Great and Small* by James Herriot.

Journalism

Some forms of **journalism** can fall into the category of literary non-fiction—e.g., travel writing, nature writing, sports writing, the interview, and sometimes, the essay. Some examples include Elizabeth Kolbert's "The Lost World, in the Annals of Extinction series for *The New Yorker* and Gary Smith's "Ali and His Entourage" for ***Sports Illustrated***.

Vocabulary Development

Basic Components of Vocabulary

Vocabulary

Vocabulary consists of the bank of words that children can understand and apply fluently in order to communicate effectively. A strong vocabulary and word recognition base enables children to access prior knowledge and experiences in order to make connections in written texts. A strong vocabulary also allows children to express ideas, learn new concepts, and decode the meanings of unfamiliar words by using context clues. Conversely, if a child's vocabulary knowledge is limited and does not steadily increase, reading comprehension will be negatively affected. If children become frustrated with their lack of understanding of written texts, they will likely choose to only read texts at their comfort level or refuse to read altogether. With direct instruction, educators introduce specific words to pre-teach before reading, or examine word roots, prefixes, and suffixes. Through indirect instruction, educators ensure that students are regularly exposed to new words. This engages students in high-quality conversations and social interactions and provides access to a wide variety of challenging and enjoyable reading material.

Morphology

The study of **morphology** generally deals with the structure and formation of words. A **phoneme** is the smallest unit of sound that does not necessarily carry meaning. Essentially, phonemes are combined to form words, and words are combined to form sentences. Morphology looks at the smallest meaningful part of a word, known as a **morpheme**. In contrast to a phoneme, a morpheme must carry a sound and a meaning. Free morphemes are those that can stand alone, carrying both sound and meaning, as in the following words: *girl, boy, man,* and *lady.* Just as the name suggests, bound morphemes are bound to other morphemes in order to carry meaning. Examples of bound morphemes include: *ish, ness, ly,* and *dis.*

Semantics

Semantics is the branch of linguistics that addresses meanings. Morphemes, words, phrases, and sentences all carry distinct meanings. The way these individual parts are arranged can have a significant effect on meaning. In order to construct language, children must be able to use semantics to arrange and rearrange words to achieve the particular meaning they are striving for. Activities that teach semantics revolve around teaching the arrangement of word parts (morphology) and root words, and then the teaching of vocabulary. Moving from vocabulary words into studying sentences and sentence structure leads children to learn how to use context clues to determine meaning and to understand anomalies such as metaphors, idioms, and allusions. There are five types of semantic relationships that are critical to understand:

- **Hyponyms** refer to a relationship between words where general words have multiple more-specific words (hyponyms) that fall into the same category (e.g., horse: mare, stallion, foal, Appaloosa, Clydesdale).

- **Meronyms** refer to a relationship between words where a whole word has multiple parts (meronyms) that comprise it (e.g., horse: tail, mane, hooves, ears).

- **Synonyms** refer to words that have the same meaning as another word (e.g., instructor/teacher/educator, canine/dog, feline/cat, herbivore/vegetarian).

- **Antonyms** refer to words that have the opposite meaning as another word (e.g., true/false, up/down, in/out, right/wrong).

- **Homonyms** refer to words that are spelled the same (homographs) or sound the same (homophones) but mean different things (e.g., there/their/they're, two/too/to, principal/principle, plain/plane, (kitchen) sink/ sink (down as in water)).

Syntax

With its origins from the Greek word, "syntaxis," which means arrangement, **syntax** is the study of phrase and sentence formation. The study of syntax focuses on the ways in which specific words can be combined to create coherent meaning. For example: the simple rearrangement of the words, "I can run," is different from the question, "Can I run?" which is also different from the meaningless "Run I can."

The following methods can be used to teach syntax:

- Proper Syntax Modeling: Students don't need to be corrected for improper syntax. Instead, they should be shown ways to rephrase what they said with proper syntax. If a student says, "Run I can," then the teacher should say, "Oh, you can run how fast?" This puts syntax in place with conversational skills.

- Open-Ended Sentences: Students can complete open-ended sentences with proper syntax both orally and in written format, or they can correct sentences that have improper syntax so that they make sense.

- Listening for Syntax: Syntax is auditory. Students can often hear a syntax error before they can see it in writing. Teachers should have students use word cards or word magnets to arrange and rearrange simple sentences and read them aloud to check for syntax.

- Repetition: Syntax can be practiced by using songs, poems, and rhymes for repetitive automation.

Pragmatics

Pragmatics is the study of what words mean in certain situations. It helps to understand the intentions and interpretations of intentions through words used in human interaction. Different listeners and different situations call for different language and intonations of language. When people engage in a conversation, it is usually to convey a certain message, and the message (even using the same words) can change depending on the setting and the audience. The more fluent the speaker, the more success she or he will have in conveying the intended message.

The following methods can be used to teach pragmatics:

- When students state something incorrectly, a response can be given to what they intended to say in the first place. For instance, if a student says, "That's how it didn't happen." Then the teacher might say, "Of course, that's not how it happened." Instead of putting students on defense by being corrected, this method puts them at ease and helps them learn.

- Role-playing conversations with different people in different situations can help teach pragmatics. For example, pretend playing can be used where a situation remains the same but the audience changes, or the audience stays the same but the situations change. This can be followed with a discussion about how language and intonations change too.

- Different ways to convey a message can be used, such as asking vs. persuading, or giving direct vs. indirect requests and polite vs. impolite messages.

- Various non-verbal signals can be used to see how they change pragmatics. For example, students can be encouraged to use mismatched words and facial expressions, such as angry words while smiling or happy words while pretending to cry.

Strategies to Help Read New and/or Difficult Words

Children who are developing reading fluency and comprehension skills can become frustrated when presented with unfamiliar words in a given text. With direct phonics instruction, educators can teach children to decode words and then use context clues to define the words while reading. If children have a strong enough understanding of language structures, including nouns and verbs, educators can ask them to consider what part of speech the unknown word might be based on and where it might fit into the sentence. Other useful strategies involve **self-monitoring**, in which children are asked to think as they read and ask themselves if what they have just read makes sense. Focusing on visual clues, such as drawings and photographs, may give children valuable insight into deciphering unknown words. Looking for the word in another section of the text to see how it relates to the overall meaning could give a clue to the new vocabulary word. Spelling the word out loud or looking for word chunks, prefixes, and suffixes, as well as demonstrating how to segment the unknown word into its individual syllables, may also be effective strategies to employ.

One of the most valuable strategies, however, for helping children to read and understand new words is pre-teaching. In this strategy, educators select what they evaluate to be the unfamiliar words in the text and then introduce them to the class before reading. Educators using this method should be careful not to simply ask the children to read the text and then spell the new words correctly. They should also provide clear definitions and give the children the opportunity to read these words in various sentences to decipher word meaning. This method can dramatically reduce how often children stop reading in order to reflect on unknown words. Educators are often unsure as to whether to correct every mispronounced word a child makes when reading. If the mispronounced word still makes sense, it is sometimes better to allow the child to continue to read, since the more the child stops, the more the child's reading comprehension and fluency are negatively affected.

Reading, Inquiry, and Research

Locating Information

In informational texts, certain features function to organize the information and also act as guides, which in turn supports the reader's overall comprehension.

Headings include titles and subtitles that identify the topic of study. They also help a reader to arrive at a clearer understanding with regard to the text's main idea. Headings can help readers make connections between background knowledge and the information in the text, which helps them make predictions before reading begins. Headings also strategically organize a text into sections so that one section at a time can be studied.

Sidebars are found in the right or left margins of informational texts. Sidebars often provide the reader with helpful, additional information about a topic that appears on that particular page. By providing examples, interesting facts, definitions of key terms, and more, sidebars emphasize important information that the author wishes to convey.

Hyperlinks are in-text links to specific website addresses that a reader may wish to visit to further their understanding of a specific topic. When authors insert hyperlinks into modern informational texts, they create a text that is more interactive, providing further resources for children to strengthen their comprehension of a given topic.

Study and Inquiry Skills

With a wealth of information at people's fingertips in this digital age, it's important to know not only the type of information one is looking for, but also in what medium he or she is most likely to find it. Information needs to be specific and reliable. For example, if someone is repairing a car, an encyclopedia would be mostly useless. While an encyclopedia might include information about cars, an

owner's manual will contain the specific information needed for repairs. Information must also be reliable or credible so that it can be trusted. A well-known newspaper may have reliable information, but a peer-reviewed journal article will have likely gone through a more rigorous check for validity. Determining **bias** can be helpful in determining credibility. If the information source (person, organization, or company) has something to gain from the reader forming a certain view on a topic, it's likely the information is skewed. For example, if trying to find the unemployment rate, the Bureau of Labor Statistics is a more credible source than a politician's speech.

Primary sources are best defined as records or items that serve as evidence of periods of history. To be considered primary, the source documents or objects must have been created during the time period in which they reference. Examples include diaries, newspaper articles, speeches, government documents, photographs, and historical artifacts. In today's digital age, primary sources, which were once in print, are often embedded in secondary sources. **Secondary sources**—such as websites, history books, databases, or reviews—contain analysis or commentary on primary sources. Secondary sources borrow information from primary sources through the process of quoting, summarizing, or paraphrasing.

Today's students often complete research online through **electronic sources**. Electronic sources offer advantages over print, and can be accessed on virtually any computer, while libraries or other research centers are limited to fixed locations and specific catalogs. Electronic sources are also efficient and yield massive amounts of data in seconds. The user can tailor a search based on key words, publication years, and article length. Lastly, many **databases** provide the user with instant citations, saving the user the trouble of manually assembling sources for a bibliography.

Although electronic sources yield powerful results, researchers must use caution. While there are many reputable and reliable sources on the internet, just as many are unreliable or biased sources. It's up to the researcher to examine and verify the reliability of sources. *Wikipedia*, for example, may or may not be accurate, depending on the contributor. Many databases, such as *EBSCO* or *SIRS*, offer peer-reviewed articles, meaning the publications have been reviewed for the quality and accuracy of their content.

Developing a Topic Sentence

Good writers get to the point quickly. This is accomplished by developing a strong and effective topic sentence that details the author's purpose and answers questions such as: *What does the author intend to explain or impress?* or *What does the author want the reader to believe?* The **topic sentence** is normally found at the beginning of a supporting paragraph and usually gives purpose to a single paragraph. When reading, critical readers should find the topic sentence in each paragraph. If all information points back to one sentence, it's the topic sentence.

Use of Evidence to Support Conclusions

Using only one form of supporting evidence is not nearly as effective as using a variety to support a claim. Presenting only a list of statistics can be boring to the reader, but providing a true story that's both interesting and humanizing helps. In addition, one example isn't always enough to prove the writer's larger point, so combining it with other examples in the writing is extremely effective. Thus, when reading a passage, readers should not just look for a single form of supporting evidence.

For example, although most people can't argue with the statement, "Seat belts save lives", its impact on the reader is much greater when supported by additional content. The writer can support this idea by:

- Providing statistics on the rate of highway fatalities alongside statistics of estimated seat belt usage.

- Explaining the science behind car accidents and what happens to a passenger who doesn't use a seat belt.

- Offering anecdotal evidence or true stories from reliable sources on how seat belts prevent fatal injuries in car crashes.

Another key aspect of supporting evidence is a **reliable source**. Does the writer include the source of the information? If so, is the source well-known and trustworthy? Is there a potential for bias? For example, a seat belt study done by a seat belt manufacturer may have its own agenda to promote.

Writing Conventions

The following table lists the stages in writing conventions:

Developmental Stages of Writing	Description	Grade-Appropriate Continuum
Scribbling	Random marks, circles, and lines that may not resemble print, but represent ideas for the young writer.	Praise the children's creativity and ask them to explain their work to you. Consider adding a sentence at the bottom of their work based on the children's ideas.
Letter-like symbols	Letter-like symbols start to randomly appear and may be mixed in with numbers and scribbles.	Praise the children's creativity and point to the letter-like symbols for discussion. Consider adding a sentence at the bottom of the work based on the children's ideas.
Strings of letters	Using strings of letters in a row, children are demonstrating the preliminary understanding of letter-to-sound relationships.	Praise the children's efforts in attempting to use letters to represent sounds. Ask the children to tell you the story or to read you the sentences and consider writing what they say at the bottom.

Developmental Stages of Writing	Description	Grade-Appropriate Continuum
The emergence of beginning sounds	Children begin to use letters to represent actual words and may string the letters together in a row that can tell a story.	Praise the children's efforts in attempting to use letters to represent actual words. Help with spacing, building sound-letter correspondence, and expanding vocabulary.
Words represented by consonants	Children begin to leave spaces between words with a possible mixture of uppercase and lowercase letters.	Praise children's work as a prompt for further explanation of the story. Prompt children to use more details and to build more sentences.
Initial, middle, final sounds	Children begin to write some basic sight words and familiar names, but all other words are spelled the way they sound.	Praise children's progress and continue to build vocabulary. Help children to organize writing with structure and sentence variety.
Transitional phase	Writing is beginning to approach conventional spelling.	Praise children's progress and model the use of effective wording by using specific vocabulary to expand ideas.
Standard spelling	Children begin to spell most words correctly, with a basic understanding that the spelling of many words is connected to the meaning.	Praise children's progress and challenge them to begin writing more complex sentences, expand ideas, and establish a clear purpose for writing.

Relationship Between Spelling and Phonological and Alphabetic Awareness

Well before children are able to read and write, they begin to develop basic listening skills and gradually begin to imitate and produce the sounds they hear. Since language is used to communicate one's needs, react to situations, share experiences, and develop an understanding of the surrounding world, these beginning stages form the foundation of a child's literacy development. Before a child reaches the

preschool years, they begin to develop the ability to recognize and manipulate the sounds in their environment.

Generally speaking, *phonological awareness* is the ability to identify and manipulate specific units of oral language, including words, syllables, onsets, and rimes. The beginning stages of phonological awareness occur when a child is able to listen to and understand the words that people speak and read and when they are further able to recognize the various sounds within these words. Phonological awareness is also defined as the ability to sound out various words by connecting the sounds heard to familiar sounds and to manipulate those sounds in order to create new sounds and words. A child is demonstrating phonological awareness when they are able to do the following:

Appropriately recognize and apply words that rhyme—*cat, bat, sat*

Identify initial letters—the *c* in *cat*

Identify middle letters—the *a* in *cat*

Identify ending letters—the *t* in *cat*

Separate simple words into their individual sounds or phonemes—c/a/t *cat*

There are many strategies educators can use to strengthen a child's phonological awareness. One effective strategy to strengthen a child's awareness of word units is clapping out the number of syllables in a word. Familiar and enjoyable songs, such as "Bingo," help children to identify individual phonemes within a word and strengthen their spelling skills, listening comprehension, and rhythm. Other strategies may include word games that challenge children to think of rhyming words or words that share the same initial, middle, or ending sounds. Creating fun and engaging ways for children to strengthen their phonological awareness will build the framework for future literary success.

Stages of Spelling Development

Spelling development occurs in stages. In order, these stages are the pre-phonetic stage, the semiphonetic stage, the phonetic stage, the transitional stage, and the conventional stage. Each stage is explained below. Ways in which phonics and vocabulary development fit into the spelling stages are discussed. Instructional strategies for each phase of spelling are suggested.

Spelling development begins with the pre-phonetic stage. This stage is marked by an incomplete understanding of the alphabetic principle. Student understanding of letter-sound correspondences is limited. During the pre-phonetic stage, students participate in precommunicative writing. Precommunicative writing appears to be a jumble of letter-like forms rather than a series of discrete letters. Students' precommunicative writing samples can be used as informal assessments of their understanding of the alphabetic principle and knowledge of letter-sound correspondences.

Pre-phonetic stage of spelling development

The pre-phonetic stage is followed by the semiphonetic stage. In this stage, a student understands that letters represent sounds. The alphabetic principle may be understood, but letter recognition may not yet be fully developed. In this stage, single letters may be used to represent entire words (e.g., *U* for *you*). Other times, multiple syllables within words may be omitted. Writing produced by students in this stage is still virtually unreadable. Teachers may ask students to provide drawings to supplement their writing to better determine what a student intended to write.

Semiphonetic stage of writing

The third stage in spelling development is the phonetic stage. In this stage, students have mastered letter-sound correspondences. Although letters may be written backward or upside down, phonetic spellers are able to write all of the letters in the alphabet. Because phonetic spellers have limited sight vocabulary, irregular words are often spelled incorrectly. However, words that are written may phonetically sound like the spoken word. Additionally, student writing becomes systematic. For example, students are likely to use one letter to represent a digraph or letter blend (e.g., *f* for /ph/).

Phonetic stage of writing

Spelling instruction of common consonant patterns, short vowel sounds, and common affixes or rimes can begin during the phonetic stage. Thus, spelling instruction during the phonetic stage coincides with the instruction of phonics and phonemic awareness that also occurs during this stage of development.

The creation of word walls is advantageous during the phonetic stage of spelling development. On a word wall, words that share common consonant-vowel patterns or letter clusters are written in groups. Students are encouraged to add words to the group. As a result, word walls promote strategic spelling, vocabulary development, common letter combinations, and common morphological units.

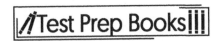

The transitional stage of spelling occurs when a student has developed a small sight vocabulary and a solid understanding of letter-sound correspondences. Thus, spelling dependence on phonology decreases. Instead, dependence on visual representation and word structure increases. As sight word vocabulary increases during the transition stage, the correct spelling of irregular words will also increase. However, students may still struggle to spell words with long vowel sounds.

Transitional stage of spelling

Differentiation of spelling instruction often begins during the transitional stage. Instruction ought to be guided by data collected through informal observations and informal assessments. Depending on individual needs, lessons may include sight word recognition, morphology, etymology, reading, and writing. It is during the transitional stage that the instruction of homophones can begin. Homophones are words that sound the same but have different spellings and meanings (e.g., *their* and *there*). Additionally, students should be expected to begin writing full sentences at the transitional stage. Writing will not only reinforce correct spelling of words but also phonics and vocabulary development.

Conventional spelling is the last and final stage of spelling development. This stage occurs after a student's sight word vocabulary recognition is well developed and the student is able to read fluently and with comprehension. By this stage, students know the basic rules of phonics. They are able to deal with consonants, multiple vowel-consonant blends, homophones, digraphs, and irregular spellings.

Due to an increase in sight word recognition at this stage, a conventional speller is able to recognize when a word is spelled incorrectly.

Conventional stage

I Have a Mouse In My Backpack

It is at the conventional spelling stage that spelling instruction can begin to focus on content-specific vocabulary words and words with unusual spellings. In order to further reinforce vocabulary development of such content-specific words and apply phonic skills, students should be encouraged to use the correct spelling of such words within various writing activities.

For even the best conventional spellers, some words will still cause consistent trouble. Students can keep track of words that they consistently spell incorrectly or find confusing in word banks so they can isolate and eventually eliminate their individualized errors. Students can use their word banks as references when they come across a word with which they struggle. Students may also spend time consciously committing the words in their banks to memory through verbal or written practice.

Effective Written Expression

Written expression refers to the ability of the writer to fluidly communicate meaning and purpose throughout the composition. Essentially, this refers not only to how clear the central focus of the piece is but how well the ideas surrounding the central focus are presented. If the writer can't successfully express the meaning and implications of the idea, the writing will not be strong.

Effective written expression utilizes detailed, clear communication. A writer doesn't need to unload elaborate diction throughout the paragraphs. Such an embellishment can be distracting to the reader,

which actually defeats the principles behind effective writing. Sentences should be direct and emphasize language that, while engaging, remains simple enough for the audience to understand. This doesn't mean abstaining from using advanced words but rather keeping sentences direct and to the point. Students should avoid rambling line after line. Avoiding exaggerating language or overdramatic phrasing is also important. Not only can this confuse the reader, it can also harm the reader's credibility.

A simple formula for effective writing is to introduce an idea, discuss it, and then make a conclusion. This applies for the written piece as a whole but must also be used within individual paragraphs. If a writer just introduces idea after idea with no substance, the reader is left with unsubstantiated claims. Without supporting evidence to understand the view, the reader is left with only opinion. With the implementation of facts and supporting details, this opinion is strengthened. Thus, the reasoning behind the central idea is clearly executed and can be considered seriously. This helps the writer achieve credibility.

Paragraph coherence is vital for effective written expression. Paragraph sequencing and information placement are essential to streamlining the entire piece. Evidence and supporting information should be used to transition from one section to another, up to the conclusion. This enables the information to be clearly expressed. The author should strive to write in a way that, as the piece progresses, the focus becomes clearer and more convincing. By the conclusion of the written piece, the author should also restate his or her thesis to solidify their views and reasoning.

Writing Mechanics

Educators must first be masters of the English language in order to teach it. Teachers serve several key roles in the classroom that all require that they know the conventions of grammar, punctuation, and spelling. Teachers are communicators. They must know how to structure their own language for clarity. They must also be able to interpret what the students are saying to accurately either affirm or revise it for correctness. Teachers are educators of language. They are the agents of change from poor-quality conventions to mastery of the concepts. Teachers are responsible for differentiating instruction so that students at all levels and aptitudes can succeed with language learning. Teachers need to be able to isolate gaps in skill sets and decide which skills need intervention in the classroom.

Teachers are evaluators. They are responsible for making key decisions about a student's educational trajectory based on their assessment of the student's capabilities.

Teachers also have great impact on how students view themselves as learners. Teachers are models. They must be superb examples of educated individuals. Just like with any other subject, people need a strong grasp of the basics of language. They will not be able to learn these things unless the teachers themselves have mastered it.

Teachers foster socialization; socialization to cultural norms and to the everyday practices of the community in which they live is of utmost importance to students' lives. These processes begin at home but continue early in a child's life at school. Teachers play a key role in guiding and scaffolding students' socialization skills. If teachers are to excel in this role, they need to be adept with the use of the English language.

Teachers need to have mastery of the conventions of English including:

- Nouns
- Collective Nouns
- Compound Subjects
- Pronouns
- Subjects, Objects, and Compounds
- Pronoun/Noun Agreement
- Indefinite Pronouns
- Choosing Pronouns
- Adjectives
- Compound Adjectives
- Verbs
- Infinitives
- Verb Tenses
- Participles
- Subject/Verb Agreement
- Active/Passive Voice
- Adverbs
- Double Negatives
- Comparisons
- Double Comparisons
- Prepositions
- Prepositional Phrases
- Conjunctions
- Interjections
- Articles
- Types of sentences
- Subjects and Predicates
- Clauses and Phrases
- Pronoun Reference Problems
- Misplaced Modifiers
- Dangling Participial Phrases
- Punctuation
- Periods
- Commas
- Semicolons and Colons
- Parentheses and Dashes
- Quotation Marks
- Apostrophes
- Hyphens
- Question Marks
- Exclamation Points
- Capitalization
- Spelling
- Noun Plurals

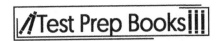

- Prefixes and Suffixes
- Spelling Hurdles
- Abbreviations
- Pronunciation
- Homonyms and other easy mix-ups

Differences Between Spoken and Written English

Register

Despite the fact that a standardized form of English is used in published academic and scientific language, several varieties of spoken and written English also exist. There are differences in how one speaks at home, with friends, to teachers, and to colleagues. In each social setting, a person's *register*—his or her level of formality—will likely change in order to appropriately address the audience. Written registers also vary, depending on a number of factors. For instance, when writing a research paper for professional purposes, formal language will be used, but when writing a letter to a friend, a person is more apt to employ a more casual register. The following statements indicate differences in register:

> *Call me back when you get this message.*

> *I look forward to hearing back from you at your earliest convenience.*

Although both statements express the writer's desire to further communicate with the receiver of the message, the degree of formality, the register, is strikingly different.

Dialect

A language also has several dialects, which are dependent on a great many factors. *Dialects* have specific grammatical rules and patterns that often differ from the standard rules of the language. For instance, within Britain, Canada, and the United States, there are several dialects of the English language. One need only travel from Newfoundland, in eastern Canada, to Louisiana, in the southern United States, to witness a striking difference in how the English language is spoken.

Written dialects and registers also exist. They vary, based on the type of written work, when it was created, where it was written, by whom it was written, for what purposes, and for what audience it was intended. Authors of dramas, stories, and poetry employ the use of dialect for a multitude of reasons. For instance, when authors wish to develop a clear picture of the setting and characters within a drama, dialect plays a significant role. Here are some examples of dialect:

> "Bess, you is my woman now…"—from George Gershwin's opera, *Porgy and Bess*

> "That ain't no matter."—from Mark Twain's novel, *Huckleberry Finn*

With the careful and skillful placement of written dialect, the author conveys the character's personality, situation, and social class.

Written Communication

Writing in Connection with Listening, Reading, and Speaking

Identifying Research-Based Approaches to Formative and Summative Assessment

It is almost as important to provide feedback and evaluate a student's skill level as it is to teach. Most classes utilize both formative and summative assessments as a grading template. Although assessment and grading are not the same thing, assessments are often used to award a grade. A **formative assessment** monitors the student's progress in learning and allows continuous feedback throughout the course in the form of homework and in-class assignments, such as quizzes, writing workshops, conferences, or inquiry-based writing prompts. These assessments typically make up a lower percent of the overall grade. Alternatively, a **summative assessment** compares a student's progress in learning against some sort of standard, such as against the progress of other students or by the number of correct answers. These assessments usually make up a higher percent of the overall grade and come in the form of midterm or final exams, papers, or major projects.

One evidence-based method used to assess a student's progress is a rubric. A **rubric** is an evaluation tool that explicitly states the expectations of the assignment and breaks it down into different components. Each component has a clear description and relationship to the assignment as a whole. For writing, rubrics may be **holistic**, judging the overall quality of the writing, or they can be **analytic**, in which different aspects of the writing are evaluated, e.g., structure, style, word choices, and punctuation.

Rubrics can be used in all aspects of a curriculum, including reading comprehension, oral presentations, speeches, performances, papers, projects, and listening comprehension. They are usually formative in nature, but can be summative depending on the purpose. Rubrics allow instructors to provide specific feedback and allow students to understand the expectations for an assignment.

An example of an analytic rubric is displayed below:

Name _____   Date _____

Essay Rubric	4 Mastery	3 Satisfactory	2 Needs Improvement	1 Poor
Writing Quality	-Excellent usage of voice and style -Outstanding organizational skills -Wealth of relevant information	-Style and voice of essay was interesting -Mostly organized -Useful amount of information	-Inconsistent style and voice -Lacked clear organization -Small amount of useful information	-No noticeable style or voice -Virtually no organization -No relevant information
Grammar Conventions	-Essentially no mistakes in grammar -Correct spelling throughout	-Minor amount of grammar and spelling mistakes	-Many errors in grammar conventions and spelling	-Too many grammatical errors to understand the meaning of the piece

Another research-proven strategy is **conferencing**, in which students participate in a group discussion that usually involves the teacher. Students learn best when they can share their thoughts on what they've read or written and receive feedback from their peers and instructors. For writing, conferencing is frequently done in the revision stage. Through discussion, students are also able to enhance their listening and speaking skills. Conferences can be done in a one-on-one setting, typically between a student and instructor, or in a small group of students with guidance from the instructor. They are useful in that they provide an atmosphere of respect where a student can share his or her work and thoughts without fear of judgment. They increase motivation and allow students to explore a variety of topics and discussions. Conferences also allow the instructor to provide immediate feedback or prompt students for deeper explanations of their ideas. The most successful conferences have these characteristics:

- Have a set structure
- Focus on only a few points—too many are confusing or distracting
- Are solution based
- Allow students to both discuss their thoughts/works and receive/provide feedback for others
- Encourage the use of appropriate vocabulary
- Provide motivation and personal satisfaction or pleasure from reading and writing
- Allow a time where questions can be asked and immediately answered

Rubrics and conferencing are both methods that provide useful **feedback**, one of the most important elements in the progress of a student's learning. Feedback is essentially corrective instruction delivered in writing, either verbally or non-verbally. Research has shown that the following techniques are the most effective when giving feedback:

Being Specific

For a student to know exactly how he or she is doing, feedback should be directed towards specific components of a student's writing, listening, or speaking skills, not a holistic overview. For example, writing "Excellent!" on a student's paper or homework is not useful information as it's unclear what was done well. A paper should provide useful comments throughout the body of the work, for example, "Wording is confusing here," or "Great use of adjectives." However, instructor comments should not overwhelm the student's writing; they should be used to focus their attention on specific areas of success or improvement. This encourages the student to keep doing what he or she is doing well and work on what needs improvement without being overwhelmed.

Being Sensitive

Giving feedback is precarious in nature as it entirely depends upon the emotional and mental states of the receiver. Some students do well with "tough love," while others may be discouraged and disheartened to see a slew of comments on their paper. Teachers should pay attention to how a student reacts to feedback. As a general rule, feedback should focus more on the positives so as not to damage self-esteem, while teaching students new techniques for self-correction, instead of simply criticizing what they've done. Also, it's important to try and be aware of the types of feedback each student responds the most effectively to, for example, providing oral feedback for students who don't read well.

Being Prompt

Feedback should be presented sooner rather than later, so that students will not have time to repeat mistakes they are unaware of that may become habitual. Studies have shown that students who are given immediate feedback display a greater increase in performance than those who were given feedback later in the term. As soon as the action has happened, it is important give the appropriate praise or critique so that the student associates the feedback with the action.

Being Explicit

It is important to explain the purpose of the feedback before it is given so that a student does not feel controlled, too closely examined, or competitive. This can cause the learner to feel self-conscious and discourage him or her from performing his or her best. The importance of feedback and how it is meant to improve on a personal skill set should be explained to the student.

Being Focused

Teachers should try and keep the feedback in alignment with the goal the student is expected to achieve. Too much feedback, especially if it is unrelated to the goal, can be overwhelming and distracting from the purpose of the assignment or paper.

Here are some other tips to consider when giving feedback:

- Teachers should be aware of their body language and facial expressions when giving feedback—a frown or grimace can be very discouraging, even if the written feedback was mostly positive.

- It's conducive to concentrate on one thing at a time. If a student submits a paper with a lot of errors, for example, it may be helpful to identify a prevalent pattern of error and work through strategies to correct it so that student does not feel overwhelmed.

- Using effective rubrics can make all the difference—letting students know exactly what is expected will provide them with a basis on which to model their techniques and skills.

- Students should be educated on giving feedback. This can be demonstrated by example and through instruction how to give feedback in a positive, constructive way and correct any behavior that trends toward disrespect or excessive competition. Students should also provide feedback to the teacher as well.

- Teachers should not give the same comments to every student, but make them personal.

- When offering criticism, teachers should always offer tips for how the student can improve.

- It's important to avoid personal comments, e.g., "You're so smart!" or "Math isn't your best subject." Rather, the comments should focus on the writing: e.g., "The organization of this paper is clear."

- Students shouldn't be compared to each other, e.g., "Look how perfectly Victor composed this sentence!" This can galvanize the students into competing with one another.

Evaluating the Effectiveness of Research-Based Approaches to Formative and Summative Assessment

Most research has already been done to evaluate the effectiveness of certain strategies of formative and summative assessments. Because there are innumerable approaches to the art of teaching, the only

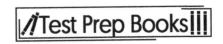

real way one can evaluate a strategy's effectiveness is to monitor how the students improve over time with any given approach. If one strategy does not seem to show much improvement, then a different one should be used. Because each student has individual needs, a teacher may need to utilize several different techniques tailored to the needs of each student.

To monitor student process, the following approaches should be considered:

- Asking questions in the classroom during and after a lecture
- Cultivating a classroom environment that encourages student questions
- Circulating around the classroom and engaging in one-on-one conferences during in-class assignments
- Giving periodic quizzes
- Leaving sufficient time for questions at the end of a lecture
- Assigning and collecting homework and returning the corrected material immediately
- Giving midterms and final exams
- Conducting regular reviews of student progress through the above methods and adjusting teaching strategies accordingly

Another strategy to assess student knowledge and identify areas in need of development is to create a K-W-L chart in preparation for a lesson that introduces a new topic. First, students are prompted for what they already know (K). Then, they are asked to consider what they want to know (W). The instructor may then choose to adjust the lesson by spending less time on areas that students are already proficient in and by spending more time on areas that students want to know more about. Finally, after the lesson, students can be asked to reflect on what they learned (L). A K-W-L chart lets students know that they are active participants in their own learning.

Promoting Writing Development

The goal of sight word instruction is to help students readily recognize regular and irregular high-frequency words in order to aid reading fluency and comprehension. Several factors affect the sequence of instruction for specific sight words. For example, before a child is exposed to sight words, he or she needs to be able to fluently recognize and say the sound of all uppercase and lowercase letters. Also, students need to be able to accurately decode target words before they recognize sight words. When irregular words are introduced, attention should be drawn to both the phonetically regular and the phonetically irregular portions of the words.

Before sight word instruction can begin, teachers need to identify high-frequency words that do and do not follow normal spelling conventions, but are used often. Teachers may choose to select words that are used often within their students' reading materials, words that students have an interest in learning, or content-specific words. Alternatively, grade-level standardized sight word lists, such as the Dolch word lists, can be referenced.

Repetition and exposure through guided and independent practice are essential in student retention of sight words. Each lesson should introduce only three to five new sight words and also review words from previous lessons. Visually similar words should not be introduced in proximity to one another.

Sample activities through which sight words can be taught are listed below.

1. Students can practice reading decodable texts and word lists.

2. Teachers should read text that contains the sight words that a class is currently learning. As a teacher reads aloud, they should pause, point to, and correctly pronounce the words. Instead of pointing to the words, teachers can underline or highlight the words as they appear in sentences that are read.

3. Flashcards can be used to practice sight word recognition.

4. Games are fun and motivating avenues through which sight words can be practiced. Examples of games that can be used to practice sight words include Bingo, Go Fish, and Memory.

5. As students learn new sight words, they can write them in a sight word "dictionary." Students should be asked to write a sentence using each sight word included within the dictionary.

The spelling of high-frequency words should be taught after students have been exposed to the words, can readily recognize the words, and can read the words. The following multisensory strategies can be used to help students master the spelling of high-frequency sight words:

1. Spell Reading: Spell reading begins when a student says the high-frequency word. Then, the student spells out the letters in the word. Lastly, the student reads the word again. Spell reading helps commit the word to a student's memory when done in repetition.

2. Air Writing: When air writing, a student uses their finger to write the letters of a word in the air.

3. Arm Tapping: During arm tapping, a student says the word, spells the word's letters on their arm, and then reads the word again.

4. Table Writing: Students write the word on the table. A substrate, where the word is written in sand or shaving cream, can be added to the table. See examples of substrates below:

5. Letter Magnet Spelling: Arranging letter magnets on a metal surface, such as a cookie sheet, is a fun way for students to learn how to spell sight words. Because this strategy is seen as a game to the student, letter magnet spelling increases student motivation to write words.

6. Material Writing: Students can use clay, play dough, Wikki sticks, or other materials to form letters that are used to spell the words.

Various Stages of Writing

Writing Skills Development
Children who receive regular and consistent encouragement to write and whose environment is rich with writing materials and resources will be more apt to strengthen their writing proficiency. Research suggests that at least an hour a day of writing practice, including skilled instruction, is necessary. Writing projects should be chosen that also involve the subjects of science, social studies, reading, or mathematics to give students well-rounded views of the purposes for writing. Piece by piece, students practice writing skills in all subjects, and collectively it should add up to more than an hour a day.

POWER Strategy for Teaching the Writing Process
The **POWER strategy** helps all students to take ownership of the writing process by prompting them to consciously focus on what they are writing.

The POWER strategy is an acronym for the following:

- Prewriting or Planning
- Organizing
- Writing a first draft
- Evaluating the writing
- Revising and rewriting

Prewriting and Planning
During the Prewriting and Planning phase, students learn to consider their audience and purpose for the writing project. Then they compile information they wish to include in the piece of writing from their background knowledge and/or new sources.

Organizing
Next, students decide on the organizational structure of their writing project. There are many types of organizational structures, but the common ones are: story/narrative, informative, opinion, persuasive, compare and contrast, explanatory, and problem/solution formats. Often graphic organizers are an important part of helping students complete this step of the writing process.

Writing
In this step, students write a complete first draft of their project. Educators may begin by using modeled writing to teach this step in the process. It may be helpful for beginning writers to work in small groups or pairs. Verbalizing their thoughts before writing them is also a helpful technique.

Evaluating
In this stage, students reread their writing and note the segments that are particularly strong or need improvement. Then they participate in peer editing. They ask each other questions about the piece. The

peers learn to provide feedback and constructive criticism to help the student improve. Scoring rubrics are a helpful tool in this phase to guide students as they edit each other's work.

Revising and Rewriting

Finally, the student incorporates any changes she or he wishes to make based on the evaluating process. Then students rewrite the piece into a final draft and publish it however it best fits the audience and purpose of the writing.

6+1 Traits Strategy for Teaching Writing

6+1 Traits is a model for teaching writing that uses a common language to explain the standards for what good writing looks like. Students learn to evaluate whether these expectations have been met in their own writing and then edit, revise, and rewrite accordingly. The 6+1 Traits are the characteristics that make writing readable and effective no matter what genre of writing is being used. The 6+1 Traits are as follows:

- Ideas
- Organization
- Voice
- Word choice
- Sentence fluency
- Conventions
- Presentation

The Ideas Trait

This trait is the content of the writing. This is where students learn to select an important topic for their writing. They are taught to narrow down and focus their idea. Then they learn to develop and elaborate on the specific idea. Finally, they investigate and discover the information and details that best convey the idea to others.

The Organization Trait

This trait teaches students how to build the framework for their writing. They choose an organizational strategy or purpose for the writing and build the details upon that structure. There are many purposes for writing, and they all have different frameworks. However, there are commonalities that students can learn to effectively organize their writing so it makes sense to the reader. Students learn to invite the reader into their work with an effective introduction. They are taught how to create thoughtful transitions between ideas and key points in their writing and how to create logical and purposeful sequencing of ideas. Finally, students are taught how to create a powerful conclusion to their piece that summarizes the information but leaves the reader with something to think about. Many students are inclined to jump into their writing without a clear direction for where it is going. The organization trait teaches them to plan and purpose their writing toward excellence.

The Voice Trait

This is the trait that gives the writing a sense of individuality and connection to the author. It shows that the writing is meaningful and that the author cares about it. It is what makes the writing uniquely the author's own. It is how the reader begins to know the author and what she or he "sounds like." Students learn to recognize "voice" in some writing samples and find their own "voice" to apply to their work. Students are taught to speak on an emotional level directly to their readers. Students experiment with

matching their style to the audience and the purpose of the writing. Students are taught to enjoy taking risks and putting their personal touch into their work.

The Word Choice Trait

This trait gives writing a sense of functional communication through precise language that is rich and enlightening. If the work is narrative, the words create images in the mind's eye; if the work is descriptive, the words clarify and expand thoughts and ideas. If the work is persuasive, the words give new perspective and invite thought. Students learn not only to choose exceptional vocabulary, but also to hone their skills for using ordinary words well. Students are taught to describe things using striking language. They learn to use exact language that is accurate, concise, precise, and lively.

The Sentence Fluency Trait

When sentences are built to fit together and move with one another to create writing that is easy to read aloud, the author has written with fluency. Students learn to eliminate awkward word patterns that otherwise would encumber the reader. Sentences and paragraphs start and stop in precisely the right places so that the writing moves well. Students are taught to establish a flow, develop a rhythm, and give cadence to their work. They edit their sentences to vary the structure and length. Educators can teach fluency through reading aloud beautifully written examples and contrasting them with less fluent work.

The Conventions Trait

Here the focus changes from creation of the piece to preparation for the reader. Instead of revision that the first five traits teach, this trait teaches editing skills. The students learn to make their writing clear and understandable through the use of proper grammar, spelling, capitalization, and punctuation. Students are taught the differences between revision and editing. They learn basic editing marks and symbols. Teachers can assist students to learn conventions through guided editing and regular practice. Expectations for correctness need to be kept developmentally appropriate. If immediate correctness is expected, students may shy away from experimenting and taking risks.

The Presentation Trait

This trait focuses on the final appearance of the work. Presentation is not a concern during the process of the other six traits, nor must perfect presentation be expected for every work a student does. Students are taught to make their work inviting and accessible to the reader of the end product. They learn to show they care about their writing when it is neat and readable. Students are taught about uniform spacing, legible handwriting, appropriate use of fonts and sizes, and how to use bullets, numbers, headings, charts, graphs, and pictures to help make the work visually appealing. Students are taught about the publishing process and are given opportunities to showcase their finished products.

Purposeful Writing

Purposeful writing practices have a significant effect on writing development. **Purposeful writing** refers to intentional writing practices for the purpose of communicating. Through learning to write well, students can begin to use writing as a method of thinking through issues and solving problems. They become more adept with questioning and investigation. Students learn to accurately convey and critique information. They can more readily express real or imagined experiences to others. Through the varied writing purposes, students learn to focus on what the audience understands, while at other times, they focus on the topic and what information they are trying to impart. Other situations call for focus on their own thinking and feelings. Writing as a whole becomes more effective and accessible as students glean skills for writing with purpose. Some of the writing purposes are as follows:

- Letter writing
- Poetry and Songs
- Creative and Narrative writing
- Informative writing
- Opinion writing
- Persuasive writing
- Compare and Contrast writing
- Explanatory/Expository writing
- Problem and Solution writing

Benefits of Technology for Writing Skills, Publication, and Teaching Writing

Teachers are learning to adapt their writing instruction to integrate today's technology standards and to enhance engagement in the writing process. The key is to still build a strong foundation of the fundamentals of writing while using current technology. Gone are the days when writing relied solely on handwritten pieces and when the tools of the trade were pencils, paper, hardback dictionaries, and encyclopedias. Online resources are now the backbone of the writing experience. It is now possible to integrate photo, video, and other interactive components into a completed project to provide a well-rounded engagement with media. In order to have an education conducive to college and career readiness and success, students need online research and digital media writing skills.

There are many compelling reasons to teach students to be digitally aware and prudent users of technology when it comes to their writing. With current digital technology, the writing process has become a much more collaborative experience. In higher education and in career settings, collaborative skills are essential. Publishing and presenting are now simplified such that completed work is often read by a wide variety of audiences. Writing can be instantly shared with parents, peers, educators, and the general public, including experts in the field. Students are more apt to take an interest in the writing process when they know that others are reading their writing. Feedback is also simplified because so many platforms allow comments from readers. Teachers can be interactive with the students throughout the process, allowing formative assessment and integration of personalized instruction. Technology is simply a new vehicle for human connection and interactivity.

A student may be exposed to a plethora of technology, but this does not mean that she or he necessarily knows how to use it for learning. The teacher is still responsible for guiding, monitoring, and scaffolding the students toward learning objectives. It is critical that educators teach students how to locate credible information and to reliably cite their sources using bibliographies. Platforms and apps for online learning are varied and plentiful. Here are some ideas for how to use technology for writing instruction in the classroom:

- Use a projector with a tablet to display notes and classwork for the group to see. This increases instructional time because notes are already available rather than having to be written in real-time. This also provides the ability to save, email, and post classwork and notes for students and parents to access on their own time. A student can work at his or her own pace and still keep up with instruction. Student screens can be displayed for peer-led teaching and sharing of class work.

- More technology in class means less paperwork. Digital drop-boxes can be used for students to turn in assignments. Teachers can save paper, keep track of student revisions of work, and give feedback electronically.

- Digital media can be used to differentiate instruction for multiple learning styles and multiple skill levels. Instead of using standardized textbook learning for everyone, teachers can create and collect resources for individualizing course content.

- Inquiry- and problem-based learning is easier with increased collaborative capabilities provided by digital tools.

- Digital textbooks and e-readers can replace hardback versions of text that are prone to damage and loss. Students can instantly access definitions for new words, as well as annotate and highlight useful information without ruining a hardbound book.

- Library databases can be used to locate reliable research information and resources. There are digital tools for tracking citation information, allowing annotations for internet content, and for storing internet content.

- Mobile devices may be used in the classroom to encourage reading and writing when students use them to text, post, blog, and tweet.

- PowerPoint and other presentation software can be used to model writing for students and to provide a platform for presenting their work.

- Students can create a classroom blog, review various blog sites, and use blogs as they would diaries or journals. They can even write from the perspective of the character in a book or a famous historical person.

- Web quests can be used to help guide students on research projects. They can get relevant information on specific topics and decide what pieces to include in their writing.

- Students can write about technology as a topic. They can "teach" someone how to use various forms of technology, specific learning platforms, or apps.

- Students can create webpages, make a class webpage, and then use it to help with home-school communication.

- Online feedback and grading systems can be used. There are many to choose from. This may allow students to see the grading rubric and ask questions or receive suggestions from the teacher.

- Students and teachers can use email to exchange ideas with other schools or experts on certain topics that are being studied in the classroom.

- Game show-style reviews can be created for units of study to use on computers or on an overhead projector.

- A wiki website can be created that allows students to collaborate, expand on each other's work, and do peer editing and revision.

- Publishing tools can be used to publish student work on the web or in class newspapers or social media sites.

Understanding the Task, Purpose, and Audience

Identifying the Task, Purpose, and Intended Audience

An author's *writing style*—the way in which words, grammar, punctuation, and sentence fluidity are used—is the most influential element in a piece of writing, and it is dependent on the purpose and the audience for whom it is intended. Together, a writing style and mode of writing form the foundation of a written work, and a good writer will choose the most effective mode and style to convey a message to readers.

Writers should first determine what they are trying to say and then choose the most effective mode of writing to communicate that message. Different writing modes and *word choices* will affect the tone of a piece—that is, its underlying attitude, emotion, or character. The argumentative mode may utilize words that are earnest, angry, passionate, or excited whereas an informative piece may have a sterile, germane, or enthusiastic tone. The tones found in narratives vary greatly, depending on the purpose of the writing. *Tone* will also be affected by the audience—teaching science to children or those who may be uninterested would be most effective with enthusiastic language and exclamation points whereas teaching science to college students may take on a more serious and professional tone, with fewer charged words and punctuation choices that are inherent to academia.

Sentence fluidity—whether sentences are long and rhythmic or short and succinct—also affects a piece of writing as it determines the way in which a piece is read. Children or audiences unfamiliar with a subject do better with short, succinct sentence structures as these break difficult concepts up into shorter points. A period, question mark, or exclamation point is literally a signal for the reader to stop and takes more time to process. Thus, longer, more complex sentences are more appropriate for adults or educated audiences as they can fit more information in between processing time.

The amount of *supporting detail* provided is also tailored to the audience. A text that introduces a new subject to its readers will focus more on broad ideas without going into greater detail whereas a text that focuses on a more specific subject is likely to provide greater detail about the ideas discussed.

Writing styles, like modes, are most effective when tailored to their audiences. Having awareness of an audience's demographic is one of the most crucial aspects of properly communicating an argument, a story, or a set of information.

Choosing the Most Appropriate Type of Writing

Before beginning any writing, it is imperative that a writer have a firm grasp on the message he or she wishes to convey and how he or she wants readers to be affected by the writing. For example, does the author want readers to be more informed about the subject? Does the writer want readers to agree with his or her opinion? Does the writer want readers to get caught up in an exciting narrative? The following steps are a guide to determining the appropriate type of writing for a task, purpose, and audience:

1. Identifying the purpose for writing the piece
2. Determining the audience
3. Adapting the writing mode, word choices, tone, and style to fit the audience and the purpose

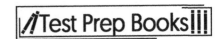

It is important to distinguish between a work's purpose and its main idea. The essential difference between the two is that the *main idea* is what the author wants to communicate about the topic at hand whereas the *primary purpose* is why the author is writing in the first place. The primary purpose is what will determine the type of writing an author will choose to utilize, not the main idea, though the two are related. For example, if an author writes an article on the mistreatment of animals in factory farms and, at the end, suggests that people should convert to vegetarianism, the main idea is that vegetarianism would reduce the poor treatment of animals. The primary purpose is to convince the reader to stop eating animals. Since the primary purpose is to galvanize an audience into action, the author would choose the argumentative writing mode.

The next step is to consider to whom the author is appealing as this will determine the type of details to be included, the diction to be used, the tone to be employed, and the sentence structure to be used. An audience can be identified by considering the following questions:

- What is the purpose for writing the piece?
- To whom is it being written?
- What is their age range?
- Are they familiar with the material being presented, or are they just being newly introduced to it?
- Where are they from?
- Is the task at hand in a professional or casual setting?
- Is the task at hand for monetary gain?

These are just a few of the numerous considerations to keep in mind, but the main idea is to become as familiar with the audience as possible. Once the audience has been understood, the author can then adapt the writing style to align with the readers' education and interests. The audience is what determines the *rhetorical appeal* the author will use—ethos, pathos, or logos. *Ethos* is a rhetorical appeal to an audience's ethics and/or morals. Ethos is most often used in argumentative and informative writing modes. *Pathos* is an appeal to the audience's emotions and sympathies, and it is found in argumentative, descriptive, and narrative writing modes. *Logos* is an appeal to the audience's logic and reason and is used primarily in informative texts as well as in supporting details for argumentative pieces. Rhetorical appeals are discussed in depth in the informational texts and rhetoric section of the test.

If the author is trying to encourage global conversion to vegetarianism, he or she may choose to use all three rhetorical appeals to reach varying personality types. Those who are less interested in the welfare of animals but are interested in facts and science would relate more to logos. Animal lovers would relate better to an emotional appeal. In general, the most effective works utilize all three appeals.

Finally, after determining the writing mode and rhetorical appeal, the author will consider word choice, sentence structure, and tone, depending on the purpose and audience. The author may choose words that convey sadness or anger when speaking about animal welfare if writing to persuade, or he or she will stick to dispassionate and matter-of-fact tones, if informing the public on the treatment of animals in factory farms. If the author is writing to a younger or less-educated audience, he or she may choose to shorten and simplify sentence structures and word choice. If appealing to an audience with more expert knowledge on a particular subject, writers will more likely employ a style of longer sentences and more complex vocabulary.

Depending on the task, the author may choose to use a first person, second person, or third person point of view. First person and second person perspectives are inherently more casual in tone, including the author and the reader in the rhetoric, while third person perspectives are often seen in more professional settings.

Evaluating the Effectiveness of a Piece of Writing

An effective and engaging piece of writing will cause the reader to forget about the author entirely. Readers will become so engrossed in the subject, argument, or story at hand that they will almost identify with it, readily adopting beliefs proposed by the author or accepting all elements of the story as believable. On the contrary, poorly written works will cause the reader to be hyperaware of the author, doubting the writer's knowledge of a subject or questioning the validity of a narrative. Persuasive or expository works that are poorly researched will have this effect, as well as poorly planned stories with significant plot holes. An author must consider the task, purpose, and audience to sculpt a piece of writing effectively.

When evaluating the effectiveness of a piece, the most important thing to consider is how well the purpose is conveyed to the audience through the mode, use of rhetoric, and writing style.

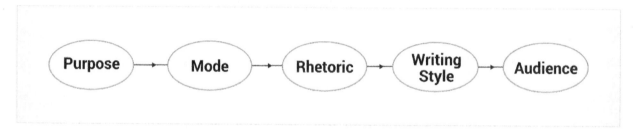

The purpose must pass through these three aspects for effective delivery to the audience. If any elements are not properly considered, the reader will be overly aware of the author, and the message will be lost. The following is a checklist for evaluating the effectiveness of a piece:

- Does the writer choose the appropriate writing mode—argumentative, narrative, descriptive, informative—for his or her purpose?

- Does the writing mode employed contain characteristics inherent to that mode?

- Does the writer consider the personalities/interests/demographics of the intended audience when choosing rhetorical appeals?

- Does the writer use appropriate vocabulary, sentence structure, voice, and tone for the audience demographic?

- Does the author properly establish himself/herself as having authority on the subject, if applicable?

- Does the piece make sense?

Another thing to consider is the medium in which the piece was written. If the medium is a blog, diary, or personal letter, the author may adopt a more casual stance towards the audience. If the piece of writing is a story in a book, a business letter or report, or a published article in a journal or if the task is to gain money or support or to get published, the author may adopt a more formal stance. Ultimately, the writer will want to be very careful in how he or she addresses the reader.

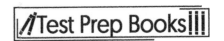

Finally, the effectiveness of a piece can be evaluated by asking how well the purpose was achieved. For example, if students are assigned to read a persuasive essay, instructors can ask whether the author influences students' opinions. Students may be assigned two differing persuasive texts with opposing perspectives and be asked which writer was more convincing. Students can then evaluate what factors contributed to this—for example, whether one author uses more credible supporting facts, appeals more effectively to readers' emotions, presents more believable personal anecdotes, or offers stronger counterargument refutation. Students can then use these evaluations to strengthen their own writing skills.

Documentation and Sources

As a reading specialist instructor, it is important to not only educate students but also to further the knowledge base of other teachers and educators. New research on learning disabilities, teaching techniques, and even psychological research is very valuable to any educational institution. This new information will impact the overall instruction of students throughout departments and potentially influence funding opportunities. Because research is constantly producing new ideas and improvements, educational institutions that incorporate it will continue their strive toward excellence. Therefore, it is important to offer the highest quality of information possible.

New information is only as good as its quality and authenticity. It is important to investigate all new research carefully, and make sure the sources are credible. Assessing the findings and claims of other professionals is important as well. If the information doesn't make sense or is poorly documented, reading specialists should consider researching the same material from a different source. When drawing from official research documentation, one must check bibliographies or specific incidents mentioned to fact-check the writer's claims. Not only does this new research impact the individual reading specialist, but also the students and the institution's integrity. Reading specialists must also be aware of trends within the research and whether the research in question is attempting to support a specific agenda or theory. Being mindful of opposing viewpoints in research topics will enable a reading instructor to offer balanced information that addresses topics.

Educational research can be quite difficult to understand and apply. When presenting information to peers, the specialist must use clear language and be prepared to address questions. Being able to present this material necessitates more than just knowledge of the research; one must be able to apply it to the current programs, or at least present ideas on how to do so. Reading instructors should ask themselves: Can this research help address current program issues? Can this research accelerate or improve student learning? Can these methodologies be seamlessly integrated, or will there be problems adjusting program parameters? Such analysis will not only determine whether the research in question has good information but also whether it's appropriate for the current needs of the school, faculty, and students.

Viewing and Representing

Written, Visual, and Oral Information from Texts and Multimedia Sources

Students in a modern classroom have access to a wide variety of instructional resources. From teacher-led instruction and classroom activities, traditional textbooks, encyclopedias, nonfiction magazines, and customized classroom libraries to desktop computers, iPads, tablets, laptops, online tutorials, and smart boards, there is a plethora of information waiting to be discovered. Learning how to integrate traditional written, visual, and oral information to other information provided on a multimedia platform can prove challenging, but it is well worth the effort. Since the vast majority of children from the primary school years and older are well equipped at using a variety of technology-based resources, educators who integrate technology in the classroom will likely succeed in helping children to progress both academically and socially. The classroom is as much a social setting as it is academic, and as society changes, so must the instructional approaches.

Time management is one of the initial tasks facing educators when setting up their academic year. Educators are responsible for teaching a wide range of subjects, specific domains within each subject, and numbers of skills within each domain. Designing long-range plans that take all of this into account and forming a framework for the academic year is the most logical starting point.

From this framework, educators can determine how to teach each discipline with an effective, time management approach. Taking the number of students, the possible varying academic and social levels, socioeconomic differences, and language barriers into account, teachers can begin to develop differentiated instructional approaches that cater to all the needs in the classroom. It is at this stage that both traditional resources and technology must find a way to complement each other in the classroom.

For instance, one effective approach is to instruct children to ensure that every research project involves a minimum of two textbook sources as well as a minimum of two technology-based sources. When introducing new topics or reinforcing a lesson, educators are still highly encouraged to use visual aids in the classroom, including word walls, personal dictionaries, and classroom labels. Modeling the effective use of hand-held books, reference guides, and magazines also provides children the opportunity to see how valuable written information continues to be in the world of education.

In order for children to experience a well rounded, quality education, instructional days should be divided between effective, quality instruction, independent exploration and learning, and positive social interaction. Since the needs of children vary in each classroom, as well as their academic and social levels, each educator's decision on how to divide instructional time will also vary. However, having access to technology is paramount in every classroom and at every grade level.

Technology in the classroom helps children to become more actively engaged and encourages independent learning with the use of student-centered, project-based activities. From virtual math tools to collaborative class blogs, there are many ways for students to effectively engage in technology in the classroom.

Although technology plays an important role in the modern classroom, it is still important for educators to guide children, helping them use the technology in an effective, efficient, and responsible manner. Teaching children about cyber-bullying, copyright, plagiarism, and digital footprints will inevitably strengthen their ability to responsibly and safely conduct themselves online.

Educators also use technology for lesson planning, assessments, and evaluation. With a number of online programs available, educators are able to provide students, colleagues, administration, and parents with effective feedback and to develop and evaluate high-quality formative and summative assessments in an efficient manner.

By combining the use of technology along with teacher-centered instruction and traditional textbooks, educators will undoubtedly help to create a classroom with children who are actively engaged throughout the instructional day.

Visual and Oral Elements

Depending on home life and first language acquisition, children generally enter the primary years of school with a basic foundation of oral development as well as basic phonemic awareness. It is imperative to a young child's continued success in language development that educators provide students with language-rich lessons and activities throughout the instructional day.

Visual Instructional Techniques

Studies continue to show a strong correlation between language development and the use of visual aids. From the primary years of education through the post-secondary years, the use of visual aids as a way to enhance reading comprehension has proven to be very effective. In the primary grades, picture books provide students with visual cues that help them to decode unknown words and strengthen reading comprehension. Visual aids support and clarify meaning, helping to make the learning and reading process more enjoyable and more interactive. When educators engage the students in a *picture walk*, skimming through picture books prior to reading, children become more motivated to read. Even reluctant readers, struggling readers, and English language learners are more apt to pick up a picture book and attempt to read it from cover to cover, enjoying the graphics and using them as powerful clues to the text's overall meaning.

Graphic novels are also becoming a popular addition to classroom and school libraries. With a structural approach that is similar to comic books, graphic novels have a strong appeal to children in the middle school years, teen years, and beyond. The visual images within graphic novels help children to make immediate connections to a story's plot and help them to understand potentially more challenging information.

As a universal learning tool, visual aids help all learners to comprehend the meaning behind the words and strengthen their ability to retain information over a longer period of time.

Oral Instructional Techniques

When children are just learning to read, they benefit greatly from shared reading and oral reading experiences. Having a teacher or a classmate read a book aloud helps emergent readers connect their phonemic awareness skills to a growing understanding and application of print awareness. This will begin to form the foundation for more advanced reading skills in later years.

Oral reading also helps children strengthen their use of vocabulary and advances their vocabulary inventory. Educators and more advanced readers who model oral reading fluency—including rate, accuracy, and prosody—demonstrate to young readers that the process of reading is highly interactive and meaningful. Educators who spend significant time engaging in classroom discussions and asking and answering questions help children develop social interaction skills, listening comprehension skills, and oral communication skills. When early and intensive instruction focuses on oral language development, educators set the groundwork for future reading success.

Oral and Visual Instructional Techniques

Multimedia presentations, such as PowerPoint or SlideShare, have been traditionally most effective at the higher education levels. However, as young children are more and more exposed to a world of technology, educators at the primary years are beginning to employ multimedia presentations in the classroom.

If carefully planned out, multimedia presentations can be used to enhance comprehension on virtually any subject. Using powerful graphic imagery that is directly relevant to the topic—coupled with effective textual language or audio—has been particularly effective in a growing number of classrooms.

Presenting students with the challenge of creating their own multimedia presentations can also be very rewarding for educators and students alike. Either independently, in pairs, or in groups, children take the learning process into their own hands with the opportunity to demonstrate the knowledge of a given subject by employing relevant written text and graphics.

Literary Text vs. Oral, Staged, or Filmed Version

Many of today's students are saturated with technology in their everyday lives. With the availability of iPads, iPods, personal computers, and smartphones, children as early as the primary grades are not only familiar with modern technology, but are becoming confident practitioners. Therefore, integrating technology in the classroom is a logical approach to helping children connect to the learning process and engage their interests.

With regard to English language arts instruction, technology can provide ample opportunities for educators to help strengthen students' critical thinking, oral communication, and reading comprehension skills. Since stories have always been used as a way of helping to explain the world and our place in it, they continue to be an integral part of any society's culture. The same story can be shared orally, in print, in film, or onstage, and each presentation provides similarities and differences with regard to the story's elements and to the audience's interpretation. By allowing children to compare and contrast various presentations of the same story, educators can increase students' motivation in English language arts.

Isolated scenes in films or documentaries can be used to begin a class discussion on a given topic. Children can openly discuss what version of the story they prefer and why. They can become detectives as they watch carefully for differences and similarities in the story's elements, such as setting, plot, and character traits. Educators who introduce a film or stage version of a literary work may wish to introduce the elements of lighting, dialogue, or special effects and begin a class discussion about how these elements, much like points of view, setting, and details in print, are critical to a film's structure.

If used strategically and with careful planning, the use of films, plays, and various technology-based story presentations can prove to be a very effective instructional strategy that strengthens students' understanding and appreciation of English language arts.

Visual and Multimedia Elements in Texts

Graphic novels, comic books, fiction, folktales, myths, and poetry often include visual elements in the story. Whether in the form of drawings, photographs, sound, video, or animation, these visual elements work to strengthen the reader's understanding and interpretation of the author's message, help to set the story's tone, bring characters into perspective, and, possibly, provide the reader with alternative interpretations of the story's main idea.

Hyperlinks included in informational texts provide the reader with additional sources of information that strengthen the author's message. Informational texts also employ the use of graphs, charts, diagrams, and maps, which either work to compare and contrast information, demonstrate cause and effect, show a chronological timeline of events, or display trends and patterns.

Effective instructional approaches to literature incorporate how to interpret the various forms of visual and multimedia elements that exist within literary and informational texts. Modeling how to use visuals in various texts appropriately will undoubtedly strengthen students' reading comprehension and critical thinking skills.

Assessment of Developing Literacy

Fostering Students' Participation in Collaborative Conversations with Diverse Partners

Effective and Responsible Practices in Communication with Children
The foundation of a child's academic, social, and emotional success in any classroom lies directly in the educator's ability to use effective communicative interactions. **DAP**, or **Developmentally Appropriate Practice**, was designed by researchers who took into consideration what is known about how children develop, as well as what is known about effective early education instruction. Classrooms with effective communication techniques will generally see enthusiastic, engaged children.

DAP focuses on these 10 basic principles that aim to help educators build an effective foundation of communication:

- Acknowledgement
- Encouragement
- Immediate and beneficial feedback
- Modeling
- Demonstrating
- Challenging
- Questioning
- Providing effective assistance
- Providing valuable information
- Giving appropriate directions

Acknowledgement
Students are not simply little subjects for educators to enlighten. They are intellectual, social, and emotional beings worthy of recognition and appreciation. Acknowledgement of students begins with understanding where they are coming from and the experiences they bring with them. When a teacher considers prior knowledge before beginning instruction, they are being considerate of the student's time and intellect. They are acknowledging that the student already has the capacity for learning and brings valid experiences and aptitudes that are useful for assimilating new information. The teacher doesn't waste time re-teaching what students have already mastered. Review is necessary, of course, but not to the extent that there is a risk of losing student engagement and interest.

Students come to learn at various stages of intellectual development. In the early stages, there is a duplicity of black-and-white thinking. Multiplicity should come next, where there is some understanding of opinion and perspective. Finally, learning to value evidence and validity helps students understand topics at various levels of complexity. When teachers take this into account, they are acknowledging the students' individuality and honoring their learning needs.

Significant differences exist in the way teaching and learning is conceptualized for various cultures. Values for particular types of learning, the beliefs about best practices, and the role of the teacher/student relationship may be strikingly different from culture to culture. The value of learning itself is a bridge for multicultural connection. When teachers recognize and celebrate cultural differences, they are acknowledging the students at the level of their individual identity.

The social trends and expectations of students and teachers grow and change over generations. The topics and ways that students are learning and teachers are teaching are likely quite different from what they were even a decade ago. Educators cannot expect students to learn the same way from generation to generation. Awareness of generational differences acknowledges the student and his or her perception of the world.

Encouragement

Ideally, students come into classrooms hopeful and willing to take risks. With this in mind, teachers have to develop the kind of classroom that fosters participation and motivation. Here are some ways that teachers can encourage classroom participation:

- Students should be praised. This helps them know they are at the center of learning. They need to feel cared for and valued. Positive behavior should be rewarded and progress acknowledged.

- Students should be allowed to have some control in their lives. Choices should be offered and mistakes forgiven.

- Excellence should be expected from students. High but realistic expectations should be held for them. The effort they put forth should be respected. The learning process, over the end product, should be valued.

- Children should be allowed to be children. There should be much activity and collaboration.

- The fun of learning should be shown to students. They should be encouraged by taking part in the planning of field trips, guest speakers, and other extraordinary activities.

- Students should be made aware of how learning relates to their lives. Teachers should teach to the interests of the students and understand where they are coming from.

- Clear and simple lessons should be presented at a pace they can all follow. Teachers should communicate clearly and enunciate understandably so students do not have to struggle to follow along. Teachers should regularly check on the students' level of understanding.

- A pleasant and comfortable environment free from obvious distractions should be created.

Immediate and Beneficial Feedback

Students need to know what they are doing well and what needs improvement. There should be no mystery about the learning targets. They need a positive self-image fostered by repeated success. Feedback should be positive and specific. Giving clear and effective feedback communicates to the student that her or his work is worthwhile, and that someone cares enough to review and consider it.

Informal feedback is part of formative assessment and should let students know where they are in the learning process and what they should do next. They should be able to formulate a plan for

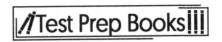

improvement and a vision of the next success they can achieve. Informal feedback is often oral and interactive.

Formal feedback is driven by objectives and rubrics that students should be given prior to a learning task. This gives them a clear goal for the activity and outlines expectations. Formal feedback should be presented in writing or another tangible format. Formal feedback is often summative in nature and may or may not be tied to grades and final assessments.

Feedback strategies are variable. Individualized adjustments can be made regarding timing, amount, mode, and audience. The timing may be immediate or delayed and given frequently or infrequently. Feedback might describe progress on many points or just a few, and it may go into great detail or be generalized. It may be oral, written, or demonstrative. It might be addressed to the individual, a small group, or the entire class. Feedback content is also infinitely variable. Feedback might focus on the work itself, the process, or the student's self-regulation but never on the student personally. Feedback comparisons might be criterion-, norm-, or self-referenced. It may function as a description of the work or an evaluation of the work but should not be judgmental. It can be both positive and negative, but any negative comments should be accompanied by suggestions for improvement. Feedback should be understandable to the student and developmentally appropriate. In some cases, feedback can be too specific so that it becomes difficult for a student to apply it to other situations. It can also be overly general, which does not give the student enough information to help with correction. Finally, feedback should communicate respect, activate motivation, and inspire thought.

Modeling, Explaining, and Demonstrating

In order to learn to read and write well, all children need effective modeling and demonstration. Educators often are content to assign reading and writing tasks and ask students to answer questions about the task in lieu of quality direct interactive instruction.

Modeling is when teachers engage in the activity of reading or writing and the children observe and imitate the procedures and strategies. Children can pick up many skills by simply watching and attempting to copy adult behaviors. Reading aloud is one of the most powerful strategies for teaching in the classroom. When being read to, students are given a model for how reading should sound and how stories are constructed. Talking about the reading selection during and after reading models an appropriate response to text. It also fosters comprehension strategies that children need in order to become effective readers. Writing down main points of the reading selection and taking notes models a function of writing. Designating a time each day for reading aloud highlights the importance of reading. High-quality literature with rich text and content should be chosen to read in the classroom. This models the evaluation of literature and the selection of quality reading material. Response groups should be formed so children have a model for collaboratively comprehending text. Modeling is an essential component of any classroom. However, modeling is not sufficient to give children enough information about how to accomplish the tasks that readers and writers actually need to be proficient.

Explanation is also a key component of classroom instruction. Adults in classrooms spend much time explaining reading and writing methods to students. Unfortunately, students often miss key messages because their attention span isn't long enough to follow wordy explanations. Explanations often involve specialized vocabulary that students may not be able to use to comprehend the instruction. Giving excellent explanations is an essential skill for teachers. Seeing teachers and other children model reading and writing and being told how to read and write is still not sufficient for teaching literacy to many struggling learners. This is where *demonstration* comes into play.

Demonstration is when a teacher not only models and explains how to do a task but also engages in thinking through the task with the students. Effective teachers narrate their thinking processes when modeling a strategy. An effective demonstration includes opportunities for the student to try the strategy with immediate feedback from the teacher. Demonstration is teaching and learning in real-time. Effective demonstration occurs in four steps: preparation, presentation, application, and evaluation.

During **preparation,** a teacher puts the students at ease with the impending learning task. He or she assesses students for prior knowledge of the information. Explaining the importance of the learning task is essential. This step may include an attention-getter or motivational strategy. Finally, preparation includes getting the students ready to observe, ensuring they can see and hear well and have appropriate note-taking supplies.

During **presentation,** the teacher tells, shows, illustrates, explains, questions, and models the task. By carefully and patiently narrating the process step-by-step, stressing key points and learning goals, the teacher presents all information and models all skills needed.

Application is guided practice. It includes students attempting the task and then having the teacher give them immediate feedback. Repetition is often used to solidify the skills. The teacher's job is to narrate the steps taken, to ask questions for a measure of understanding, and to prevent errors.

Evaluation is following up with the learning that occurred during the demonstration. The teacher reviews the objectives and evaluates whether they were covered effectively. Checking for readiness and making sure the students know how to get help if they need it are parts of this step.

Challenging and Questioning

Educators are constantly asking questions. This is because questioning serves a wide range of functions in the classroom. Teachers ask questions to involve and engage students in a lesson. Questions increase interest and motivation. A teacher asks questions to assess prior knowledge and readiness for learning. Questioning can help check for completion of learning tasks. It is key for developing critical thinking skills. Questions might be asked to review or assess mastery of learning goals. Asking questions stimulates independent and collaborative learning and invites insight and forethought.

When questioning, it is important to consider how many questions to ask. During the lesson, it is vital to know when the questions are the most appropriate. Will the questions lend meaning to the instruction? Will the questions cause students to focus on all the information presented or only on the parts that help them answer the question? Will the questions lead away from the topic? It is also important to consider how much wait-time to give students to answer the question before the teacher elaborates or asks a new question. Typically, students need to be afforded at least three seconds to formulate an answer to a question. The way a teacher responds to answers is just as important as the questions themselves. The teacher can affirm a correct response, probe the student for more information, or redirect him if the answer is wrong or misinterpreted.

It can be difficult for teachers to give lessons at the appropriate level of difficulty in a classroom of students who are at varying levels of academic readiness. How does a teacher reach a student who is struggling and one who is above grade level in the same lesson? Knowing the appropriate challenge level is essential for learning in the classroom. If a lesson is too challenging, some students will give up.

Conversely, if a lesson is not challenging enough, some students will get bored. There are many strategies that teachers can use to differentiate lessons for varying challenge levels including:

- Allowing choices
- Integrating technology
- Allowing collaboration
- Accommodating pace
- Assessing prior knowledge
- Encouraging goal setting
- Providing creative teaching
- Allowing independent learning
- Allowing students to explore their interests
- Using self-assessment

Providing Effective Assistance and Valuable Information

Students need assistance and guidance in a classroom; however, knowing how much help to offer is always a balancing act. If teachers give too much assistance, they end up doing the work for students, who then do not learn. If teachers do not offer enough assistance, students become lost, overwhelmed, and do not learn. What does the right amount of help look like for each student? Giving effective assistance to students is a foundational teaching strategy. The goal is to help students become as self-motivated and autonomous as possible.

Autonomy in the classroom begins with establishing clear and consistent classroom procedures. Students should be taught how the classroom runs and how to manage themselves. If a student knows what to do to solve simple problems such as sharpening pencils, teachers do not need to waste valuable teaching time with disruptions. Educators can continue to build autonomy by allowing freedom of choice and giving students some power.

Related to autonomy is the concept of self-motivation. Teachers can help students become self-motivated learners by making learning individualized and accessible to all. Instruction should be differentiated for levels of readiness, for personal interests and aptitudes, and for varied learning styles and multiple intelligences. Offering students choices of learning activities and methods of assessment helps individualize education. Educators should have knowledge of the Universal Design for Learning, which promotes differentiation through considering the following three premises:

1. Content should be presented in multiple ways: visual, oral, kinesthetic, etc.

2. Students should be able to show their learning in multiple ways: writing, speaking, drawing, acting, etc.

3. Engaging students should occur in multiple formats: videos, technology, group work, etc.

Teachers can also foster self-motivation by holding high expectations of students and giving them a sense of competence. When adults expect excellence from students, the students often rise to the occasion. Care must be taken that expectations are developmentally appropriate and attainable, but they should always stretch students to the top of their capabilities. Giving students a sense of competence means learning effective praise techniques. It is best to praise effort (something students can control) over intelligence (something out of their control). Students will gain a sense that they learn through their own hard work.

Giving Appropriate Directions

One of the biggest obstacles to learning is when students do not understand or cannot remember the directions they are given. Present directions in auditory and visual formats and assess for understanding by having students retell them to each other or to the teacher. Some tips for teachers to give good directions include:

- Providing directions in story form. Students can often remember stories, since they are typically more interesting and therefore, better than other forms of communication for multi-step directions.

- Starting with *"when I say go,"* which gets them to listen for all the directions before moving, then telling students what they're *"going to"* do for each step of the process. Students create pictures of themselves doing the steps in their mind's eye and assume they can do it without help.

- Being silly! Throwing in some funny character voices, different facial expressions, or random silly instructions for things they should do between steps of the real task adds interest and increases the desire of students to listen more closely.

- Asking students to speak up if they don't understand all the steps. Teachers should inform students that they want to know of any questions before the students begin the task, rather than find out in the middle of the activity that the students didn't hear or understand all the instructions at the beginning. This makes students responsible for knowing what to do.

- Begin with requiring students to only do a few things at a time. However, as they get used to working with provided instructions, they will be able to take on much more lengthy activities and remember more directions.

The Abecedarian Approach

The **Abecedarian Approach** is primarily concerned with a child's behavioral and intellectual successes from birth to adulthood. There are four main components of the Abecedarian Approach: 1) learning games; 2) conversational reading; 3) language priority; and 4) enriched caregiving. Two areas explicitly involve literacy development: conversational reading and language priority. They both involve playful, responsive approaches to rich language instruction.

The Abecedarian Approach to Conversational Reading

The Abecedarian Approach to conversational reading has been demonstrated to have significant benefits in the areas of reading fluency and comprehension. **Conversational reading** involves a conversational-style of reading instruction in which the educator plays an active role by partnering in shared reading activities. Conversational reading gets its name from being a back-and-forth reading conversation. During the reading process, educators prompt the children to "see, show, and say" what they are reading. This is referred to as the **3S Strategy**. Children may be encouraged to identify the words they know on a given page, look for rhyming words, or draw pictures that correspond to the reading. Educators take an active role in the reading process by running their fingers along the words, asking questions about the reading, prompting conversations, and strengthening comprehension, as well as pointing out interesting ideas about the reading to encourage a dialogue.

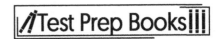

The Abecedarian Approach to Language Priority

The Abecedarian Approach uses language priority to focus on rich language stimulation. By emphasizing language throughout the day, the language priority strategy creates endless occasions for meaningful conversations. Educators work to extend conversations from a variety of different angles, promoting higher cognitive thinking and engagement. Educators will also use the **3N Approach** by *noticing* the student's current reading level, *nudging* or encouraging the student to go one step beyond this level, and *narrating* the student's activities.

Practice Questions

1. What contributes the most to schema development?
   a. Reading comprehension
   b. Structural analysis
   c. Written language
   d. Background knowledge

2. Which of the following is NOT an essential component of effective fluency instruction?
   a. Spelling
   b. Feedback
   c. Guidance
   d. Practice

3. The Directed-Reading Think-Aloud (DRTA) method helps students to do what?
   a. Build prior knowledge by exploring audiovisual resources before a reading
   b. Predict what will occur in a text and search the text to verify the predictions
   c. Identify, define, and review unfamiliar terms
   d. Understand the format of multiple types and genres of text

4. A teacher assigns a writing prompt in order to assess her students' reading skills. Which of the following can be said about this form of reading assessment?
   a. It is the most beneficial way to assess reading comprehension
   b. It is invalid because a student's ability to read and write are unrelated
   c. It is erroneous since the strength of a student's reading and writing vocabulary may differ
   d. It is the worst way to assess reading comprehension

5. When does scaffolded reading occur?
   a. A student hears a recording of herself reading a text in order to set personal reading goals.
   b. A student receives assistance and feedback on strategies to utilize while reading from someone else.
   c. A student is given extra time to find the answers to predetermined questions.
   d. A student is pulled out of a class to receive services elsewhere.

6. What are the three interconnected indicators of reading fluency?
   a. Phonetics, word morphology, and listening comprehension
   b. Accuracy, rate, and prosody
   c. Syntax, semantics, and vocabulary
   d. Word exposure, phonetics, and decodable skills

7. Which of the following about effective independent reading is NOT true?
   a. Students should read texts that are below their reading levels during independent reading.
   b. Students need to first demonstrate fluency before reading independently.
   c. Students who don't yet display automaticity should whisper to themselves when reading aloud.
   d. Students who demonstrate automaticity in decoding should be held accountable during independent reading.

8. Timed oral reading can be used to assess which of the following?
   a. Phonics
   b. Listening comprehension
   c. Reading rate
   d. Background knowledge

9. Syntax is best described as what?
   a. The arrangement of words into sentences
   b. The study of language meaning
   c. The study of grammar and language structure
   d. The proper formatting of a written text

10. What do informal reading assessments allow that standardized reading assessments do NOT allow?
   a. The application of grade-level norms towards a student's reading proficiency
   b. The personalization of reading assessments in order to differentiate instruction based on the need(s) of individual students
   c. The avoidance of partialities in the interpretation of reading assessments
   d. The comparison of an individual's reading performance to that of other students in the class

11. When building a class library, a teacher should be cognizant of the importance of what?
   a. Providing fiction that contains concepts relating to the background knowledge of all students in the class.
   b. Utilizing only nonfictional text that correlates to state and national standards in order to reinforce academic concept knowledge.
   c. Utilizing a single genre of text in order to reduce confusion of written structures.
   d. Including a wide range of fiction and nonfiction texts at multiple reading levels.

12. Samantha is in second grade and struggles with fluency. Which of the following strategies is likely to be most effective in improving Samantha's reading fluency?
   a. The teacher prompts Samantha when she pauses upon coming across an unknown word when reading aloud.
   b. The teacher records Samantha as she reads aloud.
   c. The teacher reads a passage out loud several times to Samantha and then has Samantha read the same passage.
   d. The teacher uses read-alouds and verbalizes contextual strategies that can be used to identify unfamiliar words.

13. Reading fluency is best described as the ability to do what?
   a. Read smoothly and accurately
   b. Comprehend what is read
   c. Demonstrate phonetic awareness
   d. Properly pronounce a list of words

14. Poems are often an effective device when teaching what skill?
   a. Fluency
   b. Spelling
   c. Writing
   d. Word decoding

15. A teacher needs to assess students' accuracy in reading grade-appropriate, high frequency, and irregular sight words. Which of the following strategies would be most appropriate for this purpose?

    a. The teacher gives students a list of words to study for a spelling test that will be administered the following week.

    b. The teacher allows each student to bring their favorite book from home and has each student read their selected text aloud independently.

    c. The teacher administers the Stanford Structural Analysis assessment to determine students' rote memory and application of morphemes contained within the words.

    d. The teacher records how many words each student reads correctly when reading aloud a list of a teacher-selected, grade-appropriate words.

16. What type of texts are considered nonfiction?

    a. Folktales

    b. Memoirs

    c. Fables

    d. Short stories

17. What is a summative assessment?

    a. A formal assessment that is given at the end of a unit of study

    b. An informal assessment that is given at the end of a unit of study

    c. An assessment that is given daily and is usually only a few questions in length, based on the day's objective

    d. An assessment given at the end of the week that is usually based on observation

18. How are typographic features useful when teaching reading comprehension?

    a. Typographic features are graphics used to illustrate the story and help students visualize the text.

    b. Typographic features give the answers in boldfaced print.

    c. Typographic features are not helpful when teaching reading comprehension and should not be used.

    d. Typographic features are print in boldface, italics, and subheadings, used to display changes in topics or to highlight important vocabulary or content.

19. What do English Language Learners need to identify prior to comprehending text?

    a. Vocabulary

    b. Figurative language

    c. Author's purpose

    d. Setting

20. What kind of assessment is most beneficial for students with special needs?

    a. Frequent and ongoing

    b. Weekly

    c. Monthly

    d. Summative assessments only at the end of a unit of study

21. Which is NOT a reason that independent reading is important for developing reading comprehension?
    a. To develop a lifelong love of reading
    b. To encourage students to read a genre they enjoy
    c. So that students can read at their own pace
    d. To visit the reading corner, which is an area of the classroom that is restful and enjoyable

22. Why are purposeful read alouds by a teacher important to enhance reading comprehension?
    a. They encourage students to unwind from a long day and reading lesson.
    b. They encourage students to listen for emphasis and voice.
    c. They encourage students to compare the author's purpose versus the teacher's objective.
    d. They encourage students to work on important work from earlier in the day while listening to a story.

23. Which of the following is the study of what words mean in certain situations?
    a. Morphology
    b. Pragmatics
    c. Syntax
    d. Semantics

24. What is "text evidence" when referring to answering a comprehension question?
    a. Taking phrases directly from the text itself to answer a question
    b. Using a variety of resources to find the answer
    c. Using technology and websites to locate an answer
    d. Paraphrasing and using a student's own words to answer the question

25. What allows readers to effectively translate print into recognizable speech?
    a. Fluency
    b. Spelling
    c. Phonics
    d. Word decoding

26. Which of the following is the MOST important reason why group-based discussions in the classroom enhance reading comprehension?
    a. They promote student discussions without the teacher present.
    b. They promote student discussions with a friend.
    c. They promote student discussions so that those who didn't understand the text can get answers from another student.
    d. They give all students a voice and allow them to share their answer, rather than one student sharing an answer with the class

27. Which of the following skills is NOT useful when initially helping students understand and comprehend a piece of text?
    a. Graphic organizers
    b. Note-taking
    c. Small intervention groups
    d. Extension projects and papers

93

28. Why are intervention groups important to advanced learners?
    a. They are not useful, as they do not need intervention in a particular skill
    b. They can be used to teach struggling students
    c. They can be given more advanced and complex work
    d. They can be given tasks to do in the classroom while others are meeting for intervention

29. Which of the following can be useful when working with intervention groups of struggling readers?
    a. Having the teacher read aloud a text to the students while they take notes
    b. Having students read the text silently
    c. Giving independent work and explaining the directions in detail before they take it back to their seat
    d. Providing games for them to play while the teacher observes

30. What should be taught and mastered first when teaching reading comprehension?
    a. Theme
    b. Word analysis and fluency
    c. Text evidence
    d. Writing

31. What is the method called that teachers use before and after reading to improve critical thinking and comprehension?
    a. Self-monitoring comprehension
    b. KWL charts
    c. Metacognitive skills
    d. Directed reading-thinking activities

32. When a student looks back at a previous reading section for information, he or she is using which of the following?
    a. Self-monitoring comprehension
    b. KWL charts
    c. Metacognitive skills
    d. Directed reading-thinking activities

33. Which choice of skills is NOT part of Bloom's Taxonomy?
    a. Remembering and understanding
    b. Applying and analyzing
    c. Listening and speaking
    d. Evaluating and creating

34. What is the spelling stage of a student who looks at a word and is able to tell the teacher that the letters spell C-A-T, but the who cannot actually say the word?
    a. Alphabetic Spelling
    b. Within Word Pattern Spelling
    c. Derivational Relations Spelling
    d. Emergent Spelling

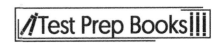

35. Predicting, Summarizing, Questioning, and Clarifying are steps of what?
    a. Reciprocal teaching
    b. Comprehensive teaching
    c. Activation teaching
    d. Summative teaching

36. When a student asks, "What do I know?", "What do I want to know?", and "What have I learned?" and records the answers in a table, he or she is using which of the following?
    a. Self-monitoring comprehension
    b. KWL charts
    c. Metacognitive skills
    d. Directed reading-thinking activities

37. What technique might an author use to let the reader know that the main character was in a car crash as a child?
    a. Point of view
    b. Characterization
    c. Figurative language
    d. Flashback

38. A graphic organizer is a method of achieving what?
    a. Integrating knowledge and ideas
    b. Generating questions
    c. Determining point of view
    d. Determining the author's purpose

39. A student is trying to decide if a character is telling the truth about having stolen candy. After the student reads that the character is playing with an empty candy wrapper in her pocket, the student decides the character is guilty. This is an example of what?
    a. Flashback
    b. Making inferences
    c. Style
    d. Figurative language

40. What is the method of categorizing text by its structure and literary elements called?
    a. Fiction
    b. Nonfiction
    c. Genre
    d. Plot

41. A reader is distracted from following a story because he's having trouble understanding why a character has decided to cut school, so the reader jumps to the next page to find out where the character is headed. This is an example of what?
    a. Self-monitoring comprehension
    b. KWL charts
    c. Metacognitive skills
    d. Directed reading-thinking activities

42. Phonemic Awareness, Phonics, Fluency, Vocabulary, and Comprehension are the five basic elements of what?
    a. Bloom's Taxonomy
    b. Spelling instruction
    c. Reading education
    d. Genre

43. A child reads the story *Little Red Riding Hood* aloud. He easily pronounces the words, uses an apprehensive tone to show that the main character should not be leaving the path, adds a scary voice for the Big Bad Wolf, and reads the story at a pace that engages the class. What are these promising signs of?
    a. Reading fluency
    b. Phonemic awareness
    c. Reading comprehension
    d. Working memory

44. A student is trying to read the word "preferred." She first recognizes the word "red" at the end, then sounds out the rest of the word by breaking it down into "pre," then "fer," then "red." Finally she puts it together and says "preferred." This student is displaying what attribute?
    a. Phonemic awareness
    b. Phonics
    c. Fluency
    d. Vocabulary

45. A class silently reads a passage on the American Revolution. Once they are done, the teacher asks who were the two sides fighting, why were they fighting, and who won. What skill is the teacher gauging?
    a. Orthographic development
    b. Fluency
    c. Comprehension
    d. Phonics

46. In the word *shut*, the *sh* is an example of what?
    a. Consonant digraph
    b. Sound segmentation
    c. Vowel digraph
    d. Rime

47. When students identify the phonemes in spoken words, they are practicing which of the following?
    a. Sound blending
    b. Substitution
    c. Rhyming
    d. Segmentation

48. What is the alphabetic principle?
    a. The understanding that letters represent sounds in words.
    b. The ability to combine letters to correctly spell words.
    c. The proper use of punctuation within writing.
    d. The memorization of all the letters in the alphabet.

49. Print awareness includes all EXCEPT which of the following concepts?
    a. The differentiation of uppercase and lowercase letters
    b. The identification of word boundaries
    c. The proper tracking of words
    d. The spelling of sight words

50. When teachers point to words during shared readings, what are they modeling?
    I. Word boundaries
    II. Directionality
    III. One-to-one correspondence
    a. I and II
    b. I and III
    c. II and III
    d. I, II, and III

51. Structural analysis would be the most appropriate strategy in determining the meaning of which of the following words?
    a. Extra
    b. Improbable
    c. Likely
    d. Wonder

52. A student spells *eagle* as *EGL*. This student is performing at which stage of spelling?
    a. Conventional
    b. Phonetic
    c. Semiphonetic
    d. Transitional

53. Spelling instruction should include which of the following?
    I. Word walls
    II. Daily reading opportunities
    III. Daily writing opportunities
    IV. Weekly spelling inventories with words students have studied during the week
    a. I and IV
    b. I, II, and III
    c. I, II, and IV
    d. I, II, III, and IV

54. A kindergarten student is having difficulty distinguishing the letters *b* and *d*. The teacher should do which of the following?
    a. Have the student use a think-aloud to verbalize the directions of the shapes used when writing each letter.
    b. Have the student identify the letters within grade-appropriate texts.
    c. Have the student write each letter five times.
    d. Have the student write a sentence in which all of the letters start with either *b* or *d*.

55. When differentiating phonics instruction for English-language learners (ELLs), teachers should do which of the following?
    a. Increase the rate of instruction
    b. Begin with the identification of word boundaries
    c. Focus on syllabication
    d. Capitalize on the transfer of relevant skills from the learners' original language(s)

56. Which of the following is the most appropriate assessment of spelling for students who are performing at the pre-phonetic stage?
    a. Sight word drills
    b. Phonemic awareness tests
    c. Writing samples
    d. Concepts about print (CAP) test

57. Phonological awareness is best assessed through which of the following?
    a. Identification of rimes or onsets within words
    b. Identification of letter-sound correspondences
    c. Comprehension of an audio book
    d. Writing samples

58. The identification of morphemes within words occurs during the instruction of what?
    a. Structural analysis
    b. Syllabic analysis
    c. Phonics
    d. The alphabetic principle

59. Which of the following pairs of words are homophones?
    a. Playful and replay
    b. To and too
    c. Was and were
    d. Gloomy and sad

60. Nursery rhymes are used in kindergarten to develop what?
    a. Print awareness
    b. Phoneme recognition
    c. Syllabication
    d. Structural analysis

61. High-frequency words such as *be, the*, and *or* are taught during the instruction of what?
    a. Phonics skills
    b. Sight word recognition
    c. Vocabulary development
    d. Structural analysis

62. To thoroughly assess students' phonics skills, teachers should administer assessments that require students to do which of the following?
    a. Decode in context only
    b. Decode in isolation only
    c. Both A and B
    d. Neither A nor B

63. A student is having difficulty pronouncing a word that she comes across when reading aloud. Which of the following is most likely NOT a reason for the difficulty that the student is experiencing?
    a. Poor word recognition
    b. A lack of content vocabulary
    c. Inadequate background knowledge
    d. Repeated readings

64. Which is the largest contributor to the development of students' written vocabulary?
    a. Reading
    b. Directed reading
    c. Direct teaching
    d. Modeling

65. The study of roots, suffixes, and prefixes is called what?
    a. Listening comprehension
    b. Word consciousness
    c. Word morphology
    d. Textual analysis

66. It is important to choose a variety of texts to elicit higher-level thinking skills. Which of the following text groupings would be appropriate to reach this goal?
    a. Basal readers, fantasy texts, and sci-fi novels
    b. Nonfiction, fiction, cultural pieces, and United States documents
    c. Scholastic magazine articles
    d. Textbooks and high-interest blogs

67. Informational text should comprise what percentage of all text used in instruction by the time students reach the twelfth grade?
    a. 25 percent
    b. 55 percent
    c. 50 percent
    d. 70 percent

68. A teacher wants to help her students write a nonfiction essay on how the Pueblos built their homes. Before they write, she helps the students make clay from corn starch and water, draw a plan for the house with a ruler, and build it using the clay and leaves from the schoolyard. These exercises are examples of what?
    a. Proficiency
    b. Collaboration
    c. Constructive writing
    d. Cross-curricular integration

69. A first grader that is in a classroom's reading center appears to be frustrated. How can the teacher best help this student find a book that is at the appropriate reading level?
    a. Have the student do a five-finger test for vocabulary
    b. Pick a new book for the student
    c. Have the student try to figure it out on their own
    d. Have a peer read the book to the student

70. Which element is important for a teacher to consider when planning a lesson?
    I. Pacing
    II. Intervention groups
    III. Modeling and direct instruction
    a. III only
    b. I and II
    c. I and III
    d. I, II, and III

71. What is an effective strategy when working with a child who has an Individualized Education Program (IEP)?
    I. Provide remediation during which the teacher works with the student on a particular skill
    II. Allow the student to work independently
    III. Chart the student's performance on a particular skill on a weekly basis in order to observe the student's growth over time
    a. II and III
    b. I and II
    c. I and III
    d. I, II, and III

72. Which trait teaches students to build the framework of their writing?
    a. Conventions
    b. Word choice
    c. Ideas
    d. Organization

73. What is the goal of a reading specialist position at a school site?
    I. To inform staff of changes in the curriculum
    II. To offer reading lessons in the classroom
    III. To instruct staff on how to do their job
    a. II only
    b. I and II
    c. II and III
    d. I, II, and III

74. Which of the following is NOT the best way to utilize a reading center or corner in a classroom?
    a. As a spot for students to play games
    b. As a private and quiet place to chat about books
    c. As a location to provide a variety of leveled readers
    d. As fun and entertaining décor to enhance a comfortable learning environment

75. Which trait is most commonly associated with giving individuality and style to writing?
    a. Voice
    b. Word choice
    c. Presentation
    d. Ideas

Answer Explanations

1. D: A schema is a framework or structure that stores and retrieves multiple, interrelated learning elements as a single packet of knowledge. Children who have greater exposure to life events have greater schemas. Thus, students who bring extensive background knowledge to the classroom are likely to experience easier automation when reading. In this way, background knowledge and reading comprehension are directly related. Likewise, students who have greater background knowledge are able to learn a greater number of new concepts at a faster rate.

2. A: Practice is an essential component of effective fluency instruction. When teachers provide daily opportunities for students to learn words and utilize word-analysis skills, accuracy and rate will likely increase. Oral reading accompanied by guidance and feedback from teachers, peers, or parents has a significant positive impact on fluency. In order to be beneficial, such feedback needs to target specific areas in which students need improvement, as well as strategies that students can use in order to improve their areas of need. Such feedback increases students' awareness so that they can independently make needed modifications to improve fluency.

3. B: DRTA, or Directed Reading-Thinking Activity, incorporates both read-alouds and think-alouds. During a DRTA, students make predictions about what they will read in order to set a purpose for reading, give cognitive focus, and activate prior knowledge. Students use reading comprehension in order to verify their predictions.

4. C: There are five types of vocabulary: listening, speaking, written, sight, and meaning. Most often, listening vocabulary contains the greatest number of words. This is usually followed by speaking vocabulary, sight reading vocabulary, meaning vocabulary, and written vocabulary. Formal written language usually utilizes a richer vocabulary than everyday oral language. Thus, students show differing strengths in reading vocabulary and writing vocabulary. Likewise, a student's reading ability will most likely differ when assessed via a reading assessment versus a writing sample.

5. B: Scaffolded opportunities occur when a teacher helps students by giving them support, offering immediate feedback, and suggesting strategies. In order to be beneficial, such feedback needs to help students identify areas that need improvement. Much like oral reading feedback, this advice increases students' awareness so they can independently make needed modifications in order to improve fluency.

Scaffolding is lessened as the student becomes a more independent reader. Struggling readers, students with reading difficulties or disabilities, and students with special needs especially benefit from direct instruction and feedback that teaches decoding and analysis of unknown words, automaticity in key sight words, and correct expression and phrasing.

6. B: Key indicators of reading fluency include accuracy, rate, and prosody. Phonetics and decodable skills aid fluency. Syntax, semantics, word morphology, listening comprehension, and word exposure aid vocabulary development.

7. A: Once students become fluent readers, independent reading can begin. Students who don't yet display automaticity may need to read out loud or whisper to themselves during independent reading time. Independent silent reading accompanied by comprehension accountability is an appropriate strategy for students who demonstrate automaticity in their decoding skills. Also, each student should be provided with a text that matches his or her reading level.

8. C: The most common measurement of reading rate includes the oral contextual timed readings of students. During a timed reading, the number of errors made within a given amount of time is recorded. This data can be used to identify if a student's rate is improving and if the rate falls within the recommended fluency rates for their grade level.

9. A: Syntax refers to the arrangement of words and phrases to form well-developed sentences and paragraphs. Semantics has to do with language meaning. Grammar is a composite of all systems and structures utilized within a language and includes syntax, word morphology, semantics, and phonology. Cohesion and coherence of oral and written language are promoted through a full understanding of syntax, semantics, and grammar.

10. B: Informal reading assessments allow teachers to create differentiated assessments that target reading skills of individual students. In this way, teachers can gain insight into a student's reading strengths and weaknesses. Informal assessments can help teachers decide what content and strategies need to be targeted. However, standardized reading assessments provide all students with the same structure to assess multiple skills at one time. Standardized reading assessments cannot be individualized. Such assessments are best used for gaining an overview of student reading abilities.

11. D: Students within a single classroom come with various background knowledge, interests, and needs. Thus, it's unrealistic to find texts that apply to all. Students benefit when a wide range of fiction and nonfiction texts are available in a variety of genres, promoting differentiated instruction.

12. D: This answer alludes to both read-alouds and think-alouds. Modeling of fluency can be done through read-alouds. Proper pace, phrasing, and expression of text can be modeled when teachers read aloud to their students. During think-alouds, teachers verbalize their thought processes when orally reading a selection. The teacher's explanations may describe strategies they use as they read to monitor their comprehension. In this way, teachers explicitly model the metacognition processes that good readers use to construct meaning from a text.

13. A: Reading fluency is the ability to accurately read at a socially acceptable pace and with proper expression. Phonetic awareness leads to the proper pronunciation of words and fluency. Once students are able to read fluently, concentration is no longer dedicated toward the process of reading. Instead, students can concentrate on the meaning of a text. Thus, in the developmental process of reading, comprehension follows fluency.

14. A: Poems are an effective method for teaching fluency, since rhythmic sounds and rhyming words build a child's understanding of phonemic awareness.

15. D: Accuracy is measured via the percentage of words that are read correctly with in a given text. Word-reading accuracy is often measured by counting the number of errors that occur per 100 words of oral reading. This information is used to select the appropriate level of text for an individual.

16. B: Nonfiction texts include memoirs, biographies, autobiographies, and journalism. Choices *A*, *C*, and *D* are all examples of fictional prose.

17. A: Summative assessments are formal assessments that are given at the end of a unit of study. These assessments are usually longer in length. They are not completed daily. These summative assessments shouldn't be confused with informal assessments, which are used more frequently to determine mastery of the day's objective. However, summative assessments may be used to determine students' mastery, in order to form intervention groups thereafter.

18. D: Typographic features are important when teaching reading comprehension as the boldfaced, highlighted, or italics notify a student when a new vocabulary word or idea is present. Subtitles and headings can also alert a student to a change in topic or idea. These features are also important when answering questions, as a student may be able to easily find the answer with these typographic features present.

19. A: English Language Learners should master vocabulary and word usages in order to fully comprehend text. Figurative language, an author's purpose, and settings are more complex areas and are difficult for English Language Learners. These areas can be addressed once ELL students understand the meaning of words. In order to master comprehension skills, vocabulary and the English language need to be mastered first, but comprehension can still be difficult. Figurative language is culture-based, and inferences may be difficult for those with a different cultural background.

20. A: Assessments should always be frequent and ongoing for all students, but especially for those with special needs. These assessments may be informal, but given daily after direct instruction and modeling. Summative assessments are important, but this should not be the first and only assessment during a unit of study, as these types of assessments are given at the end of a unit of study. Weekly and monthly assessments are not frequent enough for instructors to identify struggling areas and for successful remediation and intervention.

21. D: Although the reading corner should be a restful and enjoyable place to encourage students to read independently, it does not enhance reading comprehension directly. Choices *A*, *B*, and *C* all encourage enhancement of reading comprehension. Giving students a chance to read independently allows them to choose books they enjoy, read at their own pace, and develop a lifelong enjoyment of reading.

22. B: Purposeful teacher read alouds allow students to listen to a story for voice emphasis and tone. This will help students when they are reading independently as well. Although students may find this time restful or a chance to catch up on old work, neither is the main purpose. Students may use this time to take notes on the reading, but students should only be listening to the story being read and not doing other work.

23. B: Pragmatics is the study of what words mean in certain situations. Choice *A*, morphology, involves the structure and formation of words. Choice *C*, syntax, refers to the order of words in a sentence. Choice *D*, semantics, addresses the distinct meanings of words.

24. A: "Text evidence" refers to taking phrases and sentences directly from the text and writing them in the answer. Students are not asked to paraphrase, nor use any other resources to address the answer. Therefore, Choices *B*, *C*, and *D* are incorrect.

25. C: Phonics allows readers to effectively translate print into recognizable speech. If children lack proficiency in phonics, their ability to read fluently and to increase vocabulary will be limited.

26. D: Text-based discussions, like think-pair-share, encourage all students to speak rather than having just one student share an answer. Each student is given time to collaborate with another student and share their thoughts. It is not intended for one student to give another student the answers, which is why Choice *C* is incorrect. Although Choices *A* and *B* might be correct, they are not the MOST important reason that text-based discussions are useful in the classroom.

27. D: Extension projects and papers should be used to challenge advanced learners, not learners developing comprehension skills. Graphic organizers, taking notes, and small intervention groups can aid reading comprehension. Graphic organizers and taking notes are great ways for a student to outline key parts of the text. Small intervention groups set up by the instructor can then focus on individual needs.

28. C: Advanced students can benefit from intervention groups by allowing the students to be challenged with more complex assignments. These assignments can be worked on independently and can include more difficult questions or higher level vocabulary. Even short projects may be beneficial for these advanced students to work on throughout the week.

29. A: Small intervention groups can benefit from a teacher reading a text or small book aloud while students listen and take notes. This helps struggling students to focus on reading comprehension rather than having to decode words. Intervention time is not meant for a teacher to give independent work nor to just provide observation without support.

30. B: Word analysis and fluency should be mastered before teaching theme, text evidence, and writing. For English Language Learners and struggling readers, word analysis and fluency are often difficult barriers, which is why comprehension skills are not initially mastered. Theme is often a complex and inferential skill, which is developed later on. Text evidence is pulling answers to comprehension questions directly from a text and cannot be accomplished until readers can fluently read and understand the text. Writing skills generally come after comprehension skills are underway.

31. D: Teachers use directed reading-thinking activities before and after reading to improve critical thinking and reading comprehension. Metacognitive skills are when learners think about their thinking. Self-monitoring is when children are asked to think as they read and ask themselves if what they have just read makes sense. KWL charts help guide students to identify what they already know about a given topic.

32. C: Asking oneself a comprehension question is a metacognition skill. Readers with metacognitive skills have learned to think about thinking. It gives students control over their learning while they read. KWL charts help students to identify what they already know about a given topic.

33. C: Listening and speaking are not part of Bloom's Taxonomy. The six parts are remembering, understanding, applying, analyzing, evaluating, and creating.

34. D: During the Emergent Spelling stage, children can identify letters but not the corresponding sounds. The other choices are all fictitious.

35. A: Reciprocal teaching involves predicting, summarizing, questioning, and clarifying. The other choices are all fictitious.

36. B: KWL charts are an effective method of activating prior knowledge and taking advantage of students' curiosity. Students can create a KWL (*Know/Want to know/Learned*) chart to prepare for any unit of instruction and to generate questions about a topic.

37. D: Flashback is a technique used to give more background information in a story. None of the other concepts are directly related to going back in time.

38. A: Graphic organizers are a method of integrating knowledge and ideas. A graphic organizer can be one of many different visual tools for connecting concepts to help students understand information.

39. B: Making inferences is a method of deriving meaning in writing that is intended by the author but not explicitly stated. A flashback is a scene set earlier than the main story. Style is a general term for the way something is done. Figurative language is text that is not to be taken literally.

40. C: Genre is a means of categorizing text by its structure and literary elements. Fiction and nonfiction are both genre categories. Plot is the sequence of events that make a story happen.

41. A: Scanning future portions of the text for information that helps resolve a question is an example of self-monitoring. Self-monitoring takes advantage of students' natural ability to recognize when they understand the reading and when they do not. KWL charts are used to help guide students to identify what they already know about a given topic. Metacognitive skills are when learners think about their thinking. Directed reading-thinking activities are done before and after reading to improve critical thinking and reading comprehension skills.

42. C: The five basic components of reading education are phonemic awareness, phonics, fluency, vocabulary, and comprehension.

43. A: If a child can accurately read text with consistent speed and appropriate expression while demonstrating comprehension, the child is said to have reading fluency skills. Without the ability to read fluently, a child's reading comprehension (Choice *C*) will be limited.

44. B: Phonics is the ability to apply letter-sound relationships and letter patterns in order to accurately pronounce written words. Phonemic awareness is the understanding that words are comprised of a combination of sounds. Fluency is an automatic recognition and accurate interpretation of text. Vocabulary is the body of words that a person knows.

45. C: Comprehension is the level of content understanding that a student demonstrates after reading. Orthographic development is a cumulative process for learning to read, with each skill building on the previously mastered skill. Fluency is an automatic recognition and accurate interpretation of text. Phonics is the ability to apply letter-sound relationships and letter patterns in order to accurately pronounce written words.

46. A: The *sh* is an example of a consonant digraph. Consonant digraphs are combinations of two or three consonants that work together to make a single sound. Examples of consonant digraphs are *sh*, *ch*, and *th*. Choice *B*, sound segmentation, is used to identify component phonemes in a word, such as separating the /t/, /u/, and /b/ for *tub*. Choice *C*, vowel digraph, is a set of two vowels that make up a single sound, such as *ow*, *ae*, or *ie*. Choice *D*, rime, is the sound that follows a word's onset, such as the /at/ in *cat*.

47. D: Sound segmentation is the identification of all the component phonemes in a word. An example would be the student identifying each separate sound, /t/, /u/, and /b/, in the word *tub*. Choice *A*, sound blending, is the blending together of two or more sounds in a word, such as /ch/ or /sh/. Choice *B*, substitution, occurs when a phoneme is substituted within a word for another phoneme, such as substituting the sound /b/ in *bun* to /r/ to create *run*. Choice *C*, rhyming, is an effective tool to utilize during the analytic phase of phonics development because rhyming words are often identical except for their beginning letters.

48. A: The alphabetical principle is the understanding that letters represent sounds in words. It is through the alphabetic principle that students learn the interrelationships between letter-sound (grapheme-phoneme) correspondences, phonemic awareness, and early decoding skills (such as sounding out and blending letter sounds).

49. D: Print awareness includes all except the spelling of sight words. Print awareness includes Choice *A*, the differentiation of uppercase and lowercase letters, so that students can understand which words begin a sentence. Choice *B*, the identification of word boundaries, is also included in print awareness; that is, students should be made aware that words are made up of letters and that spaces appear between words, etc. Choice *C*, the proper tracking of words, is also included in print awareness; this is the realization that print is organized in a particular way, so books must be tracked and held accordingly.

50. D: Word boundaries is included as one of the factors modeled because students should be able to identify which letters make up a word as well as the spaces before and after the letters that make up words. Directionality is the ability to track words as they are being read, so this is also modeled. One-to-one correspondence, the last factor listed, is the ability to match written letters to words to a spoken word when reading. It is another thing teachers model when they point to words while they read.

51. B: Structural analysis focuses on the meaning of morphemes. Morphemes include base words, prefixes, and word endings (inflections and suffixes) that are found within longer words. Students can use structural analysis skill to find familiar word parts within an unfamiliar word in order to decode the word and determine the definition of the new word. The prefix im- (meaning not) in the word "improbable" can help students derive the definition of an event that is not likely to occur.

52. B: The student is performing at the phonetic stage. Phonetic spellers will spell a word as it sounds. The speller perceives and represents all of the phonemes in a word. However, because phonetic spellers have limited sight word vocabulary, irregular words are often spelled incorrectly.

53. B: The creation of word walls, Choice *I*, is advantageous during the phonetic stage of spelling development. On a word wall, words that share common consonant-vowel patterns or letter clusters are written in groups. Choices *II* and *III*, daily reading and writing opportunities, are also important in spelling instructions. Students need daily opportunities in order to review and practice spelling development. Daily journals or exit tickets are cognitive writing strategies effective in helping students reflect on what they have learned. A spelling inventory, Choice *IV*, is different than a traditional spelling test because students are not allowed to study the words prior to the administration of a spelling inventory. Therefore, this option is incorrect as it mentions the inventory contains words students have studied all week.

54. A: The teacher should have the student use a think-aloud to verbalize the directions of the shapes used when writing each letter. During think-alouds, teachers voice the metacognitive process that occurs when writing each part of a given letter. Students should be encouraged to do likewise when practicing writing the letters.

55. D: Teachers should capitalize on the transfer of relevant skills from the learner's original language(s). In this way, extra attention and instructional emphasis can be applied toward the teaching of sounds and meanings of words that are nontransferable between the two languages.

56. C: Writing samples are the most appropriate assessment of spelling for students who are performing at the pre-phonetic stage. During the pre-phonetic stage, students participate in precommunicative writing. Precommunicative writing appears to be a jumble of letter-like forms rather than a series of discrete letters. Samples of students' precommunicative writing can be used to assess their understanding of the alphabetic principle and their knowledge of letter-sound correspondences.

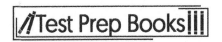

57. A: Phonological awareness is best assessed through identification of rimes or onsets within words. Instruction of phonological awareness includes detecting and identifying word boundaries, syllables, onset/rime, and rhyming words.

58. A: The identification of morphemes within words occurs during the instruction of structural analysis. Structural analysis is a word recognition skill that focuses on the meaning of word parts, or morphemes, during the introduction of a new word. Choice *B*, syllabic analysis, is a word analysis skill that helps students split words into syllables. Choice *C*, phonics, is the direct correspondence between and blending of letters and sounds. Choice *D*, the alphabetic principle, teaches that letters or other characters represent sounds.

59. B: Homophones are words that are pronounced the same way but differ in meaning and/or spelling. The pair *to* and *too* is an example of a homophone because they are pronounced the same way, but differ in both meaning and spelling. Choices *A*, *C*, and *D* are not homophones because they do not sound the same when spoken aloud.

60. B: Nursery rhymes are used in kindergarten to develop phoneme recognition. Rhyming words are often almost identical except for their beginning letter(s), so rhyming is a great strategy to implement during the analytic phase of phoneme development.

61. B: High-frequency words are taught during the instruction of sight word recognition. Sight words, sometimes referred to as high-frequency words, are words that are used often but may not follow the regular principles of phonics. Sight words may also be defined as words that students are able to recognize and read without having to sound out.

62. C: Both *A* and *B*. Decoding should be assessed in context in addition to isolation. During such assessments, the students read passages from reading-level appropriate texts aloud to the teacher so that the teacher is better able to analyze a student's approach to figuring out unknown words. Decoding should also be assessed in isolation. In these types of assessments, students are given a list of words and/or phonics patterns. Initially, high-frequency words that follow predictable phonics patterns are presented. The words that are presented become more challenging as a student masters less difficult words.

63. D: An individual's sight vocabulary includes the words that he or she can recognize and correctly pronounce when reading. Limited sight vocabulary can be caused by poor word recognition, a lack of content vocabulary, and inadequate background knowledge. Although proper pronunciation may affect the ability to spell a word, the ability to properly spell a word is less likely to affect a student's ability to properly pronounce that word.

64. A: There is a positive correlation between a student's exposure to text and the academic achievement of that individual. Therefore, students should be given ample opportunities to read independently as much text as possible in order to gain vocabulary and background knowledge.

65. C: By definition, morphology is the identification and use of morphemes such as root words and affixes. Listening comprehension refers to the processes involved in understanding spoken language. Word consciousness refers to the knowledge required for students to learn and effectively utilize language. Textual analysis is an approach that researchers use to gain information and describe the characteristics of a recorded or visual message.

66. B: Students should read a wide variety of literary and informational texts to prepare for college. Texts may extend across a wide variety of genres, timelines, and cultural works. Nonfiction, fiction, cultural pieces, and United States documents are all excellent examples of texts to use during reading instruction.

67. D: Students should be exposed to 70 percent of nonfiction text during reading instruction by the time they reach the twelfth grade. By eighth grade, students should be exposed to 55 percent of nonfiction text. Students should be exposed to a 50/50 balance from kindergarten to fifth grade.

68. D: Cross-curricular integration is choosing to teach writing projects that include the subjects of science, social studies, mathematics, reading, etc.

69. A: Young students should use the five-finger test to select an appropriate-level text. Using the five-finger test, a student selects a page within a text that he or she wants to read. The student holds up a finger for each word he or she is unable to read on that page. If the student has five fingers up after reading the entire page, then the student should stop and choose a book at an easier reading level. If there are not a variety of books of various reading levels from which a student can choose, then the student is likely to become frustrated. Such frustration may cause the student to stop reading for pleasure and see reading as a chore.

70. D: Elements of a good lesson are all of the listed criteria. Pacing, modeling, direct instruction, and intervention are necessary to build a strong reading lesson. Teachers need to account for time given by a district for reading. That time should include whole-class instruction of new reading skills. Teachers should then assess students formatively during guided and independent practice in order to break students into groups based on their performance levels.

71. C: It is important for teachers to allocate time to work one-on-one with students who have IEPs. Students with IEPs may need to have skills retaught. Measuring the growth of students with IEPs can be done by charting their performance levels on a weekly basis. If there is little or no growth, a teacher may need to revisit his or her pacing or the form of instruction being used with the student(s).

72. D: Organization is the trait that teaches students how to build the framework of their writing. Students choose an organizational strategy or purpose for the writing and build the details upon that structure. There are many purposes for writing, and they all have different frameworks.

73. B: The role of a reading specialist is not to tell teachers how to do their jobs, but rather to assist them. One role of a reading coach is to help teachers in their classrooms with assessing students or even teach lessons for teachers. Another role of a reading specialist is to inform staff of district changes at staff meetings, in-services, or in professional development opportunities. Such changes may include alterations of curriculum or state standards.

74. A: A reading corner is not designed to be a "hang out" for students. Rather, it is a place for students to share thoughts on books or discuss recommendations. A reading corner should have a fun atmosphere to enhance students' interest in reading and be filled with a variety of genres and levels.

75. A: Voice is the primary trait that shows the individual writing style of an author. It is based on an author's choice of common syntax, diction, punctuation, character development, dialogue, etc.

Mathematics

Mathematics and Instruction

Applying Research-Based Theories of Learning Mathematics

The most effective teachers apply research-based theories and principles into their classroom. Some examples of such theories and principles are the following:

1. Begin each day with a quick review of the previous lesson. Reviewing allows students to make connections between old and new material.

2. Present new material in short intervals afterwards in which students get a chance to practice each step. It is proven that students can only grasp so much information at once, and breaking up the lesson allows for there to be a better chance of the material being placed in one's memory.

3. Ask many questions throughout the lecture to see if the students understand the material. Students need time to practice the material in class, and seeing if they are getting correct responses allows for the teacher to determine if more instruction is necessary.

4. Provide models that supplement word problems. Worked out examples allow for students to see the step-by-step process necessary to solve problems, and this approach requires less strain on their memory and more emphasis on understanding.

5. Provide more instructional support on difficult tasks that are assigned. Examples of such support could be guidance through steps from the teacher or checklists, and once some problems are completed, the idea would be to eventually withdraw the instructional support. In conclusion, many theories and principles tend to overlap some ideas, but all have been heavily researched and studied to show their success with use in the classroom.

Linguistic, Cultural, and Socioeconomic Diversity of Students

In the classroom, teachers can aim to close the achievement gap that currently exists between students of different cultures and socioeconomic backgrounds. They can honor the diversity of their students by using it to their advantage. Students will have different backgrounds in literature, art, music, languages, politics, entertainment, and food. Teachers have the ability to introduce diverse and new concepts to students, and in doing so, it will make them better suited for the real world. Collaborative activities amongst students of different backgrounds should be welcomed and integrated into daily activities. Teachers can show that they genuinely care about the diversity of their students by taking time to learn about their different cultures, which supports their students' individual needs. Once they learn a little more about each student, that individualized information can be used to create lessons that relate to students on a more personal level.

In mathematics, word problems and problems involving real-world applications such as units of measurement are what relates instructional material to the real world. Teachers have the ability to create their own word problems based on cultural values of their students. For example, when teaching students how to use a clock to tell time, if there are students who speak Spanish in the classroom, the teacher could introduce the process in both English and Spanish. In that case, numbers from 1 to 12

Test Prep Books

could be reviewed in Spanish as well. Also, simple word problems focusing on different mathematical concepts can be changed to represent a scenario relating to some of the students' cultural backgrounds.

Concrete, Symbolic, and Abstract Representations of Mathematical Knowledge

When concepts are introduced into the mathematics classroom, there is a three-part strategy that can be used for instruction purposes. This strategy involves breaking up instruction into the concrete, symbolic, and abstract phase. In the concrete phase, the teacher introduces the concept using tangible ideas and real models so that the idea can be seen in a physical sense. For example, when learning how to find the area of a rectangle, an actual rectangle composed of unit blocks can be used. The area of the rectangle would be found by counting the number of blocks. Also, at this point it could be shown that the number of blocks on the side representing its length times the number of blocks on the side representing its height equals this same quantity. The second stage, known as the symbolic stage, involves the teacher using other types of representations such as drawings, graphs, and charts, of the concrete idea to support further introduction of the concept. In the area idea, this would involve drawing a rectangle on the board and noting the length of each side. Perhaps, the actual multiplication of the length times width could be written on the board now. Finally, the last stage involves the abstract stage, in which the teacher introduces the idea on a symbolic level only. Only mathematical expressions consisting of numbers, variables, and operations are used here. In the area example, the formula of the area of the rectangle would be introduced: Area is equal to length times width, or $A = l \times w$. This three-step process is designed so that each student understands the connections between each type of representation. Research has shown that students who learn in this manner are more engaged and are more likely to be able to apply the concepts in the real world.

Manipulatives and Technological Tools

Manipulatives and technological tools are items that need to be introduced early into the mathematics classroom. They are important because they allow for other ways besides paper and pencil problems for students to enhance their understanding of mathematics. Their use allows the students to develop concrete examples that apply to abstract concepts while providing fun and engaging ways to learn math concepts. For example, base ten blocks can be used to learn addition and place value. The visualization of the math concepts and actual physical manipulation of the objects allow for great ways to conceptualize and understand the concepts being taught. Manipulatives also allow students to develop common language between their peers in the classroom and the teachers. They provide a fun and interesting way to learn new vocabulary while matching up each new term to a concrete, tangible idea. Research has also shown that classrooms that utilize manipulatives have students who are more interested in mathematics and who find more enjoyment in problem solving. Other types of manipulatives are tangrams, which consist of seven flat shapes that can be rearranged to form new shapes to teach geometry, interlocking cubes, pattern blocks, and fraction strips.

Mathematical Tasks in Individual, Small-Group, and Large-Group Settings

In the classroom, teachers can vary instruction techniques by introducing tasks to be completed individually and in small and large-group settings. To actively engage students in each type of setting, different monitoring approaches can be used. In individualized tasks, specific questions can be asked to both challenge the student and assess their progress. For example, in this setting it would be appropriate to ask how the student came up with the solution procedure on their own, to ask what patterns they saw along the way, and to ask how they relate the situation to other scenarios that have been seen before both in and out of the classroom. In small and large-group settings, questions can be

asked relating to how the group organized their thoughts, how they came up with their solution approach, if they think it is the best approach, if there is anything they would do differently, and if any members agreed or disagreed at any point along the way. There will probably be more disagreement in larger groups and more situations in which some students see different approaches as being better due to the larger group size. Each different type of setting is a chance for the students to use both their communication and math skills in various ways.

Tools to Strengthen Students' Mathematical Understanding

Many tools need to be introduced into the classroom by the teacher these days, and the large number of tools might seem discouraging. Basic tools involve chalkboard and chalk and pencil and paper. Very young students can be first introduced to base ten blocks, which allow for understanding of place value in numbers, and a 100-bead basic abacus, which allows for practice counting numbers. Then measurement devices, or manipulatives, such as protractors, compasses, and rulers, need to be used because of their applicability in the real world. Time measurement devices such as clocks and stopwatches and anything relating to counting money are also applicable to the real world. Simultaneously, computer software and interactive lessons are used in the classroom. Today, some software exists that replaces physical measurement devices. For example, software can replace ruler or compass measurements that would originally be completed on paper so that it is done on the screen. In many ways, the software allows a student to better visualize the process. Older students can support the process of learning how to plot points and graph lines with graphing software and graphing calculators. It is important that once each tool is introduced into the classroom, it is fully understood by the students before introducing another tool. All of these tools will help strengthen students' mathematical understanding. However, full understanding of a few tools is more beneficial to students than being introduced to a multitude of tools while having little understanding of each item.

Mathematics in the Texas Essential Knowledge and Skills (TEKS)

In order to engage the students, a math teacher should utilize various methods of instruction. The material should be introduced using an assortment of ways, or else most students will get bored. If every day were spent taking notes and solving problems with pencil and paper, many students would have a hard time staying motivated. Lecture is an important part of classroom time, but other items can be mixed in. Group work is a great technique to break up the monotony. Working with peers allows for the concepts to be better understood, and it provides a chance for students to practice using their new vocabulary. Technology is another way to change the traditional lecture style. Items such as mathematical software and graphing calculators are great ways to see the concepts in a new way. Also, self-guided lectures can be utilized as ways for students to learn new material by teaching the material to themselves. Depending on the situation and the students, this can be a great technique to really allow the material to sink in. Finally, visuals such as diagrams, graphs, videos, and charts should be utilized whenever possible to create a link between the abstract and a tangible idea.

Reevaluate Instruction Based on the Mathematics in the TEKS

Each teacher needs to ask the question, what do I want my students to know at the end of their time in the classroom? Lesson plans should be created that are centered around the mathematical concepts necessary to be taught throughout the year. However, a little bit of flexibility should be allowed. It is important to make sure all the necessary topics are covered; however, if an instruction technique is not working in a given classroom, there should always be a chance for adjustment. It is important to keep updating the lesson plans throughout the year. As assessments are completed, teachers can adjust their lessons based on student interest and performance, making sure to adhere to the topics listed in the TEKS. For example, if the students are not reacting well to a certain tool such as mathematical software, and it is not something that the students need to learn, the teacher should take the opportunity to find a new instruction method that replaces the software. The mathematical concepts being introduced are more important than the instruction methods.

Mathematics and Other Disciplines Such as Art, Music, Science, Social Science, and Business

The problem-solving process involves applying the skills learned in the classroom to situations in the real world. Mathematics reasoning can appear in many scenarios and in many other disciplines, such as art, music, science, social science, and business. In art, mathematical concepts like symmetry, proportion, linear perspective, and recursion appear as well as various geometric figures and properties. In music, concepts such as intervals, counting, tempo, fractions, patterns, and symbols appear, and an understanding of mathematics is required to both read and write sheet music as well as when playing a musical instrument. For example, the length of notes relates to fractions. When playing a musical instrument or singing, whole notes, half notes, quarter notes, eighth notes, and sixteenth notes are used. A whole note can be thought of as a whole pie, the number 1, or 100%. Each subsequent note is a piece of the pie. For example, an eighth note is equivalent to the fraction $\frac{1}{8}$ or the percentage 12.5%. In relation to a pie, if a pie were cut into eight equal parts, an eighth note would be one piece of the pie.

Traditionally, more time in the classroom is spent on how mathematics relates to other disciplines such as science and business. However, it is very important to show how math is used in the arts and music. Traditional word problems that relate to science applications are those that involve Newton's Second Law of motion where force is equal to mass times acceleration, population growth and decay, and calculus problems that relate an equation of motion with its velocity and acceleration through derivatives and integrals. Social science problems involve anything relating to economics, sociology, and political science. Real world situations are modeled using math equations and formulas. Finally, in business, traditional problems involve formulas involving interest.

Encouraging Mathematical Discourse

In the classroom, the teacher should pose different types of questions relating to the mathematical concepts being discussed. Each question should be both engaging and challenging and the teacher should use questions that require both oral and written response types. The teacher should also determine when it is appropriate to provide helpful information and when to let the students deal with the difficulty on their own. For example, in some scenarios, students can be allowed to ask questions to gather more information necessary to provide a solution, as in a case study environment. However, this scenario would not be appropriate in a test situation that asks specific questions that involve evaluating expressions and solving equations. Also, especially in early mathematics, testing should involve a combination of both vocabulary and skill, to ensure that the students can not only work with the concepts being taught but verbally communicate within the subject as well.

Common Misconceptions and Error Patterns

A range of assessments exists that allow a teacher to evaluate how his or her students are performing in the classroom. They can be grouped into two categories: formal and informal. Formal methods can be used to place scores on each student's achievement levels. They are a way to judge how well students

have learned concepts throughout the year. Some examples would be chapter tests, quizzes, and final exams. Each formal assessment is administered and graded in a formal manner. Each student is graded the same way, and each problem is either right or wrong, unless partial credit is given, in which a student can be right in some steps of the problem. Teachers can also utilize informal assessments throughout the year. These include any way of measuring the success of students besides a formal testing procedure. Some examples of informal assessments are experiments, group projects, and presentations. Each one of these does not have a formal method of evaluation; however, they are still beneficial tools that allow teachers to measure success in the classroom. An advantage of informal processes is that they also give the teachers a chance to assess both communication skills in addition to the mathematics material.

Relationship Between Assessment and Instruction

In the classroom, assessment should be used to guide instruction. Assessments are utilized to judge how well students are retaining the concepts being taught, while instruction is the process in which they actually learn the concepts. Assessments and instruction should be designed together in order to enhance one other. If both are not designed with each other in mind, it can impact student learning and achievement in a negative way. Each type of learning method has its own optimal assessments and assessments that do not work. For example, a vocabulary lesson in which new mathematics terms are introduced are best assessed through questions that allow the students to recall terms and definitions. Such question types are multiple-choice, matching, and fill-in-the blank. Lessons involving problem solving in which students need to apply techniques should use different assessment techniques. Multiple-choice problems should not be utilized for long problems, and assessments that involve more of an open-response problem set are better suited. In this way, the student does not focus on the answer, but instead the focus is on what process is the best approach in order to solve the problem. If multiple-choice questions are given to assess problems that involve many steps, the teacher will not be able to see where the student went wrong. The assessment should be used as a tool to help guide instruction in addition to its traditional use of giving out scores and grades.

Various Assessments in Mathematics, Including Formative and Summative Assessments

Throughout the year, different types of assessments come into play, and it is important to utilize the correct type when necessary. First, a diagnostic test can be utilized at the beginning of the year. This type of test provides insight as to how much each student knows going into the year. Teachers can plan their lessons accordingly. Formative assessment is then used throughout the year, mostly in the form of tests and quizzes, that provide regular insight on how well each student is retaining the information being taught. Formative assessments are most useful in recognizing student error patterns and can assist teachers by highlighting what skills and topics need to be revisited in their instruction. Summative assessment is testing completed at the end of the year, and it can provide a final score that summarizes how well each student did in the class. Finally, standardized testing is completed in some years, and these types of tests ask the same questions to every student of the same age at a national level. Their results provide an individual comparison of each student to national averages. Each type of assessment has its own benefits, but the formative assessments are the most useful throughout the year for teachers.

Uses of Mathematics in Careers and Professions

A great way to engage students in the mathematics classroom is to show them how math is used in the workplace. For example, teachers of younger students can introduce examples that relate to counting money and act as if they are working within a banking environment. This provides a fun way to link the classroom to a day-to-day use. Teachers of older students have the ability to introduce word problems that actually occur in a workplace. These types of situations provide practice with problem solving as well as a chance to motivate students by allowing them to see the usefulness of the problems. The question "why do I need to know this" is a common one in math classes, and any chance a teacher has to answer it with a tangible example should be taken.

A great example involves the medical field and calculating dosages for medication. For example, a nurse needs to administer 450 mg of a medication that comes as 150 mg diluted in 3 ml of fluid. The rule is to divide the total needed by the amount per measure, times the amount of liquid that comes in. Therefore, they would need to administer $\frac{450}{150} \times 3 = 9$ ml of the medication to the patient. Banking settings also provide great examples that show how math is used in professions. In lower level mathematics, simple counting can be used to highlight what a teller does, and in higher-level classes, compound interest problems can be worked through to show what a financial advisor does.

Number Concepts and Operations

Base-10 Numerals, Number Names, and Expanded Form

Numbers used in everyday life are constituted in a base-10 system. Each digit in a number, depending on its location, represents some multiple of 10, or quotient of 10 when dealing with decimals. Each digit to the left of the decimal point represents a higher multiple of 10. Each digit to the right of the decimal point represents a quotient of a higher multiple of 10 for the divisor. For example, consider the number 7,631.42. The digit one represents simply the number one. The digit 3 represents 3×10. The digit 6 represents $6 \times 10 \times 10$ (or 6×100). The digit 7 represents $7 \times 10 \times 10 \times 10$ (or 7×1000). The digit 4 represents $4 \div 10$. The digit 2 represents $(2 \div 10) \div 10$, or $2 \div (10 \times 10)$ or $2 \div 100$.

A number is written in expanded form by expressing it as the sum of the value of each of its digits. The expanded form in the example above, which is written with the highest value first down to the lowest value, is expressed as: $7,000 + 600 + 30 + 1 + .4 + .02$.

When verbally expressing a number, the integer part of the number (the numbers to the left of the decimal point) resembles the expanded form without the addition between values. In the above example, the numbers read "seven thousand six hundred thirty-one." When verbally expressing the decimal portion of a number, the number is read as a whole number, followed by the place value of the furthest digit (non-zero) to the right. In the above example, 0.42 is read "forty-two hundredths." Reading the number 7,631.42 in its entirety is expressed as "seven thousand six hundred thirty-one and forty-two hundredths." The word *and* is used between the integer and decimal parts of the number.

Composing and Decomposing Multi-Digit Numbers

Composing and decomposing numbers aids in conceptualizing what each digit of a multi-digit number represents. The standard, or typical, form in which numbers are written consists of a series of digits representing a given value based on their place value. Consider the number 592.7. This number is composed of 5 hundreds, 9 tens, 2 ones, and 7 tenths.

Composing a number requires adding the given numbers for each place value and writing the numbers in standard form. For example, composing 4 thousands, 5 hundreds, 2 tens, and 8 ones consists of adding as follows: $4,000 + 500 + 20 + 8$, to produce 4,528 (standard form).

Decomposing a number requires taking a number written in standard form and breaking it apart into the sum of each place value. For example, the number 83.17 is decomposed by breaking it into the sum of 4 values (for each of the 4 digits): 8 tens, 3 ones, 1 tenth, and 7 hundredths. The decomposed or "expanded" form of 83.17 is $80 + 3 + .1 + .07$.

Place Value of a Given Digit

The number system that is used consists of only ten different digits or characters. However, this system is used to represent an infinite number of values. The place value system makes this infinite number of values possible. The position in which a digit is written corresponds to a given value. Starting from the decimal point (which is implied, if not physically present), each subsequent place value to the left represents a value greater than the one before it. Conversely, starting from the decimal point, each subsequent place value to the right represents a value less than the one before it.

The names for the place values to the left of the decimal point are as follows:

Billions	Hundred-Millions	Ten-Millions	Millions	Hundred-Thousands	Ten-Thousands	Thousands	Hundreds	Tens	Ones

*Note that this table can be extended infinitely further to the left.

The names for the place values to the right of the decimal point are as follows:

Decimal Point (.)	Tenths	Hundredths	Thousandths	Ten-Thousandths	...

*Note that this table can be extended infinitely further to the right.

When given a multi-digit number, the value of each digit depends on its place value. Consider the number 682,174.953. Referring to the chart above, it can be determined that the digit 8 is in the ten-thousands place. It is in the fifth place to the left of the decimal point. Its value is 8 ten-thousands or 80,000. The digit 5 is two places to the right of the decimal point. Therefore, the digit 5 is in the hundredths place. Its value is 5 hundredths or $\frac{5}{100}$ (equivalent to .05).

Base-10 System

Value of Digits

In accordance with the base-10 system, the value of a digit increases by a factor of ten each place it moves to the left. For example, consider the number 7. Moving the digit one place to the left (70), increases its value by a factor of 10 ($7 \times 10 = 70$). Moving the digit two places to the left (700) increases its value by a factor of 10 twice ($7 \times 10 \times 10 = 700$). Moving the digit three places to the left (7,000) increases its value by a factor of 10 three times ($7 \times 10 \times 10 \times 10 = 7,000$), and so on.

Conversely, the value of a digit decreases by a factor of ten each place it moves to the right. (Note that multiplying by $\frac{1}{10}$ is equivalent to dividing by 10). For example, consider the number 40. Moving the digit one place to the right (4) decreases its value by a factor of 10 ($40 \div 10 = 4$). Moving the digit two places to the right (0.4), decreases its value by a factor of 10 twice ($40 \div 10 \div 10 = 0.4$) or ($40 \times \frac{1}{10} \times$

$\frac{1}{10} = 0.4$). Moving the digit three places to the right (0.04) decreases its value by a factor of 10 three times ($40 \div 10 \div 10 \div 10 = 0.04$) or ($40 \times \frac{1}{10} \times \frac{1}{10} \times \frac{1}{10} = 0.04$), and so on.

Exponents to Denote Powers of 10

The value of a given digit of a number in the base-10 system can be expressed utilizing powers of 10. A power of 10 refers to 10 raised to a given exponent such as 10^0, 10^1, 10^2, 10^3, etc. For the number 10^3, 10 is the base and 3 is the exponent. A base raised by an exponent represents how many times the base is multiplied by itself. Therefore, $10^1 = 10$, $10^2 = 10 \times 10 = 100$, $10^3 = 10 \times 10 \times 10 = 1,000$, $10^4 = 10 \times 10 \times 10 \times 10 = 10,000$, etc. Any base with a zero exponent equals one.

Powers of 10 are utilized to decompose a multi-digit number without writing all the zeroes. Consider the number 872,349. This number is decomposed to $800,000 + 70,000 + 2,000 + 300 + 40 + 9$. When utilizing powers of 10, the number 872,349 is decomposed to $(8 \times 10^5) + (7 \times 10^4) + (2 \times 10^3) + (3 \times 10^2) + (4 \times 10^1) + (9 \times 10^0)$. The power of 10 by which the digit is multiplied corresponds to the number of zeroes following the digit when expressing its value in standard form. For example, 7×10^4 is equivalent to 70,000 or 7 followed by four zeros.

Rounding Multi-Digit Numbers

Rounding numbers changes the given number to a simpler and less accurate number than the exact given number. Rounding allows for easier calculations which estimate the results of using the exact given number. The accuracy of the estimate and ease of use depends on the place value to which the number is rounded. Rounding numbers consists of:

- Determining what place value the number is being rounded to
- Examining the digit to the right of the desired place value to decide whether to round up or keep the digit
- Replacing all digits to the right of the desired place value with zeros

To round 746,311 to the nearest ten thousands, the digit in the ten thousands place should be located first. In this case, this digit is 4 (746,311). Then, the digit to its right is examined. If this digit is 5 or greater, the number will be rounded up by increasing the digit in the desired place by one. If the digit to the right of the place value being rounded is 4 or less, the number will be kept the same. For the given example, the digit being examined is a 6, which means that the number will be rounded up by increasing the digit to the left by one. Therefore, the digit 4 is changed to a 5. Finally, to write the rounded number, any digits to the left of the place value being rounded remain the same and any to its right are replaced with zeros. For the given example, rounding 746,311 to the nearest ten thousand will produce 750,000. To round 746,311 to the nearest hundred, the digit to the right of the three in the hundreds place is examined to determine whether to round up or keep the same number. In this case, that digit is a one, so the number will be kept the same and any digits to its right will be replaced with zeros. The resulting rounded number is 746,300.

Rounding place values to the right of the decimal follows the same procedure, but digits being replaced by zeros can simply be dropped. To round 3.752891 to the nearest thousandth, the desired place value is located (3.752891) and the digit to the right is examined. In this case, the digit 8 indicates that the number will be rounded up, and the 2 in the thousandths place will increase to a 3. Rounding up and replacing the digits to the right of the thousandths place produces 3.753000 which is equivalent to 3.753. Therefore, the zeros are not necessary and the rounded number should be written as 3.753.

When rounding up, if the digit to be increased is a 9, the digit to its left is increased by 1 and the digit in the desired place value is changed to a zero. For example, the number 1,598 rounded to the nearest ten is 1,600. Another example shows the number 43.72961 rounded to the nearest thousandth is 43.730 or 43.73.

Solving Multistep Mathematical and Real-World Problems

Problem Situations for Operations

Addition and subtraction are *inverse operations*. Adding a number and then subtracting the same number will cancel each other out, resulting in the original number, and vice versa. For example, $8 + 7 - 7 = 8$ and $137 - 100 + 100 = 137$. Similarly, multiplication and division are inverse operations. Therefore, multiplying by a number and then dividing by the same number results in the original number, and vice versa. For example, $8 \times 2 \div 2 = 8$ and $12 \div 4 \times 4 = 12$. Inverse operations are used to work backwards to solve problems. In the case that 7 and a number add to 18, the inverse operation of subtraction is used to find the unknown value ($18 - 7 = 11$). If a school's entire 4th grade was divided evenly into 3 classes each with 22 students, the inverse operation of multiplication is used to determine the total students in the grade ($22 \times 3 = 66$). Additional scenarios involving inverse operations are included in the tables below.

There are a variety of real-world situations in which one or more of the operators is used to solve a problem. The tables below display the most common scenarios.

Addition & Subtraction

	Unknown Result	**Unknown Change**	**Unknown Start**
Adding to	5 students were in class. 4 more students arrived. How many students are in class? $5 + 4 = ?$	8 students were in class. More students arrived late. There are now 18 students in class. How many students arrived late? $8 + ? = 18$ Solved by inverse operations $18 - 8 = ?$	Some students were in class early. 11 more students arrived. There are now 17 students in class. How many students were in class early? $? + 11 = 17$ Solved by inverse operations $17 - 11 = ?$
Taking from	15 students were in class. 5 students left class. How many students are in class now? $15 - 5 = ?$	12 students were in class. Some students left class. There are now 8 students in class. How many students left class? $12 - ? = 8$ Solved by inverse operations $8 + ? = 12 \rightarrow 12 - 8 = ?$	Some students were in class. 3 students left class. Then there were 13 students in class. How many students were in class before? $? - 3 = 13$ Solved by inverse operations $13 + 3 = ?$

	Unknown Total	Unknown Addends (Both)	Unknown Addends (One)
Putting together/ taking apart	The homework assignment is 10 addition problems and 8 subtraction problems. How many problems are in the homework assignment? $10 + 8 =?$	Bobby has $9. How much can Bobby spend on candy and how much can Bobby spend on toys? $9 =? +?$	Bobby has 12 pairs of pants. 5 pairs of pants are shorts, and the rest are long. How many pairs of long pants does he have? $12 = 5+?$ Solved by inverse operations $12- 5 =?$

	Unknown Difference	Unknown Larger Value	Unknown Smaller Value
Comparing	Bobby has 5 toys. Tommy has 8 toys. How many more toys does Tommy have than Bobby? $5+? = 8$ Solved by inverse operations $8- 5 =?$ Bobby has $6. Tommy has $10. How many fewer dollars does Bobby have than Tommy? $10- 6 =?$	Tommy has 2 more toys than Bobby. Bobby has 4 toys. How many toys does Tommy have? $2 + 4 =?$ Bobby has 3 fewer dollars than Tommy. Bobby has $8. How many dollars does Tommy have? $? - 3 = 8$ Solved by inverse operations $8 + 3 =?$	Tommy has 6 more toys than Bobby. Tommy has 10 toys. How many toys does Bobby have? $? +6 = 10$ Solved by inverse operations $10- 6 =?$ Bobby has $5 less than Tommy. Tommy has $9. How many dollars does Bobby have? $9 - 5 =?$

Multiplication and Division

	Unknown Product	Unknown Group Size	Unknown Number of Groups
Equal groups	There are 5 students, and each student has 4 pieces of candy. How many pieces of candy are there in all? $5 \times 4 = ?$	14 pieces of candy are shared equally by 7 students. How many pieces of candy does each student have? $7 \times ? = 14$ Solved by inverse operations $14 \div 7 = ?$	If 18 pieces of candy are to be given out 3 to each student, how many students will get candy? $? \times 3 = 18$ Solved by inverse operations $18 \div 3 = ?$

	Unknown Product	Unknown Factor	Unknown Factor
Arrays	There are 5 rows of students with 3 students in each row. How many students are there? $5 \times 3 = ?$	If 16 students are arranged into 4 equal rows, how many students will be in each row? $4 \times ? = 16$ Solved by inverse operations $16 \div 4 = ?$	If 24 students are arranged into an array with 6 columns, how many rows are there? $? \times 6 = 24$ Solved by inverse operations $24 \div 6 = ?$

	Larger Unknown	Smaller Unknown	Multiplier Unknown
Comparing	A small popcorn costs $1.50. A large popcorn costs 3 times as much as a small popcorn. How much does a large popcorn cost? $1.50 \times 3 = ?$	A large soda costs $6 and that is 2 times as much as a small soda costs. How much does a small soda cost? $2 \times ? = 6$ Solved by inverse operations $6 \div 2 = ?$	A large pretzel costs $3 and a small pretzel costs $2. How many times as much does the large pretzel cost as the small pretzel? $? \times 2 = 3$ Solved by inverse operations $3 \div 2 = ?$

Remainders in Division Problems

If a given total cannot be divided evenly into a given number of groups, the amount left over is the remainder. Consider the following scenario: 32 textbooks must be packed into boxes for storage. Each box holds 6 textbooks. How many boxes are needed? To determine the answer, 32 is divided by 6, resulting in 5 with a remainder of 2. A remainder may be interpreted three ways:

- Add 1 to the quotient
  How many boxes will be needed? Six boxes will be needed because five will not be enough.

- Use only the quotient
  How many boxes will be full? Five boxes will be full.

- Use only the remainder
  If you only have 5 boxes, how many books will not fit? Two books will not fit.

Strategies and Algorithms to Perform Operations on Rational Numbers

A rational number is any number that can be written in the form of a ratio or fraction. Integers can be written as fractions with a denominator of 1 ($5 = \frac{5}{1}$; $-342 = \frac{-342}{1}$; etc.). Decimals that terminate and/or repeat can also be written as fractions ($0.47 = \frac{47}{100}$; $0.\overline{33} = \frac{1}{3}$). For more on converting decimals to fractions, see the section *Converting Between Fractions, Decimals, and Percent*.

When adding or subtracting fractions, the numbers must have the same denominators. In these cases, numerators are added or subtracted and denominators are kept the same. For example, $\frac{2}{7} + \frac{3}{7} = \frac{5}{7}$ and $\frac{4}{5} - \frac{3}{5} = \frac{1}{5}$. If the fractions to be added or subtracted do not have the same denominator, a common denominator must be found. This is accomplished by changing one or both fractions to a different but equivalent fraction. Consider the example $\frac{1}{6} + \frac{4}{9}$. First, a common denominator must be found. One method is to find the least common multiple (LCM) of the denominators 6 and 9. This is the lowest number that both 6 and 9 will divide into evenly. In this case the LCM is 18. Both fractions should be changed to equivalent fractions with a denominator of 18. To obtain the numerator of the new fraction, the old numerator is multiplied by the same number by which the old denominator is multiplied. For the fraction $\frac{1}{6}$, 6 multiplied by 3 will produce a denominator of 18. Therefore, the numerator is multiplied by 3 to produce the new numerator $\left(\frac{1\times3}{6\times3} = \frac{3}{18}\right)$. For the fraction $\frac{4}{9}$, multiplying both the numerator and denominator by 2 produces $\frac{8}{18}$. Since the two new fractions have common denominators, they can be added $\left(\frac{3}{18} + \frac{8}{18} = \frac{11}{18}\right)$.

When multiplying or dividing rational numbers, these numbers may be converted to fractions and multiplied or divided accordingly. When multiplying fractions, all numerators are multiplied by each other and all denominators are multiplied by each other. For example, $\frac{1}{3} \times \frac{6}{5} = \frac{1\times6}{3\times5} = \frac{6}{15}$ and $\frac{-1}{2} \times \frac{3}{1} \times \frac{11}{100} = \frac{-1\times3\times11}{2\times1\times100} = \frac{-33}{200}$. When dividing fractions, the problem is converted by multiplying by the reciprocal of the divisor. This is done by changing division to multiplication and "flipping" the second fraction, or divisor. For example, $\frac{1}{2} \div \frac{3}{5} \rightarrow \frac{1}{2} \times \frac{5}{3}$ and $\frac{5}{1} \div \frac{1}{3} \rightarrow \frac{5}{1} \times \frac{3}{1}$. To complete the problem, the rules for multiplying fractions should be followed.

Note that when adding, subtracting, multiplying, and dividing mixed numbers (ex. $4\frac{1}{2}$), it is easiest to convert these to improper fractions (larger numerator than denominator). To do so, the denominator is kept the same. To obtain the numerator, the whole number is multiplied by the denominator and added to the numerator. For example, $4\frac{1}{2} = \frac{9}{2}$ and $7\frac{2}{3} = \frac{23}{3}$. Also, note that answers involving fractions should be converted to the simplest form.

Rational Numbers and Their Operations

Irregular Products and Quotients

The following shows examples where multiplication does not result in a product greater than both factors, and where division does not result in a quotient smaller than the dividend.

If multiplying numbers where one or more has a value less than one, the product will not be greater than both factors. For example, $6 \times \frac{1}{2} = 3$ and $0.75 \times 0.2 = 0.15$. When dividing by a number less than

one, the resulting quotient will be greater than the dividend. For example, $8 \div \frac{1}{2} = 16$, because division turns into a multiplication problem, $8 \div \frac{1}{2} \rightarrow 8 \times \frac{2}{1}$. Another example is $0.5 \div 0.2$, which results in 2.5. The problem can be stated by asking how many times 0.2 will go into 0.5. The number being divided is larger than the number that goes into it, so the result will be a number larger than both factors.

Composing and Decomposing Fractions

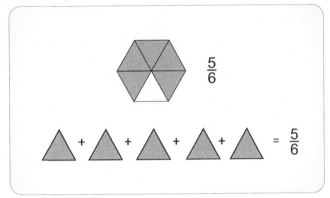

Fractions can be broken apart into sums of fractions with the same denominator. For example, the fraction $\frac{5}{6}$ can be decomposed into sums of fractions with all denominators equal to 6 and the numerators adding to 5. The fraction $\frac{5}{6}$ is decomposed as: $\frac{3}{6} + \frac{2}{6}$; or $\frac{2}{6} + \frac{2}{6} + \frac{1}{6}$; or $\frac{3}{6} + \frac{1}{6} + \frac{1}{6}$; or $\frac{1}{6} + \frac{1}{6} + \frac{1}{6} + \frac{2}{6}$; or $\frac{1}{6} + \frac{1}{6} + \frac{1}{6} + \frac{1}{6} + \frac{1}{6}$.

A unit fraction is a fraction in which the numerator is 1. If decomposing a fraction into unit fractions, the sum will consist of a unit fraction added the number of times equal to the numerator. For example, $\frac{3}{4} = \frac{1}{4} + \frac{1}{4} + \frac{1}{4}$ (unit fractions $\frac{1}{4}$ added 3 times). Composing fractions is simply the opposite of decomposing. It is the process of adding fractions with the same denominators to produce a single fraction. For example, $\frac{3}{7} + \frac{2}{7} = \frac{5}{7}$ and $\frac{1}{5} + \frac{1}{5} + \frac{1}{5} = \frac{3}{5}$.

Decrease in Value of a Unit Fraction

A unit fraction is one in which the numerator is 1 ($\frac{1}{2}, \frac{1}{3}, \frac{1}{8}, \frac{1}{20}$, etc.). The denominator indicates the number of *equal pieces* that the whole is divided into. The greater the number of pieces, the smaller each piece will be. Therefore, the greater the denominator of a unit fraction, the smaller it is in value. Unit fractions can also be compared by converting them to decimals. For example, $\frac{1}{2} = 0.5, \frac{1}{3} = 0.\overline{3}, \frac{1}{8} = 0.125, \frac{1}{20} = 0.05$, etc.

Use of the Same Whole when Comparing Fractions

Fractions all represent parts of the same whole. Fractions may have different denominators, but they represent parts of the same one whole, like a pizza. For example, the fractions $\frac{5}{7}$ and $\frac{2}{3}$ can be difficult to compare because they have different denominators. The first fraction may represent a whole divided into seven parts, where five parts are used. The second fraction represents the same whole divided into three parts, where two are used. It may be helpful to convert one or more of the fractions so that they have common denominators for converting to equivalent fractions by finding the LCM of the denominator. Comparing is much easier if fractions are converted to the equivalent fractions of $\frac{15}{21}$ and $\frac{14}{21}$. These fractions show a whole divided into 21 parts, where the numerators can be compared because the denominators are the same.

Order of Operations

When reviewing calculations consisting of more than one operation, the order in which the operations are performed affects the resulting answer. Consider $5 \times 2 + 7$. Performing multiplication then addition results in an answer of 17 ($5 \times 2 = 10$; $10 + 7 = 17$). However, if the problem is written $5 \times (2 + 7)$, the order of operations dictates that the operation inside the parenthesis must be performed first. The resulting answer is 45 ($2 + 7 = 9$, then $5 \times 9 = 45$).

The order in which operations should be performed is remembered using the acronym PEMDAS. PEMDAS stands for parenthesis, exponents, multiplication/division, and addition/subtraction. Multiplication and division are performed in the same step, working from left to right with whichever comes first. Addition and subtraction are performed in the same step, working from left to right with whichever comes first.

Consider the following example: $8 \div 4 + 8(7 - 7)$. Performing the operation inside the parenthesis produces $8 \div 4 + 8(0)$ or $8 \div 4 + 8 \times 0$. There are no exponents, so multiplication and division are performed next from left to right resulting in: $2 + 8 \times 0$, then $2 + 0$. Finally, addition and subtraction are performed to obtain an answer of 2. Now consider the following example: $6 \times 3 + 3^2 - 6$. Parentheses are not applicable. Exponents are evaluated first, $6 \times 3 + 9 - 6$. Then multiplication/division forms $18 + 9 - 6$. At last, addition/subtraction leads to the final answer of 21.

Properties of Operations

Properties of operations exist that make calculations easier and solve problems for missing values. The following table summarizes commonly used properties of real numbers.

Property	Addition	Multiplication
Commutative	$a + b = b + a$	$a \times b = b \times a$
Associative	$(a + b) + c = a + (b + c)$	$(a \times b) \times c = a \times (b \times c)$
Identity	$a + 0 = a$; $0 + a = a$	$a \times 1 = a$; $1 \times a = a$
Inverse	$a + (-a) = 0$	$a \times \frac{1}{a} = 1$; $a \neq 0$
Distributive	$a(b + c) = ab + ac$	

The commutative property of addition states that the order in which numbers are added does not change the sum. Similarly, the commutative property of multiplication states that the order in which numbers are multiplied does not change the product. The associative property of addition and multiplication state that the grouping of numbers being added or multiplied does not change the sum or product, respectively. The commutative and associative properties are useful for performing calculations. For example, $(47 + 25) + 3$ is equivalent to $(47 + 3) + 25$, which is easier to calculate.

The identity property of addition states that adding zero to any number does not change its value. The identity property of multiplication states that multiplying a number by one does not change its value. The inverse property of addition states that the sum of a number and its opposite equals zero.

Opposites are numbers that are the same with different signs (ex. 5 and -5; $-\frac{1}{2}$ and $\frac{1}{2}$). The inverse property of multiplication states that the product of a number (other than zero) and its reciprocal equals one. Reciprocal numbers have numerators and denominators that are inverted (ex. $\frac{2}{5}$ and $\frac{5}{2}$). Inverse properties are useful for canceling quantities to find missing values (see algebra content). For example, $a + 7 = 12$ is solved by adding the inverse of 7 (which is -7) to both sides in order to isolate a.

The distributive property states that multiplying a sum (or difference) by a number produces the same result as multiplying each value in the sum (or difference) by the number and adding (or subtracting) the products. Consider the following scenario: You are buying three tickets for a baseball game. Each ticket costs $18. You are also charged a fee of $2 per ticket for purchasing the tickets online. The cost is calculated: $3 \times 18 + 3 \times 2$. Using the distributive property, the cost can also be calculated $3(18 + 2)$.

Representing Rational Numbers and Their Operations

Concrete Models

Concrete objects are used to develop a tangible understanding of operations of rational numbers. Tools such as tiles, blocks, beads, and hundred charts are used to model problems. For example, a hundred chart (10×10) and beads can be used to model multiplication. If multiplying 5 by 4, beads are placed across 5 rows and down 4 columns producing a product of 20. Similarly, tiles can be used to model division by splitting the total into equal groups. If dividing 12 by 4, 12 tiles are placed one at a time into 4 groups. The result is 4 groups of 3. This is also an effective method for visualizing the concept of remainders.

Representations of objects can be used to expand on the concrete models of operations. Pictures, dots, and tallies can help model these concepts. Utilizing concrete models and representations creates a foundation upon which to build an abstract understanding of the operations.

Rational Numbers on a Number Line

A number line typically consists of integers (...3, 2, 1, 0, -1, -2, -3...), and is used to visually represent the value of a rational number. Each rational number has a distinct position on the line determined by comparing its value with the displayed values on the line. For example, if plotting -1.5 on the number line below, it is necessary to recognize that the value of -1.5 is 0.5 less than -1 and 0.5 greater than -2. Therefore, -1.5 is plotted halfway between -1 and -2.

Number lines can also be useful for visualizing sums and differences of rational numbers. Adding a value indicates moving to the right (values increase to the right), and subtracting a value indicates moving to the left (numbers decrease to the left). For example, $5 - 7$ is displayed by starting at 5 and moving to the left 7 spaces, if the number line is in increments of 1. This will result in an answer of -2.

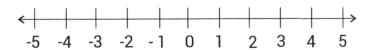

Multiplication and Division Problems

Multiplication and division are inverse operations that can be represented by using rectangular arrays, area models, and equations. Rectangular arrays include an arrangement of rows and columns that correspond to the factors and display product totals.

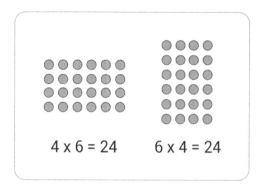

$$4 \times 6 = 24 \qquad 6 \times 4 = 24$$

Another method of multiplication can be done with the use of an *area model*. An area model is a rectangle that is divided into rows and columns that match up to the number of place values within each number. For example, $29 \times 65 = (25 + 4) \times (60 + 5)$. The products of those 4 numbers are found within the rectangle and then summed up to get the answer. The entire process is:

$$(60 \times 25) + (5 \times 25) + (60 \times 4) + (5 \times 4) = 1,500 + 240 + 125 + 20 = 1,885$$

Here is the actual area model:

	25	**4**
60	60x25 1,500	60x4 240
5	5x25 125	5x4 20

```
    1 , 5 0 0
        2 4 0
        1 2 5
  +        2 0
    1 , 8 8 5
```

Dividing a number by a single digit or two digits can be turned into repeated subtraction problems. An area model can be used throughout the problem that represents multiples of the divisor. For example, the answer to $8580 \div 55$ can be found by subtracting 55 from 8580 one at a time and counting the total number of subtractions necessary.

However, a simpler process involves using larger multiples of 55. First, $100 \times 55 = 5,500$ is subtracted from 8,580, and 3,080 is leftover. Next, $50 \times 55 = 2,750$ is subtracted from 3,080 to obtain 380. $5 \times 55 = 275$ is subtracted from 330 to obtain 55, and finally, $1 \times 55 = 55$ is subtracted from 55 to obtain zero. Therefore, there is no remainder, and the answer is $100 + 50 + 5 + 1 = 156$.

Here is a picture of the area model and the repeated subtraction process:

Comparing, Classifying, and Ordering Rational Numbers

A **rational number** is any number that can be written as a fraction or ratio. Within the set of rational numbers, several subsets exist that are referenced throughout the mathematics topics. Counting numbers are the first numbers learned as a child. Counting numbers consist of 1, 2, 3, 4, and so on. Whole numbers include all counting numbers and zero (0, 1, 2, 3, 4, …). Integers include counting numbers, their opposites, and zero (…, -3, -2, -1, 0, 1, 2, 3, …). Rational numbers are inclusive of integers, fractions, and decimals that terminate, or end (1.7, 0.04213) or repeat ($0.136\overline{5}$).

When comparing or ordering numbers, the numbers should be written in the same format (decimal or fraction), if possible. For example, $\sqrt{49}$, 7.3, and $\frac{15}{2}$ are easier to order if each one is converted to a decimal, such as 7, 7.3, and 7.5 (converting fractions and decimals is covered in the following section). A number line is used to order and compare the numbers. Any number that is to the right of another number is greater than that number. Conversely, a number positioned to the left of a given number is less than that number.

Converting Between Fractions, Decimals, and Percent

To convert a fraction to a decimal, the numerator is divided by the denominator. For example, $\frac{3}{8}$ can be converted to a decimal by dividing 3 by 8 ($\frac{3}{8} = 0.375$). To convert a decimal to a fraction, the decimal point is dropped, and the value is written as the numerator. The denominator is the place value farthest to the right with a digit other than zero. For example, to convert .48 to a fraction, the numerator is 48, and the denominator is 100 (the digit 8 is in the hundredths place). Therefore, $.48 = \frac{48}{100}$. Fractions should be written in the simplest form, or reduced. To reduce a fraction, the numerator and denominator are divided by the largest common factor. In the previous example, 48 and 100 are both divisible by 4. Dividing the numerator and denominator by 4 results in a reduced fraction of $\frac{12}{25}$.

To convert a decimal to a percent, the number is multiplied by 100. To convert .13 to a percent, .13 is multiplied by 100 to get 13 percent. To convert a fraction to a percent, the fraction is converted to a decimal and then multiplied by 100. For example, $\frac{1}{5} = .20$ and .20 multiplied by 100 produces 20 percent.

To convert a percent to a decimal, the value is divided by 100. For example, 125 percent is equal to 1.25 ($\frac{125}{100}$). To convert a percent to a fraction, the percent sign is dropped, and the value is written as the numerator with a denominator of 100. For example, $80\% = \frac{80}{100}$. This fraction can be reduced ($\frac{80}{100} = \frac{4}{5}$).

Understanding Proportional Relationships and Percent

Applying Ratios and Unit Rates

A ratio is a comparison of two quantities that represent separate groups. For example, if a recipe calls for 2 eggs for every 3 cups of milk, this is expressed as a ratio. Ratios can be written three ways:

- With the word "to"
- Using a colon
- As a fraction.

In the previous example, the ratio of eggs to cups of milk is written as 2 to 3, 2:3, or $\frac{2}{3}$. When writing ratios, the order is very important. The ratio of eggs to cups of milk is not the same as the ratio of cups of milk to eggs, 3:2.

In simplest form, both quantities of a ratio should be written as integers. These should also be reduced just as a fraction is reduced. For example, 5:10 is reduced to 1:2. Given a ratio where one or both quantities are expressed as a decimal or fraction, multiply both by the same number to produce integers. To write the ratio $\frac{1}{3}$ to 2 in simplest form, both quantities are multiplied by 3. The resulting ratio is 1 to 6.

A problem involving ratios may give a comparison between two groups. The problem may then provide a total and ask for a part, or provide a part and ask for a total. Consider the following: The ratio of boys to girls in the 11th grade class is 5:4. If there are a total of 270 11th grade students, how many are girls? The total number of *ratio pieces* should be determined first. The total number of 11th grade students is divided into 9 pieces. The ratio of boys to total students is 5:9, and the ratio of girls to total students is 4:9. Knowing the total number of students, the number of girls is determined by setting up a proportion: $\frac{4}{9} = \frac{x}{270}$.

A rate is a ratio comparing two quantities expressed in different units. A unit rate is a ratio in which the second quantity is one unit. Rates often include the word *per*. Examples include miles per hour, beats per minute, and price per pound. The word per is represented with a / symbol or abbreviated with the letter *p* and units abbreviated. For example, miles per hour is written as mi/h. When given a rate that is not in its simplest form (the second quantity is not one unit), both quantities are divided by the value of

the second quantity. If 99 heartbeats were recorded in $1\frac{1}{2}$ minutes, both quantities are divided by $1\frac{1}{2}$ to determine the heart rate of 66 beats per minute.

Percent

The word percent means per hundred. Similar to a unit rate in which the second quantity is always one unit, a percent is a rate where the second quantity is always 100 units. If the results of a poll state that 47 percent of people support a given policy, this indicates that 47 out of every 100 individuals polled were in support. In other words, 47 per 100 support the policy. If an upgraded model of a car costs 110 percent of the cost of the base model, for every $100 that is spent for the base model, $110 must be spent to purchase the upgraded model. In other words, the upgraded model costs $110 per $100 for the cost of the base model.

When dealing with percentages, the numbers can be evaluated as a value in hundredths. For example, 15 percent is expressed as fifteen hundredths and is written as $\frac{15}{100}$ or 0.15.

Unit-Rate Problems

A rate is a ratio in which two terms are in different units. When rates are expressed as a quantity of one, they are considered unit rates. To determine a unit rate, the first quantity is divided by the second. Knowing a unit rate makes calculations easier than simply having a rate. For example, suppose a 3 pound bag of onions costs $1.77. To calculate the price of 5 pounds of onions, a proportion could show: $\frac{3}{1.77} = \frac{5}{x}$. However, by knowing the unit rate, the value of pounds of onions is multiplied by the unit price. The unit price is calculated: $\$1.77/3lb = \$0.59/lb$. Multiplying the weight of the onions by the unit price yields: $5lb \times \frac{\$0.59}{lb} = \$2.95$. The *lb.* units cancel out.

Similar to unit-rate problems, unit conversions appear in real-world scenarios including cooking, measurement, construction, and currency. Given the conversion rate, unit conversions are written as a fraction (ratio) and multiplied by a quantity in one unit to convert it to the corresponding unit. To determine how many minutes are in $3\frac{1}{2}$ hours, the conversion rate of 60 minutes to 1 hour is written as $\frac{60\ min}{1h}$. Multiplying the quantity by the conversion rate results in $3\frac{1}{2}h \times \frac{60\ min}{1h} = 210\ min$. (The h unit is canceled.) To convert a quantity in minutes to hours, the fraction for the conversion rate is flipped to cancel the *min* unit. To convert 195 minutes to hours, $195min \times \frac{1h}{60\ min}$ is multiplied. The result is $\frac{195h}{60}$ which reduces to $3\frac{1}{4}h$.

Converting units may require more than one multiplication. The key is to set up conversion rates so that units cancel each other out and the desired unit is left. To convert 3.25 yards to inches, given that 1yd = 3ft and 12in = 1ft, the calculation is performed by multiplying 3.25 yd $\times \frac{3ft}{1yd} \times \frac{12in}{1ft}$. The yd and ft units will cancel, resulting in 117in.

Using Proportional Relationships

A proportion is a statement consisting of two equal ratios. Proportions will typically give three of four quantities and require solving for the missing value. The key to solving proportions is to set them up properly. Consider the following: 7 gallons of gas costs $14.70. How many gallons can you get for $20?

The information is written as equal ratios with a variable representing the missing quantity:

$$\left(\frac{gallons}{cost} = \frac{gallons}{cost}\right) : \frac{7}{14.70} = \frac{x}{20}$$

To solve for x, the proportion is cross-multiplied. This means the numerator of the first ratio is multiplied by the denominator of the second, and vice versa. The resulting products are shown equal to each other. Cross-multiplying results in $(7)(20) = (14.7)(x)$. By solving the equation for x (see the algebra content), the answer is that 9.5 gallons of gas may be purchased for $20.

Percent problems can also be solved by setting up proportions. Examples of common percent problems are:

    a. What is 15% of 25?
    b. What percent of 45 is 3?
    c. 5 is $\frac{1}{2}$% of what number?

Setting up the proper proportion is made easier by following the format: $\frac{is}{of} = \frac{percent}{100}$. A variable is used to represent the missing value. The proportions for each of the three examples are set up as follows:

    a. $\frac{x}{25} = \frac{15}{100}$

    b. $\frac{3}{45} = \frac{x}{100}$

    c. $\frac{5}{x} = \frac{\frac{1}{2}}{100}$

By cross-multiplying and solving the resulting equation for the variable, the missing values are determined to be:

    a. 3.75
    b. $6.\bar{6}$%
    c. 1,000

Basic Concepts of Number Theory

Prime and Composite Numbers

Whole numbers are classified as either prime or composite. A prime number can only be divided evenly by itself and one. For example, the number 11 can only be divided evenly by 11 and one; therefore, 11 is a prime number. A helpful way to visualize a prime number is to use concrete objects and try to divide them into equal piles. If dividing 11 coins, the only way to divide them into equal piles is to create 1 pile of 11 coins or to create 11 piles of 1 coin each. Other examples of prime numbers include 2, 3, 5, 7, 13, 17, and 19.

A composite number is any whole number that is not a prime number. A composite number is a number that can be divided evenly by one or more numbers other than itself and one. For example, the number 6 can be divided evenly by 2 and 3. Therefore, 6 is a composite number. If dividing 6 coins into equal piles, the possibilities are 1 pile of 6 coins, 2 piles of 3 coins, 3 piles of 2 coins, or 6 piles of 1 coin. Other examples of composite numbers include 4, 8, 9, 10, 12, 14, 15, 16, 18, and 20.

To determine if a number is a prime or composite number, the number is divided by every whole number greater than one and less than its own value. If it divides evenly by any of these numbers, then the number is composite. If it does not divide evenly by any of these numbers, then the number is prime. For example, when attempting to divide the number 5 by 2, 3, and 4, none of these numbers divide evenly. Therefore, 5 must be a prime number.

Factors and Multiples of Numbers

The factors of a number are all integers that can be multiplied by another integer to produce the given number. For example, 2 is multiplied by 3 to produce 6. Therefore, 2 and 3 are both factors of 6. Similarly, $1 \times 6 = 6$ and $2 \times 3 = 6$, so 1, 2, 3, and 6 are all factors of 6. Another way to explain a factor is to say that a given number divides evenly by each of its factors to produce an integer. For example, 6 does not divide evenly by 5. Therefore, 5 is not a factor of 6.

Multiples of a given number are found by taking that number and multiplying it by any other whole number. For example, 3 is a factor of 6, 9, and 12. Therefore, 6, 9, and 12 are multiples of 3. The multiples of any number are an infinite list. For example, the multiples of 5 are 5, 10, 15, 20, and so on. This list continues without end. A list of multiples is used in finding the least common multiple, or LCM, for fractions when a common denominator is needed. The denominators are written down and their multiples listed until a common number is found in both lists. This common number is the LCM.

Prime factorization breaks down each factor of a whole number until only prime numbers remain. All composite numbers can be factored into prime numbers. For example, the prime factors of 12 are 2, 2, and 3 ($2 \times 2 \times 3 = 12$). To produce the prime factors of a number, the number is factored, and any composite numbers are continuously factored until the result is the product of prime factors only. A factor tree, such as the one below, is helpful when exploring this concept.

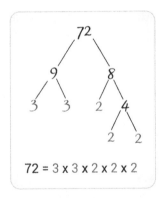

72 = 3 x 3 x 2 x 2 x 2

Determining the Reasonableness of Results

When solving math word problems, the solution obtained should make sense within the given scenario. The step of checking the solution will reduce the possibility of a calculation error or a solution that may be *mathematically* correct but not applicable in the real world. Consider the following scenarios:

A problem states that Lisa got 24 out of 32 questions correct on a test and asks to find the percentage of correct answers. To solve the problem, a student divided 32 by 24 to get 1.33, and then multiplied by 100 to get 133 percent. By examining the solution within the context of the problem, the student should recognize that getting all 32 questions correct will produce a perfect score of 100 percent. Therefore, a score of 133 percent with 8 incorrect answers does not make sense, and the calculations should be checked.

A problem states that the maximum weight on a bridge cannot exceed 22,000 pounds. The problem asks to find the maximum number of cars that can be on the bridge at one time if each car weighs 4,000 pounds. To solve this problem, a student divided 22,000 by 4,000 to get an answer of 5.5. By examining the solution within the context of the problem, the student should recognize that although the calculations are mathematically correct, the solution does not make sense. Half of a car on a bridge is not possible, so the student should determine that a maximum of 5 cars can be on the bridge at the same time.

Mental Math Estimation

Once a result is determined to be logical within the context of a given problem, the result should be evaluated by its nearness to the expected answer. This is performed by approximating given values to perform mental math. Numbers should be rounded to the nearest value possible to check the initial results.

Consider the following example: A problem states that a customer is buying a new sound system for their home. The customer purchases a stereo for $435, 2 speakers for $67 each, and the necessary cables for $12. The customer chooses an option that allows him to spread the costs over equal payments for 4 months. How much will the monthly payments be?

After making calculations for the problem, a student determines that the monthly payment will be $145.25. To check the accuracy of the results, the student rounds each cost to the nearest ten (440 + 70 + 70 + 10) and determines that the total is approximately $590. Dividing by 4 months gives an approximate monthly payment of $147.50. Therefore, the student can conclude that the solution of $145.25 is very close to what should be expected.

When rounding, the place-value that is used in rounding can make a difference. Suppose the student had rounded to the nearest hundred for the estimation. The result ($400 + 100 + 100 + 0 = 600$; $600 \div 4 = 150$) will show that the answer is reasonable, but not as close to the actual value as rounding to the nearest ten.

Patterns and Algebra

Solving for X in Proportions

Proportions are commonly used in word problems to find unknown values, such as x, that are some percent or fraction of a known number. Proportions are solved by cross-multiplying and then dividing to arrive at x. The following examples show how this is done:

1. $\frac{75\%}{90\%} = \frac{25\%}{x}$

To solve for x, the fractions must be cross-multiplied: ($75\%x = 90\% \times 25\%$). To make things easier, the percentages can be converted to decimals: ($0.9 \times 0.25 = 0.225 = 0.75x$). To get rid of the coefficient of x, each side must be divided by that same coefficient to get the answer $x = 0.3$. The question could ask for the answer as a percentage or fraction in lowest terms, which are 30% and $\frac{3}{10}$, respectively.

2. $\frac{x}{12} = \frac{30}{96}$

Cross-multiply: $96x = 30 \times 12$

Multiply: $96x = 360$

Divide: $x = 360 \div 96$

Answer: $x = 3.75$

3. $\frac{0.5}{3} = \frac{x}{6}$

Cross-multiply: $3x = 0.5 \times 6$

Multiply: $3x = 3$

Divide: $x = 3 \div 3$

Answer: $x = 1$

Observant test takers may have noticed there's a faster way to arrive at the answer. If there is an obvious operation being performed on the proportion, the same operation can be used on the other side of the proportion to solve for x. For example, in the first practice problem, 75% became 25% when divided by 3, and upon doing the same to 90%, the correct answer of 30% would have been found with much less legwork. However, these questions aren't always so intuitive, so it's a good idea for test takers to work through the steps, even if the answer seems apparent from the onset.

Translating Words into Math

To translate a word problem into an expression, test takers should look for key words indicating addition, subtraction, multiplication, or division:

- *Addition*: add, altogether, together, plus, increased by, more than, in all, sum, and total
- *Subtraction*: minus, less than, difference, decreased by, fewer than, remain, and take away
- *Multiplication*: times, twice, of, double, and triple
- *Division*: divided by, cut up, half, quotient of, split, and shared equally

If a question asks to give words to a mathematical expression and says "equals," then an = sign must be included in the answer. Similarly, "less than or equal to" is expressed by the inequality symbol ≤, and "greater than or equal" to is expressed as ≥. Furthermore, "less than" is represented by <, and "greater than" is expressed by >.

Word Problems

Word problems can appear daunting, but prepared test takers shouldn't let the verbiage psyche them out. No matter the scenario or specifics, the key to answering them is to translate the words into a math problem. It is critical to keep in mind what the question is asking and what operations could lead to that answer. The following word problems highlight the most commonly tested question types.

Working with Money

Walter's Coffee Shop sells a variety of drinks and breakfast treats.

Price List	
Hot Coffee	$2.00
Slow Drip Iced Coffee	$3.00
Latte	$4.00
Muffins	$2.00
Crepe	$4.00
Egg Sandwich	$5.00

Costs	
Hot Coffee	$0.25
Slow Drip Iced Coffee	$0.75
Latte	$1.00
Muffins	$1.00
Crepe	$2.00
Egg Sandwich	$3.00

Walter's utilities, rent, and labor costs him $500 per day. Today, Walter sold 200 hot coffees, 100 slow drip iced coffees, 50 lattes, 75 muffins, 45 crepes, and 60 egg sandwiches. What was Walter's total profit today? To accurately answer this type of question, the first step is to determine the total cost of making his drinks and treats, then determine how much revenue he earned from selling those products. After arriving at these two totals, the profit is measured by deducting the total cost from the total revenue.

Walter's costs for today:

200 hot coffees	$\times$ $0.25	= $50
100 slow drip iced coffees	$\times$ $0.75	= $75
50 lattes	$\times$ $1.00	= $50
75 muffins	$\times$ $1.00	= $75
45 crepes	$\times$ $2.00	= $90
60 egg sandwiches	$\times$ $3.00	= $180
Utilities, Rent, and Labor		= $500
Total costs		= $1,020

Walter's revenue for today:

200 hot coffees	$\times$ $2.00	= $400
100 slow drip iced coffees	$\times$ $3.00	= $300
50 lattes	$\times$ $4.00	= $200
75 muffins	$\times$ $2.00	= $150
45 crepes	$\times$ $4.00	= $180
60 egg sandwiches	$\times$ $5.00	= $300
Total revenue		= $1,530

Walter's $Profit = Revenue - Costs = \$1{,}530 - \$1{,}020 = \$510$

This strategy can be applied to other question types. For example, calculating salary after deductions, balancing a checkbook, and calculating a dinner bill are common word problems similar to business planning. In all cases, the most important step is remembering to use the correct operations. When a balance is increased, addition is used. When a balance is decreased, the problem requires subtraction. Common sense and organization are one's greatest assets when answering word problems.

Unit Rate

Unit rate word problems ask test takers to calculate the rate or quantity of something in a different value. For example, a problem might say that a car drove a certain number of miles in a certain number of minutes and then ask how many miles per hour the car was traveling. These questions involve solving proportions. Consider the following examples:

1. Alexandra made $96 during the first 3 hours of her shift as a temporary worker at a law office. She will continue to earn money at this rate until she finishes in 5 more hours. How much does Alexandra make per hour? How much money will Alexandra have made at the end of the day?

This problem can be solved in two ways. The first is to set up a proportion, as the rate of pay is constant. The second is to determine her hourly rate, multiply the 5 hours by that rate, and then adding the $96.

To set up a proportion, the money already earned (numerator) is placed over the hours already worked (denominator) on one side of an equation. The other side has x over 8 hours (the total hours worked in the day). It looks like this: $\frac{96}{3} = \frac{x}{8}$. Now, cross-multiply yields $768 = 3x$. To get x, the 768 is divided by 3, which leaves $x = 256$. Alternatively, as x is the numerator of one of the proportions, multiplying by its denominator will reduce the solution by one step. Thus, Alexandra will make $256 at the end of the day. To calculate her hourly rate, the total is divided by 8, giving $32 per hour.

Alternatively, it is possible to figure out the hourly rate by dividing $96 by 3 hours to get $32 per hour. Now her total pay can be figured by multiplying $32 per hour by 8 hours, which comes out to $256.

2. Jonathan is reading a novel. So far, he has read 215 of the 335 total pages. It takes Jonathan 25 minutes to read 10 pages, and the rate is constant. How long does it take Jonathan to read one page? How much longer will it take him to finish the novel? Express the answer in time.

To calculate how long it takes Jonathan to read one page, 25 minutes is divided by 10 pages to determine the page per minute rate. Thus, it takes 2.5 minutes to read one page.

Jonathan must read 120 more pages to complete the novel. (This is calculated by subtracting the pages already read from the total.) Now, his rate per page is multiplied by the number of pages. Thus, $120 \times 2.5 = 300$. Expressed in time, 300 minutes is equal to 5 hours.

3. At a hotel, $\frac{4}{5}$ of the 120 rooms are booked for Saturday. On Sunday, $\frac{3}{4}$ of the rooms are booked. On which day are more of the rooms booked, and by how many more?

The first step is to calculate the number of rooms booked for each day. This is done by multiplying the fraction of the rooms booked by the total number of rooms.

$$\text{Saturday: } \frac{4}{5} \times 120 = \frac{4}{5} \times \frac{120}{1} = \frac{480}{5} = 96 \text{ rooms}$$

$$\text{Sunday: } \frac{3}{4} \times 120 = \frac{3}{4} \times \frac{120}{1} = \frac{360}{4} = 90 \text{ rooms}$$

Thus, more rooms were booked on Saturday by 6 rooms.

4. In a veterinary hospital, the veterinarian-to-pet ratio is 1:9. The ratio is always constant. If there are 45 pets in the hospital, how many veterinarians are currently in the veterinary hospital?

A proportion is set up to solve for the number of veterinarians: $\frac{1}{9} = \frac{x}{45}$

Cross-multiplying results in $9x = 45$, which works out to 5 veterinarians.

Alternatively, as there are always 9 times as many pets as veterinarians, is it possible to divide the number of pets (45) by 9. This also arrives at the correct answer of 5 veterinarians.

5. At a general practice law firm, 30% of the lawyers work solely on tort cases. If 9 lawyers work solely on tort cases, how many lawyers work at the firm?

The first step is to solve for the total number of lawyers working at the firm, which will be represented here with x. The problem states that 9 lawyers work solely on torts cases, and they make up 30% of the total lawyers at the firm. Thus, 30% multiplied by the total, x, will equal 9. Written as equation, this is: $30\% \times x = 9$.

It's easier to deal with the equation after converting the percentage to a decimal, leaving $0.3x = 9$. Thus, $x = \frac{9}{0.3} = 30$ lawyers working at the firm.

6. Xavier was hospitalized with pneumonia. He was originally given 35mg of antibiotics. Later, after his condition continued to worsen, Xavier's dosage was increased to 60mg. What was the percent increase of the antibiotics? Round the percentage to the nearest tenth.

An increase or decrease in percentage can be calculated by dividing the difference in amounts by the original amount and multiplying by 100. Written as an equation, the formula is:

$$\frac{new\ quantity - old\ quantity}{old\ quantity} \times 100$$

Here, the question states that the dosage was increased from 35mg to 60mg, so these values are plugged into the formula to find the percentage increase.

$$\frac{60 - 35}{35} \times 100 = \frac{25}{35} \times 100 = .7142 \times 100 = 71.4\%$$

FOIL Method

FOIL is a technique for generating polynomials through the multiplication of binomials. A **polynomial** is an expression of multiple variables (for example, x, y, z) in at least three terms involving only the four basic operations and exponents. FOIL is an acronym for First, Outer, Inner, and Last. "First" represents the multiplication of the terms appearing first in the binomials. "Outer" means multiplying the outermost terms. "Inner" means multiplying the terms inside. "Last" means multiplying the last terms of each binomial.

After completing FOIL and solving the operations, **like terms** are combined. To identify like terms, test takers should look for terms with the same variable and the same exponent. For example, in $4x^2 - x^2 + 15x + 2x^2 - 8$, the $4x^2$, $-x^2$, and $2x^2$ are all like terms because they have the variable (x) and

exponent (2). Thus, after combining the like terms, the polynomial has been simplified to $5x^2 + 15x - 8$.

The purpose of FOIL is to simplify an equation involving multiple variables and operations. Although it sounds complicated, working through some examples will provide some clarity:

1. Simplify $(x + 10)(x + 4)$ =

$$\underset{\text{First}}{(x \times x)} \quad + \quad \underset{\text{Outer}}{(x \times 4)} \quad + \quad \underset{\text{Inner}}{(10 \times x)} \quad + \quad \underset{\text{Last}}{(10 \times 4)}$$

After multiplying these binomials, it's time to solve the operations and combine like terms. Thus, the expression becomes: $2x^2 + 4x + 10x + 40 = 2x^2 + 14x + 40$.

2. Simplify $2x(4x^3 - 7y^2 + 3x^2 + 4)$

Here, a monomial $(2x)$ is multiplied into a polynomial $(4x^3 - 7y^2 + 3x^2 + 4)$. Using the distributive property, the monomial gets multiplied by each term in the polynomial. This becomes $2x(4x^3) - 2x(7y^2) + 2x(3x^2) + 2x(4)$.

Now, each monomial is simplified, starting with the coefficients:

$$(2 \times 4)(x \times x^3) - (2 \times 7)(x \times y^2) + (2 \times 3)(x \times x^2) + (2 \times 4)(x)$$

When multiplying powers with the same base, their exponents are added. Remember, a variable with no listed exponent has an exponent of 1, and exponents of distinct variables cannot be combined. This produces the answer:

$$8x^{1+3} - 14xy^2 + 6x^{1+2} + 8x = 8x^4 - 14xy^2 + 6x^3 + 8x$$

3. Simplify $(8x^{10}y^2z^4) \div (4x^2y^4z^7)$

The first step is to divide the coefficients of the first two polynomials: $8 \div 4 = 2$. The second step is to divide exponents with the same variable, which requires subtracting the exponents. This results in: $2(x^{10-2}y^{2-4}z^{4-7}) = 2x^8y^{-2}z^{-3}$.

However, the most simplified answer should include only positive exponents. Thus, $y^{-2}z^{-3}$ needs to be converted into fractions, respectively $\frac{1}{y^2}$ and $\frac{1}{z^3}$. Since the $2x^8$ has a positive exponent, it is placed in the numerator, and $\frac{1}{y^2}$ and $\frac{1}{z^3}$ are combined into the denominator, leaving $\frac{2x^8}{y^2z^3}$ as the final answer.

Rational Expressions

A **rational expression** is a fraction where the numerator and denominator are both polynomials. Some examples of rational expressions include the following: $\frac{4x^3y^5}{3z^4}$, $\frac{4x^3+3x}{x^2}$, and $\frac{x^2+7x+10}{x+2}$. Since these refer to expressions and not equations, they can be simplified but not solved. Using the rules in the previous *Exponents* and *Roots* sections, some rational expressions with monomials can be simplified. Other rational expressions such as the last example, $\frac{x^2+7x+10}{x+2}$, require more steps to be simplified. First, the polynomial on top can be factored from $x^2 + 7x + 10$ into $(x + 5)(x + 2)$. Then the common factors can be canceled and the expression can be simplified to $(x + 5)$.

The following problem is an example of using rational expressions:

Reggie wants to lay sod in his rectangular backyard. The length of the yard is given by the expression $4x + 2$ and the width is unknown. The area of the yard is $20x + 10$. Reggie needs to find the width of the yard. Knowing that the area of a rectangle is length multiplied by width, an expression can be written to find the width: $\frac{20x+10}{4x+2}$, area divided by length. Simplifying this expression by factoring out 10 on the top and 2 on the bottom leads to this expression: $\frac{10(2x+1)}{2(2x+1)}$. Cancelling out the $2x + 1$ results in $\frac{10}{2} = 5$. The width of the yard is found to be 5 by simplifying the rational expression.

Rational Equations

A **rational equation** can be as simple as an equation with a ratio of polynomials, $\frac{p(x)}{q(x)}$, set equal to a value, where $p(x)$ and $q(x)$ are both polynomials. A rational equation has an equal sign, which is different from expressions. This leads to solutions, or numbers that make the equation true.

It is possible to solve rational equations by trying to get all of the x terms out of the denominator and then isolating them on one side of the equation. For example, to solve the equation $\frac{3x+2}{2x+3} = 4$, both sides get multiplied by $(2x + 3)$. This will cancel on the left side to yield $3x + 2 = 4(2x + 3)$, then $3x + 2 = 8x + 12$. Now, subtract $8x$ from both sides, which yields $-5x + 2 = 12$. Subtracting 2 from both sides results in $-5x = 10$. Finally, both sides get divided by -5 to obtain $x = -2$.

Sometimes, when solving rational equations, it can be easier to try to simplify the rational expression by factoring the numerator and denominator first, then cancelling out common factors. For example, to solve $\frac{2x^2-8x+6}{x^2-3x+2} = 1$, the first step is to factor $2x^2 - 8x + 6 = 2(x^2 - 4x + 3) = 2(x - 1)(x - 3)$. Then, factor $x^2 - 3x + 2$ into $(x - 1)(x - 2)$. This turns the original equation into $\frac{2(x-1)(x-3)}{(x-1)(x-2)} = 1$. The common factor of $(x - 1)$ can be canceled, leaving $\frac{2(x-3)}{x-1} = 1$. Now the same method used in the previous example can be followed. Multiplying both sides by $x - 1$ and performing the multiplication on the left yields $2x - 6 = x - 1$, which can be simplified to $x = 5$.

Rational Functions

A **rational function** is similar to an equation, but it includes two variables. In general, a rational function is in the form: $f(x) = \frac{p(x)}{q(x)}$, where $p(x)$ and $q(x)$ are polynomials. Refer to the *Functions* section (which follows) for a more detailed definition of functions. Rational functions are defined everywhere except

where the denominator is equal to zero. When the denominator is equal to zero, this indicates either a hole in the graph or an asymptote. An example of a function with an asymptote is shown below.

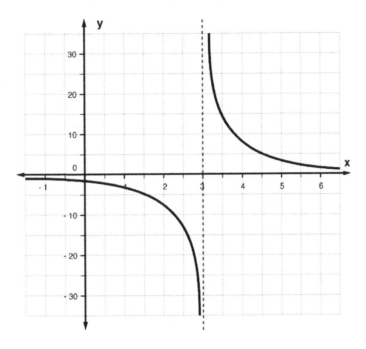

Algebraic Functions

A function is called **algebraic** if it is built up from polynomials by adding, subtracting, multiplying, dividing, and taking radicals. This means that, for example, the variable can never appear in an exponent. Thus, polynomials and rational functions are algebraic, but exponential functions are not algebraic. It turns out that logarithms and trigonometric functions are not algebraic either.

A function of the form $f(x) = a_nx^n + a_{n-1}x^{n-1} + a_{n-2}x^{n-2} + \cdots + a_1x + a_0$ is called a **polynomial function**. The value of n is called the **degree** of the polynomial. In the case where $n = 1$, it is called a **linear function**. In the case where $n = 2$, it is called a **quadratic function**. In the case where $n = 3$, it is called a **cubic function**.

When n is even, the polynomial is called **even**, and not all real numbers will be in its range. When n is odd, the polynomial is called **odd**, and the range includes all real numbers.

The graph of a quadratic function $f(x) = ax^2 + bx + c$ will be a **parabola**. To see whether or not the parabola opens up or down, it's necessary to check the coefficient of x^2, which is the value a. If the coefficient is positive, then the parabola opens upward. If the coefficient is negative, then the parabola opens downward.

The quantity $D = b^2 - 4ac$ is called the **discriminant** of the parabola. If the discriminant is positive, then the parabola has two real zeros. If the discriminant is negative, then it has no real zeros. If the discriminant is zero, then the parabola's highest or lowest point is on the x-axis, and it has a single real zero.

The highest or lowest point of the parabola is called the **vertex**. The coordinates of the vertex are given by the point $(-\frac{b}{2a}, -\frac{D}{4a})$. The roots of a quadratic function can be found with the quadratic formula, which is:

$$x = \frac{-b \pm \sqrt{b^2 - 4ac}}{2a}$$

A **rational function** is a function $f(x) = \frac{p(x)}{q(x)}$, where p and q are both polynomials. The domain of f will be all real numbers except the (real) roots of q. At these roots, the graph of f will have a **vertical asymptote,** unless they are also roots of p. Here is an example to consider:

$$p(x) = p_n x^n + p_{n-1} x^{n-1} + p_{n-2} x^{n-2} + \cdots + p_1 x + p_0$$

$$q(x) = q_m x^m + q_{m-1} x^{m-1} + q_{m-2} x^{m-2} + \cdots + q_1 x + q_0$$

When the degree of p is less than the degree of q, there will be a **horizontal asymptote** of $y = 0$. If p and q have the same degree, there will be a horizontal asymptote of $y = \frac{p_n}{q_n}$. If the degree of p is exactly one greater than the degree of q, then f will have an oblique asymptote along the line:

$$y = \frac{p_n}{q_{n-1}} x + \frac{p_{n-1}}{q_{n-1}}$$

Exponential Functions

An **exponential function** is a function of the form $f(x) = b^x$, where b is a positive real number other than 1. In such a function, b is called the **base**.

The **domain** of an exponential function is all real numbers, and the **range** is all positive real numbers. There will always be a horizontal asymptote of $y = 0$ on one side. If b is greater than 1, then the graph will be increasing when moving to the right. If b is less than 1, then the graph will be decreasing when moving to the right. Exponential functions are one-to-one. The basic exponential function graph will go through the point (0, 1).

The following example demonstartes this more clearly:

Solve $5^{x+1} = 25$.

The first step is to get the x out of the exponent by rewriting the equation $5^{x+1} = 5^2$ so that both sides have a base of 5. Since the bases are the same, the exponents must be equal to each other. This leaves $x + 1 = 2$ or $x = 1$. To check the answer, the x-value of 1 can be substituted back into the original equation.

Logarithmic Functions

A **logarithmic function** is an inverse for an exponential function. The inverse of the base b exponential function is written as $\log_b(x)$, and is called the **base b logarithm**. The domain of a logarithm is all positive real numbers. It has the properties that $\log_b(b^x) = x$. For positive real values of x, $b^{\log_b(x)} = x$.

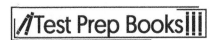

When there is no chance of confusion, the parentheses are sometimes skipped for logarithmic functions: $\log_b(x)$ may be written as $\log_b x$. For the special number e, the base e logarithm is called the **natural logarithm** and is written as $\ln x$. Logarithms are one-to-one.

When working with logarithmic functions, it is important to remember the following properties. Each one can be derived from the definition of the logarithm as the inverse to an exponential function:

- $\log_b 1 = 0$
- $\log_b b = 1$
- $\log_b b^p = p$
- $\log_b MN = \log_b M + \log_b N$
- $\log_b \frac{M}{N} = \log_b M - \log_b N$
- $\log_b M^p = p \log_b M$

When solving equations involving exponentials and logarithms, the following fact should be used:

If f is a one-to-one function, $a = b$ is equivalent to $f(a) = f(b)$.

Using this, together with the fact that logarithms and exponentials are inverses, allows for manipulations of the equations to isolate the variable as is demonstrated in the following example:

Solve $4 = \ln(x - 4)$.

Using the definition of a logarithm, the equation can be changed to $e^4 = e^{\ln(x-4)}$. The functions on the right side cancel with a result of $e^4 = x - 4$. This then gives $x = 4 + e^4$.

Trigonometric Functions

Trigonometric functions are built out of two basic functions, the **sine** and **cosine**, written as $\sin \theta$ and $\cos \theta$, respectively. Note that similar to logarithms, it is customary to drop the parentheses as long as the result is not confusing.

Sine and cosine are defined using the **unit circle**. If θ is the angle going counterclockwise around the origin from the x-axis, then the point on the unit circle in that direction will have the coordinates ($\cos \theta$, $\sin \theta$).

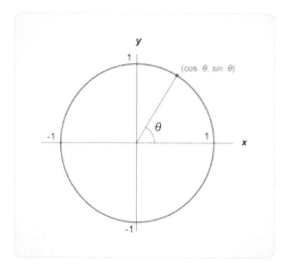

Since the angle returns to the start every 2π radians (or 360 degrees), the graph of these functions is **periodic**, with period 2π. This means that the graph repeats itself as one moves along the x-axis because $\sin \theta = \sin(\theta + 2\pi)$. Cosine works similarly.

From the unit circle definition, the sine function starts at 0 when $\theta = 0$. It grows to 1 as θ grows to $\pi/2$, and then back to 0 at $\theta = \pi$. Then it decreases to -1 as θ grows to $3\pi/2$, and goes back up to 0 at $\theta = 2\pi$.

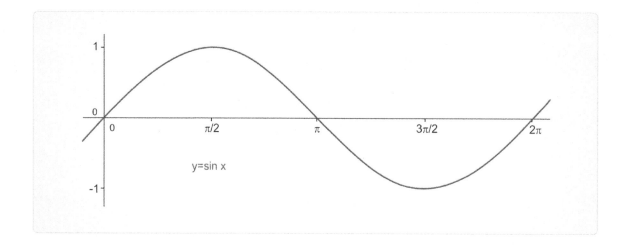

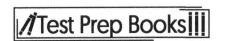

The graph of the cosine is similar. The cosine graph will start at 1, decreasing to 0 at $\pi/2$ and continuing to decrease to -1 at $\theta = \pi$. Then, it grows to 0 as θ grows to $3\pi/2$ and back up to 1 at $\theta = 2\pi$.

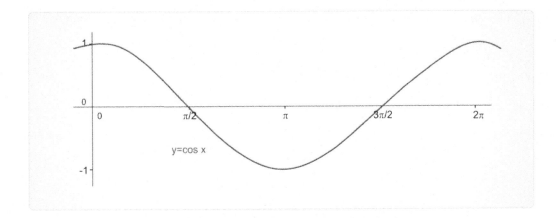

Another trigonometric function that is frequently used, is the **tangent** function. This is defined as the following equation: $\tan\theta = \frac{\sin\theta}{\cos\theta}$.

The tangent function is a period of π rather than 2π because the sine and cosine functions have the same absolute values after a change in the angle of π, but they flip their signs. Since the tangent is a ratio of the two functions, the changes in signs cancel.

The tangent function will be zero when sine is zero, and it will have a vertical asymptote whenever cosine is zero. The following graph shows the tangent function:

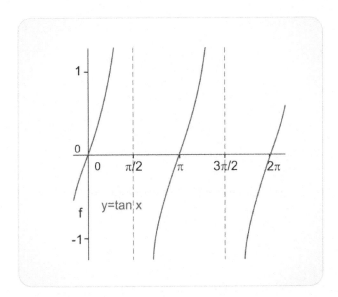

Three other trigonometric functions are sometimes useful. These are the **reciprocal** trigonometric functions, so named because they are just the reciprocals of sine, cosine, and tangent. They are the

cosecant, defined as $\csc\theta = \frac{1}{\sin\theta}$, the **secant**, $\sec\theta = \frac{1}{\cos\theta}$, and the **cotangent**, $\cot\theta = \frac{1}{\tan\theta}$. Note that from the definition of tangent, $\cot\theta = \frac{\cos\theta}{\sin\theta}$.

In addition, there are three identities that relate the trigonometric functions to one another:

- $\cos\theta = \sin(\frac{\pi}{2} - \theta)$
- $\csc\theta = \sec\left(\frac{\pi}{2} - \theta\right)$
- $\cot\theta = \tan(\frac{\pi}{2} - \theta)$

Here is a list of commonly-needed values for trigonometric functions, given in radians, for the first quadrant:

Table for trigonometric functions

$\sin 0 = 0$	$\cos 0 = 1$	$\tan 0 = 0$
$\sin\frac{\pi}{6} = \frac{1}{2}$	$\cos\frac{\pi}{6} = \frac{\sqrt{3}}{2}$	$\tan\frac{\pi}{6} = \frac{\sqrt{3}}{3}$
$\sin\frac{\pi}{4} = \frac{\sqrt{2}}{2}$	$\cos\frac{\pi}{4} = \frac{\sqrt{2}}{2}$	$\tan\frac{\pi}{4} = 1$
$\sin\frac{\pi}{3} = \frac{\sqrt{3}}{2}$	$\cos\frac{\pi}{3} = \frac{1}{2}$	$\tan\frac{\pi}{3} = \sqrt{3}$
$\sin\frac{\pi}{2} = 1$	$\cos\frac{\pi}{2} = 0$	$\tan\frac{\pi}{2} = undefined$
$\csc 0 = undefined$	$\sec 0 = 1$	$\cot 0 = undefined$
$\csc\frac{\pi}{6} = 2$	$\sec\frac{\pi}{6} = \frac{2\sqrt{3}}{3}$	$\cot\frac{\pi}{6} = \sqrt{3}$
$\csc\frac{\pi}{4} = \sqrt{2}$	$\sec\frac{\pi}{4} = \sqrt{2}$	$\cot\frac{\pi}{4} = 1$
$\csc\frac{\pi}{3} = \frac{2\sqrt{3}}{3}$	$\sec\frac{\pi}{3} = 2$	$\cot\frac{\pi}{3} = \frac{\sqrt{3}}{3}$
$\csc\frac{\pi}{2} = 1$	$\sec\frac{\pi}{2} = undefined$	$\cot\frac{\pi}{2} = 0$

To find the trigonometric values in other quadrants, complementary angles can be used. The **complementary angle** is the smallest angle between the x-axis and the given angle.

Once the complementary angle is known, the following rule is used:

> For an angle θ with complementary angle x, the absolute value of a trigonometric function evaluated at θ is the same as the absolute value when evaluated at x.

The correct sign for sine and cosine is determined by the x and y coordinates on the unit circle.

- Sine will be positive in quadrants I and II and negative in quadrants III and IV.
- Cosine will be positive in quadrants I and IV, and negative in II and III.
- Tangent will be positive in I and III, and negative in II and IV.

The signs of the reciprocal functions will be the same as the sign of the function of which they are the reciprocal. For example:

Find $\sin\frac{3\pi}{4}$.

The reference angle must be found first. This angle is in the II quadrant, and the angle between it and the x-axis is $\frac{\pi}{4}$. Now, $\sin\frac{\pi}{4} = \frac{\sqrt{2}}{2}$. Since this is in the II quadrant, sine takes on positive values (the y coordinate is positive in the II quadrant). Therefore, $\sin\frac{3\pi}{4} = \frac{\sqrt{2}}{2}$.

In addition to the six trigonometric functions defined above, there are inverses for these functions. However, since the trigonometric functions are not one-to-one, one can only construct inverses for them on a restricted domain.

Usually, the domain chosen will be $[0, \pi)$ for cosine and $(-\frac{\pi}{2}, \frac{\pi}{2}]$ for sine. The inverse for tangent can use either of these domains. The inverse functions for the trigonometric functions are also called **arc functions.** In addition to being written with a -1 as the exponent to denote that the function is an inverse, they will sometimes be written with an "a" or "arc" in front of the function name, so $\cos^{-1}\theta = a\cos\theta = \arccos\theta$.

When solving equations that involve trigonometric functions, there are often multiple solutions. For example, $2\sin\theta = \sqrt{2}$ can be simplified to $\sin\theta = \frac{\sqrt{2}}{2}$. This has solutions $\theta = \frac{\pi}{4}, \frac{3\pi}{4}$, but in addition, because of the periodicity, any integer multiple of 2π can also be added to these solutions to find another solution.

The full set of solutions is $\theta = \frac{\pi}{4} + 2\pi k, \frac{3\pi}{4} + 2\pi k$ for all integer values of k. It is very important to remember to find all possible solutions when dealing with equations that involve trigonometric functions.

The name *trigonometric* comes from the fact that these functions play an important role in the geometry of triangles, particularly right triangles. Consider the right triangle shown in this figure:

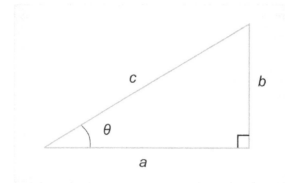

The following hold true:

- $c \sin \theta = b$.
- $c \cos \theta = a$.
- $\tan \theta = \frac{b}{a}$.
- $b \csc \theta = c$.
- $a \sec \theta = c$.
- $\cot \theta = \frac{a}{b}$.

It is important to remember that the angles of a triangle must add up to π radians (180 degrees).

Geometry and Measurement

Shapes and Solids

Perimeter is the distance measurement around something. It can be thought of as the length of the boundary, like a fence. In contrast, area is the space occupied by a defined enclosure, like a field enclosed by a fence.

The perimeter of a square is measured by adding together all of the sides. Since a square has four equal sides, its perimeter can be calculated by multiplying the length of one side by 4. Thus, the formula is $P = 4 \times s$, where s equals one side. The area of a square is calculated by squaring the length of one side, which is expressed as the formula $A = s^2$.

Like a square, a rectangle's perimeter is measured by adding together all of the sides. But as the sides are unequal, the formula is different. A rectangle has equal values for its lengths (long sides) and equal values for its widths (short sides), so the perimeter formula for a rectangle is $P = l + l + w + w = 2l + 2w$, where l equals length and w equals width. The area is found by multiplying the length by the width, so the formula is $A = l \times w$.

A triangle's perimeter is measured by adding together the three sides, so the formula is $P = a + b + c$, where $a, b,$ and c are the values of the three sides. The area is calculated by multiplying the length of the base times the height times ½, so the formula is $A = \frac{1}{2} \times b \times h = \frac{bh}{2}$. The base is the bottom of

the triangle, and the height is the distance from the base to the peak. If a problem asks one to calculate the area of a triangle, it will provide the base and height.

A circle's perimeter—also known as its **circumference**—is measured by multiplying the **diameter** (the straight line measured from one side, through the center, to the direct opposite side of the circle) by π, so the formula is $\pi \times d$. This is sometimes expressed by the formula $C = 2 \times \pi \times r$, where r is the **radius** of the circle. These formulas are equivalent, as the radius equals half of the diameter. The area of a circle is calculated with the formula $A = \pi \times r^2$. The test will indicate either to leave the answer with π attached or to calculate to the nearest decimal place, which means multiplying by 3.14 for π.

The perimeter of a parallelogram is measured by adding the lengths and widths together. Thus, the formula is the same as for a rectangle, $P = l + l + w + w = 2l + 2w$. However, the area formula differs from the rectangle. For a parallelogram, the area is calculated by multiplying the length by the height: $A = h \times l$

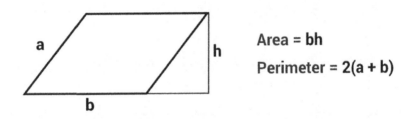

The perimeter of a trapezoid is calculated by adding the two unequal bases and two equal sides, so the formula is $P = a + b_1 + c + b_2$. Although unlikely to be a test question, the formula for the area of a trapezoid is $A = \frac{b_1 + b_2}{2} \times h$, where h equals height, and b_1 and b_2 equal the bases.

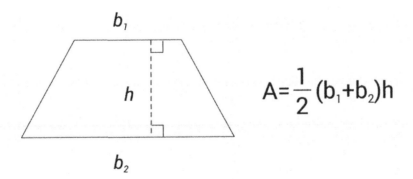

Congruence and Similarity

Triangles are similar if they have the same angle measurements, and their sides are proportional to one another. Triangles are **congruent** if the angles of the triangles are equal in measurement and the sides of the triangles are equal in measurement.

There are five ways to show that triangles are congruent:

1. SSS (Side-Side-Side Postulate) – when all three corresponding sides are equal in length, then the two triangles are congruent.

2. SAS (Side-Angle-Side Postulate) – if a pair of corresponding sides and the angle in between those two sides are equal, then the two triangles are congruent.

3. ASA (Angle-Side-Angle Postulate) – if a pair of corresponding angles are equal and the side lengths within those angles are equal, then the two triangles are equal.

4. AAS (Angle-Angle-Side Postulate) – when a pair of corresponding angles for two triangles and a non-included side are equal, then the two triangles are congruent.

5. HL (Hypotenuse-Leg Theorem) – if two right triangles have the same hypotenuse length, and one of the other sides in each triangle are of the same length, then the two triangles are congruent.

If two triangles are discovered to be similar or congruent, this information can assist in determining unknown parts of triangles, such as missing angles and sides.

The example below involves the question of congruent triangles. The first step is to examine whether the triangles are congruent. If the triangles are congruent, then the measure of a missing angle can be found.

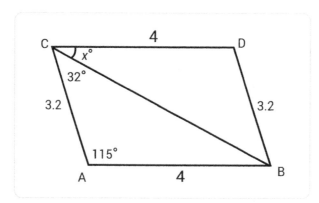

The above diagram provides values for angle measurements and side lengths in triangles CAB and CDB. Note that side CA is 3.2 and side DB is 3.2. Side CD is 4 and side AB is 4. Furthermore, line CB is congruent to itself by the reflexive property. Therefore, the two triangles are congruent by SSS (Side-Side-Side). Because the two triangles are congruent, all of the corresponding parts of the triangles are also congruent. Therefore, angle x is congruent to the inside of the angle for which a measurement is not provided in triangle CAB. Thus, 115º + 32º = 147º. A triangle's angles sum to 180º, therefore, 180º – 147º = 33º. Angle x = 33º, because the two triangles are reversed.

Surface Area and Volume

Surface area and volume are two- and three-dimensional measurements. Surface area measures the total surface space of an object, like the six sides of a cube. Questions about surface area will ask how much of something is needed to cover a three-dimensional object, like wrapping a present. **Volume** is the measurement of how much space an object occupies, like how much space is in the cube. Volume

questions will ask how much of something is needed to completely fill the object. The most common surface area and volume questions deal with spheres, cubes, and rectangular prisms.

The formula for a cube's surface area is $SA = 6 \times s^2$, where s is the length of a side. A cube has 6 equal sides, so the formula expresses the area of all the sides. Volume is simply measured by taking the cube of the length, so the formula is $V = s^3$.

The surface area formula for a rectangular prism or a general box is SA = $2(lw + lh + wh)$, where l is the length, h is the height, and w is the width. The volume formula is $V = l \times w \times h$, which is the cube's volume formula adjusted for the unequal lengths of a box's sides.

The formula for a sphere's surface area is $SA = 4\pi r^2$, where r is the sphere's radius. The surface area formula is the area for a circle multiplied by four. To measure volume, the formula is V = $\frac{4}{3}\pi r^3$.

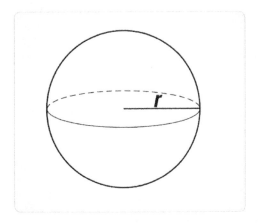

A **rectangular pyramid** is a figure with a rectangular base and four triangular sides that meet at a single vertex. If the rectangle has sides of lengths x and y, then the volume will be given by $V = \frac{1}{3}xyh$.

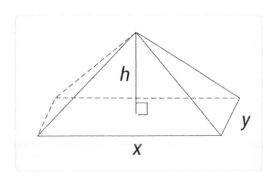

To find the surface area, the dimensions of each triangle must be known. However, these dimensions can differ depending on the problem in question. Therefore, there is no general formula for calculating total surface area.

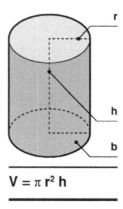

$$V = \pi\, r^2\, h$$

The formula to find the volume of a cylinder is $\pi r^2 h$. This formula contains the formula for the area of a circle (πr^2) because the base of a cylinder is a circle. To calculate the volume of a cylinder, the slices of circles needed to build the entire height of the cylinder are added together. For example, if the radius is 5 feet and the height of the cylinder is 10 feet, the cylinder's volume is calculated by using the following equation: $\pi 5^2 \times 10$. Substituting 3.14 for π, the volume is 785.4 ft³.

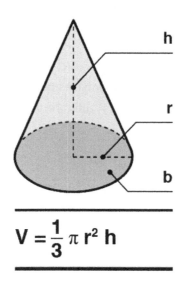

$$V = \frac{1}{3}\, \pi\, r^2\, h$$

The formula used to calculate the volume of a cone is $\frac{1}{3}\pi r^2 h$. Essentially, the area of the base of the cone is multiplied by the cone's height. In a real-life example where the radius of a cone is 2 meters and the height of a cone is 5 meters, the volume of the cone is calculated by utilizing the formula $\frac{1}{3}\pi 2^2 \times 5 = 21$. After substituting 3.14 for π, the volume is 785.4 ft³.

Solving for Missing Values in Triangles

Suppose that Lara is 5 feet tall and is standing 30 feet from the base of a light pole, and her shadow is 6 feet long. How high is the light on the pole? To figure this out, it helps to make a sketch of the situation:

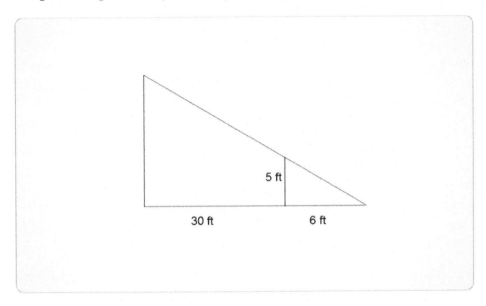

The light pole is the left side of the triangle. Lara is the 5-foot vertical line. Test takers should notice that there are two right triangles here, and that they have all the same angles as one another. Therefore, they form similar triangles. So, the ratio of proportionality between them must be found.

The bases of these triangles are known. The small triangle, formed by Lara and her shadow, has a base of 6 feet. The large triangle, formed by the light pole along with the line from the base of the pole out to the end of Lara's shadow is $30 + 6 = 36$ feet long. So, the ratio of the big triangle to the little triangle is $\frac{36}{6} = 6$. The height of the little triangle is 5 feet. Therefore, the height of the big triangle will be $6 \cdot 5 = 30$ feet, meaning that the light is 30 feet up the pole.

The Pythagorean Theorem

The **Pythagorean theorem** states that for right triangles, the sum of the squares of the two shorter sides is equal to the square of the longest side (also called the **hypotenuse**). The longest side will always be the side opposite to the 90° angle. If this side is called c, and the other two sides are a and b, then the Pythagorean theorem states that $c^2 = a^2 + b^2$. Since lengths are always positive, this also can be written as $c = \sqrt{a^2 + b^2}$. A diagram to show the parts of a triangle using the Pythagorean theorem is below.

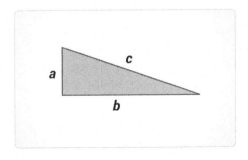

As an example of the theorem, suppose that Shirley has a rectangular field that is 5 feet wide and 12 feet long, and she wants to split it in half using a fence that goes from one corner to the opposite corner. How long will this fence need to be? To figure this out, note that this makes the field into two right triangles, whose hypotenuse will be the fence dividing it in half. Therefore, the fence length is given by $\sqrt{5^2 + 12^2} = \sqrt{169} = 13$ feet long.

One last useful relationship between the trigonometric functions introduced in the *Functions* section is the **Pythagorean identity**, which states that $\sin^2 \theta + \cos^2 \theta = 1$. Note that for trigonometric functions, the exponent is sometimes written next to the function name, so $\sin^2 \theta = (\sin \theta)^2$, and so on. The same is sometimes also done for logarithmic functions. The Pythagorean identity has two other forms which are often useful: $1 + \cot^2 \theta = \csc^2 \theta$ and $\tan^2 \theta + 1 = \sec^2 \theta$.

As mentioned, although the trigonometric functions are not one-to-one, it is possible to define inverses for them on limited domains. These are also called the *arc* functions. The inverse function for sine is called the **arcsine** and is written as either $\sin^{-1} x$ or as $\text{asin } x$, and similarly for the other five trigonometric functions. The range of the arcsine and arccosecant is usually taken to be $[-\frac{\pi}{2}, \frac{\pi}{2}]$. The range of the arccosine, arcsecant, arctangent, and arccotangent are generally taken to be $[0, \pi]$. Some specific values for these inverse functions can be read off published tables.

When solving an equation using these inverses, unless the domain is specifically restricted, all possible angles which satisfy the equation must be considered. For example, when solving $\cos(x - 1) = \frac{\sqrt{2}}{2}$, arccosine is applied to both sides, which yields $x - 1 = \text{acos } \frac{\sqrt{2}}{2}$. From the available tables, cosine takes the value $\frac{\sqrt{2}}{2}$ for any angle $2\pi k \pm \frac{\pi}{4}$, where k is an arbitrary integer. The equation becomes $x - 1 = 2\pi k \pm \frac{\pi}{4}$, or $x = 2\pi k \pm \frac{\pi}{4} + 1$.

Performing Algebraic Operations on Functions

As mentioned, it is possible to perform algebraic operations between functions, meaning they can be added, subtracted, multiplied, or divided. In fact, all the trigonometric functions are formed this way from sine and cosine. More generally, everything stated regarding arithmetic operations on functions can be done for trigonometric and logarithmic functions. However, sometimes it will be possible to use their definition to simplify the result.

For example, given $f(x) = \sin x + 1, g(x) = \cos x$, find $\frac{f(x)}{g(x)}$. This will, of course, be $\frac{\sin x + 1}{\cos x}$; however, this can be further simplified using the identities of trigonometric functions. The expression can be rewritten as $\frac{\sin x}{\cos x} + \frac{1}{\cos x} = \tan x + \sec x$.

Identifying and Using Composite Functions

Everything previously explained about composing functions can be applied to exponential, logarithmic, and trigonometric functions as well. For example, given $f(x) = 5^x, g(x) = \cos x$, one may form the composition $(g \circ f)(x) = \cos(5^x)$. The ability to recognize such compositions will be particularly important when discussing calculus, where more examples will be considered.

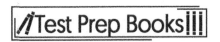

Conics

The graph of an equation of the form $y = ax^2 + bx + c$ or $x = ay^2 + by + c$ is called a **parabola.**

The graph of an equation of the form $\frac{x^2}{a^2} - \frac{y^2}{b^2} = 1$ or $-\frac{x^2}{a^2} + \frac{y^2}{b^2} = 1$ is called a **hyperbola**.

The graph of an equation of the form $\frac{(x-x_0)^2}{a^2} + \frac{(y-y_0)^2}{b^2} = 1$ is called an **ellipse**. If $a = b$ then this is a circle with **radius** $r = \frac{1}{a}$.

Probability and Statistics

Center and Spread of Distributions

Descriptive statistics are utilized to gain an understanding of properties of a data set. This entails examining the center, spread, and shape of the sample data.

Center
The **center** of the sample set can be represented by its mean, median or mode. The **mean** is the average of the data set. It is calculated by adding the data values together and dividing this sum by the sample size (the number of data points). The **median** is the value of the data point in the middle when the sample is arranged in numerical order. If the sample has an even number of data points, the mean of the two middle values is the median. The **mode** is the value which appears most often in a data set. It is possible to have multiple modes (if different values repeat equally as often) or no mode (if no value repeats).

Spread
Methods for determining the **spread** of the sample include calculating the range and standard deviation for the data. The *range* is calculated by subtracting the lowest value from the highest value in the set. The **standard deviation** of the sample can be calculated using the formula:

$$\sigma = \sqrt{\frac{\sum(x - \bar{x})^2}{n - 1}}$$

$\bar{x}$ = sample mean
n = sample size

Shape
The **shape** of the sample when displayed as a histogram or frequency distribution plot helps to determine if the sample is normally distributed (bell-shaped curve), symmetrical, or displays skewness (lack of symmetry), or kurtosis. **Kurtosis** is a measure of whether the data are heavy-tailed (high number of outliers) or light-tailed (low number of outliers).

Data Collection Methods

Statistical inference, based in probability theory, makes calculated assumptions about an entire population based on data from a sample set from that population.

Population Parameters

A population is the entire set of people or things of interest. For example, if researchers wanted to determine the number of hours of sleep per night for college females in the U.S, the population would consist of *every* college female in the country. A **sample** is a subset of the population that may be used for the study. A sample might consist of 100 students per school from 20 different colleges in the country. From the results of the survey, a sample statistic can be calculated. A **sample statistic** is a numerical characteristic of the sample data including mean and variance. A sample statistic can be used to estimate a corresponding **population parameter**, which is a numerical characteristic of the entire population.

Confidence Intervals

A population parameter estimated using a sample statistic may be very accurate or relatively inaccurate based on errors in sampling. A **confidence interval** indicates a range of values likely to include the true population parameter. A given confidence interval such as 95% means that the true population parameter will occur within the interval for 95% of samples.

Measurement Error

The accuracy of a population parameter based on a sample statistic may also be affected by measurement error. **Measurement error** can be divided into random error and systematic error. An example of **random error** for the previous scenario would be a student reporting 8 hours of sleep when she actually sleeps 7 hours per night. **Systematic errors** are those attributed to the measurement system. If the sleep survey gave response options of 2,4,6,8, or 10 hours. This would lead to systematic measurement error because certain values could not be accurately reported.

Evaluating Reports and Determining the Appropriateness of Data Collection Methods

The presentation of statistics can be manipulated to produce a desired outcome. For example, in the statement "four out of five dentists recommend our toothpaste", critical readers should wonder: *who are the five dentists?* While the wording is similar, this statement is very different from "four out of every five dentists recommend our toothpaste." The context of the numerical values allows one to decipher the meaning, intent, and significance of the survey or study.

When analyzing a report, the researchers who conducted the study and their intent must be considered. Was it performed by a neutral party or by a person or group with a vested interest? The sampling method and the data collection method should also be evaluated. Was it a true random sample of the population or was one subgroup over- or underrepresented? Lastly, the measurement system used to obtain the data should be assessed. Was the system accurate and precise or was it a flawed system?

Understanding and Modeling Relationships in Bivariate Data

The simplest type of correlation between two variables is a **linear correlation**. If the independent variable is x and the dependent variable is y, then a linear correlation means $y = mx + b$. If m is positive, then y will increase as x increases. While if m is negative, then y decreases while x increases. The variable b represents the value of y when x is 0.

Calculating Probabilities, Including Related Sample Spaces

Probability, represented by variable *p*, always has a value from 0 to 1. The total probability for all the possible outcomes (sample space) should equal 1.

The probability of a single outcome x_i can be expressed $p(x_i) = \frac{1}{n}$, where *n* is the total number of possible outcomes. A good example of this is a fair six-sided die, in which the possible outcomes are 1, 2, 3, 4, 5, and 6, and the individual probability of each of these six outcomes is $\frac{1}{6}$.

The probability of an outcome occurring from a range *A* of possible outcomes is written as $P(A)$. To compute this, the probabilities for each outcome in *A* are added together. To use the example of a fair six-sided die, a problem may ask one to find the probability of getting a 2 or lower when it is rolled. The possible rolls are 1, 2, 3, 4, 5, and 6. So, to get a 2 or lower, one must roll a 1 or a 2. Each probability is $\frac{1}{6}$, and adding them together to get $p(1) + p(2) = \frac{1}{6} + \frac{1}{6} = \frac{1}{3}$.

Here are a few types of probability distributions that are standard and have standard names:

- The **binomial distribution**: This distribution describes the probability of getting *k* successes in *n* trials, where each trial can either succeed or fail. If the probability of a single trial being a success is denoted by *p*, then, the probability of getting *k* successes in *n* trials is:

$$\frac{n!}{k!\,(n-k)!} p^k (1-p)^{n-k}$$

- A **Poisson distribution**: This describes the probability of getting *k* events in a fixed interval of time. If the average number of events during this time interval is denoted by λ, then the probability of getting *k* events during this time interval is given by $\frac{\lambda^k e^{-\lambda}}{k!}$.

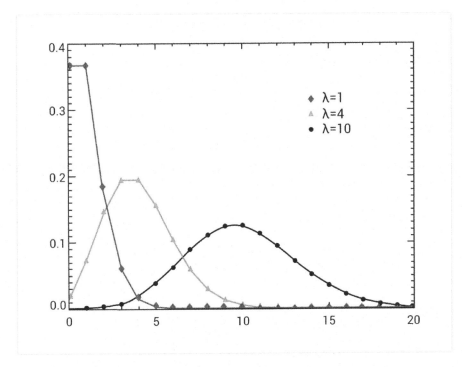

Conditional Probabilities

In some cases, it may be known that the outcome lies within the subset of possibilities *B*, and a problem will ask for probability that the outcome will end up being inside another subset of possibilities *A*. This kind of problem is called a **conditional probability**.

As an application of this, one can imagine a fair die is rolled. It is known that the roll's value lies between 1 and 4, inclusive, but the number of sides that the die has is not known (not all dice are six-sided). A problem may ask for the probability the roll was higher than 2. In this case, the total number of sides of the die is unimportant, and, since this is a fair die, the probability distribution is uniform across all possibilities. Therefore, it is possible to apply the formula $\frac{|A \cap B|}{|B|}$. $A \cap B$ means "*A* intersect *B*," and is the set of all outcomes that lie in both *A* and *B*. In this particular problem, *B* is {1, 2, 3, 4} and $A \cap B$ is {3, 4}. Therefore, $\frac{|A \cap B|}{|B|} = \frac{2}{4} = \frac{1}{2}$.

In many cases, changing the order of the conditional probabilities will greatly affect the outcome. For example, if a person has received a military medal, it is certain the person must have served in the military. However, given that a person served in the military, the probability of them receiving a military medal may not be very high.

In some special cases, however, the order in which the conditional probabilities are taken will not change the final probability. In this case, *A* and *B* are said to be **independent**. One situation in which one would expect that the outcomes should be independent is in rolling a pair of dice. If someone rolls two dice (a white die and a black die), then one would expect that the number that is obtained from the white die should not depend upon the number that is obtained from the black die, or vice versa. The same principle applies to a situation in which one rolls a single die repeatedly. A similar situation applies to flipping a coin repeatedly: whether the next flip is heads or tails will not depend upon what results have been obtained in previous flips.

Mathematical Processes

Logical Reasoning in Mathematics

Reasoning in mathematics involves figuring out how to solve a problem, using a tool or software correctly, or achieving any other type of goal in the classroom. Students learn to determine what is being asked for and decide what they think the best approach will be. Specifically, logic is introduced when determining whether statements and conjectures are true or false. An example of a true statement is "the sum of two even numbers results in an even number." An example of a false statement is "the sum of two even numbers results in an odd number." Logical reasoning can be used to show the first statement is true by a formal proof, and it can also be used to show the second example is false by an example disproving it. Such an example would be $4 + 6 = 10$, and it is known as a counterexample.

Ultimately, formal reasoning is used to prove theorems, and a famous proof that uses such a formalized mechanism is the Pythagorean Theorem. The proof involves a step-by-step logical process of using properties of right triangles to prove that $a^2 + b^2 = c^2$. In the classroom, such formal reasoning is taught in Geometry, Trigonometry, etc., but informal logic is used every day.

Informal reasoning is an important part of the classroom as well. Hands-on activities are great ways to introduce informal reasoning. For example, before geometric shapes are introduced through definitions and theorems, physical representations can be passed around from student to student. In this situation, the students can form their own thoughts and ideas about each shape, which will help them later as they have to conduct the formal reasoning at test time.

Deriving Valid Conclusions from a Set of Premises

The legitimacy of a conclusion is always based on the correctness of the argument. The argument is only deemed to be valid if every single premise is accurately used in a correct order to build the argument. If a premise is wrong, then the entire argument is invalid. This thought process applies to formal proving techniques, such as in geometry, and in other situations such as solving equations in algebra. Each step in the solution procedure involves justification as to why it can be done, and if something is done incorrectly, then the conclusion is most likely wrong.

Teachers should pay attention to the way students think and build their reasoning as they work through problems in the classroom. The process in which a student builds an argument or solves a problem can vary student to student. If the teacher sees a common mistake being made, time should be spent clarifying the error to the entire class so that it does not continue to happen. Also, teachers need to understand that in some situations there are many ways to obtain a solution, and they should make their students aware of that fact as well.

Inductive Reasoning and Deductive Methods to Evaluate Validity of Conjectures

A **deductive** argument is one in which the goal is to show that a conjecture must be true. Logical reasoning is used to find statements and conjectures that are always true to come up with a conclusion that has to be true. Geometry and Trigonometry problems involve deductive reasoning. In order to prove a statement or theorem, facts are used to build an argument that makes up a formal proof. If one of the premises used is incorrect, the entire proof is wrong. Deductive reasoning would be used in the following setting: Every time a train stops at the station, people get off the train. For every person getting off the train, two people board the train. If 13 people get off the train, deductive reasoning is used to determine that 26 people will subsequently board the train. This amount is based on the known premises, so $13 \times 2 = 26$ new passengers.

An **inductive** argument is one in which the goal is to show that the conjecture is probably true. If the premises, meaning the conjectures used to build the argument, are true, then the conclusion is most likely true. Inductive reasoning involves more of an estimation. The premises are observations that are not necessarily true. For example, if a person boards an airplane from Los Angeles to Phoenix, and no children are on the plane, he or she could conclude that children do not fly that route. However, this is based on the one-time observation and is not always going to be a true statement.

Reasonableness of a Solution

Once a math problem is solved, the answer should be checked if possible to see if it is correct. For example, in most equations, once the variable is solved for, it can be checked in the original equation to see if it makes a true statement. If it creates a false statement, then the solution does not work, and a mistake has been made somewhere. If it is not possible to check the answer completely, a sanity check can be completed. For example, the scale of the answer should be considered. Basically, does the size of the answer make sense? If the problem involved finding a dollar amount necessary to perform a task, and the answer found was less than $0.00001, then the answer does not really make sense. Similarly, if the task was to build a fence, and the solution stated that over a million feet of fencing was necessary, something was probably incorrect. In either case, the problem-solving steps should be revisited to see if an error was made. All solutions should be deemed reasonable. The teacher should stress this concept in the classroom. Not only is it important to set up and solve the problem correctly, but it is always helpful to make sure the answer makes sense.

Connections Among Concepts in Areas of Mathematics

Coordinate geometry is the link that connects algebra and geometry. Throughout its use, equivalent representations in both fields can be associated. Consider a rectangle in geometry. Typical lessons involve calculating the area and perimeter of the shape and discussing properties of angles and lines that make up the figure.

A rectangle can be inserted into the Cartesian coordinate plane as such:

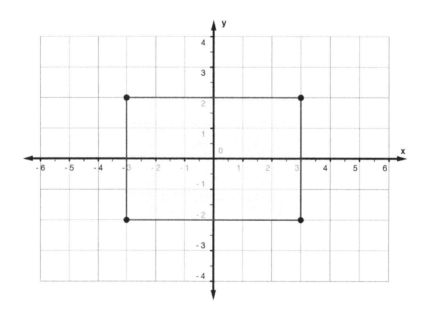

Two of the sides run parallel to the x-axis, and the other two sides run parallel to the y-axis. The length of each side can be determined by counting the number of tick marks on each axis that the shape includes. Each point on the rectangle corresponds to an ordered pair (x,y) in the plane, and the distance between any two points $(x_1, y_1), (x_2, y_2)$ can be calculated using the distance formula $d = \sqrt{(x_2 - x_1)^2 + (y_2 - y_1)^2}$. The equation of each line can be determined using algebraic rules. For example, the bottom line is equivalent to $y = -3, -3 \leq x \leq 3$. All two-dimensional shapes can be inserted into the xy-plane in a similar manner. Some traditional geometric proofs can be completed using algebra using the coordinate system relationship. For example, the Pythagorean Theorem can be proved using traditional side lengths *a, b,* and *c,* or a right triangle can be placed inside the xy-plane, and side lengths can be found using the distance formula. Each proof uses the same properties, but different methodologies.

Three dimensional geometric shapes can also be represented in a coordinate system. If a third axis, the z-axis, is introduced into an xy-plane, the three-dimensional world is defined. The x and y axes represent

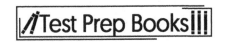
a horizontal plane, and the z-axis runs vertical through the origin. Each point in this space is an ordered triple (x,y,z).

The following shows a pyramid in the three-dimensional coordinate system with vertices labeled and one vertex located at the origin:

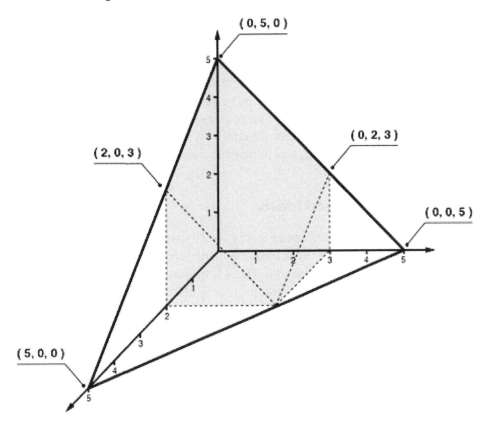

Solving Math Problems

Often, there are a variety of ways to solve a math problem. For example, the perimeter of a rectangle can be found by finding the sum of all four sides or by using the formula $p = 2 \times l + 2 \times w$, where l is the length and w is the width of the rectangle. Also, in many instances, theorems can be proved using different approaches. Premises can be used in an alternate order, or an entire different set of premises might be used. Sometimes one approach is better than the others, meaning it is probably a faster and more efficient way of doing something. Consider the derivative in Calculus. It is first introduced in its limit definition into the classroom. This is known as the dreaded "long way" to students, and they usually do not enjoy calculating derivatives this way. However, derivative rules, proven with use of the limit definition, such as the product and quotient rules, are used to shorten the process. It is important to understand both techniques, but probably use the quicker method.

Appropriate Mathematical Language

Being able to transition back and forth between mathematical expressions and verbal statements that represent the same concept is an important part of mathematical development. A student should be able to see an equation or an expression and read it as though it is a sentence in the English language. Also, he or she should be able to represent it verbally in more than one way. For example, consider the equation $2x + 3 = 5$. It can be read literally as "two times x plus 3 equals 5." However, it can also be read as "three more than double x is equivalent to 5" or "the sum of two times *x* and 3 is the same as 5." Each mathematical operation translates to multiple words in the English language, and each grade level has its own requirements for what should be understood and used in the classroom.

Expressions that represent the addition process are *sum, in addition to, plus, entire, total, increase, more than, combined,* and *in all.* Expressions that can be used to express subtraction verbally are *minus, difference, less than, decrease, reduce, fewer,* and *remain.* Multiplication can be stated as *product, multiply, times,* and *part of* if fractions are involved. Also, words like *twice, triple, four times,* etc. also represent multiplication. Finally, verbal cues that represent division are *quotient, divide, split, each, per, equal parts, average,* and *shared.* Note that sometimes multiplication and division can be used interchangeably. For example, multiplying times ¼ is the same as dividing by 4. Also, it must be recognized by the student if the statement represents an expression or an equation. An expression just needs to be evaluated and is not set equal to any quantity. A statement representing an equation would need to be solved for the missing quantity, and phrases corresponding to "is equal to" are used in this case.

Representations of Mathematical Ideals

In the classroom, mathematical concepts can be introduced in a number of ways, and each student has a best way in which he or she processes the information. The teacher should utilize all such methods so that the different learning styles are represented. There are visual learners that understand concepts better using pictorial representations such as graphs, charts, animations, and diagrams, quantitative learners who grasp concepts better with symbolic representations such as equations and formulas, and verbal learners who understand the material best through discussion and brainstorming.

Consider the introduction of volume of a sphere in the classroom. Visual learners would do best with seeing a drawing of a sphere, with its diameter and radius labeled. With both labeled, they can see that the diameter is twice the radius. Once graphics are shown, the formula can be introduced. Then, practical applications can be discussed. Real-life scenarios might help some learners grasp the concept more. A fun example might be determining the volume of an orange. It can be cut in half to measure either the radius or diameter so that the formula can be used. Throughout this lesson, a variety of representations are used and each one appeals to a different type of learner. Also, what can be discussed, depending on the grade level, is how the concept or formula was derived. In the case of volume of a sphere, this would be a Calculus problem, which involves integration. When students are able to see where a concept comes from, it gives them a more concrete understanding of the material. Sometimes it might even help them out when it comes to test time. If they forget a formula at test time, but remember how to derive it, it might save the day if they have to use the formula at some point.

Estimation

There is a difference between an exact answer and an estimation. Sometimes answering a question with an estimate is good enough; however, an exact answer is often required. Also, using an estimate as a ballpark to tell if an exact answer is reasonable is sometimes a good technique to use as well. For example, consider the situation if a student has to buy lunch at school, and they only have $5 to do so. A sandwich is $2.29, a piece of fruit is $0.75, and a drink is $1.25. An estimate might be enough to tell if he or she had enough money. A good estimate would be to round each cost to whole dollar amounts. Therefore, the estimate would be that lunch would cost $2.00 for the sandwich, $1.00 for the fruit, and $1.00 for the drink, which adds up to $4.00. The estimate would be that $5.00 is enough to pay for lunch. The exact amount is $4.29, so the estimate does the trick. However, sometimes estimation could

steer someone in the wrong direction. Consider a situation where the sandwich was $2.45, the fruit was $1.25, and the drink was $1.35. Rounding to the nearest dollar would still result in an estimate of $4.00; however, the exact amount in this scenario is $5.05. Therefore, the student would not have enough money. Perhaps rounding to the nearest $0.50 would be a better estimation process. Exact calculations are usually the best, but estimations are useful if they are done correctly.

Mathematical Manipulatives

Mathematical manipulatives and appropriate technological tools can be introduced into the classroom at any age. They consist of innovative ways to allow students to see concepts in a more tangible way and introduce more ways to communicate verbally using the math concepts being discussed. They can be used alongside paper and pencil problems to enhance a student's understanding even more. Common manipulatives include base-ten blocks, tangrams, rulers, protractors, compasses, measuring cups, playing cards, scales, thermometers, and abacuses. Each type of manipulative relates to several math concepts. For example, compasses and protractors can be used throughout many geometry lessons. Blocks can be used in basic addition and in a lesson involving areas of squares and rectangles. In addition to providing concrete examples, manipulatives also promote engagement and interest amongst the students, which results in a positive learning environment.

Technology, in the form of different types of calculators and mathematical software, can also be used to enhance the classroom experience. Graphing calculators can be used to enhance the graphing process and assist in statistics. Scientific calculators are helpful with logarithmic and exponential expressions. Finally, financial calculators can assist with any lesson involving interest problems. Teachers do have to make sure calculators are used as a tool to enhance learning, and not as a substitute for learning the concepts. Students should not rely heavily on them for simple calculations. Software in the classroom has many uses as well. It can help to introduce concepts by showing visualizations, and it can help to reinforce concepts through the use of drills, games, and online homework, quizzes, and tests.

History and Evolution of Mathematical Concepts

Studying the history and evolution in the mathematics classroom is a great way for the students to create a better relationship with the concepts being studied. There are many famous mathematicians that can be studied, and a great way to introduce this into the classroom is to have each student research a topic or person related to the history of math and present on it. In this exercise, students can learn about the history of math from their classmates, which breaks up the monotony of a traditional history lecture.

Students should realize that mathematical documentation dates back to 2000 BC, and many math concepts date back to an even older time period than the historic documents. From those ancient times to modern day times, there have been many different periods of mathematical discovery, and each individual period had concepts that were refined. This refinement continues today, so it is important to note that the evolution of mathematics has not stopped and that it continues through present day.

For example, number systems and concepts relating to counting and arithmetic date back to prehistoric times. It is thought that prehistoric math dates back to approximately 20,000 B.C., however, number systems have been updated along the way. For example, Babylonian mathematics, formed in ancient Mesopotamia, involve the derivation of algebraic concepts and fractions. They also evolved number systems by introducing the concept of place value around about 2,000 B.C. Their place value was based on 60, versus our current system based on 10, and they were the first to work with numbers less than one. What they did not do, was introduce a decimal point. Decimals were originally introduced in ancient China but were not widely used until about 500 years ago. The modern decimal point did not come into play until the 17th century. Place value and decimals is just one example of many that has evolved through time.

Cultural Contributions to Mathematics

Many different cultures have made contributions to the field of mathematics. A history of mathematics lecture is the perfect time to highlight this fact; however, as each concept is introduced, its origin can also be discussed at that time. For example, number systems were introduced by the Romans, the bulk of arithmetic was founded by the Egyptians, and the first trigonometric concept was introduced by the Indians. More concepts within geometry and trigonometry were discovered by the Greeks, and many algebraic ideas were discovered by the Tehranians. Many developments were made during the Scientific Revolution, which spanned the 17th and 18th centuries. During this time, the German mathematician Gottfried Leibniz developed Calculus and Leohnard Euler, also a German, defined the square root of -1 to be the imaginary number i and first used the Greek letter π to represent the ratio of a circle's circumference to its diameter. More modern-day mathematics started in the 19th century, and this time frame included more work on complex variables by the German mathematician Carl Gauss, development on non-Euclidean geometry by many Russian, Hungarian, and German mathematicians, and a number of additions to the field by the German Albert Einstein.

In present day, mathematicians in many cultures are constantly at work evolving the subject, and research is done daily at many universities spanning the globe. As crazy as it seems, many historical conjectures continue to not be proven, and attempts are made constantly with goals of determining ways to prove them. Mathematics has been very impactful across society and different cultures. Problem-solving abilities span the globe, and such linkage allows people to relate globally. In all cultures, mathematics plays a large role in intellectual development, and many mental abilities of children are formed through this field.

Financial Literary Concepts

Financial literacy is a classroom topic that is very useful for students as they interact in the real world. They will work with various models, tools, and techniques within this area. Students learn to conduct their financial matters while mitigating risks, protecting their assets, and conducting a continual management of their own finances in the form of savings and debt. It is important for students to learn these skills early because they will use them throughout their lives. These topics provide an interesting way to relate mathematical concepts to real-life applications.

Students must learn about the purpose of financial institutions, specifically how most people deal with them on a regular basis. Transactions such as making investments, taking out loans, and depositing money are concepts that should be introduced to the students. Role-play scenarios within the classroom are great ways for the students to become more familiar with these concepts. Students should be familiarized with what a savings account means and know that there are multiple ways to save money in addition to savings accounts. Each method has its own advantages and disadvantages. Regular savings accounts are easy to use but have low interest rates. Money market accounts are not very risky, have higher interest rates, but have higher minimum balances. Certificates of deposit (CDs) allow interest to be accrued over the lifetime of the certificate, and even though they have high interest rates, if the money is taken out early, there is a penalty.

In addition to banking, students should be introduced to the different type of taxes at a young age and know that all taxes are required by law. Specifically, income tax is money paid to the federal government based on one's salary. A person's gross income is his or her income before any taxes are taken out, and net income is total income once all deductions are removed. Sales tax is money collected by a store or service provider in addition to the goods or service cost and is paid to the local government. Property tax is money paid to the local government by a property owner that is based on the value of one's property. Finally, payroll tax is paid to the federal government by an employer, and its amount is based on the total payroll of the company.

Finally, students should be introduced to various payment and credit options at this age. Checks, debit and credit cards, and electronic payments can be discussed and differentiated in the classroom. Not all payment methods are created equal, and each has its own advantages and disadvantages. For example, debit cards are directly linked to checking accounts while credit cards are used to borrow money from financial institutions and come at a cost in the form of paid back interest. Electronic payments are payments that can use different security mechanisms, allowing for a more secure payment. Different credit options include lines of credit which include auto loans, student loans, and mortgages.

Financial Resources

In addition to financial literacy relating to banking, students can be introduced to concepts that will allow them to maintain financial security throughout their lifetime. These crucial conversations provide a solid foundation in a young age that will form a basis to help them throughout all time. Students are introduced to expenses, which are payments made for either goods and services, and will be able to distinguish between fixed and variable expenses. Fixed expenses do not change based on the amount of goods sold or services rendered. Rent, salaries, and mortgage payments are all examples of fixed expenses. Contrasting fixed expenses, a variable expense changes based the amount of goods sold or services rendered. An hourly wage is an example of a variable expense because it varies based on the number of hours worked. Other examples of variable expenses are shipping costs and commissions. Shipping costs vary based on the weight of the item and commissions vary based on the quantity sold. Another important concept that students will learn at a young age is how to calculate profit in a given situation. They will learn that profit is the result when all expenses and costs are subtracted from total revenue. For example, if a student sells a book on Amazon, his or her total profit is the monetary amount received for the book minus shipping and packaging costs. Or if he or she starts a lemonade stand, it must be understood that total profit has to take into consideration the amount spent on materials.

In order to maintain financial security, keeping financial records is crucial, and such records can also be introduced at an early age in the classroom. A financial record is a document that keeps track of all financial transactions of either a person or a business. An example of a widely used financial record is a budget. Each student can learn how to track income and expenses while keeping a budget. Keeping a budget is an important concept for everyday life that allows one to help reach financial goals. A budget summarizes how much income is necessary to outweigh expenses, and such budgets can be computed on different time frames. Typically, budgets are calculated monthly or yearly. Teachers can administer a simple in-class example of a budget and discuss actions that can be taken if expenses exceed income. All sources of income are documented, making sure to take into consideration the difference between gross and net income. Also, all costs and expenses need to be documented, making clear that fixed expenses will not vary monthly, but variable expenses could vary month to month. Because of the variation in expenses, budgets can differ each month. The overall goal is to have net income outweigh all costs and expenses, however, this is not always the case. Students can learn ways to either boost income or reduce expenses that will allow for a more balanced budget.

Practice Questions

1. Which of the following is the result of simplifying the expression: $\frac{4a^{-1}b^3}{a^4b^{-2}} \times \frac{3a}{b}$?

    a. $12a^3b^5$

    b. $12\frac{b^4}{a^4}$

    c. $\frac{12}{a^4}$

    d. $7\frac{b^4}{a}$

2. What is the product of two irrational numbers?

    a. Irrational

    b. Rational

    c. Irrational or rational

    d. Complex and imaginary

3. The graph shows the position of a car over a 10-second time interval. Which of the following is the correct interpretation of the graph for the interval 1 to 3 seconds?

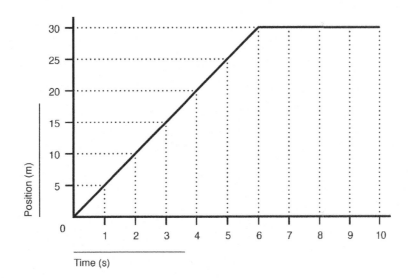

    a. The car remains in the same position.

    b. The car is traveling at a speed of 5m/s.

    c. The car is traveling up a hill.

    d. The car is traveling at 5 mph.

4. How is the number -4 classified?

    a. Real, rational, integer, whole, natural

    b. Real, rational, integer, natural

    c. Real, rational, integer

    d. Real, irrational

5. $4\frac{1}{3} + 3\frac{3}{4} =$

    a. $6\frac{5}{12}$

    b. $8\frac{1}{12}$

    c. $8\frac{2}{3}$

    d. $7\frac{7}{12}$

6. Five of six numbers have a sum of 25. The average of all six numbers is 6. What is the sixth **number?**
    a. 8
    b. 10
    c. 11
    d. 12

7. 4.67 miles is equivalent to how many kilometers to three significant digits?
    a. 7.514 km
    b. 7.51 km
    c. 2.90 km
    d. 2.902 km

8. If $\frac{5}{2} \div \frac{1}{3} = n$, then n is between:
    a. 5 and 7
    b. 7 and 9
    c. 9 and 11
    d. 3 and 5

9. A closet is filled with red, blue, and green shirts. If $\frac{1}{3}$ of the shirts are green and $\frac{2}{5}$ are red, what fraction of the shirts are blue?

    a. $\frac{4}{15}$

    b. $\frac{1}{5}$

    c. $\frac{7}{15}$

    d. $\frac{1}{2}$

10. Shawna buys $2\frac{1}{2}$ gallons of paint. If she uses $\frac{1}{3}$ of it on the first day, how much does she have left?

    a. $1\frac{5}{6}$ gallons

    b. $1\frac{1}{2}$ gallons

    c. $1\frac{2}{3}$ gallons

    d. 2 gallons

11. How will $\frac{4}{5}$ be written as a percent?

    a. 40%

    b. 125%

    c. 90%

    d. 80%

12. What are all the factors of 12?

    a. 12, 24, 36

    b. 1, 2, 4, 6, 12

    c. 12, 24, 36, 48

    d. 1, 2, 3, 4, 6, 12

13. At the beginning of the day, Xavier has 20 apples. At lunch, he meets his sister Emma and gives her half of his apples. After lunch, he stops by his neighbor Jim's house and gives him 6 of his apples. He then uses ¾ of his remaining apples to make an apple pie for dessert at dinner. At the end of the day, how many apples does Xavier have left?

    a. 4

    b. 6

    c. 2

    d. 1

14. How will the number 847.89632 be written if rounded to the nearest hundredth?

    a. 847.90

    b. 900

    c. 847.89

    d. 847.896

15. What is the value of the sum of $\frac{1}{3}$ and $\frac{2}{5}$?

    a. $\frac{3}{8}$

    b. $\frac{11}{15}$

    c. $\frac{11}{30}$

    d. $\frac{4}{5}$

16. Add and express in reduced form $5/12 + 4/9$.

    a. 9/17

    b. 1/3

    c. 31/36

    d. 3/5

17. Divide and reduce $4/13 \div 27/169$.

    a. 52/27

    b. 51/27

    c. 52/29

    d. 51/29

18. Express as a reduced mixed number 54/15.
    a. 3 3/5
    b. 3 1/15
    c. 3 3/54
    d. 3 1/54

19. In the problem $5 \times 6 + 4 \div 2 - 1$, which operation should be completed first?
    a. Multiplication
    b. Addition
    c. Division
    d. Subtraction

20. Express as an improper fraction 8 3/7.
    a. 11/7
    b. 21/8
    c. 5/3
    d. 59/7

21. Express as an improper fraction 11 5/8.
    a. 55/8
    b. 93/8
    c. 16/11
    d. 19/5

22. Round to the nearest tenth: 8.067
    a. 8.07
    b. 8.1
    c. 8.00
    d. 8.11

23. When rounding 245.2678 to the nearest thousandth, which place value would be used to decide whether to round up or round down?
    a. Ten-thousandth
    b. Thousandth
    c. Hundredth
    d. Thousand

24. What is the simplified form of the expression $1.2 \times 10^{12} \div 3.0 \times 10^{8}$?
    a. $0.4 * 10^{4}$
    b. $4.0 * 10^{4}$
    c. $4.0 * 10^{3}$
    d. $3.6 * 10^{20}$

25. You measure the width of your door to be 36 inches. The true width of the door is 35.75 inches. What is the relative error in your measurement?
    a. 0.7%
    b. 0.007%
    c. 0.99%
    d. 0.1%

26. The phone bill is calculated each month using the equation $c = 50g + 75$. The cost of the phone bill per month is represented by c, and g represents the gigabytes of data used that month. What is the value and interpretation of the slope of this equation?
    a. 75 dollars per day
    b. 75 gigabytes per day
    c. 50 dollars per day
    d. 50 dollars per gigabyte

27. Mom's car drove 72 miles in 90 minutes. How fast did she drive in feet per second?
    a. 0.8 feet per second
    b. 48.9 feet per second
    c. 0.009 feet per second
    d. 70.4 feet per second

28. $3\frac{2}{3} - 1\frac{4}{5} =$
    a. $1\frac{13}{15}$
    b. $\frac{14}{15}$
    c. $2\frac{2}{3}$
    d. $\frac{4}{5}$

29. Twenty is 40% of what number?
    a. 50
    b. 8
    c. 200
    d. 5000

30. Which equation is not a function?
    a. $y = |x|$
    b. $y = \sqrt{x}$
    c. $x = 3$
    d. $y = 4$

31. What is the domain for the function $y = \sqrt{x}$?
    a. All real numbers
    b. $x \geq 0$
    c. $x > 0$
    d. $y \geq 0$

32. Jessica buys 10 cans of paint. Red paint costs $1 per can and blue paint costs $2 per can. In total, she spends $16. How many red cans did she buy?
    a. 2
    b. 3
    c. 4
    d. 5

33. Which of the following is NOT a way to write 40 percent of N?

   a. $(0.4)N$

   b. $\frac{2}{5}N$

   c. $40N$

   d. $\frac{4N}{10}$

34. Four people split a bill. The first person pays for $\frac{1}{5}$, the second person pays for $\frac{1}{4}$, and the third person pays for $\frac{1}{3}$. What fraction of the bill does the fourth person pay?

   a. $\frac{13}{60}$

   b. $\frac{47}{60}$

   c. $\frac{1}{4}$

   d. $\frac{4}{15}$

35. 6 is 30% of what number?

   a. 18

   b. 20

   c. 24

   d. 26

36. $52.3 \times 10^{-3} =$

   a. 0.00523

   b. 0.0523

   c. 0.523

   d. 523

37. Which of the following numbers has the greatest value?

   a. 1.4378

   b. 1.07548

   c. 1.43592

   d. 0.89409

38. The value of 6 x 12 is the same as:

   a. 2 x 4 x 4 x 2

   b. 7 x 4 x 3

   c. 6 x 6 x 3

   d. 3 x 3 x 4 x 2

39. This chart indicates how many sales of CDs, vinyl records, and MP3 downloads occurred over the last year. Approximately what percentage of the total sales was from CDs?

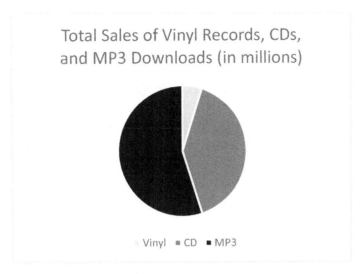

Total Sales of Vinyl Records, CDs, and MP3 Downloads (in millions)

Vinyl ▪ CD ▪ MP3

    a. 55%
    b. 25%
    c. 40%
    d. 5%

40. After a 20% sale discount, Frank purchased a new refrigerator for $850. How much did he save from the original price?
    a. $170
    b. $212.50
    c. $105.75
    d. $200

41. Which of the following is largest?
    a. 0.45
    b. 0.096
    c. 0.3
    d. 0.313

42. What is the value of b in this equation?
$$5b - 4 = 2b + 17$$

    a. 13
    b. 24
    c. 7
    d. 21

43. A school has 15 teachers and 20 teaching assistants. They have 200 students. What is the ratio of faculty to students?
    a. 3:20
    b. 4:17
    c. 3:2
    d. 7:40

44. Express the solution to the following problem in decimal form:
$$\frac{3}{5} \times \frac{7}{10} \div \frac{1}{2}$$

    a. 0.042
    b. 84%
    c. 0.84
    d. 0.42

45. A student gets an 85% on a test with 20 questions. How many answers did the student solve correctly?
    a. 15
    b. 16
    c. 17
    d. 18

46. If Sarah reads at an average rate of 21 pages in four nights, how long will it take her to read 140 pages?
    a. 6 nights
    b. 26 nights
    c. 8 nights
    d. 27 nights

47. Alan currently weighs 200 pounds, but he wants to lose weight to get down to 175 pounds. What is this difference in kilograms? (1 pound is approximately equal to 0.45 kilograms.)
    a. 9 kg
    b. 11.25 kg
    c. 78.75 kg
    d. 90 kg

48. Johnny earns $2334.50 from his job each month. He pays $1437 for monthly expenses. Johnny is planning a vacation in 3 months' time that he estimates will cost $1750 total. How much will Johnny have left over from three months' of saving once he pays for his vacation?
    a. $948.50
    b. $584.50
    c. $852.50
    d. $942.50

49. What is $\frac{420}{98}$ rounded to the nearest integer?
    a. 3
    b. 4
    c. 5
    d. 6

Answer Explanations

1. B: To simplify the given equation, the first step is to make all exponents positive by moving them to the opposite place in the fraction. This expression becomes $\frac{4b^3b^2}{a^1a^4} \times \frac{3a}{b}$. Then the rules for exponents can be used to simplify. Multiplying the same bases means the exponents can be added. Dividing the same bases means the exponents are subtracted. The resulting expression becomes $12\, b^4/a^4$.

2. C: The product of two irrational numbers can be rational or irrational. Sometimes, the irrational parts of the two numbers cancel each other out, leaving a rational number. For example, $\sqrt{2} \times \sqrt{2} = 2$ because the roots cancel each other out. Technically, the product of two irrational numbers can be complex because complex numbers can have either the real or imaginary part (in this case, the imaginary part) equal zero and still be considered a complex number. However, Choice D is incorrect because the product of two irrational numbers is not an imaginary number so saying the product is complex *and* imaginary is incorrect.

3. B: The car is traveling at a speed of five meters per second. On the interval from one to three seconds, the position changes by ten meters. By making this change in position over time into a rate, the speed becomes ten meters in two seconds or five meters in one second.

4. C: The number negative four is classified as a real number because it exists and is not imaginary. It is rational because it does not have a decimal that never ends. It is an integer because it does not have a fractional component. The next classification would be whole numbers, for which negative four does not qualify because it is negative. Choice D is wrong because -4 is not considered an irrational number because it does not have a never-ending decimal component.

5. B: $4\frac{1}{3} + 3\frac{3}{4} = 4 + 3 + \frac{1}{3} + \frac{3}{4} = 7 + \frac{1}{3} + \frac{3}{4}$. Adding the fractions gives $\frac{1}{3} + \frac{3}{4} = \frac{4}{12} + \frac{9}{12} = \frac{13}{12} = 1 + \frac{1}{12}$.
Thus, $7 + \frac{1}{3} + \frac{3}{4} = 7 + 1 + \frac{1}{12} = 8\frac{1}{12}$.

6. C: The average is calculated by adding all six numbers, then dividing by 6. The first five numbers have a sum of 25. If the total divided by 6 is equal to 6, then the total itself must be 36. The sixth number must be 36 − 25 = 11.

7. B: The answer choices for this question are tricky. Converting to kilometers from miles will yield the choice 7.514 kilometers when using the conversion 1 mi = 1.609 km. However, because the value in miles is written to three significant figures, the answer choice should also yield a value in three significant figures, making 7.51 kilometers the correct answer. Choices C and D could seem correct if someone flipped the conversion upside-down—that is, if they divided by 1.609 instead of multiplied by it.

$$4.67\ mi \times \frac{(1.609\ km)}{(1\ mi)} = 7.51\ km$$

8. B: $\frac{5}{2} \div \frac{1}{3} = \frac{5}{2} \times \frac{3}{1} = \frac{15}{2} = 7.5$.

9. A: The total fraction taken up by green and red shirts will be $\frac{1}{3} + \frac{2}{5} = \frac{5}{15} + \frac{6}{15} = \frac{11}{15}$. The remaining fraction is $1 - \frac{11}{15} = \frac{15}{15} - \frac{11}{15} = \frac{4}{15}$.

10. C: If she has used 1/3 of the paint, she has 2/3 remaining. $2\frac{1}{2}$ gallons are the same as $\frac{5}{2}$ gallons. The calculation is $\frac{2}{3} \times \frac{5}{2} = \frac{5}{3} = 1\frac{2}{3}$ gallons.

11. D: 80%. To convert a fraction to a percent, the fraction is first converted to a decimal. To do so, the numerator is divided by the denominator: $4 \div 5 = 0.8$. To convert a decimal to a percent, the number is multiplied by 100: $0.8 \times 100 = 80\%$.

12. D: 1, 2, 3, 4, 6, 12. A given number divides evenly by each of its factors to produce an integer (no decimals). The number 5, 7, 8, 9, 10, 11 (and their opposites) do not divide evenly into 12. Therefore, these numbers are not factors.

13. D: This problem can be solved using basic arithmetic. Xavier starts with 20 apples, then gives his sister half, so 20 divided by 2.

$$\frac{20}{2} = 10$$

He then gives his neighbor 6, so 6 is subtracted from 10.

$$10 - 6 = 4$$

Lastly, he uses ¾ of his apples to make an apple pie, so to find remaining apples, the first step is to subtract ¾ from one and then multiply the difference by 4.

$$\left(1 - \frac{3}{4}\right) \times 4 = ?$$

$$\left(\frac{4}{4} - \frac{3}{4}\right) \times 4 = ?$$

$$\left(\frac{1}{4}\right) \times 4 = 1$$

14. A: 847.90. The hundredths place value is located two digits to the right of the decimal point (the digit 9 in the original number). The digit to the right of the place value is examined to decide whether to round up or keep the digit. In this case, the digit 6 is 5 or greater so the hundredth place is rounded up. When rounding up, if the digit to be increased is a 9, the digit to its left is increased by one and the digit in the desired place value is made a zero. Therefore, the number is rounded to 847.90.

15. B: $\frac{11}{15}$. Fractions must have like denominators to be added. The least common multiple of the denominators 3 and 5 is found. The LCM is 15, so both fractions should be changed to equivalent fractions with a denominator of 15. To determine the numerator of the new fraction, the old numerator is multiplied by the same number by which the old denominator is multiplied to obtain the new denominator. For the fraction $\frac{2}{5}$, multiplying both the numerator and denominator by 3 produces $\frac{6}{15}$. When fractions have like denominators, they are added by adding the numerators and keeping the denominator the same: $\frac{5}{15} + \frac{6}{15} = \frac{11}{15}$.

16. C: 31/36

Set up the problem and find a common denominator for both fractions.

$$\frac{5}{12} + \frac{4}{9}$$

Multiply each fraction across by 1 to convert to a common denominator.

$$\frac{5}{12} \times \frac{3}{3} + \frac{4}{9} \times \frac{4}{4}$$

Once over the same denominator, add across the top. The total is over the common denominator.

$$\frac{15 + 16}{36} = \frac{31}{36}$$

17. A: 52/27

Set up the division problem.

$$\frac{4}{13} \div \frac{27}{169}$$

Flip the second fraction to get its reciprocal for multiplication.

$$\frac{4}{13} \times \frac{169}{27}$$

Simplify and reduce the fraction.

$$\frac{4}{1} \times \frac{13}{27}$$

Multiply across the top and across the bottom to solve.

$$\frac{4 \times 13}{1 \times 27} = \frac{52}{27}$$

18. A: 3 3/5

Divide.

$$15 \overline{)54} \quad \begin{array}{r} 3 \\ -45 \\ \hline 9 \end{array}$$

The result is 3 9/15.

Reduce the remainder for the final answer.

3 3/5

19. A: Using the order of operations, multiplication and division are computed first from left to right. Multiplication is on the left; therefore, multiplication should be performed first.

20. D: 59/7

The original number was 8 3/7. Multiply the denominator by the whole number portion. Add the numerator and put the total over the original denominator.

$$\frac{(8 \times 7) + 3}{7} = \frac{59}{7}$$

21. B: 93/8

The original number was 11 5/8. Multiply the denominator by the whole number portion. Add the numerator and put the total over the original denominator.

$$\frac{(8 \times 11) + 5}{8} = \frac{93}{8}$$

22. B: 8.1

To round 8.067 to the nearest tenths, use the digit in the hundredths.

6 in the hundredths is greater than 5, so round up in the tenths.

8.0̲67

0 becomes a 1.

8.1

23. A: The place value to the right of the thousandth place, which would be the ten-thousandth place, is what gets used. The value in the thousandth place is 7. The number in the place value to its right is greater than 4, so the 7 gets bumped up to 8. Everything to its right turns to a zero, to get 245.2680. The zero is dropped because it is part of the decimal.

24. C: Scientific notation division can be solved by grouping the first terms together and grouping the tens together. The first terms can be divided, and the tens terms can be simplified using the rules for exponents. The initial expression becomes 0.4×10^4. This is not in scientific notation because the first number is not between 1 and 10. Shifting the decimal and subtracting one from the exponent, the answer becomes 4.0×10^3./**125. A:** The relative error can be found by finding the absolute error and making it a percent of the true value. The absolute error is $36 - 35.75 = 0.25$. This error is then divided by 35.75—the true value—to find 0.7%.

26. D: The slope from this equation is 50, and it is interpreted as the cost per gigabyte used. Since the g-value represents number of gigabytes and the equation is set equal to the cost in dollars, the slope relates these two values. For every gigabyte used on the phone, the bill goes up 50 dollars.

27. D: This problem can be solved by using unit conversions. The initial units are miles per minute. The final units need to be feet per second. Converting miles to feet uses the equivalence statement 1 mile = 5,280 feet. Converting minutes to seconds uses the equivalence statement 1 minute = 60 seconds. Setting up the ratios to convert the units is shown in the following equation:

$$\frac{72\ miles}{90\ minutes} * \frac{1\ minute}{60\ seconds} * \frac{5280\ feet}{1\ mile} = 70.4 \text{ feet per second}$$

The initial units cancel out, and the new, desired units are left.

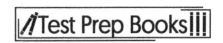

28. A: First, convert the mixed numbers to improper fractions: $\frac{11}{3} - \frac{9}{5}$. Then, use 15 as a common denominator:

$$\frac{11}{3} - \frac{9}{5} = : \frac{55}{15} - \frac{27}{15} = \frac{28}{15} = 1\frac{13}{15}$$

29. A: Setting up a proportion is the easiest way to represent this situation. The proportion becomes $\frac{20}{x} = \frac{40}{100}$, where cross-multiplication can be used to solve for x. Here, $40x = 2000$, so $x = 50$.

30. C: The equation $x = 3$ is not a function because it does not pass the vertical line test. This test is made from the definition of a function, where each x-value must be mapped to one and only one y-value. This equation is a vertical line, so the x-value of 3 is mapped with an infinite number of y-values.

31. B: The domain is all possible input values, or x-values. For this equation, the domain is every number greater than or equal to zero. There are no negative numbers in the domain because taking the square root of a negative number results in an imaginary number.

32. C: We are trying to find x, the number of red cans. The equation can be set up like this:

$$x + 2(10 - x) = 16$$

The left x is actually multiplied by $1, the price per red can. Since we know Jessica bought 10 total cans, $10 - x$ is the number blue cans that she bought. We multiply the number of blue cans by $2, the price per blue can.

That should all equal $16, the total amount of money that Jessica spent. Working that out gives us:

$$x + 20 - 2x = 16$$

$$20 - x = 16$$

$$x = 4$$

33. C: $40N$ would be 4000% of N. It's possible to check that each of the others is actually 40% of N.

34. A: To find the fraction of the bill that the first three people pay, the fractions need to be added, which means finding common denominator. The common denominator will be 60. $\frac{1}{5} + \frac{1}{4} + \frac{1}{3} = \frac{12}{60} + \frac{15}{60} + \frac{20}{60} = \frac{47}{60}$. The remainder of the bill is $1 - \frac{47}{60} = \frac{60}{60} - \frac{47}{60} = \frac{13}{60}$.

35. B: 30% is 3/10. The number itself must be 10/3 of 6, or $\frac{10}{3} \times 6 = 10 \times 2 = 20$.

36. B: Multiplying by 10^{-3} means moving the decimal point three places to the left, putting in zeroes as necessary.

37. A: Compare each numeral after the decimal point to figure out which overall number is greatest. In answers A (1.43785) and C (1.43592), both have the same tenths (4) and hundredths (3). However, the thousandths is greater in answer A (7), so A has the greatest value overall.

38. D: By grouping the four numbers in the answer into factors of the two numbers of the question (6 and 12), it can be determined that (3 x 2) x (4 x 3) = 6 x 12. Alternatively, each of the answer choices could be prime factored or multiplied out and compared to the original value. 6×12 has a value of 72 and a prime factorization of $2^3 \times 3^2$. The answer choices respectively have values of 64, 84, 108, 72, and 144 and prime factorizations of 2^6, $2^2 \times 3 \times 7$, $2^2 \times 3^3$, and $2^3 \times 3^2$, so answer *D* is the correct choice.

39. C: The sum total percentage of a pie chart must equal 100%. Since the CD sales take up less than half of the chart and more than a quarter (25%), it can be determined to be 40% overall. This can also be measured with a protractor. The angle of a circle is 360°. Since 25% of 360 would be 90° and 50% would be 180°, the angle percentage of CD sales falls in between; therefore, it would be answer *C*.

40. B: Since $850 is the price *after* a 20% discount, $850 represents 80% of the original price. To determine the original price, set up a proportion with the ratio of the sale price (850) to original price (unknown) equal to the ratio of sale percentage:

$$\frac{850}{x} = \frac{80}{100}$$

(where *x* represents the unknown original price)

To solve a proportion, cross multiply the numerators and denominators and set the products equal to each other: (850)(100) = (80)(x). Multiplying each side results in the equation 85,000=80x.

To solve for *x*, divide both sides by 80: $\frac{85,000}{80} = \frac{80x}{80}$, resulting in *x*=1062.5. Remember that *x* represents the original price. Subtracting the sale price from the original price ($1062.50-$850) indicates that Frank saved $212.50.

41. A: To figure out which is largest, look at the first non-zero digits. Answer *B*'s first nonzero digit is in the hundredths place. The other three all have nonzero digits in the tenths place, so it must be *A*, *C*, or *D*. Of these, *A* has the largest first nonzero digit.

42. C: To solve for the value of b, both sides of the equation need to be equalized.

Start by cancelling out the lower value of -4 by adding 4 to both sides:

$$5b - 4 = 2b + 17$$

$$5b - 4 + 4 = 2b + 17 + 4$$

$$5b = 2b + 21$$

The variable *b* is the same on each side, so subtract the lower 2b from each side:

$$5b = 2b + 21$$

$$5b - 2b = 2b + 21 - 2b$$

$$3b = 21$$

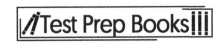

Then divide both sides by 3 to get the value of *b*:

$$3b = 21$$

$$\frac{3b}{3} = \frac{21}{3}$$

$$b = 7$$

43. D: The total faculty is 15 + 20 = 35. So the ratio is 35:200. Then, divide both of these numbers by 5, since 5 is a common factor to both, with a result of 7:40.

44. C: The first step in solving this problem is expressing the result in fraction form. Separate this problem first by solving the division operation of the last two fractions. When dividing one fraction by another, invert or flip the second fraction and then multiply the numerator and denominator.

$$\frac{7}{10} \times \frac{2}{1} = \frac{14}{10}$$

Next, multiply the first fraction with this value:

$$\frac{3}{5} \times \frac{14}{10} = \frac{42}{50}$$

Decimals are expressions of 1 or 100%, so multiply both the numerator and denominator by 2 to get the fraction as an expression of 100.

$$\frac{42}{50} \times \frac{2}{2} = \frac{84}{100}$$

In decimal form, this would be expressed as 0.84.

45. C: 85% of a number means that number should be multiplied by 0.85: $0.85 \times 20 = \frac{85}{100} \times \frac{20}{1}$, which can be simplified to $\frac{17}{20} \times \frac{20}{1} = 17$. The answer is *C*.

46. D: This problem can be solved by setting up a proportion involving the given information and the unknown value. The proportion is:

$$\frac{21 \ pages}{4 \ nights} = \frac{140 \ pages}{x \ nights}$$

Solving the proportion by cross-multiplying, the equation becomes $21x = 4 * 140$, where $x = 26.67$. Since it is not an exact number of nights, the answer is rounded up to 27 nights. Twenty-six nights would not give Sarah enough time.

47. B: Using the conversion rate, multiply the projected weight loss of 25 lb by $0.45 \frac{kg}{lb}$ to get the amount in kilograms (11.25 kg).

48. D: First, subtract $1437 from $2334.50 to find Johnny's monthly savings; this equals $897.50. Then, multiply this amount by 3 to find out how much he will have (in three months) before he pays for his vacation: this equals $2692.50. Finally, subtract the cost of the vacation ($1750) from this amount to find how much Johnny will have left: $942.50.

49. B: Dividing by 98 can be approximated by dividing by 100, which would mean shifting the decimal point of the numerator to the left by 2. The result is 4.2, which rounds to 4.

Social Studies

Social Science Instruction

An early education social studies curriculum should offer content that is comprehensive and thematic, introducing a variety of viewpoints on historical events and highlighting the relevance of connecting the past with the present. Teachers must know how to guide students in obtaining, evaluating, and processing the information associated with these topics. Although the school's textbook is a ready resource, teachers should suggest and encourage alternate sources of information, such as the library, field trips, maps, and other visual material, interviews, and discussions of current events. These opportunities allow students to analyze information and increase their societal understanding. Classroom activities can help students apply previously acquired learning through problem solving, such as performing their own mock election in order to gain a better grasp of the election process. Encouraging students to investigate social studies topics that interest them and involve real-world projects helps them to become objective observers and develop a sense of public duty. When students can interpret, organize, and present what they have learned through a variety of methods, it promotes a deeper understanding and application of wider social studies themes.

Social Studies Content and Performance Standards of the TEKS

In total, the social studies Texas Essential Knowledge and Skills (TEKS) are organized into eight strands: 1) history, 2) geography, 3) economics, 4) government, 5) citizenship, 6) culture, 7) science, technology, and society, and 8) social studies skills. The goal of these eight strands is to prepare students for college-level history, which demands that they analyze history from multiple perspectives. The first five strands introduce students to various fields or disciplines in the social sciences. The sixth and seventh strands introduce students to broader themes that guide each of the fields or disciplines. And the final strand introduces students to skills that allow them to access each of the previous seven strands. These strands are embedded in the vertical alignment of the social studies TEKS, though some grade levels may emphasize certain strands for the sake of vertical progression.

Vertical Alignment of the Social Science in the TEKS

The social sciences Texas Essential Knowledge and Skills (TEKS) are horizontally aligned across several academic disciplines, preparing teachers and students alike for embarking on interdisciplinary studies. In addition, the social sciences TEKS are vertically aligned, paving a curricular pathway from kindergarten-level historical inquiry to college readiness. The social sciences TEKS are meant to be consistent and cumulative across all grade levels so Texas students can gradually gain momentum in their learning trajectory. The social sciences TEKS's vertical alignment allows students to start with the personal (self, family, classroom) and gradually expand outward to a globalized perspective (people and places in the contemporary world). The vertical alignment for the social sciences TEKS is as follows:

- Sixth grade: People and places in the contemporary world
- Fifth grade: United States history
- Fourth grade: Texas in the Western Hemisphere
- Third grade: Communities past and present, including Texas and the nation
- Second grade: Local community, Texas, nation
- First grade: Classroom, school, and local community

- Kindergarten: Self, family, and classroom

The purpose of this broad, multi-context curriculum is to gradually expand students' historical horizons so they are better prepared as engaged family members, community members, and global citizens. One major purpose of this vertical alignment is to promote a variety of civic competencies (microcosmic and macrocosmic) over a seven-year period. The progression from the self to the globe is strategic in drawing connections between personal identity, historical agency, and civic engagement. Overall, the goal is to create active and informed citizens for the state of Texas and the world. Drawing energy from such broad-ranging disciplines as political science, geography, environmental science, economics, education, history, sociology, and psychology, the vertical alignment of social sciences TEKS attempts to prepare students for interdisciplinary college classrooms.

Uses Social Studies Terminology Correctly

Literacy should be a top concern in all K–12 classrooms. However, there is no denying that social studies classrooms are some of the most demanding for students when it comes to literacy and language acquisition. In social studies, students will not only have to comprehend basic verbs, nouns, and adjectives, but they will also have to understand complex social studies terms for particular contexts, places, eras, persons, movements, and groups. Social studies standards across different states typically demand that students obtain a relative amount of terminological specificity. In other words, literacy in a social studies classroom can be hyperspecific, which poses problems with students of all learning types and grade levels. In particular, social studies terminology can pose problems for Section 504 students, special education (SPED) students, and English language learners (ELLs). It is important that social studies teachers introduce students to best practices such as 1) using study cards, cognitive maps, and organizational charts for understanding social studies terms, 2) finding individualized structures and styles for note-taking, 3) employing memory games and mnemonic devices for recalling important information, and 4) using timelines and charts for understanding the importance of context, time, and sequence when it comes to social studies terms. Understanding and using social studies terminology correctly is almost always contingent on properly understanding the notion of time and context in history.

Stages for Implementing Effective Learning Experiences

Teachers must first assist students with understanding their own identities before they try to expose them to diverse identities and communities within the social sciences. Implementing social and emotional learning (SEL) activities can help students understand themselves as well as their peers. SEL activities, such as personal reflections or class diaries, can help students in the social sciences prepare for interacting within the broader world. SEL activities help students understand the idea of community while also helping them *build* community in the classroom. Student growth and development in the social sciences should begin with identity and gradually branch out to classroom community, family, and personal community. Once students understand themselves better and the ways in which their ideas and emotions operate, then they will be more ready to comprehend the similarities and differences they have with their teachers and peers. As the complex components of the in-class community are more readily understood, students should be ready to deconstruct their relationships to their individual families and communities.

Teachers should prompt students to understand the *why* of their beliefs and emotions as well as the source. This is crucial in a social sciences classroom because students are consistently analyzing identity, culture, society, and social relations. Without this basic foundation, it is difficult for students to respect

their own cultures. Moreover, it may be difficult for them to share about their own cultures and collaborate with people who may reside outside of their cultures. The routines and expectations of every social sciences classroom should therefore be mandated by some sort of community agreement or constitution. To design and implement effective learning experiences, the entire community must "buy into" a particular social contract. Teachers should create nonnegotiable aspects of class culture, but they should also call upon students as experts and engineers of their own context. Social science classes with poor management typically fail to implement "student voice and choice" when it comes to routines and expectations, especially for working cooperatively within the community.

Current Technology as a Tool for Teaching

Computer technology—especially with regard to the Internet, smartphones, tablets, and social media—is progressing at a rate that is often difficult for teachers to "keep up" with what is pertinent, effective, and relevant for their students. With the world becoming increasingly connected (and separated) by technology, it is important for every student in the social sciences to be exposed to contemporary techniques and practices for incorporating technology into the classroom. Students must know how to use the Internet, smartphones, tablets, and social media in their social sciences classroom to adequately prepare for the next era of college learning and professional research. Teachers must acquaint themselves with up-to-date, research-based practices for incorporating technology in the classroom. Specifically, in a social studies classroom, students must be prepared to access sources online and differentiate whether they are primary or secondary sources. More importantly, students must be able to assess whether the sources are legitimate enough to incorporate into research or presentations. Teachers should explicitly teach students how to research on technological devices while also teaching them how to assess the validity of sources and databases. In an increasingly digitized world, it is important to expose students to digital museums and databases. It is also important to use technology—specifically social media and smartphone apps—to "hook" students onto a particular topic or area of inquiry.

Applies Developmentally Appropriate Instructional Practices

Teachers should strive to move beyond textbooks in the classroom, introducing students to a variety of primary and secondary sources. Written secondary sources can include professional monographs, popular histories, historical fiction, magazines, newspapers, and scholarly journals and articles. Written primary sources can include journals, diaries, newspaper clippings, government documents, context-specific literature, letters, biographies and autobiographies, folklore, and cultural mythology. Students should also be exposed to visual sources such as political cartoons, artwork, ads, signs, graphs, charts, tables, photographs, and videos. Students can also be introduced to relevant musical works. As digital archives and histories are becoming more relevant in 21st century classroom, it's important that students are exposed to computer-based resources.

Promoting Use of Social Science Skills

In social studies, vocabulary terms typically focus on particular people, places, groups, or features that happened or existed in the past (or present). Social studies vocabulary terms can be particularly challenging because there is a certain specificity that goes along with complex identities, groups, and events. To promote student understanding of these complex vocabulary terms, it is important that teachers connect the terms to larger concepts (i.e., "words or phrases that refer to categories of information"). Concepts allow social studies students to organize large amounts of information using historical context and change over time. When analyzing concepts, students should pay close attention to the definition of the concept and examples of the concept. For example, one concept that can be bequeathed to students is the concept of "war in American history." Under the umbrella of this concept, students can chronologically or thematically organize such disparate vocabulary terms as *French and Indian War, American Revolution, War of 1812, Mexican-American War, Civil War, Spanish-American War, World War I,* and *World War II.* Students may even broaden this concept to include such terms as *Cold War* and *War on Drugs.*

To promote study skills in the classroom, teachers can introduce students to such strategies as using study cards. This is particularly helpful for visual learners who need to see a certain term or concept to make an impression in their minds. Additionally, teachers can introduce students to the "art of note-taking," which will help them succeed in both K–12 and higher-education classrooms. Students should be explicitly taught how to underline, highlight, color-code, and take notes in the margins. Test-taking skills should also be explicitly taught to students—students should know the E.R.A. approach to standardized tests that encourages them to "Examine the Question," "Recall What They Know," and "Apply What They Know." Lastly, students should be exposed to research tools such as libraries, databases, archives, citation styles, and public museums. To be prepared for the twenty-first century, students should also be exposed to digital versions of these tools. It is quite possible that students can even go on "digital tours" of museum collections, thanks to the Internet and computer technologies.

Instruction that Relates Skills and Ideas Across Different Social Science Disciplines

Over the course of the last twenty-five years, the K–12 and higher-education systems in the United States have been gradually adopting interdisciplinary practices that encourage teachers and students to integrate skills, concepts, and ideas across a variety of different disciplines. This has become especially true in the social sciences at the K–12 level, where teachers and students must continually combine theories and practices from such disparate fields as history, political science, social studies, geography, psychology, government, ethics, economics, environmental studies, and sociology. Additionally, twenty-first-century teachers and students will be expected to make connections between the social sciences, sciences, arts, and mathematics. While teachers should strive to enrich their knowledge of content in their particular field of inquiry, they should also strive to make connections between fields. This means they should employ instructional practices in the classroom that explicitly and implicitly expose students to the interconnected nature of all learning. One way this could be accomplished is through collaboration with colleagues who are experts in other fields. Another way is by introducing textbooks, articles, and materials from other fields into content-specific social science classrooms. Lastly, teachers can help students to relate skills, concepts, and ideas across different social science disciplines by incorporating project-based learning (PBL) activities into the classroom that require students to analyze/approach/solve real-world problems through collaboration with peers, professionals, and public agencies with unique, discipline-specific experiences. PBL activities ensure that students not only grasp interdisciplinary content, but also *apply* this content to real-life problems, projects, and scenarios.

Making Connections Between Knowledge in the Social Sciences and Other Areas

As mentioned earlier, teachers must extend interdisciplinary study to include fields and content areas that exist outside the traditional social sciences (i.e., history, political science, social studies, geography, psychology, government, ethics, economics, environmental studies, and sociology). The future of the social sciences depends heavily on communication with fields that traditionally fall under the STEM (Science, Technology, Engineering, and Math) or STEAM (Science, Technology, Engineering, Art, and Math) categories. Disassociating the social sciences from these other fields is not beneficial for young students. In an increasingly technological world, students must be prepared to incorporate skills, ideas,

concepts, and practices from STEM and STEAM courses into their social science classrooms. It is difficult to imagine future historians, political scientists, social studies teachers, geographers, psychologists, government officials, ethicists, economists, environmentalists, and sociologists functioning without science, technology, engineering, art, and mathematics. Future historians, for example, will likely have to be forensic computer scientists who sift through old files and data to better understand history and historical agents. Whenever possible, teachers should explicitly expose students to the ways in which these fields perpetually affect each other within the global economy and popular culture.

Uses Effective Instructional Strategies

Besides traditional lectures, textbook work, PowerPoints, and direct instruction, teachers can diversify pedagogical methods in their classrooms by incorporating inquiry-based practices, project-based learning, field work, role plays, sociodramas, skits, simulations, field trips, student-specific academic interventions, debates, and identity-based social-emotional learning activities into social science courses. The goal is to differentiate sources, instruction, and assessments so all students have access to social science content.

Social Science Issues and Trends

Social science students should not solely be focused on history and the past. Students should be exposed to disciplines such as political science, social studies, geography, psychology, government, ethics, economics, environmental studies, and sociology. These disciplines all emphasize present-day issues and trends in society; students should use these disciplines to determine the essence of their own historical context. Students must be able to not only understand social science concepts, but also apply the problem-solving and decision-making skills of the social sciences to the real world. Even history can help students better understand the present and have enough foresight to protect the future. The social sciences, in this sense, are as much about civic engagement as they are about content acquisition.

Maps and Other Graphics

Students should not only be able to analyze maps and other infographics, but they should also be able to create graphs, charts, tables, documents, maps, timelines, and other visual materials to represent geographic, political, historical, economic, and cultural features. Students should be made aware of the different options they have to present data. They should understand that maps visually display geographic features, and they can be used to illustrate key relationships in human geography and natural geography. Maps can indicate themes in history, politics, economics, culture, social relationships, demographic distributions, and climate change. Students can also choose to display data or information in a variety of graphs: Bar graphs compare two or more things with parallel bars; line graphs show change over time with strategic points placed carefully between vertical and horizontal axes; and pie graphs divide wholes into percentages or parts. Likewise, students can choose to use timelines or tables to present data/information. Timelines arrange events or ideas into chronological order, and tables arrange words or numbers into columns or rows. These are just some of the visual tools teachers and students can use to help visually convey their historical questions or ideas.

Methods for Assessing Social Science Concepts

Differentiated assessments are crucial for tailoring the educational environment for individual learning types. Teachers must be aware and sensitive to the neurodiversity in their classrooms. When designing social science assessments, teachers should keep in mind the unique learning types and cognitive skills

of English Language Learners (ELLs), Section 504 students, Gifted and Talented (GT) students, and Special Education (SPED) students. In addition, teachers in K-6 social science classrooms must be sensitive to culture. Whenever possible, social science teachers should make their materials and assessments personally and culturally relevant.

Students should be comfortable exploring and expressing their identities in social science classrooms. For students to excel at historical inquiry, it's important that they understand their own genders, sexual orientations, races, ethnicities, political affiliations, religious beliefs, and socioeconomic statuses to better understand how these categories drive the decisions of historical actors and even their peers. The TEKS performance standards act as a means for assessing the needs of each student; moreover, the TEKS performance standards encourage cultural diversity. Contrary to popular belief, these standards don't limit one's ability to implement varied assessments; rather, the TEKS were created as guideposts for implementing diverse assessments that account for the varied interests and skills present in every classroom. Whenever possible, use the TEKS for direction, and employ kinesthetic-, auditory-, oral-, written-, and visual-based assessments for every student. Also try to vary assessments by incorporating design-thinking, inquiry-based learning, project-based learning, and student voice and choice. Inevitably, a good teacher will respond to student needs and concerns and offer alternative assessments without diminishing the crucial nature of the TEKS.

Value of Social Studies Education

Teachers and students must also engage parents/caregivers, colleagues/peers, and the community to convey the overall importance of a social studies education. When challenged about the importance of a social studies education, teachers and students can illustrate the ways in which a social studies education can help people become better writers, researchers, and presenters. Moreover, a quality social studies education will also make teachers and students better problem solvers, decision makers, and civic engagers. A knowledge of social studies can help teachers and students understand many problems faced in present-day global society. Politicians, businessmen, and common citizens all could benefit from enriching their historical consciousness so that they can effectively diagnose and implement positive changes for their government, customers, families, or fellow citizens. Social studies can help rebuild communities and prevent international conflicts; it can help teachers and students become better citizens in an often-conflicted global society.

History

Texas History

Texas history can be divided into eight categories: 1) pre-colonial Texas, 2) first contact and colonial Texas, 3) the Mexican National Period, 4) revolution and the Republic of Texas, 5) U.S. annexation and the Mexican-American War, 6) antebellum slavery and the Civil War, 7) Reconstruction and post-Reconstruction, 8) 20th Century advancement, and 9) immigration and migration to the Sunbelt south.

Pre-Colonial Texas

Texas was home to Paleoindians during the prehistoric period. In fact, people have lived in Texas for over 12,000 years. Anthropologists and archaeologists working in Texas have discovered artifacts of the Clovis culture that developed in North America some 11,000–12,000 years ago. During the First Agricultural Revolution, many hunter-gatherers of nomadic Paleoindian groups began to settle permanently or semi-permanently in Texas. These earliest Native American groups included the

Karankawas, the Coahuiltecans, the Caddos, the Witchitas, the Atakapas, the Jumanos, the Tonkawas, and the Apaches. Additionally, many Native Americans resettled in Texas during the era of Indian Removal and Manifest Destiny. These included the Comanches and Kiowas.

First Contact and Colonial Texas

In the 1500s, Spanish conquistadors and French settlers began exploring the Gulf Coast region. In 1519, Spanish explorer Alonso Alvarez de Pineda became one of the first conquistadors to probe the Texas coast. There is no evidence that he reached the Texas mainland, but his expedition increased Spanish interest in Texas. Spanish explorer Panfilo de Narvaez's expedition became the first to explore the Texas mainland, albeit accidentally. During this expedition, Narvaez's ships wrecked, and explorer Alvar Nunez Cabeza de Vaca was taken in by Karankawa Indians. This first contact, which occurred in 1528, encouraged Cabeza de Vaca to continue his travels, even after he was captured and placed in captivity by Coahuiltecan Indians. Between 1528 and 1536, Cabeza de Vaca and a band of other shipwrecked survivors wandered across Texas and modern-day Mexico. Eventually they reached Mexico City in 1536 with the help of Spanish soldiers they encountered on their journey.

Cabeza de Vaca later published an account of his expedition, which caught the attention of Spanish viceroys and explorers. This led conquistador Francisco Vasquez de Coronado to embark on a journey with a force of over 1,300 men in 1540 in search of gold. While Coronado never found gold, he and his men did become some of the first Europeans to see the Grand Canyon and travel through modern-day West Texas. By the 1600s, after years of expeditions, the Spanish colonial government began establishing missions along the frontiers of modern-day Mexico, New Mexico, California, and Texas. Some settlements sprouted up along the Rio Grande in South Texas. French explorer Robert de La Salle led several expeditions in East Texas in the 1680s. Control over East Texas shifted hands from the Spanish and French on multiple occasions in the late 1600s and early 1700s until Spain took possession due to the missionary efforts of men like Father Francisco Hidalgo, a Franciscan priest who established missions in East Texas for the Spanish crown. Throughout the 1700s, Spain continued to establish missions, presidios, and ranches throughout Texas. Life in Spanish Texas during this era was marked by extreme isolation, loose government control, and border skirmishes. The Spanish crown had a hard time controlling the region based on its remoteness and a lack of manpower.

The Mexican National Period

Following Mexican independence from Spain in September 1821, Texas became part of the new Republic of Mexico. Young Tejano ranchers, now generations removed from their grandparents' settlement in the region, became the new lifeblood of Texas under Mexican national rule. During this era, Texas became a key frontier for both Mexico and the United States. The Mexican government created plans to colonize the region while many Anglo-Americans also founded frontier homes on Mexican land. Catalyzed by the free labor of slaves, farming and ranching became the economic cornerstones of the regions. Gradually, Texans established a unique cultural identity that resisted the loose control of the Mexican Republic.

Revolution and the Republic of Texas

Eventually, Mexican and Texan identities became so distinct that the Texans decided to rebel against the centralist Mexican government. The ensuing Texas Revolution, which took place in 1835 and 1836, allowed Texas to declare independence from Mexico. A flood of United States volunteers assisted in helping Texans find the Republic of Texas, which officially received its independence via the Consultation of 1836. The Republic of Texas was a short-lived nation because its people quickly accepted annexation by the United States of America in 1845.

U.S. Annexation and the Mexican-American War

President John Tyler initiated an annexation bill in March 1845, which President James K. Polk officially signed in December 1845. The Republic of Texas officially revoked its sovereignty, lawfully agreeing to become the 28th state of the Union in February 1846. The Mexican-American War (1846–1848), in many ways, was a direct response to President Polk's annexation of Texas. The war ended in the Treaty of Guadalupe, which resulted in a Mexican Cession that officially brought parts of Texas, New Mexico, Arizona, and California within the territory of the United States. One social impact of U.S. annexation and the Mexican-American War was increased political tensions over the role of slavery in new territories.

Antebellum Slavery and the Civil War

Texas became part of the South's valuable cotton belt, a regional plantation economy built on the free labor of slaves. Growing national divisions over slavery divided the nation. Most Texas politicians were tied to the cotton economy and sided with the pro-slavery politicians of the broader South. Additionally, these slavery advocates emphasized state-based sovereignty, choosing to believe the rights of states outweighed the overreach of federal government. The state of Texas joined the Confederates States of America on March 2, 1861 as the seventh state to secede from the Union. Texas troops proved to be a cornerstone of the Confederate militia during the Civil War.

Reconstruction and Post-Reconstruction

After the Civil War, the United States entered an era known as Reconstruction. During Reconstruction, the Texas government, like many Southern states, passed black codes that denied civil rights to former slaves. In the wake of emancipation, freed African-Americans were once again second-class citizens. Texas politics became intermingled with the violence of the Ku Klux Klan (KKK), as many Texans participated in the public murder of freed blacks. Many Republican politicians, such as Texas Governor Edmund J. Davis, chose to fight the intimidation tactics of the KKK and assist African-Americans in protecting their civil rights. Davis was a fervent advocate of using public funding to educate African-Americans as equals. Nevertheless, as Reconstruction waned in the South, Texas joined other Southern states in adopting segregationist Jim Crow laws. Segregation (the separation of whites and blacks in public spaces) became a keystone of Texas politics well into the 1950s and 1960s. The Civil Rights Movement of that era ended legal segregation in the South.

20th Century Advancement

The 20th century not only witnessed the extension of voting rights to women in Texas, but also the civil liberties of African-Americans. Economically, the 20th century saw Texas become a gas and petroleum powerhouse. During the Cold War, Houston joined Cape Canaveral as an epicenter of NASA's space race. The oil and space industries carried Texas well into the 21st century, bringing millions of professionals to the Sunbelt South. Population increases during this era paved the way for environmental devastation. Today, Texas cities still struggle to cope with the rampant excesses of 20th century industrialization and urbanization.

Immigration and Migration to the Sunbelt South

In the 20th and 21st centuries, immigration and migration to the Sunbelt South transformed the racial, ethnic, and religious fiber of Texas. Immigration from Mexico and Latin America has helped "Hispanicize" Texas culture. Young professionals from all racial, ethnic, and religious backgrounds gravitate toward the budding tech industries in Austin, Houston, San Antonio, and Dallas. Many Texas cities are bursting at the seams with diversity and population growth. This immigration and migration

has made Texas a diverse economic powerhouse, though this rapid influx of new residents has stirred racial tensions and has complicated city planning.

Major Contributions of Classical Civilizations

There were a number of powerful civilizations during the classical period. Mesopotamia was home to one of the earliest civilizations between the Euphrates and the Tigris rivers in the Near East. The rivers provided water and vegetation for early humans, but they were surrounded by desert. This led to the beginning of irrigation efforts to expand water and agriculture across the region, which resulted in the area being known as the Fertile Crescent.

The organization necessary to initiate canals and other projects led to the formation of cities and hierarchies, which would have considerable influence on the structure of later civilizations. For instance, the new hierarchies established different classes within the societies, such as kings, priests, artisans, and workers. Over time, these city-states expanded to encompass outside territories, and the city of Akkad became the world's first empire in 2350 B.C. In addition, Mesopotamian scribes developed systemized drawings called pictograms, which were the first system of writing in the world; furthermore, the creation of wedge-shaped cuneiform tablets preserved written records for multiple generations.

Later, Mesopotamian kingdoms made further advancements. For instance, Babylon established a sophisticated mathematical system based on numbers from one to sixty; this not only influenced modern concepts, such as the number of minutes in each hour, but also created the framework for math equations and theories. In addition, the Babylonian king Hammurabi established a complex set of laws, known as the Code of Hammurabi, which would set a precedent for future legal systems.

Meanwhile, another major civilization began to form around the Nile River in Africa. The Nile's relatively predictable nature allowed farmers to use the river's water and the silt from floods to grow many crops along its banks, which led to further advancements in irrigation. Egyptian rulers mobilized the kingdom's population for incredible construction projects, including the famous pyramids. Egyptians also improved pictographic writing with their more complex system of hieroglyphs, which allowed for more diverse styles of writing. The advancements in writing can be seen through the Egyptians' complex system of religion, with documents such as the *Book of the Dead* outlining not only systems of worship and pantheons of deities but also a deeper, more philosophical concept of the afterlife.

While civilizations in Egypt and Mesopotamia helped to establish class systems and empires, other forms of government emerged in Greece. Despite common ties between different cities, such as the Olympic Games, each settlement, known as a polis, had its own unique culture. Many of the cities were oligarchies, in which a council of distinguished leaders monopolized the government; others were dictatorships ruled by tyrants. Athens was a notable exception by practicing an early form of democracy in which free, landholding men could participate, but it offered more freedom of thought than other systems.

Taking advantage of their proximity to the Mediterranean Sea, Greek cities sent expeditions to establish colonies abroad that developed their own local traditions. In the process, Greek merchants interacted with Phoenician traders, who had developed an alphabetic writing system built on sounds instead of pictures. This diverse network of exchanges made Greece a vibrant center of art, science, and philosophy. For example, the Greek doctor Hippocrates established a system of ethics for doctors called the Hippocratic Oath, which continues to guide the modern medical profession. Complex forms of literature were created, including the epic poem "The Iliad," and theatrical productions were also developed. Athens in particular sought to spread its vision of democratic freedom throughout the world, which led to the devastating Peloponnesian War between allies of Athens and those of oligarchic Sparta from 431 to 404 B.C.

Alexander the Great helped disseminate Greek culture to new regions. Alexander was in fact an heir to the throne of Macedon, which was a warrior kingdom to the north of Greece. After finishing his father's work of unifying Greece under Macedonian control, Alexander successfully conquered Mesopotamia, which had been part of the Persian Empire. The spread of Greek institutions throughout the Mediterranean and Near East led to a period of Hellenization, during which various civilizations assimilated Greek culture; this allowed Greek traditions, such as architecture and philosophy, to endure into the present day.

Greek ideas were later assimilated, along with many other concepts, into the Roman Empire. Located west of Greece on the Italian peninsula, the city of Rome gradually conquered its neighbors and expanded its territories abroad; by 44 B.C., Rome had conquered much of Western Europe, northern Africa, and the Near East. Romans were very creative, and they adapted new ideas and innovated new technologies to strengthen their power. For instance, Romans built on the engineering knowledge of Greeks to create arched pathways, known as aqueducts, to transport water for long distances and devise advanced plumbing systems.

One of Rome's greatest legacies was its system of government. Early Rome was a republic, a democratic system in which leaders are elected by the people. Although the process still heavily favored wealthy elites, the republican system was a key inspiration for later institutions such as the United States. Octavian "Augustus" Caesar later made Rome into an empire, and the senate had only a symbolic role in the government. The new imperial system built on the examples of earlier empires to establish a vibrant dynasty that used a sophisticated legal code and a well-trained military to enforce order across vast regions. Even after Rome itself fell to barbarian invaders in fifth century A.D., the eastern half of the empire survived as the Byzantine Empire until 1453 A.D. Furthermore, the Roman Empire's institutions continued to influence and inspire later medieval kingdoms, including the Holy Roman Empire; even rulers in the twentieth century called themselves Kaiser and Tsar, titles which stem from the word "Caesar."

In addition, the Roman Empire was host to the spread of new religious ideas. In the region of Israel, the religion of Judaism presented a new approach to worship via monotheism, which is the belief in the existence of a single deity. An offshoot of Judaism called Christianity spread across the Roman Empire and gained popularity. While Rome initially suppressed the religion, it later backed Christianity and allowed the religious system to endure as a powerful force in medieval times.

Colonization and Expansion in U.S. History

When examining how Europeans explored what would become the United States of America, one must first examine why Europeans came to explore the New World as a whole. In the fifteenth century, tensions increased between the Eastern and Mediterranean nations of Europe and the expanding Ottoman Empire to the east. As war and piracy spread across the Mediterranean, the once-prosperous trade routes across Asia's Silk Road began to decline, and nations across Europe began to explore alternative routes for trade.

Italian explorer Christopher Columbus proposed a westward route. Contrary to popular lore, the main challenge that Columbus faced in finding backers was not proving that the world was round. Much of

Europe's educated elite knew that the world was round; the real issue was that they rightly believed that a westward route to Asia, assuming a lack of obstacles, would be too long to be practical. Nevertheless, Columbus set sail in 1492 after obtaining support from Spain and arrived in the West Indies three months later.

Spain launched further expeditions to the new continents and established *New Spain*. The colony consisted not only of Central America and Mexico, but also the American Southwest and Florida. France claimed much of what would become Canada, along with the Mississippi River region and the Midwest. In addition, the Dutch established colonies that covered New Jersey, New York, and Connecticut. Each nation managed its colonies differently, and thus influenced how they would assimilate into the United States. For instance, Spain strove to establish a system of Christian missions throughout its territory, while France focused on trading networks and had limited infrastructure in regions such as the Midwest.

Even in cases of limited colonial growth, the land of America was hardly vacant, because a diverse array of Native American nations and groups were already present. Throughout much of colonial history, European settlers commonly misperceived native peoples as a singular, static entity. In reality, Native Americans had a variety of traditions depending on their history and environment, and their culture continued to change through the course of interactions with European settlers; for instance, tribes such as the Cheyenne and Comanche used horses, which were introduced by white settlers, to become powerful warrior nations. However, a few generalizations can be made: many, but not all, tribes were matrilineal, which gave women a fair degree of power, and land was commonly seen as belonging to everyone. These differences, particularly European settlers' continual focus on land ownership, contributed to increasing prejudice and violence.

Situated on the Atlantic Coast, the Thirteen Colonies that would become the United States of America constituted only a small portion of North America. Even those colonies had significant differences that stemmed from their different origins. For instance, the Virginia colony under John Smith in 1607 started with male bachelors seeking gold, whereas families of Puritans settled Massachusetts. As a result, the Thirteen Colonies—Virginia, Massachusetts, Connecticut, Maryland, New York, New Jersey, Pennsylvania, Delaware, Rhode Island, New Hampshire, Georgia, North Carolina, and South Carolina—had different structures and customs that would each influence the United States.

Competition among several imperial powers in eastern areas of North America led to conflicts that would later bring about the independence of the United States. The French and Indian War from 1754 to 1763, which was a subsidiary war of the Seven Years' War, ended with Great Britain claiming France's Canadian territories as well as the Ohio Valley. The same war was costly for all the powers involved, which led to increased taxes on the Thirteen Colonies. In addition, the new lands to the west of the colonies attracted new settlers, and they came into conflict with Native Americans and British troops that were trying to maintain the traditional boundaries. These growing tensions with Great Britain, as well as other issues, eventually led to the American Revolution, which ended with Britain relinquishing its control of the colonies.

Britain continued to hold onto its other colonies, such as Canada and the West Indies, which reflects the continued power of multiple nations across North America, even as the United States began to expand across the continent. Many Americans advocated expansion regardless of the land's current inhabitants, but the results were often mixed. Still, events both abroad and within North America contributed to the growth of the United States. For instance, the rising tumult in France during the French Revolution and the rise of Napoleon led France to sell the Louisiana Purchase, a large chunk of land consisting not only of Louisiana but also much of the Midwest, to the United States in 1803. Meanwhile, as Spanish power declined, Mexico claimed independence in 1821, but the new nation became increasingly vulnerable to foreign pressure. In the Mexican-American War from 1846 to 1848, Mexico surrendered territory to the United States that eventually became California, Nevada, Utah, and New Mexico, as well as parts of Arizona, Colorado, and Wyoming.

Even as the United States sought new inland territory, American interests were also expanding overseas via trade. As early as 1784, the ship *Empress of China* traveled to China to establish trading connections. American interests had international dimensions throughout the nation's history. For instance, during the presidency of Andrew Jackson, the ship *Potomac* was dispatched to the Pacific island of Sumatra in 1832 to avenge the deaths of American sailors. This incident exemplifies how U.S. foreign trade connected with imperial expansion.

This combination of continental and seaward growth adds a deeper layer to American development, because it was not purely focused on western expansion. For example, take the 1849 Gold Rush; a large number of Americans and other immigrants traveled to California by ship and settled western territories before more eastern areas, such as Nevada and Idaho. Therefore, the United States' early history of colonization and expansion is a complex network of diverse cultures.

American Revolution and the Founding of the Nation

The American Revolution largely occurred as a result of changing values in the Thirteen Colonies that broke from their traditional relationship with England. Early on in the colonization of North America, the colonial social structure tried to mirror the stratified order of Great Britain. In England, the landed elites were seen as intellectually and morally superior to the common man, which led to a paternalistic relationship. This style of governance was similarly applied to the colonial system; government was left to the property-owning upper class, and the colonies as a whole could be seen as a child dutifully serving "Mother England."

However, the colonies' distance from England meant that actual, hereditary aristocrats from Britain only formed a small percentage of the overall population and did not even fill all the positions of power. By the mid-eighteenth century, much of the American upper class consisted of local families who acquired status through business rather than lineage. Despite this, representatives from Britain were appointed to govern the colonies. As a result, a rift began to form between the colonists and British officials.

Tensions began to rise in the aftermath of the French and Indian War of 1754 to 1763. To recover the financial costs of the long conflict, Great Britain drew upon its colonies to provide the desired resources. Since the American colonists did not fully subscribe to the paternal connection, taxation to increase British revenue, such as the Stamp Act of 1765, was met with increasing resistance. Britain sent soldiers to the colonies and enacted the 1765 Quartering Act to require colonists to house the troops. In 1773, the new Tea Act, which created a monopoly, led some colonists to raid a ship and destroy its contents in the Boston Tea Party.

Uncertain about whether they should remain loyal to Britain, representatives from twelve colonies formed the First Continental Congress in 1774 to discuss what they should do next. When Patriot militiamen at Lexington and Concord fought British soldiers in April 1775, the Revolutionary War began. While the rebel forces worked to present the struggle as a united, patriotic effort, the colonies remained divided throughout the war. Thousands of colonists, known as Loyalists or Tories, supported Britain. Even the revolutionaries proved to be significantly fragmented, and many militias only served in their home states. The Continental Congress was also divided over whether to reconcile with Britain or push

for full separation. These issues hindered the ability of the revolutionary armies to resist the British, who had superior training and resources at their disposal.

Even so, the Continental Army, under General George Washington, gradually built up a force that utilized Prussian military training and backwoods guerrilla tactics to make up for their limited resources. Although the British forces continued to win significant battles, the Continental Army gradually reduced Britain's will to fight as the years passed. Furthermore, Americans appealed to the rivalry that other European nations had with the British Empire. The support was initially limited to indirect assistance, but aid gradually increased. After the American victory at the Battle of Saratoga in 1777, France and other nations began to actively support the American cause by providing much-needed troops and equipment.

In 1781, the primary British army under General Cornwallis was defeated by an American and French coalition at Virginia, which paved the way for negotiations. The Treaty of Paris in 1783 ended the war, recognized the former colonies' independence from Great Britain, and gave America control over territory between the Appalachian Mountains and Mississippi River. However, the state of the new nation was still uncertain. The new nation's government initially stemmed from the state-based structure of the Continental Congress and was incorporated into the Articles of Confederation in 1777.

The Articles of Confederation emphasized the ideals of the American Revolution, particularly the concept of freedom from unjust government. Unfortunately, the resulting limitations on the national government left most policies—even ones with national ramifications—up to individual states. For instance, states sometimes simply decided to not pay taxes. Many representatives did not see much value in the National Congress and simply did not attend the meetings. Some progress was still made during the period, such as the Northwest Ordinance of 1787, which organized the western territories into new states; nevertheless, the disjointed links in the state-oriented government inhibited significant progress.

Although many citizens felt satisfied with this decentralized system of government, key intellectuals and leaders in America became increasingly disturbed by the lack of unity. An especially potent fear among them was the potential that, despite achieving official independence, other powers could threaten America's autonomy. In 1786, poor farmers in Massachusetts launched an insurrection, known as Shays' Rebellion, which sparked fears of additional uprisings and led to the creation of the *Constitutional Convention* in 1787.

While the convention initially intended to correct issues within the Articles of Confederation, speakers, such as James Madison, compellingly argued for the delegates to devise a new system of government that was more centralized than its predecessor. The Constitution was not fully supported by all citizens, and there was much debate about whether or not to support the new government. Even so, in 1788, the Constitution was ratified. Later additions, such as the Bill of Rights, would help protect individual liberty by giving specific rights to citizens. In 1789, George Washington became the first president of the newly created executive branch of the government, and America entered a new stage of history.

U.S. History from Founding to Present

One early development was the growth of political parties—something that Washington tried and failed to stop from forming. Federalists, such as Alexander Hamilton, wanted to expand the national government's power, while Democratic-Republicans, such as Thomas Jefferson, favored states' rights.

The United States suffered multiple defeats by Britain in the War of 1812, but individual American victories, such as the Battle of New Orleans, still strengthened nationalistic pride.

In the aftermath of the war, the Federalists were absorbed into the Democratic-Republicans, which began the Era of Good Feelings. However, two new parties eventually emerged. The Democrats, whose leader Andrew Jackson became president in 1828, favored "Jacksonian" democracy, which emphasized mass participation in elections. However, Jackson's policies largely favored white male landowners and suppressed opposing views. The Whigs supported Federalist policies but also drew on democratic principles, particularly with marginalized groups such as African Americans and women.

At the same time, settlers continued to expand west in search of new land and fortune. The Louisiana Purchase of 1803 opened up large amounts of land west of the Mississippi River, and adventurers pushed past even those boundaries toward the western coast. The vision of westward growth into the frontier is a key part of American popular culture, but the expansion was often erratic and depended on a combination of incentives and assurances of relative security. Hence, some areas, such as California and Oregon, were settled more quickly than other areas to the east. Some historians have pointed to the growth of the frontier as a means through which American democracy expanded.

However, the matter of western lands became an increasingly volatile issue as the controversy over slavery heightened. Not all northerners supported abolition, but many saw the practice as outdated and did not want it to expand. Abolitionists formed the Republican Party, and their candidate, Abraham Lincoln, was elected as president in 1860. In response, southern states seceded and formed the Confederate States of America. The ensuing Civil War lasted from 1861 to 1865 and had significant consequences. Slavery was abolished in the United States, and the power of individual states was drastically curtailed. After being reunified, southern states worked to retain control over freed slaves, and the Reconstruction period was followed by Jim Crow segregation. As a result, blacks were barred from public education, unable to vote, and forced to accept their status as second-class citizens.

After the Civil War, the United States increasingly industrialized and became part of the larger Industrial Revolution, which took place throughout the western world. Steps toward industrialization had already begun as early as Jackson's presidency, but the full development of American industry took place in the second half of the nineteenth century. Railroads helped link cities like Chicago to locations across the West, which allowed for rapid transfer of materials. New technologies, such as electricity, allowed leisure time for those with enough wealth. Even so, the Gilded Age was also a period of disparities, and wealthy entrepreneurs rose while impoverished workers struggled to make their voices heard.

The late nineteenth and early twentieth century not only marked U.S. expansion within North America but also internationally. For instance, after the Spanish-American War in 1898, the United States claimed control over Guam, Puerto Rico, and the Philippines. Rivalries in Europe culminated in World War I, in which great powers ranging from France to Russia vied for control in a bloody struggle. Americans did not enter the war until 1917, but we had a critical role in the final phase of the war. During the peace treaty process, President Woodrow Wilson sought to establish a League of Nations in order to promote global harmony, but his efforts only achieved limited success.

After World War I, the United States largely stayed out of international politics for the next two decades. Still, American businesses continued overseas ventures and strengthened the economy in the 1920s. However, massive speculation in the stock market in 1929 triggered the Great Depression—a financial crisis that spread worldwide as nations withdrew from the global economy. The crisis shepherded in the

presidency of Franklin D. Roosevelt, who reformed the Democratic Party and implemented new federal programs known as the New Deal.

The Great Depression had ramifications worldwide and encouraged the rise of fascist governments in Italy and Germany. Highly dictatorial, fascism emphasized nationalism and militarism. World War II began when the Axis powers of Germany, Italy, and Japan built up their military forces and launched invasions against neighboring nations in 1939. As part of the Allies, which also included Britain, France, and the Soviet Union, America defeated the Axis powers in 1945 and asserted itself as a global force.

The Union of Soviet Socialist Republics had emerged through the Bolshevik Revolution in 1917 in Russia and militantly supported Communism—a socialist system of government that called for the overthrow of capitalism. Although the Soviet Union formed an alliance with the United States during World War II, relations chilled, and the Cold War began in 1947. Although no true war was declared between the two nations, both the Union of Soviet Socialist Republics and the United States engaged in indirect conflict by supporting and overthrowing foreign governments.

Meanwhile, the Civil Rights Movement began to grow as marginalized groups objected to racial segregation and abuse by whites across the nation. Civil rights leaders, such as Martin Luther King Jr., argued for nonviolent resistance, but others, such as Malcolm X, advocated more radical approaches. Civil rights groups became increasingly discontented during the Vietnam War because they felt they were being drafted for a foreign war that ignored domestic problems. Even so, significant reforms, such as the Voting Rights Act of 1965, opened up new opportunities for freedom and equality in America.

In 1991, the Soviet Union collapsed, leaving the United States as the dominant global power. However, as the United States struggled to fill the void left by the Soviet Union, questions arose about America's role in the world. Terrorist acts, such as the 9/11 attack on the World Trade Center in 2001, have shed doubt on the United States' ability to enforce its authority on an international scale.

Twentieth-Century Developments in the United States

Although the United States began industrializing in the second half of the nineteenth century, American technology continued to develop in new directions throughout the course of the twentieth century. A key example was the invention of the modern assembly line. Assembly lines and conveyor belts had already become a prominent part of industrial work, but Henry Ford combined conveyor belts with the system of assembly workers in 1913 in order to produce Model T automobiles. This streamlined production system, in which multiple parts were assembled by different teams along the conveyors, allowed industries in the United States to grow ever larger.

Ford's assembly lines also promoted the growth of the automobile as a means of transportation. Early cars were an expensive and impractical novelty and were primarily the toys of the rich. The Model T, on the other hand, was relatively affordable, which made the car available to a wider array of consumers. Many of the automobiles' early issues, such as radiator leaks and fragile tires, were gradually corrected, and this made the car more appealing than horses. With the support of President Eisenhower, the Federal Aid Highway Act of 1956 paved the way for a network of interstates and highways across the nation.

At the same time, a revolutionary approach to transportation was emerging: flight. Blimps and balloons were already gaining popularity by the turn of the twentieth century, but aviators struggled to create an airplane. The first critical success was by the Wright Brothers in 1903, and they demonstrated that aircrafts did not need to be lighter than air. In time, airplanes surpassed the popularity of balloons and blimps, which tended to be more volatile. Aircraft also added a new dimension to warfare, and aircraft carriers became an integral piece of the American navy during World War II.

Furthermore, by demonstrating that heavier-than-air vehicles could actually carry passengers upward, the stage was set for the space race in the second half of the twentieth century. In 1958, the U.S. government created the National Aeronautics and Space Administration (NASA) to head the budding initiative to extend American power into space. After the Soviet Union successfully launched the Sputnik satellite into Earth's orbit in 1957 and sent the first human in space in 1961, the United States intensified its own space program through the Apollo missions. Apollo 11 successfully landed on the moon in 1969 with Buzz Aldrin and Neil Armstrong. Later ventures into space would focus on space shuttles and satellites, and the latter significantly enhanced communications worldwide.

Indeed, the twentieth century also made considerable advancements in communications and media. Inventions such as the radio greatly boosted communication across the nation and world, such that news could be reported immediately rather than take days. Furthermore, motion pictures evolved from black-and-white movies at theaters to full-color television sets in households. From animation to live films, television matured into a compelling art form in popular culture. Live-action footage gave a new layer to news broadcasts and proved instrumental in the public's reaction to events, such as the Civil Rights Movement and the Vietnam War. With the success of the space program, satellites became a fundamental piece of Earth's communications network by transmitting signals across the planet instantaneously.

Further communications advancements resulted from the development of computer technology. The early computers in the twentieth century were enormous behemoths that were too bulky and expensive for anything but government institutions. However, computers gradually became smaller while still storing large amounts of data. A turning point came with the 1976 release of the Apple computer by entrepreneurs Steve Wozniak and Steve Jobs. The computer had a simplistic design that made it marketable for a mass consumer audience, and computers eventually became household items. Similarly, the networks that would become the Internet originated as government systems, but in time they were extended to commercial avenues that became a vibrant element of modern communications.

However, other advancements in American science during the twentieth century were aimed toward more lethal purposes. In response to the multiple wars throughout the century, the United States built up a powerful military force, and new technologies were devised for that purpose. One of the deadliest creations was the atomic bomb, which split molecular atoms to produce powerful explosions; in addition to the sheer force of the bombs, the aftereffects included toxic radiation and electronic shutdowns. Developed and used in the last days of World War II, the nuclear bomb was the United States' most powerful weapon during the Cold War.

On the other hand, the twentieth century also marked new approaches to the natural environments in America. In reaction to the depletion of natural habitats by industrialization and overhunting, President Theodore Roosevelt helped preserve areas for what would become the National Parks in 1916. Laws, such as the Clean Water Act of 1972, helped improve the health of ecosystems, which benefitted not only wildlife but people across the nation. This also led to the development of alternative energy sources such as wind and solar power.

America continues to change and grow into the twenty-first century by building on preexisting ideas but also pioneering new concepts. As globalization becomes an increasingly prominent phenomenon, American businesses strive to adapt their products to consumers worldwide while also funneling in new

ideas from other nations. Yet many of the current developments in American enterprises stem in part from earlier events in American history. For instance, the environmental movement has expanded to address new issues such as global warming. NASA continues its space exploration endeavors, but entrepreneurs hope one day to travel to Mars. Therefore, the history of technology within the United States remains an engaging and relevant subject in the present.

Twentieth-Century Development in World History

At the turn of the twentieth century, imperialism had led to powers, such as France, the United States, and Japan, to establish spheres of influence throughout the world. The combination of imperial competition and military rivalries led to the outbreak of World War I when Archduke Ferdinand of Austria was assassinated in 1914. The war pitted the Allies, including England, France, and Russia, against the Central Powers of Austria-Hungary, Germany, and the Ottoman Empire—a large Islamic realm that encompassed Turkey, Palestine, Saudi Arabia, and Iraq. The rapid advances in military technology turned the war into a prolonged bloodbath that took its toll on all sides. By the end of the war in 1918, the Ottoman Empire had collapsed, the Austrian-Hungarian Empire was split into multiple countries, and Russia had descended into a civil war that would lead to the rise of the Soviet Union and Communism.

The Treaty of Versailles ended the war, but the triumphant Allies also levied heavy fines on Germany, which led to resentment that would be accentuated by the Great Depression of the 1930s. The Great Depression destabilized the global economy and led to the rise of fascism, a militarized and dictatorial system of government, in nations such as Germany and Italy. The rapid expansion of the Axis Powers of Germany, Italy, and Japan led to the outbreak of World War II. The war was even more global than the previous conflicts, with battles occurring in Europe, Africa, and Asia. World War II encouraged the development of new technologies, such as advanced radar and nuclear weapons, that would continue to influence the course of future wars.

In the aftermath of World War II, the United Nations was formed as a step toward promoting international cooperation. Based on the preceding League of Nations, the United Nations included countries from around the world and gave them a voice in world policies. The formation of the United Nations coincided with the independence of formerly colonized states in Africa and Asia, and those countries joined the world body. A primary goal of the United Nations was to limit the extent of future wars and prevent a third world war; while the United Nations could not prevent the outbreak of wars, it nevertheless tried to peacefully resolve them. In addition to promoting world peace, the United Nations also helped protect human rights.

Even so, the primary leadership in the early United Nations was held by the United States and its allies, which contributed to tensions with the Soviet Union. The United States and the Soviet Union, while never declaring war on each other, fueled a number of proxy wars and coups across the world in what would be known as the Cold War. Cold War divisions were especially noticeable in Europe, where communist regimes ruled the eastern region and democratic governments controlled the western portion. These indirect struggles often involved interference with foreign politics, and sometimes local people began to resent Soviet or American attempts to influence their countries. For instance, American and Soviet interventions in Iran and Afghanistan contributed to fundamentalist Islamic movements. The Cold War ended when the Soviet Union collapsed in 1991, but the conflict affected nations across the globe and continues to influence current issues.

Another key development during the twentieth century, as noted earlier with the United Nations, was that most colonized nations broke free from imperial control and asserted their independence. Although these nations achieved autonomy and recognition in the United Nations, they still suffered from the legacies of imperialism. The borders of many countries in Africa and Asia were arbitrarily determined by colonists with little regard to the arrangement of native populations. Therefore, many former colonies have suffered conflicts between different ethnic groups; this was also the case with the British colony in India, which became independent in 1947. Violence occurred when it split into India and Pakistan because the borders were largely based on religious differences. In addition, former colonial powers continue to assert economic control that inhibits the growth of native economies. On the other hand, the end of direct imperialism has helped a number of nations, such as India and Iran, rise as world powers that have significant influence on the world as a whole.

Additionally, there were considerable environmental reforms worldwide during the twentieth century. In reaction to the growing effects of industrialization, organizations around the world protested policies that damaged the environment. Many of these movements were locally based, but others expanded to address various environmental threats across the globe. The United Nations helped carry these environmental reforms forward by making them part of international policies. For instance, in 1997, many members of the United Nations signed a treaty, known as the *Kyoto Protocol*, that tried to reduce global carbon dioxide emissions.

Most significantly, the twentieth century marked increasing globalization. The process had already been under way in the nineteenth century as technological improvements and imperial expansions connected different parts of the world, but the late twentieth century brought globalization to a new level. Trade became international, and local customs from different lands also gained prominence worldwide. Cultural exchanges occur on a frequent basis, and many people have begun to ponder the consequences of such rapid exchanges. One example of globalization was the 1993 establishment of the European Union—an economic and political alliance between several European nations.

Cross-Cultural Comparisons in World History Instruction

Cross-cultural interactions are the very heart of world history and must be closely examined to understand the world's historical patterns. One of the main reasons why cross-cultural studies are so important is because cultures are not necessarily synonymous with political entities, such as states. Many countries, ranging from China to Greece, historically have many subcultures that should be considered individually. For example, a study of culture in the United States would need to consider multiple ethnic and regional groups. Even individual states and cities have their own traditions. On the other hand, these multiple cultures often coalesce into a larger, national culture that defines the overall society and politics of the nation. Therefore, cross-cultural studies of different subgroups in a larger body allow people to understand how the different parts of a culture interact and connect with each other.

Furthermore, cultures are not always restricted by the borders of nations, and cultural phenomena may extend through multiple countries. This can be seen in the spread of the Spanish language across Central and South America as well as other regions. The Spanish language and other various traditions tie the different countries together with a common culture. Even so, each nation changes the culture and gives it a unique style. A study of the culture in a single nation may be very insightful, but it would be incomplete if it failed to account for aspects of the culture beyond that country. In addition, this means that different cultures can overlap with each other and that the cultures of different countries may intersect in ways that their borders do not. By examining multiple cultures and how they are linked with

each other, larger cultural patterns become apparent, which makes these studies critical in world history.

Throughout history, cultures have not existed in isolation but rather have been affected by other traditions. A key influence in how different cultures develop is not only their setting and history but how they interact with neighboring cultures. For instance, the conflict from 499 to 449 B.C. between the Persian Empire and the Greek city-states helped to influence the course of Greek culture as a whole by creating a national sense of dichotomy between the Greek ideal of freedom and Persian autocracy. Aside from direct impacts such as wars, cultures can influence each other through interactions that spread some concepts while also adopting new ideas from their neighbors. Pasta became a phenomenon in Italy in part because the Silk Road linked Italy with China, which already had similar foods.

The pervasiveness of globalization in the present day has increased the importance of cross-cultural comparison and made it a topic of immediate relevance. The world now has a truly global market in which travel, communications, and trade function on an international scale. This means that people of different cultures can now interact with each other much more easily than in earlier centuries, which allows for a rapid exchange of ideas and goods between cultures. Furthermore, despite the international scope of modern trade, many globalized markets strive to build on the appeal of local cultures. Doing so gives the products a genuine and unique quality that resonates with consumers. Yet it is critical to realize how local cultures are transformed and combined with concepts from other cultures in the global market. For example, sushi is a traditional food in Japan, but its export to other nations has led chefs to create new culinary fusions, such as sushi tacos.

Cross-cultural comparisons also help to reveal common patterns in human society. Sometimes different cultures develop similar concepts without directly interacting with each other. For instance, both the Mayan culture in Central America and the ancient Egyptians independently developed pyramid structures. Although the similarities have sparked rumors that these civilizations were connected, it is most likely that each version originated independently. Close examination of the two types of pyramids and their respective cultures reveals significant differences amidst the similarities. These comparisons are important because they show how human cultures converge and diverge in their patterns of growth. A key function of historical study is to gain a better understanding and appreciation of how humanity develops. By examining the commonalities and differences between cultures, people can begin to theorize what factors influence the course of civilizations. However, such studies must account for the complex manners through which cultures interact with each other.

Geography and Culture

World and Regional Geography

Geography is essential in understanding the world as a whole. This requires a study of spatial distribution, which examines how various locations and physical features are arranged in the world. The most common element in geography is the region, which refers to a specific area that is separate from surrounding ones. Regions can be defined based on a variety of factors, including environmental, economic, or political features, and these different kinds of regions can overlap with each other.

It is also important to know the difference between location and place. A location, defined either through its physical position or through its relation to other locations, determines where something is, and this characteristic is static. A place, on the other hand, describes a combination of physical and human elements in relation to each other; the determination of place is therefore changeable depending on the movement of individuals and groups.

Geography is visually conveyed using maps, and a collection of maps is called an atlas. To illustrate some key points about geography, please refer to the map below.

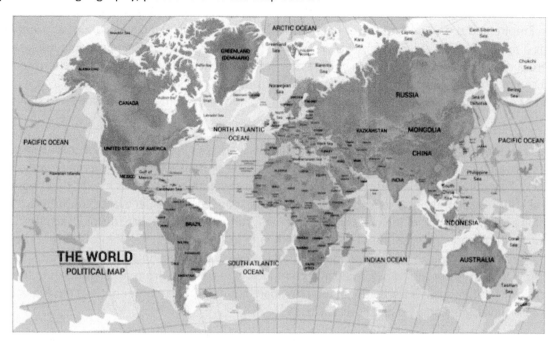

This is a traditional map of the world that displays all of the countries and six of the seven continents. Countries, the most common approach to political regions, can be identified by their labels. The continents are not identified on this map, with the exception of Australia, but they are larger landmasses that encompass most of the countries in their respective areas; the other five visible continents are North America, South America, Europe, Africa, and Asia. The seventh continent, Antarctica, is found at the South Pole and has been omitted from the map.

The absence of Antarctica leads into the issues of distortion, in which geographical features are altered on a map. Some degree of distortion is to be expected with a two-dimensional flat map of the world because Earth is a sphere. A map projection transforms a spherical map of the world into a flattened perspective, but the process generally alters the spatial appearance of landmasses. For instance, Greenland often appears, such as in the map above, larger than it really is.

Furthermore, Antarctica's exclusion from the map is, in fact, a different sort of distortion—that of the mapmakers' biases. Mapmakers determine which features are included on the map and which ones are not. Antarctica, for example, is often missing from maps because, unlike the other continents, it has a limited human population. Moreover, a study of the world reveals that many of the distinctions on maps are human constructions.

Even so, maps can still reveal key features about the world. For instance, the map above has areas that seem almost three-dimensional and jut out. They represent mountains and are an example of

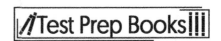

topography, which is a method used to display the differing elevations of the terrain. A more detailed topographical map can be viewed below.

On some colored maps, the oceans, represented in blue between the continents, vary in coloration depending on depth. The differences demonstrate *bathymetry*, which is the study of the ocean floor's depth. Paler areas represent less depth, while darker spots reflect greater depth.

Please also note the many lines running horizontally and vertically along the map. The horizontal lines, known as *parallels,* mark the calculated latitude of those locations and reveal how far north or south these areas are from the equator, which bisects the map horizontally. Generally, with exceptions depending on specific environments, climates closer to the equator are warmer because this region receives the most direct sunlight. The equator also serves to split the globe between the Northern and Southern hemispheres.

Longitude, as signified by the vertical lines, determines how far east or west different regions are from each other. The lines of longitude, known as *meridians,* are also the basis for time zones, which allocate different times to regions depending on their position eastward and westward of the prime meridian. As one travels west between time zones, the given time moves backward accordingly. Conversely, if one travels east, the time moves forward.

There are two particularly significant longitude-associated dividers in this regard. The prime [Greenwich] meridian, as displayed below, is defined as zero degrees in longitude, and thus determines the other lines. The line, in fact, circles the globe north and south, and it therefore divides the world into the Eastern and Western hemispheres. It is important to not confuse the Greenwich meridian with the International Date Line, which is an invisible line in the Pacific Ocean that was created to represent the change between calendar days. By traveling westward across the International Date Line, a traveler would essentially leap forward a day. For example, a person departing from the United States on Sunday would arrive in Japan on Monday. By traveling eastward across the line, a traveler would go backward a day. For example, a person departing from China on Monday would arrive in Canada on Sunday.

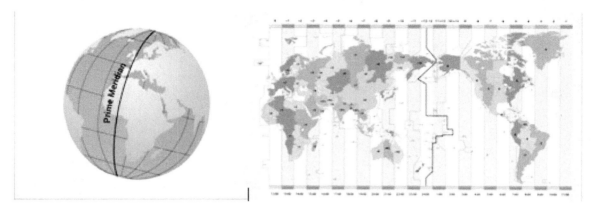

Although world maps are useful in showing the overall arrangement of continents and nations, it is also important at times to look more closely at individual countries because they have unique features that are only visible on more detailed maps.

For example, take the following map of the United States of America. It should be noted that the country is split into multiple states that have their own culture and localized governments. Other countries are often split into various divisions, such as provinces, and while these features are ignored for the sake of clarity on larger maps, they are important when studying specific nations. Individual states can be further subdivided into counties and townships, and they may have their own maps that can be examined for closer analysis.

Finally, one of the first steps in examining any map should be to locate the map's key or legend, which will explain what features different symbols represent on the map. As these symbols can be arbitrary depending on the maker, a key will help to clarify the different meanings.

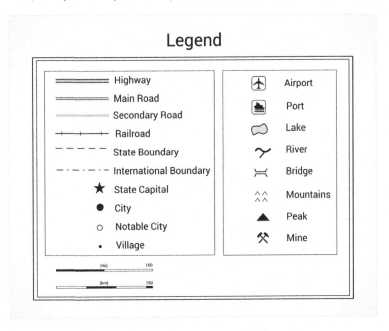

Interaction of Physical and Human Systems

Humans have always interacted with nature, and humanity has been shaped by, and, in turn, reshaped environments. Using tools to accomplish things they cannot do on their own, humans have proven highly adaptable to different environments. However, the specific ecosystems have helped to shape human development as individuals and as groups. Earth is highly diverse and has many different ecosystems, each with its own flora and fauna. The specific resources available in different places have, therefore, influenced how humans develop.

Water, in particular, has proved vital in determining the course of human civilizations. As humans require water daily to survive, even more than they do food, proximity to water has always been of utmost necessity. Many human settlements originated adjacent to sources, and only in time expanded to other areas. Water is also essential for the growth of plants, which form a considerable portion of the human diet. In the wild, edible plants grow in places where they can thrive but may not be conveniently located for harvesting by humans. Therefore, humans gradually learned to grow plants themselves in places of their own choice. Humans also diverted water sources to new areas for themselves and to irrigate crops, thus transforming ecosystems.

Another important factor in the relationships between humans and nature has been the role of other animals. From small pests, such as weevils and rodents, to predators, including crocodiles and bears, many species of animals have often posed threats to humans, and conflict increased as humans expanded into environments inhabited by other creatures. On the other hand, animals are invaluable to humans because they can provide sustenance and clothing. This led to hunting and domestication of animal species. Domestication of both plants and animals involves humans breeding species to fit their own needs, which leads to new qualities that would normally not appear in the wild.

However, despite the considerable role that humans can play in altering environments, these changes have remained limited to local levels for much of human history. This does not mean that humans did not affect their ecosystems; some Native American tribes, for instance, used regular fires or hunting methods to maintain environments suitable for their needs. Even so, for much of human existence, nature was seen not simply as an obstacle but rather a power of its own right that was above human interference. Natural phenomena such as severe weather, diseases, and famine all kept human populations in check. Many pantheons of deities center on the gods' roles as arbitrary powers in the natural world, which reflects the lack of influence that humans had in the larger course of environmental changes.

Therefore, natural resources such as water and food were often seen as forces to be respected. Natural environments were recognized as vital regions, and alterations to fully exploit the resources were limited so that the resources could remain adequately sustainable. Riparian customs meant that water was the right of those with immediate access to it, and ownership changed accordingly with who lived nearby. However, increasing industrialization meant that natural resources such as water and lumber became resources that could be commoditized. In addition, appropriation gave water rights to those individuals or businesses that had first used the resource instead of being based on physical proximity.

Another instrumental change in the relationship between humans and nature is the increasing global connections worldwide. In many cases, earlier changes to environments occurred at local levels, with travel between different regions requiring considerable time and effort. The ability to travel around the world quickly has sharply altered that dynamic. Many local ecosystems, and the human cultures that developed accordingly, originated in separate circumstances that created unique plants and animals. Now products from one part of the world can be transported to entirely different environments and create new exchanges of goods. In some cases, the transferred species escape into the wild, and they often have traits for which the local environments are not prepared. This can result in invasive species that quickly grow and overpower native species.

A key symbol of artificial environments created by humans since early civilization has been the city, which is a human center of habitation that exists separate from the countryside around it. The creation of cities usually requires significant changes to the environment in which it is located, and the city must provide for the needs of residents without being compromised by nature. Yet the city has always remained connected to the rest of the world and to nature. Because a city generally lacks the capacity for agriculture and few natural resources are located within its confines, urban populations rely on resources from outlying areas for nourishment. The city, in turn, acts as a processing center for nearby settlements and offers rural workers and farmers the opportunity to sell their goods to a larger market.

Furthermore, the city, while an artificial construct, is still an environment in its own right. Although many species of animals have perished with the creation of cities, others, such as coyotes and pigeons, have adapted to urban life, thereby creating new ecosystems within cities. Natural connections within cities used to be stronger and more common because people would raise livestock within the city and regularly reuse garbage for livestock feed. While less hygienic, this helped stimulate natural cycles within the city. Recent efforts in many cities to create natural pockets, such as parks and community gardens, have also strengthened the ties between cities and the natural world. In a sense, the city reflects humanity's mixed relationship with nature as a whole: while humans continue to reshape the environment, they also remain linked to nature.

Uses of Geography

Geography helps people better understand the role that location plays in the past, present, and future. Historians make frequent use of maps in their studies to get a clearer picture of how history unfolded. Since the beginning of history, many different groups have fought conflicts that originated from struggles for land or other resources; therefore, knowing the location and borders of different empires and kingdoms helps reveal how they interacted with each other. In addition, environmental factors, such as access to water and the proximity of mountains, often help to shape the course of civilizations. Even single events and battles make more sense with maps that show how the warring sides met and maneuvered.

Furthermore, determining the geography of historical events, in particular geographical change over time, is essential due to the role that physical settings play in the present. Many important geographic landmarks continue to exist in the world, and they are often commemorated for their roles in history. Yet the physical geography has sometimes changed significantly. For instance, the Aswan Dam significantly reshaped the flow of the Nile River, which was the heart of ancient Egyptian society; without knowledge of the past geography, it is difficult to fully understand the civilization's context and how it differs from the present reality.

History also depends on archaeology, the study of human artifacts, for the evidence necessary to make conclusions about cultures. These items are generally buried, which helps preserve the artifacts yet makes it difficult to locate them. Historical geography helps in that regard by ascertaining key sites of human activity that could potentially retain artifacts. These insights help archaeologists discover new aspects of ancient cultures, which in turn strengthen historical arguments. Maps themselves sometimes serve as artifacts in their own right because they help reveal how humans of earlier periods viewed the world.

Along with the historical implications, knowledge of the world's geography remains important for people in the present day. The most immediate use of geography is in navigation. Tools such as Global Positioning Systems have helped improve navigation, but they too represent an approach to geography that demonstrates how it continues to have a fundamental role in human society. Humans have even begun mapping the trajectories of planets and even their individual terrains.

However, beyond the direct uses for navigation, geography is invaluable in comprehending modern cultures and events. Whether through their proximity to other nations or their relation to environmental features, such as forests and deserts, societies remain deeply connected to their geographical settings. Therefore, to fully understand current affairs, such as wars and poverty, people must have a firm grasp on geographic settings. For instance, a study of nations in Africa, many of which continue to suffer from poverty, would require a close examination of geographic factors. The borders of many African countries were arbitrarily determined during the colonial period, and the conflicts of ethnic groups divided by these borders have influenced current struggles. On the environmental end, some nations have been significantly affected by desertification and deforestation, which makes studies of their ecological geography important as well.

Two recent key developments have made geography more important than ever before. The first change is the globalization of culture, economics, and politics. For much of human history, geography was most important at localized scales. Many people spent their entire lives in isolated communities, with intermittent trade between different centers. Geography was still important, but many people did not need to be familiar with anything other than their immediate locations. Today, on the other hand, places around the world are intricately connected to each other. Travel is relatively easy and quick and enables people to venture between different regions like never before. Areas that used to be geographically isolated from each other can now exchange ideas and products on an unprecedented scale.

In addition, due to the multinational relationship of politics, conflicts that would have been geographically isolated in the past can have international ramifications. Latin American revolutions, such as in Nicaragua during the Cold War, were seen as having larger implications in the struggle between American democracy and Soviet communism, which led to foreign interventions and wars that affected multiple countries. Therefore, geography is critical to not only addressing the current effects of globalization but also understanding how global interactions may influence international politics and economics in the future.

The second major factor in geography's role in modern events is the rising importance of environmental policies and climate change. Scientific developments have increasingly revealed how the planet as a whole can be considered a large ecosystem in its own right, with its own strengths and frailties. A change in one part of the environment, such as industrialization in India and China, can have larger consequences for neighboring regions and for the world as a whole. Geographical insights help to show how the world functions and how humans can work to improve their relationship with the natural world.

Moreover, as climate changes become more evident in the world, geography helps illustrate the effects of new environmental phenomena. For instance, scientists have studied the topography of nations to determine how rising sea levels will alter the land via flooding, and local and national governments are using these findings to prepare for the coming changes. Furthermore, the continued scrutiny of the state of Earth's geography reveals how climate change is transforming the planet at this very moment, as regional climates shift and islands vanish under the sea. As a result, geography will continue to have a role in future developments.

Different Cultural Backgrounds

When studying different cultures, it is important to realize that cultures are always changing in response to individuals and groups within it. Therefore, one must avoid stereotyping members of a certain culture or overgeneralizing. For example, American culture is highly diverse with multiple ethnic groups. Many ethnic communities have resided in the United States for generations, so it is incorrect to label them as a foreign culture, yet each group must be closely examined to understand American culture as a whole.

This diversity within larger classifications of cultures can be seen with Native Americans. There are many different tribes of Native Americans, and each has its own unique history and characteristics. Nevertheless, a few general qualities describe most Native American groups. First of all, Native Americans continue to struggle to escape the poverty that they were historically forced into during white settlement of the United States. Many, but not all, tribes have been traditionally matrilineal—with ancestry defined through female lineage—and emphasized communal sharing and a sustainable relationship with nature, but the American government often suppressed these customs. This has led many Native Americans to begin protecting their surviving heritage, including their rights to traditional religious practices and access to historical artifacts.

South of the United States, Mexico has a vibrant yet troubled culture. Mexico was one of the principal colonies of Spain, and the culture is therefore a diverse blend of Spanish and native customs. One

enduring legacy of Spain's rule is the prominence of Roman Catholicism, albeit mixed with pre-Spanish concepts; for instance, the traditional Day of the Dead embodies both pre-Columbian and Christian ideals. On the other hand, the Spanish system of large estates created significant class disparities. Furthermore, Mexico's war for independence and conflicts with other nations drastically destabilized its government, and the nation continues to struggle with corruption and violence. Still, Mexico retains a rich culture that celebrates its complex history. Mexican families are generally large and cooperate to help each other.

French national identity is relatively new because regional ties were prevalent until the French Revolution in the 1790s. A rising sense of nationalism unites French culture today, but various regions maintain their own local traditions. Much of France has been traditionally agricultural, but the globalization of the food trade has disrupted local markets and led to mass migration to cities. Reflecting Catholic values, most of France's families follow a nuclear model of a two-parent household with children.

South Africa is culturally and ethnically diverse, but historically white settlers used apartheid to oppress and isolate other groups. However, previously marginalized ethnic groups are now actively working to assert their own identity within South Africa. Rural communities tend to be more traditional, while people within cities have adopted new values. South Africa is largely patriarchal with defined gender roles that give men dominance over women. Efforts to strengthen South Africa's industries have depleted many of its natural resources and created a growing environmental crisis that is particularly devastating to rural populations.

Laying claim to the legacies of ancient Persia, Iran's culture was at the crossroads of trade routes between multiple continents for centuries, which gave it a long and diverse background. Iran is primarily Islamic, with the majority of Muslims belonging to the Shi'a faith. They believe that their religious leaders, imams, are divinely appointed as the religious successors, known as caliphs, to the prophet Muhammad; even so, other religions such as Judaism and Zoroastrianism are also practiced in the country. Iran's patriarchal culture generally restricts the role of women, but women have nevertheless become more involved in the civil service, sciences, and other fields.

Russia's culture is built on a rich history but has been especially influenced by the dominance of communism until the Soviet Union's dissolution in 1991. The use of state police and other agents to enforce government policies led to a sense of paranoia and distrust of anyone outside the family. On the other hand, this situation created strong support networks within families that led to strong relationships with relatives. The Soviet Union's drive to industrialize also led to numerous current environmental issues across Russia.

As with Russia, the People's Republic of China's modern culture is deeply influenced by decades of Communist rule. Under the leadership of Mao, China enacted massive efforts to strengthen Chinese industry and agriculture at the cost of environmental damage; China continues to undergo intense industrial operations in the present, which has caused pollution in the cities. On the other hand, China takes great pride in its long traditions and history that date back thousands of years. China has been traditionally patriarchal, and children have been expected to respect and care for their elders. Chinese culture is not monolithic, and there are many different ethnic groups within the country, including the Han, Manchu, and Uyghur. However, the one-child policy from 1978 to 2015 has destabilized long-term family dynamics by putting considerable pressure on single children to look after their parents.

Japan's family structure has also been disrupted in the modern era. Japanese culture is built on a sense of interdependence within families and the community as a whole, but a low birthrate has led to a rising number of elderly relatives and few children, which has unsettled the traditional foundation. Even so, Japan embraces a blend of modern advancements and traditional customs. Japanese culture is built on multiple layers of social status, and people use different forms of language depending on their relationship with others. As a result, traditional Japanese society is highly formal, but recent generations have become more open to new ideas. As Japan's islands have limited space and resources, it has been at the forefront of many natural conservation efforts, although some controversial traditions, such as whaling, still persist.

Economics

Terms and Concepts of Economics

Economics form a key component of human society. Studies of economies can be divided between macroeconomics, which considers the larger economy as a whole, and microeconomics, which focuses on the actions of smaller groups, households, and individuals. However, the most basic principle of economics comes down to resources. A resource can be defined as an object or material that can be used for some purpose. Natural resources come directly from the environment, whereas items altered through human activity are considered manufactured goods. Resources can be further divided into renewable resources, which are gradually replenished given enough time and proper circumstances, and nonrenewable resources, which regenerate slowly or not at all. In addition, there are four main types of economic resources: land, which includes most natural resources; labor, the services provided by individuals to create products; capital, which encompasses human-manufactured resources; and entrepreneurship, the process in which individuals utilize available resources for business ventures that generate new products.

Early on, human civilizations functioned using a barter system, where people would trade certain goods for other items. It remains common in some parts of the world today. However, the difficulty of storing and transporting products, such as livestock and minerals, for exchange, led to the development of monetary systems. Money is an object, such as a coin or a paper bill, which can be exchanged for any commercial product given enough money. It is important to note that money on its own often has no worth; paper money, for example, is a rather flimsy material with little actual use outside of its monetary worth. It only has value when members of a society agree that it can be used to make purchases.

Due to the artificial nature of money within societies, prices fluctuate depending on the supply and demand of products. Supply refers to the available quantity of a specific good or resource. In contrast, demand accounts for the quantity that buyers wish to obtain. These two factors influence several economic patterns. The law of supply states that the quantity available for purchase is directly related to the price, while the law of demand states that the price of an item is inversely related to the demand for the item. Thus, raising prices increases supply and reduces demand.

Furthermore, the value of money in part depends on the amount that is circulated in the market. A surplus of money has the potential to devalue the currency, which lowers the worth of each unit of money. This process, called inflation, has a detrimental effect on the economy as prices generally increase. However, the opposite trend, deflation, can also be detrimental; thus, political leaders usually strive to find a stable balance between the two ends of the spectrum. By finding equilibrium between supply and demand, an economy's prices remain relatively stable.

Economies, by nature, have limited access to certain resources, which creates a conflict between supply and demand. Scarcity occurs when the demand for a product exceeds its availability. Scarcity in part depends on the choices of individuals as they determine which products they want more than others. Choices, in turn, are influenced by the perceived costs of pursuing certain options over others. The costs and benefits of specific choices often differ depending on the individuals' perceptions of the options. When people believe that a certain service's or product's benefits outweigh its necessary costs, they may choose to pay more for the desired benefits. It is important to realize that the laws of supply and demand are not absolute, and they may fluctuate depending on the situation.

Supply and demand can be further affected by monopolies, in which an individual or group holds sole or primary access to a given product or service. The individuals controlling a monopoly can limit the supply in a manner that best suits themselves but not necessarily the consumers. Monopolies are often asserted through the creation of barriers that limit access to the resources or services. For instance, patents give exclusive rights for inventions and discoveries to their respective creators or the firms that sponsored them. Without restraints, a monopoly can significantly limit economic development and prosperity of a society.

Effects of Economics on Population, Resources, and Technology

Economics are closely linked with the flow of resources, technology, and population in societies. The use of natural resources, such as water and fossil fuels, has always depended in part on the pressures of the economy. A supply of a specific good may be limited in the market, but with sufficient demand the sellers are incentivized to increase the available quantity. Unfortunately, the demand for certain objects can often be unlimited, and a high price or limited supply may prevent consumers from obtaining the product or service. If the sellers succumb to the consumers' demand and continue to exploit a scarce resource, supply could potentially be exhausted.

The resources for most products, both renewable and nonrenewable, are finite. This is a particularly difficult issue with nonrenewable resources, but even renewable resources often have limits: organic products such as trees and animals require stable populations and sufficient habitats to support those populations. Furthermore, the costs of certain decisions can have detrimental effects on other resources. For example, industrialization provides economic benefits in many countries but also has had the negative effect of polluting surrounding environments; the pollution, in turn, often eliminates or harms fish, plants, and other potential resources.

The control of resources within an economy is particularly important in determining how resources are used. While the demand may change with the choices of consumers, the range of supply depends on the objectives of the people producing the goods. They determine how much of their supply they allot for sale, and in the case of monopolies, they might have sole access to the resource. They might choose to limit their use of the resources or instead gather more to meet the demand. As they pay for the products, consumers can choose which sellers they rely on for the supply. In the case of a monopoly, though, consumers have little influence over the company's decision because there is no alternative supplier. Therefore, the function of supply within an economy can drastically influence how the resources are exploited.

The availability of resources, in turn, affects the human population. Humans require basic resources such as food and water for survival, as well as additional resources for healthy lifestyles. Therefore, access to these resources helps determine the survival rate of humans. For much of human existence, economies have had limited ability to extract resources from the natural world, which restricted the growth rate of populations. However, the development of new technologies, combined with increasing demand for certain products, has pushed resource use to a new level. On the one hand, this led to higher living standards that ensured that fewer people would die. However, this has also brought mass population growth. Admittedly, countries with higher standards of living often have lower birthrates. Even so, the increasing exploitation of resources has sharply increased the world's population as a whole to unsustainable levels. The rising population leads, in turn, to more demand for resources that cannot be met. This creates poverty, reduced living conditions, and higher death rates. As a result, economics can significantly influence local and world population levels.

Technology is also intricately related to population, resources, and economics. The role of demand within economies has incentivized people to innovate new technologies that enable societies to have a higher quality of life and greater access to resources. Entrepreneurs expand technologies by finding ways to create new products for the market. The Industrial Revolution, in particular, illustrates the relationship between economics and technology because the ambitions of businessmen led to new infrastructure that enabled more efficient and sophisticated use of resources. Many of these inventions reduced the amount of work necessary for individuals and allowed the development of leisure activities, which in turn created new economic markets. However, economic systems can also limit the growth of technology. In the case of monopolies, the lack of alternative suppliers reduces the incentive to meet and exceed consumer expectations. Moreover, as demonstrated by the effects of economics on resources, technology's increasing ability to extract resources can lead to their depletion and create significant issues that need to be addressed.

Government's Role in Economics and the Impact of Economics on Government

Governments have considerable influence over the flow of economies, which makes it important to understand the relationships between them. When a government has full control over the economic decisions of a nation, it is called a command system. This was the case in many absolute monarchies such as eighteenth-century France; King Louis XIV built his economy on the concept of mercantilism, which believed that the state should manage all resources, particularly by accumulating gold and silver. This system of economics discouraged exports and thereby limited trade.

In contrast, the market system is guided by the concept of capitalism, in which individuals and businesses have the freedom to manage their economic decisions. This allows for private property and increases the opportunities for entrepreneurship and trade. Early proponents of capitalism emphasized *laissez-faire* policies, which means "let it be," and argued that the government should not be involved with the economy at all. They believe the market is guided by the concept of self-interest and that individuals will optimally work for their personal success. However, individuals' interests do not necessarily correlate with the needs of the overall economy. For instance, during a financial recession, consumers may decide to save up their money rather than make purchases; doing so helps them in the short run but further reduces demand in a slumping economy. Therefore, most capitalist governments still assert a degree of control over their economies while still allowing for private business.

Likewise, many command system economies, such as monarchical France, still relied heavily on private businesses maintained by wealthy businessmen. With the end of most absolute monarchies, communism has been the primary form of command system economies in the modern era. Communism is a form of socialism that emphasizes communal ownership of property and government control over production. The high degree of government control gives more stability to the economy, but it also creates considerable flaws. The monopolization of the economy by the government limits its ability to respond to local economic conditions because certain regions often have unique resources and needs.

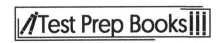

With the collapse of the Soviet Union and other communist states, command systems have been largely replaced with market systems.

The U.S. government helps to manage the nation's economy through a market system in several ways. First and foremost, the federal government is responsible for the production of money for use within the economy; depending on how the government manages the monetary flow, it may lead to a stable economy, deflation, or inflation. Second, state and federal governments impose taxes on individuals, corporations, and goods. For instance, a tariff might be imposed on imports in order to stimulate demand for local goods in the economy. Third, the government can pass laws that require additional regulation or inspections. In addition, the government has passed antitrust laws to inhibit the growth of private monopolies, which could limit free growth in the market system. Debates continue over whether the government should take further action to manage private industries or reduce its control over the private sector.

Just as governments can affect the direction of the economy, the state of the economy can have significant implications on government policies. Financial stability is critical in maintaining a prosperous state. A healthy economy will allow for new developments that contribute to the nation's growth and create jobs. On the other hand, an economic crisis, such as a recession or depression, can gravely damage a government's stability. Without a stable economy, business opportunities plummet, and people begin to lose income and employment. This, in turn, leads to frustration and discontent in the population, which can lead to criticism of the government. This could very well lead to demands for new leadership to resolve the economic crisis.

The dangers of a destabilized economy can be seen with the downfall of the French monarchy. The mercantilist approach to economics stifled French trade. Furthermore, regional aristocracies remained exempt from government taxes, which limited the government's revenues. This was compounded by expensive wars and poor harvests that led to criticism of King Louis XIV's government. The problems persisted for decades, and Louis XIV was forced to convene the Estates-General, a legislative body of representatives from across France, to address the crisis. The economic crises at the end of the eighteenth century were critical in the beginning of the French Revolution. Those financial issues, in turn, at least partially stemmed from both the government's control of the economy through mercantilism and its inability to impose economic authority over local regions.

Government and Citizenship

Connections Between Causes and Effects

When examining the historical narratives of events, it is important to understand the relationship between causes and effects. A cause can be defined as something, whether an event, social change, or other factor, that contributes to the occurrence of certain events; the results of causes are called effects. Those terms may seem simple enough, but they have drastic implications on how one explores history. Events such as the American Revolution or the Civil Rights Movement may appear to occur spontaneously, but a closer examination will reveal that these events depended on earlier phenomena and patterns that influenced the course of history.

For example, although the battles at Concord and Lexington may seem to be instantaneous eruptions of violence during the American Revolution, they stemmed from a variety of factors. The most obvious influences behind those two battles were the assortment of taxes and policies imposed on the Thirteen Colonies following the French and Indian War from 1754 to 1763. Taxation without direct representation, combined with the deployment of British soldiers to enforce these policies, greatly increased American resistance. Earlier events, such as the Boston Massacre and the Boston Tea Party, similarly stemmed from conflicts between British soldiers and local colonists over perceived tyranny and rebelliousness. Therefore, the start of the American Revolution progressed from preceding developments.

Furthermore, there can be multiple causes and effects for any situation. The existence of multiple causes can be seen through the settling of the American West. Many historians have emphasized the role of manifest destiny—the national vision of expanding across the continent—as a driving force behind the growth of the United States. Yet there were many different influences behind the expansion westward. Northern abolitionists and southern planters saw the frontier as a way to either extend or limit slavery. Economic opportunities in the West also encouraged travel westward, as did the gradual pacification of Native American tribes.

Even an individual cause can be subdivided into smaller factors or stretched out in a gradual process. Although there were numerous issues that led to the Civil War, slavery was the primary cause. However, that topic stretched back to the very founding of the nation, and the existence of slavery was a controversial topic during the creation of the Declaration of Independence and the Constitution. The abolition movement as a whole did not start until the 1830s, but nevertheless, slavery is a cause that gradually grew more important over the following decades. In addition, opponents of slavery were divided by different motivations—some believed that it stifled the economy, while others focused on moral issues.

On the other end of the spectrum, a single event can have numerous results. The rise of the telegraph, for example, had several effects on American history. The telegraph allowed news to travel much quicker and turned events into immediate national news, such as the sinking of the USS Maine, which sparked the Spanish-American War. In addition, the telegraph helped make railroads run more efficiently by improving the links between stations. The faster speed of both travel and communications led to a shift in time itself, and localized times were replaced by standardized time zones across the nation.

The importance of grasping cause-and-effect relationships is critical in interpreting the growth and development of the Civil Rights Movement. Historical narratives of the movement often focus on charismatic individuals, such as Martin Luther King Jr., and they certainly played a key leadership role. Even so, elements of the movement had already emerged in previous decades through the growth of the National Association for the Advancement of Colored People (NAACP) and other organizations. Several factors proved critical to the formation of civil rights organizations during the 1950s. African American veterans returning from World War II, as well as those continuing to serve in the military, called for equal rights. Furthermore, the United States' role as a key member of the United Nations, which included African countries, required the federal government to take racial discrimination seriously.

A specific example in the Civil Rights Movement is the sit-ins during 1960, in which black and white students defied segregation policies in restaurants and other establishments. The wave is often thought to originate from spontaneous activism by students in Greensboro, North Carolina. However, there had already been other sit-ins, such as at Royal Ice Cream Parlor in Durham, North Carolina, in 1957. In fact, the sit-ins would not have spread as quickly without a preexisting network of activists across the nation, which in part stemmed from the growth of organizations through various local and national movements.

By looking at such cases closely, it becomes clear that no event occurs without one—if not multiple—causes behind it, and that each historical event can have a variety of direct and indirect consequences.

One of the most critical elements of cause-and-effect relationships is how they are relevant not only in studying history but also in contemporary events. Much of the current political debate about social security and health care stems from FDR's New Deal in the 1930s, and at the time some people criticized the programs for being too extensive, while others argued that he did not go far enough with his vision. Current environmental concerns have their origins in long-term issues that reach back centuries. The United States' mixed history of global isolation and foreign intervention continues to influence foreign policy approaches today. Most of all, people must realize that events and developments today will likely have a number of consequences later on. Therefore, the study of cause and effect remains vital in understanding the past, the present, and the future.

Nature, Purpose, and Forms of Government

The United States of America's government, as outlined by the Constitution, is designed to serve as a compromise between democracy and preceding monarchical systems. The American Revolution brought independence from Britain and freedom from its aristocratic system of governance. On the other hand, the short-lived Articles of Confederation revealed the significant weaknesses of state-based governance with limited national control. By dividing power between local, state, and federal governments, the United States can uphold its value of individual liberties while, nevertheless, giving a sense of order to the country.

The federal government, which is in charge of laws that affect the entire nation, is split into three main branches: executive, judicial, and legislative. It is important to realize that the three segments of the federal government are intended to stand as equal counterparts to the others, and that none of them are "in charge." The executive branch centers on the president, the vice president, and the cabinet. The president and vice president are elected every four years. Also known as the commander-in-chief, the president is the official head of state and serves as the nation's head diplomat and military leader. The vice president acts as the president of the Senate in the legislative branch, while the president appoints members of the cabinet to lead agencies, including the Treasury and Department of Defense. However, the president can only sign and veto laws and cannot initiate them himself.

Instead, the legislative branch, specifically Congress, proposes and debates laws. Congress is bicameral because it is divided into two separate legislative houses. Each state's representation in the House of Representatives is determined proportionally by population, with the total number of voting seats limited to 435. The Senate, in contrast, has only two members per state and a total of one hundred senators. Members of both houses are intended to represent the interests of the constituents in their home states and to bring their concerns to a national level. Ideas for laws, called bills, are proposed in either chamber and then are voted upon according to the body's rules; should the bill pass the first round of voting, the other legislative chamber must approve it before it can be sent to the president. Congress also has a variety of other powers, such as the rights to declare war, collect taxes, and impeach the president.

The judicial branch, though it cannot pass laws itself, serves to interpret the laws. At the federal level, this is done through several tiers of judicial bodies. At the top, the Supreme Court consists of judges appointed by the president; these judges serve for life, unless they resign from their position or are removed by Congress for improper behavior. The Supreme Court's decisions in trials and other judgments rest on the justices' interpretations of the Constitution and enacted laws. As the Constitution remains fundamental to the American legal system, the Supreme Court's rulings on how laws follow or fail to uphold the Constitution have powerful implications on future rulings. Beneath the Supreme Court, there are a number of other federal judicial bodies—courts of appeals, district courts, and courts of special jurisdiction.

While the federal government manages the nation as a whole, state governments address issues pertaining to their specific territory. In the past, states claimed the right, known as nullification, to refuse to enforce federal laws that they considered unconstitutional. However, conflicts between state and federal authority, particularly in the South in regard to first, slavery, and later, discrimination, have led to increased federal power, and states cannot defy federal laws. Even so, the Tenth Amendment limits federal power to those specifically granted in the Constitution, and the rest of the powers are retained by the states and citizens. Therefore, individual state governments are left in charge of decisions with immediate effects on their citizens, such as state laws and taxes. Like the federal government, state governments consist of executive, judicial, and legislative branches, but the exact configuration of those branches varies between states. For instance, while most states follow the bicameral structure of Congress, Nebraska has only a single legislative chamber. State governments have considerable authority within their states, but they cannot impose their power on other states, nor can they secede from the United States.

Local governments, which include town governments, county boards, library districts, and other agencies, are especially variable in their composition. They often reflect the overall views of their state governments but also have their own values, rules, and structures. Generally, local governments function in a democratic fashion, although the exact form of government depends on its role. Depending on the location within the state, local government may have considerable or minimal authority based on the population and prosperity of the area; some counties may have strong influence in the state, while others may have a limited impact.

Native American tribes are treated as dependent nations that answer to the federal government but may be immune to state jurisdiction. As with local governments, the exact form of governance is left up to the tribes, which ranges from small councils to complex systems of government. Other U.S. territories, including the District of Columbia (site of Washington, D.C.) and acquired islands, such as Guam and Puerto Rico, have representation within Congress, but their legislators cannot vote on bills.

As members of a democracy, U.S. citizens are empowered to elect most government leaders, but the process varies between branch and level of government. Presidential elections at the national scale use the Electoral College system. Rather than electing the president directly, citizens cast their ballots to select electors, who generally vote for a specific candidate, that represent each state in the college. Legislative branches at the federal and state level are also determined by elections, albeit without an Electoral College. In some areas, judges are elected, but in other states judges are appointed by elected officials. It should also be noted that the two-party system was not built into the Constitution but gradually emerged over time.

Key Documents and Speeches in U.S. History

With more than two hundred years of history, American leaders have produced a number of important documents and speeches. One of the most essential is the Declaration of Independence, which the Second Continental Congress ratified on July 4, 1776. Although many historians and politicians have drawn upon the words of the Declaration to demonstrate the American ideal of freedom, most of them focus on the preamble, which focuses on the necessity of fair government and the right to overthrow

tyrants. The main body of the document consists of a set of grievances against King George III. Still, this document was instrumental in American history because it asserted American independence from Great Britain. Even so, it is important to note that the Declaration did not immediately lead to the United States; the document does not outline the government of the soon-to-be independent colonies, and independence would not become reality until Britain agreed.

The colonies' first blueprint for government was the Articles of Confederation, which was ratified in 1777. The document declared that the confederacy would be called the United States of America and that the individual states would have "a firm league of friendship" with each other. The emphasis on friendship and cooperation highlights how the confederation was a voluntary effort that states could follow or ignore as they saw fit. Still, the document also revealed the importance of obeying decisions made by Congress as a whole; while this was not very effective during the confederation period, the framework would live on to a degree in the following Constitution.

Much like the Declaration of Independence, the 1787 Constitution of the United States is most remembered for the preamble, which takes a more philosophical approach. However, the body of the Constitution is highly complex, and it covers the framework and responsibilities of the different branches of the federal government and the limits to state power. These details are very important and help to define the key institutions within the government. To resolve later issues not addressed in the Constitution, the fifth article in the document establishes a process to modify the government, and the first ten amendments are known as the *Bill of Rights*. Under the Tenth Amendment, powers not specifically allotted to Congress by the Constitution are reserved for the people and to individual states.

George Washington was the first president of the United States, and his administration set many precedents for the nation, particularly with his Farewell Address. In it, he noted the rise of regional feelings, and he urged citizens to uphold their duty to the nation above sectionalism because he felt that America was strongest when united. The issue of regional conflicts and national identity would become increasingly important in years to come, especially during the Civil War. Washington also argued against intervention in European affairs, and this warning would become the cornerstone for advocates of American isolation. On the other hand, his advice that political parties are detrimental to democracy failed to halt the development of the party system.

Washington's fears about sectional conflict were confirmed at the start of the Civil War, when the southern states violently seceded from the Union. As the president during that tumultuous time, Abraham Lincoln was seen by many to embody the Union as a whole. This can be demonstrated through his Gettysburg Address in November of 1863. After the difficult and bloody Battle of Gettysburg ended in a Union victory, crowds gathered for the dedication of the Soldiers' National Cemetery. Although he was not the main speaker of the event, Lincoln's short yet eloquent speech proved to be the most significant. Drawing upon the Declaration of Independence's assertion that "all men are created equal," he argued that the current war was a test of that ideal. More than that, he emphasized the importance of the United States as a whole and argued that it must endure as a Union for the sake of the world.

Earlier that year in January, Lincoln had already indicated his opposition to slavery through the Emancipation Proclamation. Although it was an executive order instead of a law passed by Congress, this document was not challenged by the courts and helped determine the objectives of the Civil War. The proclamation asserted that all slaves in Confederate territories were free. One must note that some southern states remained in the Union, and therefore, were not affected by this proclamation. Even so, the order helped establish a basis for later laws and amendments that would end slavery in the United States.

Another presidential attempt to set a new precedent for American policy was Woodrow Wilson's Fourteen Points, which were outlined in a speech he gave to Congress in 1918 after the United States had entered World War I. Wilson saw the United States as a protector of democracy in the world and said that we could reform world policy by fighting in the war. For instance, Wilson called for an end to private negotiations, which had contributed to the secret alliances behind the war. Most of all, he argued for nations to come together in an international body to determine world policies. The negotiations after the war only partially fulfilled Wilson's ambitions by creating a weak League of Nations, but his vision of U.S. involvement in global affairs would become a key aspect of American foreign policy.

Even as the United States began playing a more active role on the international stage of politics, internal issues such as civil rights remained important, as shown in Martin Luther King Jr.'s "I Have a Dream" speech. A leader in the civil rights movement, King gave his speech as part of the 1963 March on Washington. Drawing on Lincoln's past speech at Gettysburg, King argued that America's journey to true equality was not over yet. His references to biblical passages gave the speech a spiritual tone, but he also mentioned specific locations across the nation to signify how local struggles were tied with national consequences. By emphasizing his optimism, King's speech reflects not only civil rights activism but also the American dream of freedom and progress.

Rights and Responsibilities of Citizenship in a Democracy

Citizens living in a democracy have several rights and responsibilities to uphold. The first duty is that they uphold the established laws of the government. In a democracy, a system of nationwide laws is necessary to ensure that there is some degree of order. Therefore, citizens must try to obey the laws and also help enforce them because a law that is inadequately enforced, such as early civil rights laws in the South, is almost useless. Optimally, a democratic society's laws will be accepted and followed by the community as a whole.

However, conflict can occur when an unjust law is passed. For instance, much of the civil rights movement centered around Jim Crow laws in the South that supported segregation between black and whites. Yet these practices were encoded in state laws, which created a dilemma for African Americans who wanted equality but also wanted to respect the law. Fortunately, a democracy offers a degree of protection from such laws by creating a system in which government leaders and policies are constantly open to change in accordance with the will of citizens. Citizens can influence the laws that are passed by voting for and electing members of the legislative and executive branches to represent them at the local, state, and national levels.

This, however, requires citizens to be especially vigilant in protecting their liberties because they cannot depend solely on the existing government to meet their needs. To assert their role in a democracy, citizens should be active voters and speak out on issues that concern them. Even with these safeguards, it is possible for systems to be implemented that inhibit active participation. For instance, many southern states had laws that prevented blacks from voting. Under such circumstances, civil rights leaders felt that they had no choice but to resist the laws in order to defend their personal rights. Once voting became possible, civil rights groups strove to ensure that their votes counted by changing state and national policy.

An extension of citizens' voting rights is their ability to run as elected officials. By becoming leaders in the government, citizens can demonstrate their engagement and help determine government policy. The involvement of citizens as a whole in the selection of leaders is vital in a democracy because it helps

to prevent the formation of an elite cadre that does not answer to the public. Without the engagement of citizens who run for office, voters are limited in their ability to select candidates that appeal to them. In this case, voting options would become stagnant, which inhibits the ability of the nation to grow and change over time. As long as citizens are willing to take a stand for their vision of America, America's government will remain dynamic and diverse.

These features of a democracy give it the potential to reshape itself continually in response to new developments in society. In order for a democracy to function, it is of the utmost importance that citizens care about the course of politics and be aware of current issues. Apathy among citizens is a constant problem that threatens the endurance of democracies. Citizens should have a desire to take part in the political process, or else they simply accept the status quo and fail to fulfill their role as citizens. Moreover, they must have acute knowledge of the political processes and the issues that they can address as citizens. A fear among the Founding Fathers was the prevalence of mob rule, in which the common people did not take interest in politics except to vote for their patrons; this was the usual course of politics in the colonial era, as the common people left the decisions to the established elites. Without understanding the world around them, citizens may not fully grasp the significance of political actions and thereby fail to make wise decisions in that regard. Therefore, citizens must stay informed about current affairs, ranging from local to national or global matters, so that they can properly address them as voters or elected leaders.

Furthermore, knowledge of the nation's history is essential for healthy citizenship. History continues to have an influence on present political decisions. For instance, Supreme Court rulings often take into account previous legal precedents and verdicts, so it is important to know about those past events and how they affect the current processes. It is especially critical that citizens are aware of the context in which laws were established because it helps clarify the purpose of those laws. For instance, an understanding of the problems with the Articles of Confederation allows people to comprehend some of the reasons behind the framework of the Constitution. In addition, history as a whole shapes the course of societies and the world; therefore, citizens should draw on this knowledge of the past to realize the full consequences of current actions. Issues such as climate change, conflict in the Middle East, and civil rights struggles are rooted in events and cultural developments that reach back centuries and should be addressed.

Therefore, education is a high priority in democracies because it has the potential to instill generations of citizens with the right mind-set and knowledge required to do their part in shaping the nation. Optimally, education should cover a variety of different subjects, ranging from mathematics to biology, so that individuals can explore whatever paths they wish to take in life. Even so, social studies are especially important because students should understand how democracies function and understand the history of the nation and world. Historical studies should cover national and local events as well because they help provide the basis for the understanding of contemporary politics. Social studies courses should also address the histories of foreign nations because contemporary politics increasingly has global consequences. In addition, history lessons should remain open to multiple perspectives, even those that might criticize a nation's past actions, because citizens should be exposed to diverse perspectives that they can apply as voters and leaders.

Practice Questions

1. Which of the following correctly lists the Thirteen Colonies?
   a. Connecticut, Delaware, Georgia, Maryland, Massachusetts, New Hampshire, New Jersey, New York, North Carolina, Pennsylvania, Rhode Island, South Carolina, Virginia
   b. Carolina, Connecticut, Delaware, Maryland, Massachusetts, New Hampshire, New Jersey, New York, Ohio, Pennsylvania, Rhode Island, Virginia, West Virginia
   c. Connecticut, Delaware, Georgia, Maine, Massachusetts, New Hampshire, New Jersey, New York, North Carolina, South Carolina, Pennsylvania, Vermont, Virginia
   d. Canada, Connecticut, Delaware, Georgia, Florida, Maryland, Massachusetts, New Hampshire, New York, North Carolina, Rhode Island, South Carolina, Virginia

2. Which of the following was NOT an issue contributing to the American Revolution?
   a. Increased taxes on the colonies
   b. Britain's defeat in the French and Indian War
   c. The stationing of British soldiers in colonists' homes
   d. Changes in class relations

3. The election of a presidential candidate from which party led to the Civil War?
   a. Democrat
   b. Whig
   c. Republican
   d. Federalist

4. Which of the following was NOT an important invention in the twentieth century?
   a. Airplanes
   b. Telegraph
   c. Television
   d. Computers

5. Which of the following sets comprises a primary cause and effect of the American Revolution?
   a. A cause was the taxation of the colonies, and an effect was the civil rights movement.
   b. A cause was the Declaration of Independence, and an effect was the Constitution.
   c. A cause was the French and Indian War, and an effect was the Bill of Rights.
   d. A cause was the debate over slavery, and an effect was the Seven Years' War.

6. What are the two main parts of the federal legislative branch?
   a. President and vice president
   b. Federal and state
   c. District court and court of appeals
   d. Senate and House of Representatives

7. What was a concern that George Washington warned of in his Farewell Address?
   a. The danger of political parties
   b. To be prepared to intervene in Europe's affairs
   c. The abolition of slavery
   d. To protect states' rights through sectionalism

8. What is NOT a responsibility for citizens of democracy?
   a. To stay aware of current issues and history
   b. To avoid political action
   c. To actively vote in elections
   d. To understand and obey laws

9. Which of the following statements is true?
   a. Times zones are defined by their latitude.
   b. Eastern and Western hemispheres are defined by the prime meridian.
   c. A place is constant, while a location is changeable with the movement of people.
   d. A continent is one of six especially large landmasses in the world.

10. Which of the following statements is true?
    a. Water usage has largely shifted from appropriation to riparian.
    b. Native Americans lived in harmony with nature by never disrupting it.
    c. Cities are fully isolated environments.
    d. Invasive species can have catastrophic impacts on ecosystems.

11. Which of the following are reasons that geography is important to the examination of history?

    I. Historians make use of maps in their studies to get a clear picture of how history unfolded.
    II. Knowing the borders of different lands helps historians learn different cultures' interactions.
    III. Geography is closely linked with the flow of resources, technology, and population in societies.
    IV. Environmental factors, such as access to water and proximity of mountains, help shape the course of civilization.
       a. I, II, and III only
       b. II, III, and IV only
       c. I, II, and IV only
       d. I, III, and IV only

12. Which of the following statements is true?
    a. All Native American tribes are matrilineal.
    b. Japan is struggling to manage its high birthrate.
    c. Shi'a Muslims traditionally follow imams.
    d. Mexico's culture is deeply tied to its Protestant roots.

13. Which of the following advancements was NOT invented by Greek culture?
    a. The alphabet
    b. The Hippocratic Oath
    c. Democratic government
    d. Theater

14. Which of the following was an important development in the twentieth century?
    a. The United States and the Soviet Union officially declared war on each other in the Cold War.
    b. The League of Nations signed the Kyoto Protocol.
    c. World War I ended when the United States defeated Japan.
    d. India violently partitioned into India and Pakistan after the end of colonialism.

15. Which of the following is NOT an example of cross-cultural interactions?
    a. Egyptian and Mayan pyramids
    b. The Spanish language
    c. Styles of sushi
    d. Study of Chinese culture

16. Which of the following is true?
    a. The barter system no longer exists.
    b. Economic resources can be divided into four categories: natural, capital, manufactured, and nonrenewable.
    c. Individuals help to determine the scarcity of items through their choices.
    d. According to the law of supply, as the price of a product increases, the supply of the product will decrease.

17. What is NOT an effect of monopolies?
    a. Promote a diverse variety of independent businesses
    b. Inhibit developments that would be problematic for business
    c. Control the supply of resources
    d. Limit the degree of choice for consumers

18. Which method is NOT a way that governments manage economies in a market system?
    a. Laissez-faire
    b. Absolute monarchy
    c. Capitalism
    d. Self-interest

19. Which of the following nations did NOT establish colonies in what would become the United States?
    a. Italy
    b. England
    c. France
    d. Spain

20. Which of the following statements about the U.S. Constitution is true?
    a. It was signed on July 4, 1776.
    b. It was enacted at the end of the Revolutionary War.
    c. New York failed to ratify it, but it still passed by majority.
    d. It replaced the Articles of Confederation.

21. Which of the following locations was NOT subjected to American imperialism?
    a. Philippines
    b. Puerto Rico
    c. Canada
    d. Guam

22. What is a power that Congress has?
    a. To appoint the cabinet
    b. Right of nullification
    c. To impeach the president
    d. To interpret laws through courts

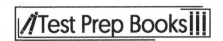

23. Which of the following is true?
    a. The Emancipation Proclamation ended slavery in the United States.
    b. President Wilson called for the foundation of the United Nations in his Fourteen Points.
    c. The Constitution of 1787 and the Bill of Rights were ratified simultaneously.
    d. The Declaration of Independence was primarily concerned with the colonists' complaints against King George III.

24. *The entire Roman Empire was destroyed in the fifth century A.D.* Is this statement true or false?
    a. True; it was conquered by barbarians in that era.
    b. True; it was destroyed by a civil war during that time period.
    c. False; the western half survived as the Holy Roman Empire.
    d. False; the eastern half, known as the Byzantine Empire, survived until 1453 A.D.

25. Which of the statements about the United Nations is false?
    a. It ensured the continuance of an alliance between the United States and Soviet Union.
    b. It was based on the idea for the League of Nations.
    c. It helps to promote human rights.
    d. It includes many former colonies from around the world.

26. Which of the following gentlemen was not instrumental in leading the charge for discussion at the Constitutional Convention held in Philadelphia in 1787?
    a. George Washington
    b. Alexander Hamilton
    c. Thomas Jefferson
    d. James Madison

27. Which American Indian tribe led a nomadic lifestyle and lived in teepees that were easily moved from place to place?
    a. Plains
    b. Southwest
    c. Eastern
    d. Northwest

28. What was Britain's first permanent settlement in North America?
    a. Plymouth, Massachusetts
    b. Roanoke, Virginia
    c. Jamestown, Virginia
    d. L'Anse Meadows, Newfoundland

29. What was the controlling act imposed by the British on American colonists that taxed imported lead, glass, paints, paper, and tea, and prompted the colonies to unite against British rule?
    a. The Stamp Act
    b. The Sugar Act
    c. The Currency Act
    d. The Townsend Act

30. Where did the first shot of the American Revolution take place?
    a. At the Boston Massacre
    b. During the Boston Tea Party
    c. On Lexington Green
    d. At the Battle of Trenton

31. The Revolutionary War's final battle took place on October 19, 1781, when British General Lord Cornwallis surrendered to Washington's troops at what location?
    a. Yorktown, Virginia
    b. Valley Forge, Pennsylvania
    c. Trenton, New Jersey
    d. Saratoga, New York

32. What important U.S. structure was burned during the War of 1812?
    a. The Washington Monument
    b. Independence Hall
    c. The White House
    d. The Statue of Liberty

33. Who was elected President of the Confederate States of America during the Civil War?
    a. Robert E. Lee
    b. Jefferson Davis
    c. William T. Sherman
    d. Abraham Lincoln

34. The period of business and industrial growth from 1876 through the turn of the twentieth century was deemed by author Mark Twain as what?
    a. Manifest Destiny
    b. The Columbian Exchange
    c. The New Deal
    d. The Gilded Age

35. When did World War I begin?
    a. 1915
    b. 1917
    c. 1914
    d. 1918

36. Which of the following countries was a U.S. ally during World War II?
    a. The Soviet Union
    b. Italy
    c. Germany
    d. Japan

37. The North Atlantic Treaty Organization (NATO) was formed between which countries or regions?
    a. Canada, the U.S., and South America
    b. Western Europe, the U.S., and Canada
    c. The U.S., Western Europe, Canada, and the Soviet Union
    d. Asia, the U.S., and Western Europe

38. Which of these events was not a driving force for the passage of the Civil Rights Act in 1964?
    a. *Brown vs. the Board of Education*
    b. Freedom rides
    c. The G.I. Bill
    d. The Montgomery bus boycott

39. What program launched by the U.S. government under President Ronald Reagan was designed to shield the U.S. from nuclear attack by the Soviet Union?
    a. The Strategic Arms Limitation Talks (SALT I and II)
    b. The Strategic Defense Initiative (SDI)
    c. The Iran-Contra Affair
    d. *Glasnost*

40. After the terrorist attacks initiated by Islamic fundamentalist Osama bin Laden on September 11, 2001, President George W. Bush ordered bombing raids on various locations in what country in an attempt to bring down bin Laden and his al-Qaeda network?
    a. Afghanistan
    b. Iraq
    c. Kuwait
    d. Pakistan

41. What are the two largest rivers in the U.S. called?
    a. The Mississippi and the Colorado
    b. The Mississippi and the Missouri
    c. The Missouri and the Ohio
    d. The Mississippi and the Ohio

42. What is used to pinpoint location on a map?
    a. Scale and longitude
    b. Contour lines and scale
    c. Latitude and longitude
    d. Latitude and contour lines

43. Under America's democratic form of government, which of the following are citizens not obligated to do?
    a. Obey the law
    b. Pay taxes
    c. Serve on a jury if asked to do so
    d. Vote in elections

Answer Explanations

1. A: Carolina is divided into two separate states—North and South. Maine was part of Nova Scotia and did not become an American territory until the War of 1812. Likewise, Vermont was not one of the original Thirteen Colonies. Canada remained a separate British colony. Finally, Florida was a Spanish territory. Therefore, by process of elimination, A is the correct list.

2. B: Britain was not defeated in the French and Indian War, and, in fact, disputes with the colonies over the new territories it won contributed to the growing tensions. All of the other options were key motivations behind the Revolutionary War.

3. C: Abraham Lincoln was elected president as part of the new Republican Party, and his plans to limit and potentially abolish slavery led the southern states to secede from the Union.

4. B: Out of the four inventions mentioned, the first telegraphs were invented in the 1830s, not in the twentieth century. In contrast, the other inventions had considerable influence over the course of the twentieth century.

5. C: The Declaration of Independence occurred during the American Revolution, so it should therefore be considered an effect, not a cause. Similarly, slavery was a cause for the later Civil War, but it was not a primary instigator for the Revolutionary War. Although a single event can have many effects long into the future, it is also important to not overstate the influence of these individual causes; the civil rights movement was only tangentially connected to the War of Independence among many other factors, and therefore it should not be considered a primary effect of it. The French and Indian War (which was part of the Seven Years' War) and the Bill of Rights, on the other hand, were respectively a cause and effect from the American Revolution, making Choice C the correct answer.

6. D: The president and vice president are part of the executive branch, not the legislative branch. The question focuses specifically on the federal level, so state government should be excluded from consideration. As for the district court and the court of appeals, they are part of the judicial branch. The legislative branch is made up of Congress, which consists of the House of Representatives and the Senate.

7. A: George Washington was a slave owner himself in life, so he did not make abolition a theme in his Farewell Address. On the other hand, he was concerned that sectionalism could potentially destroy the United States, and he warned against it. Furthermore, he believed that Americans should avoid getting involved in European affairs. However, one issue that he felt was especially problematic was the formation of political parties, and he urged against it in his farewell.

8. B: To avoid involvement in political processes such as voting is antithetical to the principles of a democracy. Therefore, the principal responsibility of citizens is the opposite, and they should be steadily engaged in the political processes that determine the course of government.

9. B: Time zones are determined by longitude, not latitude. Locations are defined in absolute terms, while places are in part defined by the population, which is subject to movement. There are seven continents in the world, not six. On the other hand, it is true that the prime meridian determines the border for the Eastern and Western hemispheres.

10. D: Riparian water usage was common in the past, but modern usage has shifted to appropriation. While often practicing sustainable methods, Native Americans used fire, agriculture, and other tools to shape the landscape for their own ends. Due to the importance of trade in providing essential resources to cities, a city is never truly separated from the outside world. However, invasive species are a formidable threat to native environments, making *D* the correct answer.

11. C: I, II, and IV only. Historians make use of maps in their studies to get a clear picture of how history unfolded, knowing the borders of different lands helps historians learn different cultures' interactions, and environmental factors, such as access to water and the proximity of mountains, help determine the course of civilization. The phrase "Geography is closely linked with the flow of resources, technology, and population in societies" is a characteristic of economics.

12. C: While many Native American tribes are matrilineal, not all of them are. Japan is currently coping with an especially low birthrate, not a high one. Mexico's religion, like that of Spain, is primarily Roman Catholic rather than Protestant. On the other hand, Shi'a Islam is based on the view that imams should be honored as Muhammad's chosen heirs to the Caliphate, making *C* correct.

13. A: Although Greeks used the alphabet as the basis for their written language, leading to a diverse array of literature, they learned about the alphabet from Phoenician traders. All the other options, in contrast, were invented in Greece.

14. D: It is important to realize that the Cold War was never an official war and that the United States and the Soviet Union instead funded proxy conflicts. The Kyoto Protocol was signed by members of the United Nations, as the League of Nations was long since defunct. While Japan was a minor participant in World War I, it was not defeated by America until World War II. The correct answer is *D*: India's partition between Hindu India and Islamic Pakistan led to large outbreaks of religious violence.

15. A: Although Egyptian and Mayan civilizations are an interesting subject for comparisons, the two cultures never interacted. The other answers are all examples of interactions between different cultures; a study of Chinese culture, for instance, would require examination of the multiple ethnic groups throughout China.

16. C: Although monetary systems were invented to solve problems with barter systems, it is wrong to assume that barter systems have ceased to exist; bartering remains a common practice throughout the world, albeit less common than money. The four main categories for economic resources are land, labor, capital, and entrepreneurship. The law of supply says that supplies will increase, not decrease, as prices increase. The correct answer is *C*, as scarcity is determined by human choice.

17. A: Rather than competition, a monopoly prevents other businesses from offering a certain product or service to consumers.

18. B: Absolute monarchies often use command system economies, but they do not represent a way that governments manage economies. Laissez-faire, capitalism, and self-interest, in contrast, are all fundamental concepts behind the market system.

19. A: England, France, and Spain all established North American colonies that would later be absorbed into the United States, but Italy, despite Christopher Columbus' role as an explorer, never established a colony in America.

20. D: The Constitution was signed in 1787; the Declaration of Independence was signed in 1776. It was successfully ratified by all the current states, including New York. Finally, the Articles of Confederation was established at the end of the American Revolution; the Constitution would replace the articles years later due to issues with the government's structure.

21. C: Although American forces made several early attempts to take Canada from Britain, the United States was never able to successfully seize this territory. On the other hand, the United States did control the Philippines, Puerto Rico, and Guam.

22. C: The executive branch determines the cabinet, while the judicial branch has the responsibility of interpreting the Constitution and laws. Even so, the legislative branch can check the president's power by impeaching him.

23. D: The Emancipation Proclamation only freed slaves in Confederate-held territories; southern states still loyal to the Union kept their slaves for the time being. Although Wilson succeeded in instituting the League of Nations, the United Nations would not emerge until decades later. The Bill of Rights was ratified after the Constitution to provide additional protection for individual liberties. However, it is true that the main body of the Declaration of Independence consisted of grievances that the colonies had against British rule.

24. D: While it is true that Rome fell to barbarians in the fifth century A.D., it would be inaccurate to say the Roman Empire had been completely destroyed. The Byzantine Empire considered itself the heir of the Roman Empire. The western sections, on the other hand, certainly collapsed; the later Holy Roman Empire tried to draw on Rome's past glory but was not a true successor.

25. A: Based on the prior League of Nations, the United Nations included many nations in postcolonial Africa and Asia and worked to support human rights. However, it failed to maintain the World War II alliance between the United States and the Soviet Union, leading to the unofficial Cold War.

26. C: At the time of the Constitutional Convention, Thomas Jefferson was in Paris serving as America's foreign minister to France. George Washington led the meeting, and Alexander Hamilton and James Madison set the tone for debate, rendering *A*, *B*, and *D* incorrect.

27. A: Plains Indians followed the buffalo across the prairies, living in tent-like teepees that were easily moved from place to place. Choice *B* is incorrect because Indians in the Southwest relied on farming for much of their food and built adobes, which are houses made out of dried clay or earth. Indians in the Eastern and Northwest sections of North America survived by hunting, gathering, farming, and fishing, and lived in wooden longhouses, plank houses, or wigwams. Thus, Choices *C* and *D* are incorrect.

28. C: Established in 1607, Jamestown, Virginia was the first permanent British settlement in the New World. Plymouth was founded a bit later in 1620 when a group of Pilgrims founded the first permanent European settlement in New England, making Choice *A* incorrect. Choice *B* is incorrect because although the Roanoke Colony was founded in 1585, it isn't considered permanent – the colony's leader, John White, went back to England for supplies two years later, and he returned to find that all of the colonists had mysteriously disappeared. Choice *D* is incorrect because L'Anse Meadows was an area in Newfoundland that was briefly settled by Scandinavian Vikings around 1000 A.D.

29. D: The British issued the Townsend Act in 1767, which taxed imported lead, glass, paints, paper, and tea, and increased the colonists' anger and further strained the relationship between England and the colonies. Choice *A*, the Stamp Act of 1765, taxed printed items, including playing cards and newspapers

printed in the colonies. Choice *B*, the Sugar Act of 1764, placed import duties on items such as molasses, sugar, coffee, and wine. Choice *C*, the Currency Act, banned the issuing of paper money in the colonies and mandated the use of gold in business dealings.

30. C: The first shot took place on Lexington Green. When the British heard that colonists were stockpiling weapons they sent troops to Concord to seize them. However, a group of approximately seventy Minutemen confronted the British soldiers on Lexington green. British troops killed five protesting colonists during the Boston Massacre in 1770, but this is not considered the first shot of the Revolution. Thus, Choice *A* is incorrect. Choice *B* is incorrect because the Boston Tea Party was when colonists dumped 342 chests of expensive tea into the Boston Harbor in defiance of the tea tax. The Revolution had already started when the Battle of Trenton took place on December 25, 1776, making Choice *D* incorrect.

31. A: British General Lord Cornwallis surrendered to Washington's troops at Yorktown, Virginia. No battles occurred at Valley Forge, but Washington's troops suffered major losses as a result of starvation, disease, and exposure to the cold, making Choice *B* incorrect. Choice *C* is incorrect because the Battle of Trenton was the first major battle of the Revolution, which occurred when Washington led his troops across the Delaware River to wage a surprise attack on British and Hessian soldiers stationed in Trenton on December 25, 1776. Choice *D*, Saratoga, New York, was the site of a major victory by General John Burgoyne in October 1777 and prompted European countries to help support the American cause.

32. C: British soldiers burned the White House during the War of 1812. Neither the Washington Monument nor the Statue of Liberty – Choices *A* and *D* – were built at the time, and Philadelphia's Independence Hall, Choice *B*, escaped conflict during this war.

33. B: Jefferson Davis was elected president of the Confederate States of America in November 1861. Choice *A*, General Robert E. Lee, was the leader of the Confederate Army. Choice *C*, William T. Sherman, was a union general famous for his march through Georgia and the burning of Atlanta in 1864. Choice *D*, Abraham Lincoln, was President of the U.S. during the Civil War.

34. D: This period was called the Gilded Age since it appeared shiny and golden on the surface, but was fueled by undercurrents of corruption led by big businessmen known as robber barons. Choice *A*, Manifest Destiny, is the concept referring to the pursuit and acquisition of new lands by the U.S., which led to the purchase of Alaska from Russia in 1867 and the annexation of Hawaii in 1898. The Columbian Exchange, Choice *B*, was an era of discovery, conquest, and colonization of the Americas by the Europeans. The New Deal, Choice *C*, was a plan launched by President Franklin Delano Roosevelt to help rebuild America's economy after the Great Depression.

35. C: World War I began in 1914 when a Serbian assassin killed Archduke Franz Ferdinand of Austria and prompted Austria-Hungary to declare war on Serbia. 1915, Choice *A*, is the year when German submarines sank the passenger ship *Lusitania*, killing 128 Americans and leading many to support U.S. efforts to enter the war. 1917, Choice *B*, is the year the U.S. entered World War I, declaring war on Germany. 1918, Choice *D*, signaled the end of the war when American troops helped defeat the German army that September. Fighting ended in November after Germany signed a peace agreement.

36. A: The Soviet Union was invaded by Germany in 1941 and allied with Britain and subsequently the U.S. President Roosevelt, British Prime Minister Winston Churchill, and Soviet director Joseph Stalin met in 1945 to plan their final assault on Germany and discuss postwar strategies. Germany aligned with Italy and Japan in 1940 to form the Axis Alliance. Their goal was to establish a German empire in Europe and place Japan in control over Asia. Thus, Choices *B*, *C*, and *D* are incorrect.

37. B: The North Atlantic Treaty Organization (NATO) was formed between Western Europe, Canada, and the U.S. in defense of Soviet hostility after the Soviet Union introduced Communism into Eastern Europe. The Soviet Union countered by creating the Warsaw Pact.

38. C: The G.I. Bill was a government program started in the 1950s that gave military veterans a free education. In the revolutionary 1954 case, *Brown vs. the Board of Education,* the Supreme Court ruled that school segregation was illegal, thereby setting the Civil Rights Movement in motion, making Choice *A* incorrect. *Freedom Rides*, Choice *B*, and the Montgomery bus boycott, Choice *D*, were among the non-violent protests against segregation that took place in the U.S. in the 1960s.

39. B: President Reagan advocated *peace through strength*, building up the U.S. military and launching the Strategic Defense Initiative (SDI), also called *Star Wars*. Choice *A*, the Strategic Arms Limitation Talks (SALT I and II), negotiated between 1972 and 1979, resulted in limits on nuclear weapons for both the U.S. and Russia. Choice *C*, the Iran-Contra Affair, was a scandal involving the secret sale of weapons to Iran in exchange for American hostages. Choice *D*, *Glasnost*, was a policy of political openness launched by Soviet leader Mikhail Gorbachev.

40. A: Afghanistan was the site of the bombing raids. Bush invaded Iraq, Choice *B*, in 2003 when Iraqi dictator Saddam Hussein defied the terms of the truce agreed upon in 1991 after the Gulf War. Kuwait, Choice *C*, was invaded by Iraq in 1990, sparking the Gulf War. Pakistan, Choice *D*, is where Osama bin Laden was killed by a group of Navy SEALs under orders from President Obama.

41. B: The Mississippi and the Missouri are the two largest rivers in the U.S., winding through the Great Plains in the center of the country. The Colorado and Ohio Rivers are about half the length of the Mississippi and Missouri.

42. C: Latitude – imaginary lines covering the globe from east to west – and longitude – imaginary lines running north to south – are used to pinpoint location on a map. Scale is used to show the relationship between the map measurements and the equivalent distance on the world's surface. Contour lines are used to show detailed elevation on a map.

43. D: Under America's democratic form of government, voting is a *right*, but it is not an *obligation*. U.S. citizens are *obliged* to obey the law, pay taxes, and serve on a jury if asked to do so, making Choices *A*, *B*, and *C* incorrect.

Science

Lab Processes, Equipment, and Safety

Appropriate and Safe Use of Materials

The appropriate and safe use of laboratory materials not only reduces the potential harm to people and the environment, but also minimizes waste and ensures accurate data collection. The following guidelines highlight the crucial skills in safely handling chemical reagents and specimens.

Identifying Hazards
The ability to identify a hazard allows one to take safety measures such as wearing the appropriate clothing and responding appropriately to spills.

Identifying Hazards

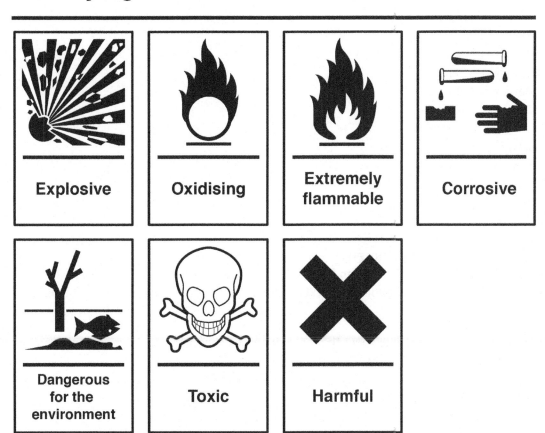

Common types of laboratory hazards include:

- Chemical hazards
- Toxins
- Corrosives
- Flammables
- Reactive substances
- Biological hazards
- Animals
- Plants
- Microbes
- Genetically-modified organisms
- Physical hazards
- Extreme heat
- Extreme cold
- Noise
- Heating devices
- Projectiles
- Electrical hazards
- Fire
- Shock
- Radiation hazards
- Ionizing radiation
- Non-iodizing radiation
- Mechanical hazards
- Machinery
- Airborne hazards
- Vapor
- Fume
- Dust

Handling Chemicals and Specimens

A **specimen** is any substance or fluid taken from a plant, animal, or other object, such as urine, blood, saliva, stool, or tissue. To safely handle chemicals and specimens, one should adhere to the following guidelines:

- Always read the safety data sheet that accompanies a chemical.
- Make sure specimens and chemicals are properly stored.
- Ensure that any first-aid equipment, including eye-washing stations, are close and ready for use.
- Keep all work stations clean and sanitized.
- Use the smallest amount of chemical or specimen possible.
- Make sure all containers are properly labeled.
- Use substitutions for more harmful chemicals whenever possible.

Safe Disposal of Materials

The following are basic requirements to follow for the disposal of chemical hazardous waste:

<u>Create a Hazardous Waste Area</u>
- Select an area near the source of the waste, out of the way of normal lab activities, and easily accessible to all lab personnel.

- Label the area "Danger—Hazardous Waste" with the following sign:

Deposit chemicals into the appropriate containers. Make sure that containers into which the chemicals will be discarded are stable enough to hold them—chemicals must not weaken or dissolve the material of the container.

- Acids and bases cannot be stored with metal.

- Hydrofluoric acid cannot be stored with glass.

- Solvents (i.e. gasoline) cannot be stored in polyethylene containers, such as a milk jug.

- Waste containers must come with lids and caps that are resistant to leakage, and containers should be closed at all times, except when opened to add more waste.

- The size of the container should be appropriate for the amount of expected waste.

- Waste containers should be placed inside a larger, empty container to catch any waste that may potentially spill or leak.

Attach a Hazardous Waste Tag

Complete and attach the following hazardous waste tag to all containers:

Hazardous Waste Tag

Front

HAZARDOUS WASTE

FEDERAL LAW PROHIBITS IMPROPER DISPOSAL

IF FOUND, CONTACT THE NEAREST POLICE OR PUBLIC SAFETY
AUTHORITY OR THE U.S. ENVIRONMENT PROTECTION AGENCY.

PROPERT D.O.T.
SHIPPING NAME _____ UN OR NA _____

GENERATOR INFORMATION:

NAME _____ ADDRESS _____

CITY _____ STATE _____ ZIP _____

EPA I.D. NO. _____ MANIFEST DOCUMENT NO. _____

EPA WASTE NO. _____ ACCUMULATION START DATE _____

HANDLE WITH CARE!

CONTAINS HAZARDOUS OR TOXIC WASTES

Back

HAZARDOUS WASTE

DO NOT REMOVE THIS TAG!

IT IS A VIOLATION OF PLANT RULES
TO DO SO WITHOUT AUTHORITY
WILL MEAN DISCIPLINARY ACTION!

IT IS HERE FOR A PURPOSE

REMARKS
_____

_____

_____

SEE OTHER SIDE

Requirements for Liquid Waste

- Don't overfill containers—be sure to leave at least 10% space between the container opening and the surface of the waste.

- Never mix liquid and solid waste.

- Double-bag small containers, such as vials, in clear plastic bags.

- Bag small containers composed of the same kind of waste.

- Attach a completed hazardous waste tag to all bags and containers.

Requirements for Solid Waste

Chemical solid waste is composed of three different categories: lab trash, dry chemicals, and sharps.

- Lab trash
- Use for waste such as Kim Wipes, disposable gloves, paper towels, and wooden stirrers
- Double-bag in clear bags
- Attach a completed hazardous waste tag to all bags
- Dry chemicals
- Return the chemical waste to the original container in which it was purchased.
- Attach a completed hazardous waste tag.
- Sharps

    o Examples include glass (broken or intact), pipettes and pipette tips, needles, X-ACTO™ knives, or anything capable of piercing, cutting, slicing, or tearing human flesh.

- Discard any used sharps into a designated sharps container with a biohazard sign.

Biohazard container

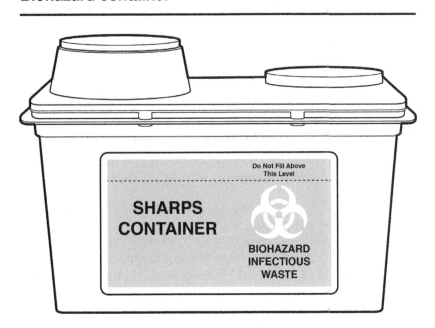

Appropriate Storage

Proper chemical storage is imperative for laboratory operations as well as the safety of all lab personnel. The following is a list of guidelines for the appropriate storage of chemicals and other hazardous materials:

1. There must be a designated place for each type of chemical.

   o Flammables and volatile poisons (poisons that easily evaporate at room temperature) must be stored in cabinets, refrigerators, or freezers marked with a flammable label.

   o Oxidizing acids, organic and mineral acids, liquid bases, liquid oxidizers, and non-volatile liquid poisons must be stored in a safety cabinet.

   o Oxidizing acids must be double-contained.

   o Solids should be stored above liquids.

   o As a rule of thumb, different compounds should be stored separately.

2. Chemicals should not be permanently stored in any fume hood.
3. All containers should be kept sealed unless in use.
4. All chemicals must be kept away from sunlight and heat.
5. All chemicals must be labeled properly.
6. No chemical, except for bleach and cleaning agents, should be stored under the sink.

Preparing Equipment for Classroom or Field Use

Conducting a science lab is one of the most exciting ways to teach science. It not only allows students to experience science as professionals but also gives them the opportunity to apply learned concepts to real-world scenarios. Before beginning a lab, instructors should:

- Know and clarify the concepts and theories upon which the experiment is based

- Test the experiment and equipment, following along in the student instruction manual to identify any potential issues

The most common preparations a science instructor will conduct are preparing solutions, staining slides, and labeling samples.

Preparing a Solution of a Given Concentration

The primary way that a solution is measured is expressed in terms of **molarity**. A solution's molarity is the number of moles per liter of a pure substance.

$$\text{Molarity (M)} = \text{moles/L}$$

A **mole** is the mass of pure substance (including atoms and all corresponding chemical units, such as elements and particles) containing the same number of constituent units as there are atoms in exactly 12.000 grams of ^{12}C. It's equivalent to 6.022×10^{23} molecules, also known as Avogadro's Number.

Most solutions are made by using a pure solid or by diluting a stock solution.

Using a Pure Solid

Instructors should follow this procedure for making a solution from a pure solid:

1. Determine the molecular mass of the solid.
2. Calculate the mass needed to make the solution.
3. Weigh out the substance and place it in the appropriate flask.
4. Dissolve solute in less water than the desired volume.
5. Fill the flask to the desired amount of solution.

Because standard weighing devices cannot measure a compound in moles, one must determine the molecular mass of a substance, which is expressed in g/mol. The molecular mass of an element can be found in a periodic table.

For example, an experiment calls for 400 mL of a 0.750 M solution of NaOH. To determine the atomic weight of the formula, one must add each element's molecular mass together.

Total molecular weight (NaOH) = 22.990 g/mol + 15.999 g/mol + 1.0078 g/mol = *39.997 g/mol* (the reported molecular weights are in five significant figures).

Once the molecular weight has been determined, the mass needed to make 400 mL of a 0.750 M solution of NaOH can be calculated by multiplying the volume of the solution (400 mL) by the molarity (0.750 mol/L) and the molecular weight of the substance (39.007 g/mol).

By entering the values, the total grams needed are calculated as follows:

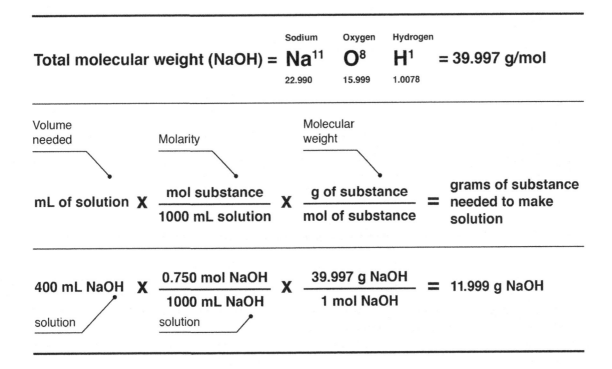

Because the required solution is given with three significant figures, the weight in grams should be measured at three significant figures as well, so 12.0 grams is necessary for this solution.

Finally, the experimenter will weigh 12.0 grams of NaOH and place it in a 500-mL volumetric flask. About 200 mL of distilled water can be added and mixed until the solute has dissolved. Then more water is added until the flask reads 400 mL.

Using a Stock Solution

Stock solutions are used frequently in labs, as many substances are considered too hazardous to have in their pure form. For example, an experiment calls for a 500 mL solution of 1.25 M of HCl (hydrochloric acid). To save space, a school's stockroom would likely have a bottle of 12.0 M HCl that would then be diluted with water to form the desired concentration. Instructors should follow the procedure below to create the desired solution using a stock:

- Calculate the appropriate volume of stock solution to add to water.
- Add the correct amount of stock to a flask containing some of the required water.
- Dilute with water until desired volume is reached.

To make a 500 mL solution of 1.25 M HCl from a 12.0 M stock of HCl, the appropriate ratio must be set up. Because the total amount of the solute doesn't change when water is added, the moles of solute from the stock solution equal the moles of solute in the dilute solution:

Moles of Solute in Stock Solution = Moles of Solute in Dilute Solution

To calculate the moles of solute, one must multiply the volume (V) of the solution times the molarity (M) of the solution: M x V.

M x V (stock) = M x V (dilute)

Or

$M_S V_S = M_D V_D$

$M_S = 12.0$ $V_S = ?$ $M_D = 1.25$ $V_D = 500$ mL

Using algebra, the necessary volume of stock solution can be solved:

$$V_S = \frac{M_D V_D}{M_S}$$

$$V_S(ml) = \frac{(1.25M)(500ml)}{12.0M} = 52.1 ml$$

Finally, 52.1 mL of the stock solution can be measured into a volumetric flask containing 200 ml of water. More water should be added until the volume reads 500 mL, and presto! There's 500 mL of a 1.25 M HCl solution. It's important to note that when diluting stock acid solutions, the acid should always be added to the water instead of the reverse. This is to prevent the acid from splashing out of the container and damaging laboratory equipment or causing bodily harm.

Staining Slides

Microscope slides are the mounts that specimens are placed upon in order to observe them under a microscope. Specimens may be **dry mounted**, or placed directly between the slide and cover slip, or they may be **wet mounted**, in which the specimen is suspended in an aqueous solution between the slide and cover slip. Staining a slide requires a wet mount.

To stain a slide, an instructor should follow this procedure:

1. Obtain a clean slide and cover slip.

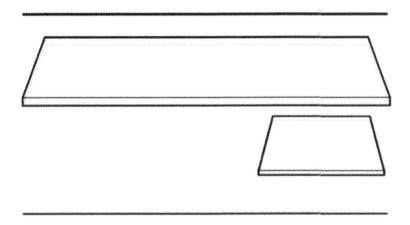

2. Place a *very thin* slice of the specimen directly in the middle of the slide.

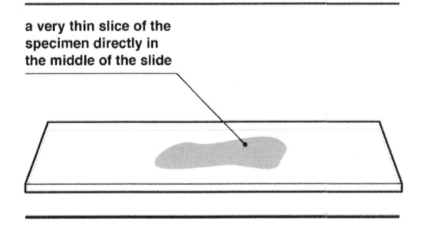

3. Add a drop of water to the specimen using a pipette.

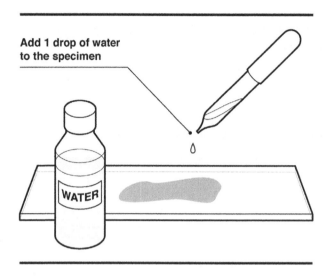

4. Add the cover slip by placing the slip on its edge and lowering it onto the specimen from a 45° angle.

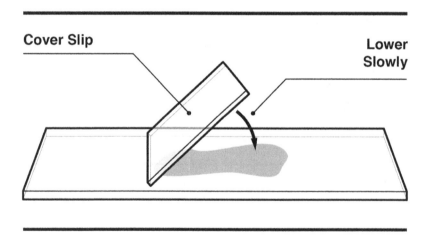

5. Add the appropriate stain (table below) on one side of the cover slip and a piece of paper towel on the other side.

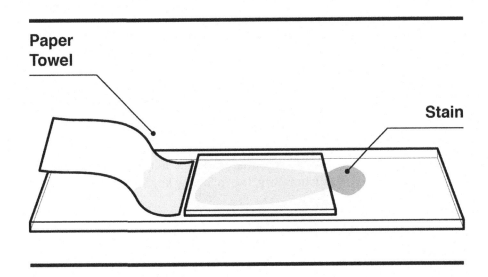

6. Press down on the paper towel so the stain is drawn through the cover slip and specimen.

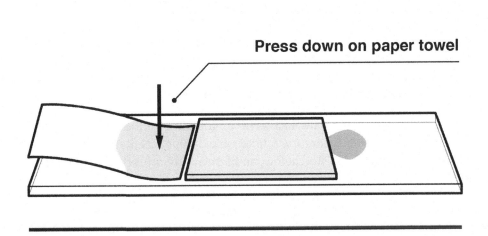

When choosing a stain, this table may be helpful:

Stain	Function	Uses
Eosin Y	Stains pink for alkaline cells (blood, cytoplasm, membranes)	Blood and bone marrow testing
Iodine	Stains brown or bluish-black for carbohydrates	Identify starches in plant and animal specimens
Gram's Stain	Stains purple for bacteria	Identify bacteria
Methylene Blue	Stains blue for acidic cells by allowing them to show against their background	Identifying acidic cell nucleic, DNA

Labeling Samples

All chemicals and collected specimens need appropriate labels to minimize confusion, which could have disastrous results. For samples within a laboratory, the following key information should be included:

- Name or initials of the researcher
- Date sample was prepared or collected
- Identification
- Chemical formula or name
- Identification number (if applicable)
- Any solvents or solutions that a sample is suspended in (such as water or acid)

History and Nature of Science

Accepted Principles and Models Develop Over Time

The very nature of scientific knowledge is that it continues to build upon itself with constant experimentation and newfound discoveries, throwing out old theories that have been proven false and replacing them with new ones. By using principles that have been developed and tested over hundreds of years, scientists and engineers have created today's technology.

Records of scientific experimentation date back as far as 400 B.C.E., although most significant discoveries didn't occur until the 17th century. A timeline of major accepted principles and models—which is by no means exhaustive—is listed below, and displays theories that were developed, discarded, and built upon:

- 1543—Nicolaus Copernicus developed the Heliocentric Model of the Solar System
- 1609—Galileo Galilei made telescopic observations of the solar system
- 1619—Johannes Kepler completed the laws of planetary motion
- 1622—Robert Boyle developed the law of ideal gas, which states that the pressure of an ideal gas is inversely proportional to the volume it occupies
- 1665—Robert Hooke discovered the biological cell
- 1672–1687—Sir Isaac Newton discovered that white light is a spectrum of different-colored rays, developed calculus, and created mathematical descriptions of force, gravity, and the laws of motion
- 1751—Benjamin Franklin discovered that lightning is electrical
- 1778–1798—Antoine Lavoisier discovered "phlogiston," later identified as oxygen; developed the law of conservation of mass and the basis for chemistry

- 1781–1800—William Herschel discovered Uranus, expanding the boundaries of the known universe and discovered infrared radiation
- 1820—Hans Christian Ørsted discovered the relationship between electricity and the magnetic field using a compass
- 1843—James Prescott Joule created the first law of thermodynamics
- 1858—Rudolf Virchow discovered that cells can only come from pre-existing cells
- 1859—Charles Darwin and Alfred Wallace developed the theory of evolution by natural selection
- 1864—James Clerk Maxwell developed the theory of electromagnetism
- 1865—Gregor Mendel identified the laws of genetic inheritance and provided the basis for genetics
- 1869—Dmitri Mendeleev created the periodic table of elements
- 1887—Alfred A. Michelson and Edward W. Morley disproved the existence of "the aether"
- 1897—J. J. Thomson discovered the electron
- 1900—Max Planck created the law of black body radiation and the basis for quantum theory
- 1905–1915—Albert Einstein developed theories of special relativity, the photoelectric effect, and general relativity
- 1911—Ernest Rutherford discovered the nucleus
- 1912—Alfred Wegener proposed continental drift, the basis for plate tectonics
- 1913—Niels Bohr created a model of the atom
- 1924—Edwin Hubble realized the Milky Way is just one of many galaxies
- 1925–1928—Major developments in quantum mechanics
- 1927—Georges Lemaitre proposed the Big Bang Theory
- 1928—Alexander Fleming discovered penicillin
- 1952—Jonas Salk developed and tested the polio vaccine
- 1953—Rosalind Franklin, Francis Crick, and James Watson discovered the helical structure of DNA
- 1983—Kary Mullis invented polymerase chain reactions
- 1997—Roslin Institute cloned the sheep Dolly
- 2001—First draft of the Human Genome Project was published
- 2006—Shinya Yamanaka generated the first induced pluripotent stem cells
- 2015—Traces of liquid water found on Mars

Major Developments in Science

Certain discoveries that revolutionized scientific understanding deserve a deeper look.

Atomic Theory

Atomic theory—a philosophical concept in ancient Greece that solidified in the 19th century—states that the universe is made up of discrete units called **atoms**. Initially believed to have been one inseparable unit, the atom was discovered to be composed of subatomic particles—protons, electrons, and neutrons—in which the protons and neutrons comprise a dense nucleus and the electrons orbit around it at mind-boggling distances. The atom is now believed to be composed of mostly space.

The Heliocentric Model of the Solar System

Before Nicolaus Copernicus, people believed Earth was the center of the universe. Copernicus placed the Sun at the center of the solar system, with the other planets revolving around it. At the time, only

Mercury, Venus, Earth, Mars, Saturn, and Jupiter were known. Evidence suggests that the ancient Greeks also used a heliocentric model of the solar system in the 3rd century B.C.E.

Gravity

Sir Isaac Newton recognized that gravity was responsible for objects falling toward the ground, which he extrapolated into a law that concluded that every object in the universe is attracted to another object through a force that is directly proportional to the product of their masses and inversely proportional to the square of the distance between them. This is called the law of universal gravitation and is expressed via the following formula:

The Law of Universal Gravitation

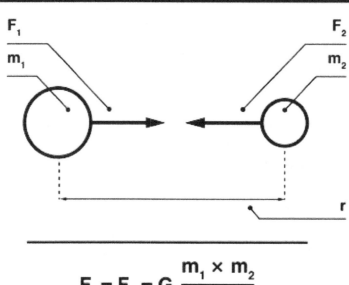

$$F_1 = F_2 = G \, \frac{m_1 \times m_2}{r^2}$$

Evolution

In 1859, Charles Darwin proposed the theory of evolution by natural selection, which explained how organisms developed *very* gradually over time as a result of mutations that enhanced an organism's ability to survive.

Key points of the theory of evolution include:

- There is genetic variation among species—meaning every species has a distinct arrangement of genes.

- Natural selection is the result of a random mutation that occurs in the genome and is favorable to the survival of the organism. For example, a random mutation that causes a moth's wings to appear white, making it harder for birds to eat them because they can't spot them against white tree branches, has a better chance of survival than dark moths. The birds eat the dark moths instead, and the white moth survives to pass on its mutation.

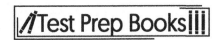
- The random mutation must be heritable—that is, it must be able to be passed on to its offspring.

- Natural selection is not the idea that organisms evolved to fit to their environment. For example, assuming that giraffes developed long necks to eat from tall trees is erroneous.

Continental Drift (Plate Tectonics)

In 1912, Alfred Wegener proposed that at one point in Earth's history, all of the continents were joined in one supercontinent (now known as Pangaea) and gradually separated to form the seven separate continents as they currently exist. The evidence, he argued, was present in the fact that fossils of similar species were found on continents several thousand miles apart. Unfortunately, Wegener had no model to explain the mechanism in which this occurred, so his theory was discarded.

However, Wegener's proposal was the foundation for **plate tectonics**, the theory that Earth's crust is composed of rigid, moving rock plates called the **lithosphere**. They move by gliding slowly over Earth's outer **mantle**, a layer of slowly moving silicate rock propelled by the hot magma below it. As hot rock from Earth's core rises to the surface, it causes the fragmented pieces of the crust to spread apart, moving away from each other. As the hot rock begins to cool, it sinks towards Earth's core, causing the plates above it to sink as well, meanwhile pushing the adjacent plates over the sinking plates. The deep trench created by the sinking and pushing is called the **subduction zone**. This process of spreading and sinking is the underlying cause of the movement of the continents.

Subduction

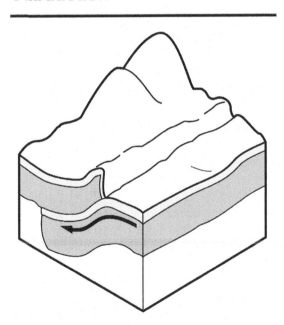

Contributions of Major Historical Figures

Many of the greatest contributors to the advancement of scientific knowledge were mentioned above. However, a brief overview of the most influential scientists is below.

Galileo Galilei

Galileo Galilei (1564–1642), considered by many to be the "Father of Modern Science," was an Italian astronomer, physicist, and philosopher. His telescopic investigations provided the basis for observational astronomy, in which he confirmed the phases of Venus, four of Jupiter's major moons, and sunspots.

Isaac Newton

Isaac Newton (1643–1727) was an English mathematician, physicist, astronomer, and philosopher. His most influential contributions were the theory of gravitation, the theory of color, the development of calculus, and the three natural laws of motion.

Charles Darwin

Charles Darwin (1809–1882) was an English biologist, whose major contributions include his theory of evolution as a result of natural selection, which provided a unifying theory for the genetic relationship and diversity of all species on Earth.

Max Planck

Max Planck (1858–1947) was a German physicist and the founder of quantum theory, a branch of theoretical physics that focuses on the relationships between subatomic particles.

Niels Bohr

Niels Bohr (1885–1962) was a Danish physicist primarily responsible for the creation of the nuclear model of the atom, which illustrates that electrons orbit around the atom's nucleus. His work received the Nobel Prize in Physics in 1922.

Albert Einstein

Albert Einstein (1879–1955), a German scientist, is possibly the most well-known scientist and contributor to modern physics. He is best known for his theory of mass-energy equivalence ($E = mc^2$) and his theories of special and general relativity. Einstein also received a Nobel Prize in Physics in 1921.

Impact on Science

Science as a Human Endeavor

Two of the worst earthquakes in history occurred in 1556 and 1976, causing 830,000 and 255,000 deaths, respectively. Earthquakes near the ocean cause massive tidal waves called tsunamis. In Indonesia in 2004, a tsunami resulted in 230,000 deaths. Seismology is the study of earthquakes. Understanding earthquakes can help predict them and possibly even prevent them.

Earthquakes have an initial source of plate movement called the focus. At the focus, there is a significant amount of tension, like the force of resistance generated by bending a wooden stick. Eventually, with enough pressure, there is so much tension that the stick breaks. The separate pieces that were once in a curved formation due to the strain will slip back into their original shape. This is called elastic rebound when it occurs at plate boundaries. After elastic rebound, the movement spreads outwards from the focus and causes waves of kinetic energy. These rolling vibrations are called seismic waves. Slipping back into place takes several adjustments called aftershocks, which are less severe than the initial movement but can still cause a significant amount of destruction. A logarithmic scale called the Richter scale

measures the amplitude of seismic waves. An earthquake magnitude of 10 has the largest amplitude, and a magnitude of 1 has the smallest.

Science as an Inquiry

Science begins with questions—it is difficult to have an answer when there are no questions. A great source of inquiry for scientists has been weather. The study of weather is called meteorology. Meteorologists measure temperature, air pressure, wind speed, wind direction, and humidity, all in hopes of predicting how and where air and water vapor will move and behave. These questions inspire meteorologists to use weather balloons and satellites to study weather and make educated guesses. As knowledge grows, technologies also improve and facilitate better weather forecasting. The impressive Doppler radar has provided scientists with meaningful data since the 1980s, allowing them to better predict the weather with more certainty.

Research

Another aspect of science is research, which is the search for answers for a scientific inquiry. One of the largest areas of scientific research is space exploration. Of course, people have always wondered about the universe, but the United States didn't make space research a priority until the 1940s and 1950s "space race" with the Soviet Union. In 1957, Russia launched a satellite called Sputnik, which fueled the intense competition between the two countries. In space research, the question that accelerated space exploration was "How can man travel into space safely?" This question fueled the creation of NASA (the National Aeronautics and Space Administration) on October 1, 1958.

NASA research continues today. They observe the sky, launch satellites and telescopes into space, and study the data collected. Currently, there are a multitude of satellites and land vehicles or "rovers" on Mars collecting data with the hope of one day finding a way for humans to live there. In fact, the target date for human occupation on Mars is somewhere in the 2030s.

Process of Science

Theories are well-supported ideas that evolve from hypotheses and experimentation. A hypothesis is an educated guess about a scientific process or object. Once every angle of investigation has been examined and all evidence supports a hypothesis, only then can it be called a theory. It is important to know that theory development is a process. As technology advances and more aspects of science can be explored, evidence might no longer support a theory. With non-supportive data, either the theory can be modified or completely thrown out while new investigations are developed to examine other explanations.

For example, plate tectonic theory didn't appear until the early 20th century. People thought Earth was static and immobile. Only after many years of investigation and evidence did skeptics finally concede that Earth's surface was broken into plates. This theory wasn't universally accepted until the late 1960s and was considered revolutionary.

Early evidence that supported plate tectonics was publicized in the 1910s by Alfred Wegener, who observed that the South American and African borders to the Atlantic Ocean seemed like they could fit together like puzzle pieces. He proposed the idea of Pangaea, a massive supercontinent that existed long ago and must have broken into pieces due to a process called continental drift. Other evidence supporting plate tectonics were similar fossils found in Africa and South America, suggesting that they were once connected. But skeptics continued to scoff at the theory. Then, in the 1960s it was discovered, with the help of early computers, that a continental shelf (an underwater boundary between plates) between the two continents had a remarkable fit that was very unlikely to be due to chance.

Concepts and Processes

Identifying Problems Based on Observations

Human beings are, by nature, very curious. Long before the scientific method was established, people have been making observations and predicting outcomes, manipulating the physical world to create extraordinary things—from the first man-made fire in 6000 B.C.E. to the satellite that orbited Pluto in 2016. Although the history of the scientific method is sporadic and attributed to many different people, it remains the most reliable way to obtain and utilize knowledge about the observable universe. The scientific method consists of the following steps:

- Make an observation
- Create a question
- Form a hypothesis
- Conduct an experiment
- Collect and analyze data
- Form a conclusion

The first step is to identify a problem based on an observation—the who, what, when, where, why, and how. An **observation** is the analysis of information using basic human senses: sight, sound, touch, taste, and smell. Observations can be two different types—qualitative or quantitative. A **qualitative** observation describes what is being observed, such as the color of a house or the smell of a flower. **Quantitative** observations measure what is being observed, such as the number of windows on a house or the intensity of a flower's smell on a scale of 1–5.

Observations lead to the identification of a problem, also called an **inference**. For example, if a fire truck is barreling down a busy street, the inferences could be:

- There's a fire.
- Someone is hurt.
- Some kid pulled the fire alarm at a local school.

Inferences are logical predictions based on experience or education that lead to the formation of a hypothesis.

Forming and Testing a Hypothesis

A **hypothesis** is a testable explanation of an observed scenario and is presented in the form of a statement. It's an attempt to answer a question based on an observation, and it allows a scientist to predict an outcome. A hypothesis makes assumptions on the relationship between two different variables, and answers the question: "If I do this, what happens to that?"

In order to form a hypothesis, there must be an independent variable and a dependent variable that can be measured. The **independent variable** is the variable that is manipulated, and the **dependent variable** is the result of the change.

For example, suppose a student wants to know how light affects plant growth. Based upon what he or she already knows, the student proposes (hypothesizes) that the more light to which a plant is exposed, the faster it will grow.

- Observation: Plants exposed to lots of light seem to grow taller.
- Question: Will plants grow faster if there's more light available?
- Hypothesis: The more light the plant has, the faster it will grow.
- Independent variable: The amount of time exposed to light (able to be manipulated)
- Dependent variable: Plant growth (the result of the manipulation)

Once a hypothesis has been formed, it must be tested to determine whether it's true or false. (How to test a hypothesis is described in a subsequent section.) After it has been tested and validated as true over and over, then a hypothesis can develop into a theory, model, or law.

Development of Theories, Models, and Laws

Theories, models, and laws have one thing in common: *they develop on the basis of scientific evidence that has been tested and verified by multiple researchers on many different occasions.* Listed below are their exact definitions:

- **Theory**: An explanation of natural patterns or occurrences—i.e., the theory of relativity, the kinetic theory of gases, etc.

- **Model**: A representation of a natural pattern or occurrence that's difficult or impossible to experience directly, usually in the form of a picture or 3-D representation—i.e., Bohr's atomic model, the double-helix model of DNA, etc.

- **Law**: A mathematical or concise description of a pattern or occurrence in the observable universe—i.e., Newton's law of gravity, the laws of thermodynamics, etc.

The terms *theory, model,* and *law* are often used interchangeably in the sciences, although there's an essential difference: theories and models are used to explain *how* and *why* something happens, while

laws describe exactly *what* happens. A common misconception is that theories develop into laws. But theories and models never become laws because they inherently describe different things.

Type	Function	Examples
Theory	To explain how and why something happens	Einstein's Theory of Special Relativity The Big Bang Theory
Model	To represent how and why something happens	A graphical model or drawing of an atom
Laws	To describe exactly what happens	$E = mc^2$ $F = ma$ $PV = nRT$

In order to ensure that scientific theories are consistent, scientists continually gather information and evidence on existing theories to improve their accuracy.

Experimental Design

To test a hypothesis, one must conduct a carefully designed experiment. There are four basic requirements that must be present for an experiment to be valid:

1. A control
2. Variables
3. A constant
4. Repeated and collected data

The **control** is a standard to which the resultant findings are compared. It's the baseline measurement that allows for scientists to determine whether the results are positive or negative. For the example of light affecting plant growth, the control may be a plant that receives no light at all.

The **independent variable** is manipulated (a good way to remember this is *I* manipulate the *I*ndependent variable), and the **dependent variable** is the result of changes to the independent variable. In the plant example, the independent variable is the amount of time exposed to light, and the dependent variable is the resulting growth (or lack thereof) of the plant. For this experiment, there may be three plants—one that receives a minimal amount of light, the control, and one that receives a lot of light.

Finally, there must be constants in an experiment. A **constant** is an element of the experiment that remains unchanged. Constants are extremely important in minimizing inconsistencies within the experiment that may lead to results outside the parameters of the hypothesis. For example, some constants in the above case are that all plants receive the same amount of water, all plants are potted in the same kind of soil, the species of the plant used in each condition is the same, and the plants are stored at the same temperature. If, for instance, the plants received different amounts of water as well as light, it would be impossible to tell whether the plants responded to changes in water or light.

Once the experiment begins, a disciplined scientist must always record the observations in meticulous detail, usually in a journal. A good journal includes dates, times, and exact values of both variables and constants. Upon reading this journal, a different scientist should be able to clearly understand the experiment and recreate it exactly. The journal includes all **collected data**, or any observed changes. In

this case, the data is rates of plant growth, as well as any other phenomena that occurred as a result of the experiment. A well-designed experiment also includes repetition in order to get the most accurate possible readings and to account for any errors, so several trials may be conducted.

Even in the presence of diligent constants, there are an infinite number of reasons that an experiment can (and will) go wrong, known as **sources of error**. All experimental results are inherently accepted as imperfect, if ever so slightly, because experiments are conducted by human beings, and no instrument can measure anything perfectly. The goal of scientists is to minimize those errors to the best of their ability. (Determining sources of error will be discussed in a subsequent section.)

Process Skills Including Observing, Comparing, Inferring, Categorizing, Generalizing, and Concluding

The skills needed to think critically, scientifically, and to follow the scientific method are referred to as **process skills**. These skills are the soil from which scientific knowledge is nurtured and grown. There are six fundamental process skills:

- **Observation**—using the senses to gather information

- **Communication**—using words, drawings, graphs, charts, or videos to effectively present observations

- **Classification**—grouping or categorizing objects or events based on certain attributes or criteria, i.e., sorting subjects into height and weight, grouping plants by species, etc.

- **Measurement**—using tools and instruments to describe dimensional variations in an object or event, such as measuring tape, graduated cylinders, clocks, etc.

- **Inference**—drawing conclusions from observations based on prior knowledge or education, i.e., "the grass is wet; it must have rained last night."

- **Prediction**—anticipating the outcome of an event based on prior knowledge or experiences, i.e., "there are many clouds in the sky; it's going to rain tonight." Prediction is the essential skill in forming a solid hypothesis.

In addition to the basic process skills, there are other skills needed in scientific experiments. One essential skill is **generalization**—a type of inference deduced by broad observations of large groups of people or objects that is used frequently in quantitative research. Because of the near-impossibility of sampling a whole population, generalizations are applied to represent a whole population as accurately as possible.

The final step of the scientific method is to make inferences from observed data, which is also known as forming a **conclusion**. Conclusions are placed at the end of scientific papers and wrap up the experimental procedure with its respective inferences. For example, if the experimental data from the plant growth experiment showed that plants with more light grew 2cm more than plants with minimal light in a given period of time, the conclusion may be that certain components of light stimulate plant growth, so the more light that a plant receives, the taller it will grow.

Nature of Scientific Knowledge

Subject to Change

The nature of science is to continuously gather knowledge in order to develop an understanding of the universe. Because of its experimental nature, there's no such thing as "absolute truth" in science. Even the oldest theories are constantly tested in order to improve our understanding or disregard those that no longer apply in light of new observations and interpretations.

Consistent with Evidence

Science is subject to change because of evidence presented in light of new findings. Science is dependent upon the inferences made from evidence obtained through observation. Introductions, expansions, and revisions of scientific theories must present evidence to ascertain that they're still true.

Based on Reproducible Evidence

Before scientific knowledge is established as true, it must be reproducible—that is, the entire experiment must be able to be duplicated by either the same scientist or a different one to ensure its validity.

Includes Unifying Concepts and Processes

Scientific knowledge must be unified, meaning there are central ideas common to all sciences from which new and improved information can grow. There are standards for unifying concepts and processes that students are required to learn in grades K–12, which include:

- Systems, Order, and Organization

  o Observing the universe in distinct parts and understanding all elements that compose these parts to form the whole—i.e., organisms, galaxies, cells, numbers, government, the entire known universe, etc.

- Evidence, Models, and Explanation

  o Scientific theories are based on collected evidence, which provides explanations and the basis for models that enhance understanding and enable scientists to make predictions.

- Change, Consistency, and Measurement

  o The natural world is consistently changing, yet many patterns are repeated over time— i.e., change of seasons, tidal phases, moon phases, etc.

- Evolution and Equilibrium

  o Organisms are genetically diverse, and traits that are advantageous for survival are passed on through the generations. Natural systems all tend towards equilibrium—a state of balance between opposing processes.

- Form and Function

  o There is a relationship between an object's structure and its function—i.e., tooth shape, cell shape, leaf thickness, etc.

Students as Learners and Science Instruction

How Prior Knowledge and Attitudes Influence Learning

While teachers are undeniably instrumental catalysts in engaging students and sparking a love of science, research has found that a child's prior knowledge, experience, and perceived utility of science drive interest and aspirations in the field. The more positive students' prior experiences with science activities have been, the more students tend to view science education as useful and exciting. Children who have been encouraged to explore different scientific concepts will view science education with enthusiasm, as it provides a vehicle by which questions can be answered and the world can be better understood. This is true especially for the practical scientific concepts that allow students to experience the world around them, such as clouds, magnets, insects, plant growth, stars, and changing seasons.

Not every child has had parental support with their natural scientific curiosity and desire to explore. Early childhood educators should recognize the differing backgrounds and degree to which each child in their classroom has had opportunities to learn, discover, and develop a positive association with science. One benefit of teaching children who are at the early stages of their formal education is that the teacher has a greater ability to influence a child's attitude toward learning, even if they have limited positive background experiences, because the child is young and impressionable.

Selecting Curricula, Content, and Activities to Meet Student Needs

One of the greatest challenges for any classroom teacher is differentiating instruction to meet the needs of each student in the classroom. Every student, regardless of their background, has an equal right to learn in school, but each child is unique. Therefore, by differentiating teaching, one can ensure that every student in the classroom can learn the material, enjoy the process of learning, and reach their potential.

The teaching philosophy of differentiating instruction is based on the premise that the student differences should guide the "what" and the "how" teachers teach. Teachers should modify their instruction so that it meets the varying learning styles, readiness levels, interests, and abilities of the students in their classroom instead of applying a one-size-fits-all approach.

There are three primary components of the curriculum that teachers can differentiate: content, process, and products.

- **Content** is the knowledge, ideas, and skills that teachers wish to impart to students, and the means by which they choose to present these concepts and skills, such as through labs, lectures, demonstrations, readings, and videos. Every student, regardless of their level, should be provided the same core content. Emerging teachers sometimes make the common mistake of watering down content for struggling students. Instead, the same concept should be taught with a varying complexity of the explanation. Teachers should disseminate content in a variety of modes, like readings, experiments, and computer simulations, exposing each student to each at different times. For example, advanced learners might be given a challenging reading, while students who are struggling or ELLs might be given a video or a classroom demonstration to watch. The means by which content is taught is one key way to differentiate instruction for learners at different levels.

- **Process** involves the various activities that deliver the content and help students develop the knowledge and skills being taught. These activities can be modified by the teacher to alter their complexity. For example, additional scaffolding can be provided for students at lower levels. Reteaching, explicit step-by-step directions, or additional resources to supplement instruction are examples of ways to scaffold what is being taught.

- **Products** are the culminating assessments or projects students complete to demonstrate the things they have learned as well as how they can extend those concepts and skills. Products can be modified by altering the level of the assessment (multiple-choice test versus essay test or group project versus solo endeavor, etc.).

Other instructional methods that aid instructional differentiation are grouping students by current level or interest, providing different "stations" in the classroom, and compacting, which helps determine each student's initial level for a given concept.

How Situations in Daily Life Relate to Science Investigation

Science is all around us. The daily lives of students involve scientific concepts directly or things that can be explored via the scientific inquiry process, so teachers can develop lessons with practical instructional material. For example, the function and history behind inventions or discoveries that have impacted daily life could be investigated, including things like refrigerators, light bulbs, microscopes, plastic, computers, antibiotics, and the pasteurization process.

A lab investigating Earth's daily rotation could involve measuring and tracking the height of each student's shadow at set intervals of time throughout the day. Children can outline their shadows with different colors of chalk for each measurement so they can obtain a visual representation of the change. The chalk outlines can also help ensure the child returns to the exact same spot for every measurement. Teachers can use this lesson design to explain how it is Earth spinning around its axis, rather than the Sun moving across the sky, that causes the changes we see in daylight. Students could then be tasked with brainstorming ideas about how this knowledge can inform decisions. For example, once they understand that the sun is highest in the sky and casts maximal sunlight in the middle of the day, they might determine this would be the warmest time to play outside in cold winter months. The varying amount of sunlight and its influence on plant growth could also be discussed. Instructional material that uses everyday products or processes makes science seem useful and can help children "buy in" to the excitement and the utility of studying it.

Common Misconceptions in Science

Educators who have spent any time teaching science at the elementary level are likely well aware that students come into the classroom with many misconceptions regarding science. It then becomes the educator's role to erase the associated mental images and ideas from these misconceptions and replace them with correct information. In general, a **misconception** is a belief that contradicts current scientific theories, thinking, laws, evidence, and facts. The following list includes some common science misconceptions held by elementary school students:

- The Sun moves around Earth and across the sky.
- Seasons occur because Earth gets closer or farther from the Sun.
- The moon is only visible at night.
- The phases of the moon are due to Earth's shadow on the moon.

- A star's brightness is only influenced by its distance from Earth.
- Clouds are formed from cotton or smoke.
- Energy is not conserved because we are running out of it.
- Batteries contain electricity inside.
- When an object is at rest, there are no forces acting upon it.
- Rocks are always heavy.
- Continents don't move.
- Smaller magnets are weaker than larger ones.
- Rivers always flow north to south.
- Only water can melt and freeze.
- Mass and weight are different terms for the same thing.
- The heavier a pendulum bob, the faster it swings.
- A gas does not have mass.
- A viscous liquid is denser than a runny one.
- Heat and temperature are different terms for the same thing.
- Pupils are black spots on the surface of our eyes.
- Offspring can inherit acquired characteristics.

Misconceptions can result from preconceived notions, vernacular issues (wherein terms have different meanings in everyday and scientific language, such as "work"), or religious or cultural beliefs, among other reasons.

Refutational teaching is a pedagogical approach that teachers can employ to help students overcome their misconceptions. **Traditional teaching** starts and ends with instruction that provides the correct facts, information, and known evidence regarding that topic. For example, when teaching about seasons, educators would assert that we experience different seasons here on Earth because the planet is tilted on its axis (about 23.4 degrees) as it rotates around the Sun. The hemisphere experiencing summer is on the part of the planet that's tilted toward the Sun during that portion of the revolution, while the hemisphere experiencing winter is tilted away from the Sun.

Traditional teaching does not delve into any common misconceptions. Refutational teaching takes things a step further by bringing up a misconception about the topic (in this case, that summer occurs because Earth is closer to the Sun and winter occurs because Earth moves further from the Sun). The teacher must then explain why this is thinking is wrong. First, the correct information is shared, rationalized (why "right" is "right"), and then the preconceived notion is debunked (why "wrong" is "wrong"). Finally, the correct facts should be reiterated to form a sandwich of truth. Presenting things in this order helps ensure children do not tune out after initially hearing their misconception asserted and then erroneously thinking they must know all the rest of what will be said.

Hands-On Learning Experience

Science instruction is often one of the most natural places in the elementary school day to incorporate hands-on learning activities. Many scientific concepts and principles can be readily explored through labs, experiments, field trips, and indoor and outdoor activities that require one or more of the five senses. In this way, teachers of science at the elementary level have the powerful tool of hands-on learning in their pockets.

Because many early elementary school students have yet to master reading, it's usually more developmentally appropriate to rely on alternative instructional materials, like labs and demonstrations, rather than readings or worksheets. Young children often prefer to learn by touching, moving, doing, exploring, and observing things, rather than simply listening or watching. Their inclination to question things lends itself quite well to the scientific inquiry process. Teachers can solicit ideas for topics that interest their students and make a list of scientific questions they have. From there, hands-on activities can be planned and implemented to help students discover the answers themselves with the supportive guidance of the teacher in the framework of a well-designed activity. This strategy can promote students' interest in the material and their understanding of the scientific process (making an observation, posing a research question, designing an experiment, gathering and analyzing data, etc.).

Higher-Level Thinking

When teachers use effective questioning strategies, they can help students achieve **higher-level thinking** and the ability to transfer concrete understanding to more abstract levels. It also can spark imagination, enhance inference skills, and provide sound critical thinking patterns that students can apply to their lives outside the classroom. While asking questions is an intuitive process, asking the "right" questions in the "right" way takes forethought and skill. Questions that are closed—answerable with a simple "yes," "no," or short response—typically are less effective at sparking further discussion and healthy debate, both of which are necessary to induce higher-level thinking. Instead of just restating facts, which is a more basic level of thinking, higher-level thinking requires students use those facts or knowledge for a secondary step. For example, students may need to connect and synthesize them, analyze them, categorize and group them, infer something from them, or apply them towards a novel situation.

Questioning strategies that promote higher-level thinking may involve the following:
- Posing open-ended questions
- Asking students to brainstorm alternative explanations to a problem or phenomenon
- Asking students to consider how some of these alternative explanations could be tested
- Tasking students with categorizing concepts and connecting previously-learned material with new ideas (what does this remind you of that we've already learned about?)
- Challenging students to make predictions and inferences (perhaps using language like "guesses" for young children) based on what has been observed

Inclusive Planning Activities

As previously mentioned, all students should have an equal opportunity to learn in the classroom. Because each child has different needs, teachers should plan lessons to accommodate as many students as possible in the classroom. Although this can be a daunting challenge, accommodating the needs of all students is one of the teacher's key responsibilities. Differentiating instruction is the process by which educators can try and fulfill this responsibility. When educators shepherd students through the curriculum in lockstep, or attempt to teach to the "middle ground," many students may fail to gain the intended skills and concepts from the lesson. Students with greater competency may be bored and become distractors to peers. Additionally, they might monopolize class discussions and answer questions before other students have the chance to consider the idea and venture an answer. Students for whom the material is too complex will struggle to follow along and keep up.

A related issue concerns the delivery method of the content and its compatibility with the learning style of each child. For example, if a teacher exclusively relies on readings and worksheets to explain the

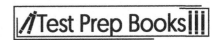

water cycle, students who are auditory learners can miss out. For these students, videos, short lectures, think-pair-share discussions, and guest interviews are likely much more effective. Teachers should spend a significant amount of time and energy planning lessons that meet the curriculum standards and the needs of each student in the classroom.

Sequencing Learning Activities

Background knowledge enables a student to more readily absorb new related concepts. Students at the early elementary level likely have obtained their background knowledge from life experiences and resources in their homes and outside school (parents, siblings, museums, books read to them) rather than from in-class instruction. Because every child hails from a different background and living situation, early childhood educators often compete with a wide variety of background knowledge in their students.

Finding means to assess the background knowledge of students regarding a certain principle (for example, food webs), gives teachers an idea of the starting point to differentiate their instruction and build upon each student's background knowledge in an effective way. Lessons must be properly paced and sequenced to progress student understanding without being overly redundant or aggressive in their aims. Educators should help add to the background knowledge for students who have limited prior learning about a topic, or who possess misconceptions and inaccuracies. This can be accomplished through additional modules and activities, child-friendly websites that explain the fundamentals of the concept, videos, picture books, and paired work with students who have a deeper understanding of the principles. The latter strategy can simultaneously deepen advanced students' understanding. Hands-on experiments are another great way to expose emerging learners to new concepts and give them part of the responsibility in learning the material and discovering the "answers" themselves.

"Exit tickets" are a quick way educators can gauge student understanding after a lesson or activity so that appropriate sequencing can be followed when planning subsequent materials and activities. These short (typically 3 to 6 question), ungraded assessments provide teachers with an easy check-in with each student without taking much class time. For young children who cannot yet write, teachers will need to be more creative with how answers are captured. In these cases, the exit ticket administration many not be quite as brief, requiring some amount of oral expression or discussion, either in groups or as a class. For classrooms that are equipped with technology for every student (such as tablets for each student or tables of students grouped together), teachers can record audio prompts that children can then select and play, and then record their own verbal response. Teachers can use the results of these check-ins to determine the pace by which they can proceed to sequence lessons and build upon the knowledge already mastered.

Science Assessment

Relationships Between a Science Curriculum, Assessment, and Instruction

Although assessment and learning are often viewed as two separate entities in education, they should actually be viewed as two sides of the same coin. Assessment results should inform teachers what they should teach and what students need to learn, and assessments should be thoughtfully designed so that students learn from them. The science curriculum is largely dictated by state and national standards, but within this framework, educators have some latitude to select topics that they think will most interest their students. More importantly, the concepts and the ways in which they are taught should be mostly informed by students' prior knowledge, readiness level, and learning style.

Preliminary assessments, or formative assessments, can be used at the beginning of a new topic to gain insight into the starting place of each student in terms of their understanding of the topic. Lessons and teaching materials can be planned once results from these pretests are analyzed. Additionally, teachers can group students based upon mastery of concepts and needs. A more advanced group might be able to take on more complicated and complex explanations of the content, while novice students might need those same concepts packaged in more basic ways.

Ongoing assessments during various units of study can help teachers take the pulse on how well students are understanding the concepts and principles being taught. Results from these assessments can enlighten educators as to which ideas need further emphasis, reteaching, supplementary materials, and alternative instructional strategies, and which skills and principles have been learned.

Finally, **summative assessments** provide useful feedback as to what students have walked away with, what they are able to reiterate, and most critically, how they are able to apply concrete concepts taught to novel or abstract situations.

Students also have the opportunity to learn from these different stages and iterations of assessments. Sometimes, it is only by having to answer questions alone and without the aid of resources that it becomes clear to students what they know versus what they don't understand about a concept. Assessments can help students figure out where they still have confusion, what further questions they may have, and what strengths and weaknesses they are experiencing as a student of science.

Assessing Science Concepts on an Ongoing Basis

In education, **assessment** is the process of systematically collecting and analyzing information about students' performance. Research has indicated that educators who employ a balanced system of ongoing, interrelated, specifically-designed assessments are able to most effectively reveal changes in students' learning and understanding over time. This has the dual benefit of informing instructional practice and motivating and instilling students' self-responsibility in their learning.

Teachers who design and administer interim assessments give themselves the opportunity to measure students' progress toward proficiency in the applicable standards and mastery of the skills and concepts being taught. This information should be used to inform instruction. If, for example, results indicate that many students are not grasping how atoms form bonds, the instructor can reteach that material, design a demonstration, or create some other alternative way to teach the concept. Interim assessments are also helpful in identifying struggling students who might need more individualized help or additional guidance and resources to learn the material.

For students, a system of ongoing assessments has multiple benefits. It gets them accustomed to the process of being evaluated, which can lessen the stress experienced when taking tests, giving oral reports, completing graded labs, and engaging in other activities where their performance will be measured. Interim assessments also provide students with feedback about their comprehension and skill attainment, which is an effective way to empower them to take responsibility for their learning and motivate them to seek additional help when necessary.

Products such as science projects, lab journals, rubrics, portfolios, student profiles, and checklists can be used as these ongoing assessments. It is important for educators to provide models of "success" so that students have an idea of what is expected and what to strive for. Finished lab reports that students can physically look at, for example, can help the teacher and students be on the same page regarding expectations.

Designs Appropriate Assessments

Educators should incorporate a range of assessments into their curriculum because doing so creates a balanced, fair, and comprehensively-informative system. Routinely administering the same type of assessment (such as a summative multiple-choice test) robs some students from an understanding of the material. It also eliminates valuable tools from the educator's arsenal, which would otherwise help guide content and instructional methods, and lead to better student outcomes.

The following, which are some of the most common types of assessments used in classrooms, should be designed and built into elementary science programs:

- **Performance Assessments**: Used to strengthen a student's higher-order thinking by measuring the ability to apply skills and material that have been learned to other applications or to complete a product or process.

- **Self-Assessments**: Involve students' evaluation of themselves personally. These are useful for helping students develop the ability to monitor their own progress and learning, identify their strengths and weaknesses, and learn when to seek help.

- **Formal Assessments**: Include standardized tests, criterion-referenced tests, norm-referenced tests, essay tests, and achievement tests. These are used to obtain scores and evaluation material for students. They contain material that has been taught and learned and reveal data that can be used to support the analyses of the test. A student's result can be used to determine proficiency of the content and/or achievement in a specific standard.

- **Informal Assessments**: Used spontaneously throughout the day, unit, or school year, these are driven by performance and content rather than data. Teachers may observe students, collect journal responses, ask questions, administer exit tickets, etc. to gather informal assessment information.

- **Formative Assessments**: Used at the beginning of the school year or unit of study to inform teaching by establishing students' starting points and readiness levels.

- **Interim Assessments**: Used periodically throughout the school year or unit of study to evaluate progress toward learning, inform necessary instruction modifications, predict students' needs and areas of weakness, and provide students with feedback about their comprehension and skill attainment.

- **Summative Assessments**: Used at the end of the school year or unit of study to measure the success of students and the instructional method and curriculum materials, and to inform future learning and teaching.

Evaluating Criteria and Assessment Results

Because elementary students are young, early in their educational careers, and still developing in every facet of their lives, educators may fail to see the importance and usefulness of involving their young students in the evaluation and assessment process. A common assumption is that children at these ages are unable to take responsibility in their learning and are uninterested in hearing what is expected of them. However, the truth is that most young pupils thrive on feeling like they have some ability to take care of themselves, make their own choices, and demonstrate their autonomy. Moreover, children tend to respond well when expectations and objectives are clear. For these reasons, it's not only effective, but also helpful, to communicate evaluation criteria and assessment results to students. The task of the educator is to communicate in a way that their young students can understand the purpose of evaluation in general, the specific criteria against which the students will be assessed and why, and how well an individual student is achieving the goals and what he or she can do to improve. Satisfying these outcomes will facilitate a successful assessment process and can help students develop their own self-assessment skills.

Scoring rubrics are particularly helpful in explicitly describing the evaluation criteria and the various benchmarks of performance along the continuum. Teachers should explain performance standards and use examples of anonymous or fabricated finished work to demonstrate models of the different levels of achievement of the standards. After using the rubric and evaluating a student's work or effort, the educator should take the time to explain the outcomes to each student. After several evaluation experiences, students should be given the opportunity to use the same rubric and practice evaluating their own work.

Teachers can lead this process by prompting students to consider what concepts they think they did well in, which concepts they are still working on, and what areas are particularly confusing. It is especially important to place significant evaluative emphasis on a student's effort and attitude in the early elementary years because it will plant the seeds of studiousness, the desire to learn, and self-efficacy in one's own learning. Students can then see that even if they aren't grasping concepts as readily or easily as peers, they aren't "failures." Finally, teachers who involve students in the evaluation process help them develop the ability to constructively critique the work of their peers. As students move through their schooling, the ability to gauge their comprehension becomes imperative for monitoring their mastery, identifying study needs, and learning when to seek additional help.

Forces and Motion

People have been studying the movement of objects since ancient times, sometimes prompted by curiosity, and sometimes by necessity. On earth, items move according to specific guidelines and have motion that is fairly predictable. In order to understand why an object moves along its path, it is important to understand what role forces have on influencing an object's movements. The term force describes an outside influence on an object. Force does not have to refer to something imparted by another object. Forces can act upon objects by touching them with a push or a pull, by friction, or without touch like a magnetic force or even gravity. Forces can affect the motion of an object.

In order to study an object's motion, the object must be locatable and describable. When locating an object's position, it can help to locate it relative to another known object, or put it into a frame of reference. This phrase means that if the placement of one object is known, it is easier to locate another object with respect to the position of the original object.

The measurement of an object's movement or change in position (x), over a change in time (t) is an object's speed. The measurement of speed with direction is velocity. A "change in position" refers to the difference in location of an object's starting point and an object's ending point. In science, the Greek letter Delta, Δ, represents a change.

Equation: $$velocity\ (v) = \frac{\Delta x}{\Delta t}$$

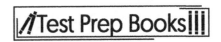

Position is measured in meters, and time is measured in seconds. The standard measurement for velocity is meters/second (m/s).

$$\frac{meters}{second} = \frac{m}{s}$$

The measurement of an object's change in velocity over time is an object's acceleration. Gravity is considered to be a form of acceleration.

Equation: $$\boldsymbol{acceleration\ (a) = \frac{\Delta v}{\Delta t}}$$

Velocity is measured in meters/second and time is measured in seconds. The standard measurement for acceleration is meters/second² (m/s²).

$$\frac{\frac{meters}{second}}{second} = \frac{meters}{second^2} = \frac{m}{s^2}$$

For example, consider a car traveling down the road. The speed can be measured by calculating how far the car is traveling over a certain period of time. However, since the car is traveling in a direction (north, east, south, west), the distance over time is actually the car's velocity. It can be confusing, as many people will often interchange the words speed and velocity. But if something is traveling a certain distance, during a certain time period, in a direction, this is the object's velocity. Velocity is speed with direction.

The change in an object's velocity over a certain amount of time is the object's acceleration. If the driver of that car keeps pressing on the gas pedal and increasing the velocity, the car would have a change in velocity over the change in time and would be accelerating. The reverse could be said if the driver were depressing the brake and the car was slowing down; it would have a negative acceleration, or be decelerating. Since acceleration also has a direction component, it is possible for a car to accelerate without changing speed. If an object changes direction, it is accelerating.

Motion creates something called momentum. This is a calculation of an object's mass multiplied by its velocity. Momentum can be described as the amount an object wants to continue moving along its current course. Momentum in a straight line is called linear momentum. Just as energy can be transferred and conserved, so can momentum.

For example, a car and a truck moving at the same velocity down a highway will not have the same momentum, because they do not have the same mass. The mass of the truck is greater than that of the car, therefore the truck will have more momentum. In a head-on collision, the vehicles would be expected to slide in the same direction of the truck's original motion because the truck has a greater momentum.

The amount of force during a length of time creates an impulse. This means that if a force acts on an object during a given amount of time, it will have a determined impulse. However, if the length of time can be extended, the force will be less, due to the conservation of momentum.

Consider another example: when catching a fast baseball, it helps soften the blow of the ball to follow through, or cradle the catch. This technique is simply extending the time of the application of the force of the ball, so the impact of the ball does not hurt the hand. As a final example, if a martial arts expert wants to break a board by executing a chop from their hand, they need to exert a force on a small point on the boards, extremely quickly. If they slow down the time of the impact from the force of their hand, they will probably injure their hand and not break the board.

Newton's Three Laws of Motion

Sir Isaac Newton spent a great deal of time studying objects, forces, and how an object's motion responds to forces. Newton made great advancements by using mathematics to describe the motion of objects and to predict future motions of objects by applying his mathematical models to situations. Through his extensive research, Newton is credited for summarizing the basic laws of motion for objects here on Earth. These laws are as follows:

First Law
The first law is the law of inertia. An object in motion remains in motion, unless acted upon by an outside force. An object at rest remains at rest, unless acted upon by an outside force. Simply put, inertia is the natural tendency of an object to continue along with what it is already doing; an outside force would have to act upon the object to make it change its course. This includes an object that is sitting still. The inertia of an object is relative to its momentum.

> Example: If a car is driving at a constant speed in a constant direction (also called a constant velocity), it would take a force in a different direction to change the path of the car. Conversely, if the car is sitting still, it would take a force greater than that of friction from any direction to make that stationary car move.

Second Law
The force (F) on an object is equal to the mass (m) multiplied by the acceleration (a) on that object. Mass (m) refers to the amount of a substance and acceleration (a) refers to a rate of velocity over time. In the case of an object falling on Earth, the value of gravity will be placed in for acceleration (a). In the case of an object at rest on Earth, gravity is placed in for acceleration (a), and the force calculated by F = ma is called Weight (W). It is important to discern that an object's mass (measured in kilograms, kg) is not the same as an object's weight (measured in Newtons, N). Weight is the mass times the gravity.

> Example: The gravity on Earth's moon is considerably less than the gravity on earth. Therefore, the weight of an object on Earth's moon would be considerably less than the weight of the object on earth. In each case, a different value for acceleration/gravity would be used in the equation F = ma. Mass is used to calculate weight, and they are not the same.

> Example: If a raisin is dropped into a bowl of pudding, it would make a small indentation and stick in the pudding a bit, but if a grapefruit is dropped into the same bowl of pudding, it would splatter the pudding out of the bowl and most likely hit the bottom of the bowl. Even though both items are accelerating at the same rate (gravity), the mass of the grapefruit is larger than that of the raisin; therefore, the force with which the grapefruit hits the bowl of pudding is considerably larger than the force from the raisin hitting the bowl of pudding.

Third Law
The third law of motion states that for every action there is an equal and opposite reaction. If someone pounds a fist on a table, the reactionary force from the table causes the person to feel a sharp force on the fist. The magnitude of the force felt on the fist increases the harder that they pound on the table. It should be noted that action/reaction pairs occur simultaneously. As the fist applies a force on the table, the table instantaneously applies an equal and opposite force on the fist.

Example: Imagine a person is wearing ice skates on ice and attempts to push on a heavy sled sitting in front of them. They will be pushed in the direction opposite of their push on the sled; the push the skater is experiencing is equal and opposite to the force they are exerting on the sled. This is a good example of how the icy surface helps to lessen the effects of friction and allows the reactionary force to be more easily observed.

Forces are anything acting upon an object either in motion or at rest; this includes friction and gravity. These forces are often depicted by using a force diagram or free body diagram. A force diagram shows an object as the focal point, with arrows denoting all the forces acting upon the object. The direction of the head of the arrow indicates the direction of the force. The object at the center can also be exerting forces on things in its surroundings.

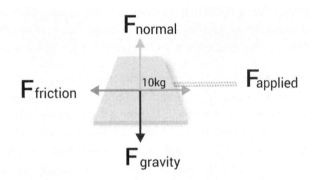

Equilibrium

If an object is in constant motion or at rest (its acceleration equals zero), the object is said to be in equilibrium. It does not imply that there are no forces acting upon the object, but that all of the forces are balanced in order for the situation to continue in its current state. This can be thought of as a "balanced"' situation.

Note that if an object is resting on top of a mountain peak or traveling at a constant velocity down the side of that mountain, both situations describe a state of equilibrium.

Falling Objects

Objects falling within Earth's atmosphere are all affected by gravity. Their rate of acceleration will be that of gravity. If two objects were dropped from a great height at the exact same time, regardless of mass, theoretically, they should hit the ground at the same time. This is due to gravity acting upon them at the same rate. In actuality, if this were attempted, the shape of the objects and external factors such as air resistance would affect their rates of fall and cause a discrepancy in when each lands. Consider the traditional illustration of this principle: a feather and a rock are released at the same time in regular air versus being released at the same time in a vacuum. In the open atmosphere, the feather would slowly loft down to the ground, due to the effects of air resistance, while the rock would quickly drop to the ground. If the feather and the rock were both released at the same time in a vacuum, they would both hit the bottom at the same time. The rate of fall is not dependent upon the mass of the item or any external factors in a vacuum (there is no air resistance in a vacuum); therefore, all that would be affecting the rate of fall would be gravity. Gravity affects every object on Earth with the same rate of acceleration.

Circular Motion

An axis is an invisible line on which an object can rotate. This is most easily observed with a toy top. There is actually a point (or rod) through the center of the top on which the top can be observed to be spinning. This is called the axis.

When objects move in a circle by spinning on their own axis, or because they are tethered around a central point (also an axis), they exhibit circular motion. Circular motion is similar in many ways to linear (straight line) motion; however, there are a few additional points to note. A spinning object is always accelerating because it is always changing direction. The force causing this constant acceleration on or around an axis is called centripetal force and is often associated with centripetal acceleration. Centripetal force always pulls toward the axis of rotation. An imaginary reactionary force, called centrifugal force, is the outward force felt when an object is undergoing circular motion. This reactionary force is not the real force; it just feels like it is there. This has also been referred to as a "fictional force." The true force is the one pulling inward, or the centripetal force.

The terms centripetal and centrifugal are often mistakenly interchanged. If the centripetal force acting on an object moving with circular motion is removed, the object will continue moving in a straight line tangent to the point on the circle where the object last experienced the centripetal force. For example, when a traditional style washing machine spins a load of clothes in order to expunge the water from the load, it spins the machine barrel in a circle at a high rate of speed. A force is pulling in toward the center of the circle (centripetal force). At the same time, the wet clothes, which are attempting to move in a straight line, are colliding with the outer wall of the barrel that is moving in a circle. The interaction between the wet clothes and barrel wall cause a reactionary force to the centripetal force and expel the water out of the small holes that line the outer wall of the barrel.

Conservation of Angular Momentum

An object moving in a circular motion also has momentum; for circular motion it is called angular momentum. This is determined by rotational inertia and rotational velocity and the distance of the mass from the axis of rotation or center of rotation. When objects are exhibiting circular motion, they also demonstrate the conservation of angular momentum, meaning that the angular momentum of a system is always constant, regardless of the placement of the mass. Rotational inertia can be affected by how far the mass of the object is placed with respect to the center of rotation (axis of rotation). The larger the distance between the mass and the center of rotation, the slower the rotational velocity. Conversely, if the mass is closer to the center of rotation, the rotational velocity increases. A change in one affects the other, thus conserving the angular momentum. This holds true as long as no external forces act upon the system.

For example, an ice skater spinning on one ice skate extends their arms out for a slower rotational velocity. When the skater brings their arms in close to their body (or lessens the distance between the mass and the center of rotation), their rotational velocity increases and they spin much faster. Some skaters extend their arms straight up above their head, which causes an extension of the axis of rotation, thus removing any distance between the mass and the center of rotation and maximizing their rotational velocity.

Another example is when a person selects a horse on a merry-go-round: the placement of their horse can affect their ride experience. All of the horses are traveling with the same rotational speed, but in order to travel along the same plane as the merry-go-round turns, a horse on the outside will have a

greater linear speed, due to it being farther away from the axis of rotation. Another way to think of it is that an outside horse has to cover a lot more ground than a horse on the inside, in order to keep up with the rotational speed of the merry-go-round platform. Thrill seekers should always select an outer horse.

Physical and Chemical Properties

In the physical sciences, it is important to break things down to their simplest components in order to truly understand why they act and react the way they do. It may seem burdensome to separate out each part of an object or to diagram each movement made by an object, but these methods provide a solid basis for understanding how to accurately depict the motion of objects and then correctly predict their future movements.

Everything around us is composed of different materials. To properly understand and sort objects, we must classify what types of materials they comprise. This includes identifying the foundational properties of each object such as its reaction to chemicals, heat, water, or other materials. Some objects might not react at all and this is an important property to note. Other properties include the physical appearance of the object or whether it has any magnetic properties. The importance of being able to sort and classify objects is the first step to understanding them.

- Matter: anything that has mass and takes up space

- Substance: a type of matter that cannot be separated out into new material through a physical reaction

- Elements: substances that cannot be broken down by either physical or chemical reactions. Elements are in the most basic form and are grouped by identified properties using the Periodic Table. The periodic table groups elements based on similar properties. Metallic elements, inert elements, and transition elements are a few categories used to organize elements on the periodic table. New elements are added as they are discovered or created, and these newer elements tend to be heavier, fall into the metal section of the periodic table, and are often unstable. Examples of elements include carbon, gold, and helium.

- Atoms: the building blocks of all elements. Atoms are the smallest particles of matter that retain their identities during chemical reactions. Atoms have a central nucleus that includes positively charged protons, and neutrons, which carry no charge. Atoms are also surrounded by electrons that carry a negative charge. The amount of each component determines what type of atom is formed when the components come together. For example, two hydrogen atoms and one oxygen atom can bond together to form water, but the hydrogen and oxygen atoms still remain true to their original identities.

- Mass: the measure of how much of a substance exists in an object. The measure of mass is not the same as weight, area, or volume.

Physical Properties vs. Chemical Properties

Both physical and chemical properties are used to sort and classify objects:

- Physical properties: refers to the appearance, mass, temperature, state, size, or color of an object or fluid; a physical change indicates a change in the appearance, mass, temperature, state, size or color of an object or fluid.

- Chemical properties: refers to the chemical makeup of an object or fluid; a chemical change refers to an alteration in the makeup of an object or fluid and forms a new solution or compound.

Reversible Change vs. Non-Reversible Change

Reversible change (physical change) is the changing of the size or shape of an object without altering its chemical makeup. Examples include the heating or cooling of water, change of state (solid, liquid, gas), the freezing of water into ice, or cutting a piece of wood in half.

When two or more materials are combined, it is called a mixture. Generally, a mixture can be separated out into the original components. When one type of matter is dissolved into another type of matter (a solid into a liquid or a liquid into another liquid), and cannot easily be separated back into its original components, it is called a solution.

States of matter refers to the form substances take such as solid, liquid, gas, or plasma. Solid refers to a rigid form of matter with a flexed shape and a fixed volume. Liquid refers to the fluid form of matter with no fixed shape and a fixed volume. Gas refers to an easily compressible fluid form of matter with no fixed shape that expands to fill any space available. Finally, plasma refers to an ionized gas where electrons flow freely from atom to atom.

> Examples: A rock is a solid because it has a fixed shape and volume. Water is considered to be a liquid because it has a set volume, but not a set shape; therefore, you could pour it into different containers of different shapes, as long as they were large enough to contain the existing volume of the water. Oxygen is considered to be a gas. Oxygen does not have a set volume or a set shape; therefore, it could expand or contract to fill a container or even a room. Gases in fluorescent lamps become plasma when electric current is applied to them.

Matter can change from one state to another in many ways, including through heating, cooling, or a change in pressure.

Changes of state are identified as:

- Melting: solid to liquid
- Sublimation: solid to gas
- Evaporation: liquid to gas
- Freezing: liquid to solid
- Condensation: gas to liquid
- Non-reversible change (chemical change): When one or more types of matter change and it results in the production of new materials. Examples include burning, rusting, and combining solutions. If a piece of paper is burned it cannot be turned back into its original state. It has forever been altered by a chemical change.

Energy and Interactions

Energy

The term **energy** typically refers to an object's ability to perform work. This can include a transfer of heat from one object to another, or from an object to its surroundings. Energy is usually measured in Joules. There are two main categories of energy: renewable and non-renewable.

- Renewable: energy produced from the exhaustion of a resource that can be replenished. Burning wood to produce heat, then replanting trees to replenish the resource is an instance of using renewable energy.

- Non-renewable: energy produced from the exhaustion of a resource that cannot be replenished. Burning coal to produce heat would be an example of a non-renewable energy. Although coal is a natural resource found in/on the earth that is mined or harvested from the earth, it cannot be regrown or replenished. Other examples include oil and natural gas (fossil fuels).

Temperature is measured in degrees Celsius (C) or Kelvin (K). Temperature should not be confused with heat. Heat is a form of energy: a change in temperature or a transfer of heat can also be a measure of energy. The amount of energy measured by the change in temperature (or a transfer) is the measure of heat.

Heat energy (thermal energy) can be transferred through the following ways:

Conduction

Conduction is the heating of one object by another through the actual touching of molecules, in order to transfer heat across the objects involved. A spiral burner on an electric stovetop heats from one molecule touching another to transfer the heat via conduction.

Convection

Heat transfer due to the movement/flow of molecules from areas of high concentration to ones of low concentration. Warmer molecules tend to rise, while colder molecules tend to sink. The heat in a house will rise from the vents in the floor to the upper levels of the structure and circulate in that manner, rising and falling with the movement of the molecules. This molecular movement helps to heat or cool a house and is often called convection current.

Radiation

The sun warms Earth through radiation or radiant energy. Radiation does not need any medium for the heat to travel; therefore, the heat from the sun can radiate to Earth across space.

Greenhouse Effect

The sun transfers heat into Earth's atmosphere through radiation traveling in waves. The atmosphere helps protect Earth from extreme exposure to the sun, while reflecting some of the waves continuously within the atmosphere, creating habitable temperatures. The rest of the waves are meant to dissipate out through the atmosphere and back into space.

Energy can be harnessed to operate objects, and this energy is obtained from various sources such as electricity, food, gasoline, batteries, wind, and sun. For example, wind turbines out in a field are turned by the natural power of the wind. The turbines then store that energy internally in power cells; that stored energy can be used to power the lights on a farm or run machinery.

Potential Energy vs. Kinetic Energy

Potential energy (gravitational potential energy, or PE) is stored energy, or energy due to an object's height above the ground. Kinetic energy (KE) is the energy of motion. If an object is moving, it has some amount of kinetic energy.

Consider a rollercoaster car sitting still on the tracks at the top of a hill. The rollercoaster has all potential energy and no kinetic energy. As it travels down the hill, the energy transfers from potential energy into kinetic energy. At the bottom of the hill, where the car is going the fastest, it has all kinetic energy, but no potential energy. If energy losses to the environment (friction, heat, sound) are ignored, the amount of potential energy at the top of the hill equals the amount of kinetic energy at the bottom of the hill.

Mechanical Energy

Mechanical energy is the sum of the potential energy plus the kinetic energy in a system, minus energy lost to non-conservative forces. Often, the effects of non-conservative forces are small enough that they can be ignored. The total mechanical energy of a system is conserved or always the same. The amount of potential energy and the amount of kinetic energy can vary to add up to this total, but the total mechanical energy in the situation remains the same.

$$ME = PE + KE$$

$$Mechanical\ Energy = Potential\ Energy + Kinetic\ Energy$$

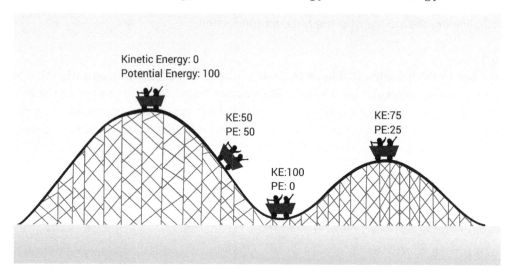

An illustration of a rollercoaster going down a hill demonstrates this point. At the top of the hill a label of $ME = PE$ describes the rollercoaster, halfway down the hill the label $ME = \frac{1}{2}PE + \frac{1}{2}KE$ describes the rollercoaster, and at the bottom of the hill, $ME = KE$ describes the rollercoaster.

Remember, energy can transfer or change forms, but it cannot be created or destroyed. This transfer can take place through waves (including light waves and sound waves), heat, impact, etc.

Simple Machines

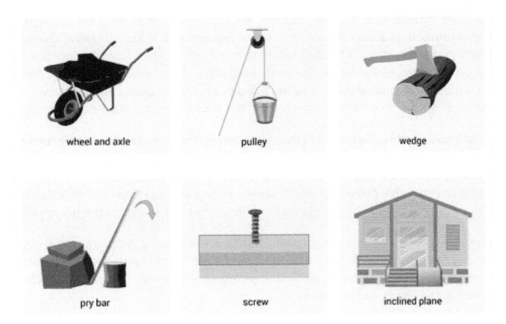

The use of simple machines can help by requiring less force to perform a task with the same result. This is also referred to as mechanical advantage.

Trying to lift a child into the air to pick an apple from a tree would require less force if the child was placed on the end of a teeter-totter and the adult pushed the other end of the teeter-totter down, in order to elevate the child to the same height to pick the apple. In this instance, the teeter-totter is a lever and provides a mechanical advantage to make the job easier.

Interactions of Energy

There is a fundamental law of thermodynamics (the study of heat and movement) called Conservation of Energy. This law states that energy cannot be created or destroyed, but rather energy is transferred to different forms involved in a process. For instance, a car pushed beginning at one end of a street will not continue down that street forever; it will gradually come to a stop some distance away from where it was originally pushed. This does not mean the energy has disappeared or has been exhausted; it means the energy has been transferred to different mediums surrounding the car. The frictional force from the road on the tires dissipates some of the energy, the air resistance from the movement of the car dissipates some of the energy, the sound from the tires on the road dissipates some of the energy, and the force of gravity pulling on the car dissipates some of the energy. Each value can be calculated in a number of ways including measuring the sound waves from the tires, measuring the temperature change in the tires, measuring the distance moved by the car from start to finish, etc. It is important to understand that many processes factor into such a small situation, but all situations follow the conservation of energy.

As in the earlier example, the rollercoaster at the top of a hill has a measurable amount of potential energy, and when it rolls down the hill, it converts most of that energy into kinetic energy. There are still additional factors like friction and air resistance working on the rollercoaster and dissipating some of the energy, but energy transfers in every situation.

Electrostatics

Electrostatics is the study of electric charges at rest. A charge comes from an atom having more or fewer electrons than protons. If an atom has more electrons than protons, it has a negative charge. If an atom has fewer electrons than protons, it has a positive charge. It is important to remember that opposite charges attract each other, while like charges repel each other. So, a negative attracts a positive, a negative repels a negative, and similarly, a positive repels a positive. Just as energy cannot be created or destroyed, neither can charge; charge is transferred. This transfer can be done through touch.

If a person wears socks and scuffs their feet across carpeting, they are transferring electrons to the carpeting through friction. If that person then goes to touch a light switch, they will receive a small shock, which is the electrons transferring from the switch to their hand. The person lost electrons to the carpet, which left them with a positive charge; therefore, the electrons from the switch attract to the person for the transfer. The shock is the electrons jumping from the switch to the person's finger.

Another method of charging an object is through induction. Induction is when a charged object is brought near, but not touched to, a neutral conducting object. The charged object will cause the electrons within the conductor to move. If the charged object is negative, the electrons will be induced away from the charged object and vice versa.

Yet another way to charge an object is through polarization. Polarization can be achieved by simply reconfiguring the electrons on an object. If a person were to rub a balloon on their hair, the balloon would then stick to a wall. This is because rubbing the balloon causes it to become negatively charged and when the balloon is held against a neutral wall, the negatively charged balloon repels all of the wall's electrons, causing a positively charged surface on the wall. This type of charge would be temporary, due to the massive size of the wall, and the charges would quickly redistribute.

Electric Current

Electrical current is the process by which electrons carry charge. In order to make the electrons move so that they can carry a charge, a change in voltage must be present. On a small scale, this is demonstrated through the electrons travelling from the light switch to a person's finger in the example where the person scuffed their socks on a carpet. The difference between the switch and the finger caused the electrons to move. On a larger and more sustained scale, this movement would need to be more controlled. This can be achieved through batteries/cells and generators. Batteries or cells have a chemical reaction that takes place inside, causing energy to be released and a charge to be able to move freely. Generators convert mechanical energy into electric energy.

If a wire is run from touching the end of a battery to the end of a light bulb, and then another is run from touching the base of the light bulb to the opposite end of the original battery, the light bulb will light up. This is due to a complete circuit being formed with the battery and the electrons being carried across the voltage drop (the two ends of the battery). The appearance of the light from the bulb is the visible heat caused by the friction of the electrons moving through the filament.

Electric Energy

Electric energy can be derived from a number of sources including coal, wind, sun, and nuclear reactions. Electricity has numerous applications, including being able to transfer into light, sound, heat, or magnetic forces.

Magnetic Forces

Magnetic forces can occur naturally in certain types of materials. If two straight rods are made from iron, they will naturally have a negative end (pole) and a positive end (pole). These charged poles react just like any charged item: opposite charges attract and like charges repel. They will attract each other when set up positive to negative, but if one rod is turned around, the two rods will repel each other due to the alignment of negative to negative and positive to positive.

These types of forces can also be created and amplified by using an electric current.

The relationship between magnetic forces and electrical forces can be explored by sending an electric current through a stretch of wire, which creates an electromagnetic force around the wire from the charge of the current, as long as the flow of electricity is sustained. This magnetic force can also attract and repel other items with magnetic properties. Depending upon the strength of the current in the wire, a smaller or larger magnetic force can be generated around this wire. As soon as the current is cut off, the magnetic force also stops.

Magnetic Energy

Magnetic energy can be harnessed, or controlled, from natural sources or from a generated source (a wire carrying electric current). Magnetic forces are used in many modern applications, including the creation of super-speed transportation. Super-magnets are used in rail systems and supply a cleaner form of energy than coal or gasoline.

Sound/Acoustic Energy

Just like light, sound travels in waves and both are forms of energy. The transmittance of a sound wave produced when plucking a guitar string sends vibrations at a specific frequency through the air, resulting in one's ear hearing a specific note or sets of notes that form a chord. If the same guitar is plugged into an electric amplifier, the strength of the wave is increased, producing what is perceived as a "louder" note. If a glass of water is set on the amplifier, the production of the sound wave can also be visually observed in the vibrations in the water. If the guitar were being plucked loudly enough and in great succession, the force created by the vibrations of the sound waves could even knock the glass off of the amplifier.

Waves can travel through different mediums. When they reach a different material (i.e., light traveling from air to water), they can bend around and through the new material. This is called refraction.

If one observes a straw in half a glass of water from above, the straw appears to be bent at the height of the water. The straw is still straight, but the observation of light passing from air to water (different materials) makes the straw seem as though it bends at the water line. This illusion occurs because the human eye can perceive the light travels differently through the two materials. The light might slow down in one material, or refract or reflect off of the material, causing differences in an object's appearance.

In another example, imagine a car driving straight along a paved road. If one or two of the tires hit the gravel along the side of the road, the entire car will pull in that direction, due to the tires in the gravel now traveling slower than the tires on the paved road. This is what happens when light travels from one medium to another: its path becomes warped, like the path of the car, rather than traveling in a straight line. This is why a straw appears to be bent when the light travels from water to air; the path is warped.

When waves encounter a barrier, like a closed door, parts of the wave may travel through tiny openings. Once a wave has moved through a narrow opening, the wave begins to spread out and may cause interference. This process is called diffraction.

Energy Transformations and Conservation

Energy Transformation

Fossil Fuels

Fossil fuels are organic compounds from dead organisms that, when burned, produce energy. Through the pressure from rock layers above them, the heat emanating from Earth's mantle, and decomposition, these once-living organisms transform into oil, coal, and natural gas. Fossil fuels provide energy for the modern world, but there is a strong push to find other ways to harness energy.

Scientists are interested in finding renewable sources of energy, such as:

- Wind: Converting kinetic energy from wind into electrical energy using windmills (turbines) is inexpensive.

- Solar: Converting light energy from the sun using solar cells and panels is a more expensive option than wind energy, and effective storage solutions need to be developed for extended cloudy days.

- Geothermal: Converting heat energy that water picks up from Earth's surface into electricity requires expensive power stations that can only exist at geographical locations where water and heat converge (close to hot springs, for example).

- Hydroelectric: Converting kinetic energy from running water to electrical energy using water turbines has a major drawback. Hydroelectric power requires dams to hold water (to slow down its movement to maximize the energy production), which are expensive and can damage ecosystems.

- Biofuels/Biomass: Converting potential energy from decomposing organic material is currently expensive and also has the potential to damage ecosystems.

Energy

Energy is everywhere and is one of the few things in the universe believed to be constant. That means that in the whole universe, if all the energy could be measured (energy in all the stars, atoms, etc.), the amount of energy that was present at the beginning of time is exactly the same as it is now. The only difference is that energy has been converted into different forms. For example, a plant gets its energy from the Sun, using it to grow bigger and stronger; therefore, the Sun's energy is converted and stored inside the plant. Then a person eats the plant, using its stored energy. In this example, energy exists in the form of light, growth, and movement (picking the plant and chewing it).

Only with the energy food provides can organisms exist. Think of a construction team and a pile of bricks and mortar. The bricks are not going to just arrange themselves into a building. However, if a construction team uses their muscles and energy, the complex building can be built. If the construction team runs out of food, though, they will become exhausted and will be unable to construct the building.

The human body is the same way. Organs (heart, brain, stomach, etc.) are like the bricks. The chemical reactions in the body are like the workers. Energy is the food that the workers need to build the organism. The food of life is sugar, specifically glucose. A candy bar, soda, or a slice of birthday cake can provide a boost of energy because of all the sugar they contain. There are many bonds between the molecules of sugar, holding them in place (like the mortar holding the bricks in a building). When the bonds are broken in digestion, all that energy is released so that living things can invest that energy into chemical reactions.

Two chemical reactions are critical for living things: photosynthesis and respiration.

Photosynthesis in the Chloroplast Provides Energy

Any producer must have a chloroplast in order to convert light energy into food, usually in the form of a carbohydrate. Chloroplasts are organelles that look like little green beans because they contain the pigment chlorophyll, which is able to absorb the sunlight's energy in the form of photons, or light rays. Some prokaryotes are also photosynthetic, and although they don't have a chloroplast because they're too simple and don't contain organelles, they have a pigment in order to make their own food.

Plants need water and sunlight to live. Plants suck up water from their roots. The sunlight they need is absorbed by the chlorophyll in chloroplasts, which are clustered and concentrated in their leaves. Interestingly, the chlorophyll actually is able to absorb every color of light except for green, which is why leaves look green: they reflect green light. If the roots take in water and the leaves take in carbon dioxide and sunlight energy, why are stems important? The stems in plants are an example of how structure helps function. The stem is like a skeleton for plants; it holds the leaves high so they can be closer to the sun.

Plants are critical for life on earth because they absorb the energy from the sun and invest it in the bonds that make sugar. Sugar passes through the food chain to provide energy for all living organisms. Plants and other autotrophs can make their own energy, while heterotrophs (which cannot make their own energy) consume the sugar, break it down, and convert it into usable energy with their mitochondria.

Structure and Function of Living Things

Characteristics of Living and Non-Living Things

There are several common traits among all living organisms, including:

- They are comprised of cells
- They contain DNA, the genetic code of life
- They grow and develop
- They reproduce
- They need food for energy
- They maintain homeostasis
- They react to their surroundings
- They evolve as a population

There are two types of cells that make up living things: simple bacterial cells (**prokaryotes**) and the complicated cells of protists, fungi, plants, and animals (**eukaryotes**). All of these have a set of instructions, DNA, which codes for the proteins that allow organisms to grow. In the case of bacteria and single-celled eukaryotes, there is simple development, such as creating structures like DNA, **ribosomes** (protein factories), and a cell membrane. Bacteria do not have complex development because they simply divide once and make a new organism; however, multicellular organisms develop more complex structures—for examples, humans have hearts, stomachs, brains, etc. A human starts as one fused cell called a **zygote**. In nine months, that zygote has developed so much that it has all the internal organs needed to support life.

Organisms cannot live without energy to fuel the necessary reactions to grow and develop. They get the energy they need either by making it themselves (if they are **producers/autotrophs** like plants) or consuming it (like animals and fungi) from an outside source. Not only do organisms use that food to grow and develop, but they also use it to stay healthy and maintain homeostasis. For example, the human body has a constant temperature of 98.6 degrees. If the temperature goes above that, the body starts to sweat to cool off. Much below that temperature, the body will shiver in order to generate energy to heat up. For survival, all organisms must be highly regulated to function, kind of like a car. Every single part has to work together in harmony in order to function properly.

Living things, such as humans, respond to their surroundings. If someone hears a loud noise, his or her head turns toward it. If something gets thrown at one's face, the person will blink. Even plants grow towards sunlight. Living things also evolve as a population. Humans today are nothing like our ancestors of long ago because as a species, humans had to continually adapt to Earth's changing environment.

An extensive explanation of these characteristics of life is beyond an early childhood curriculum, but it's helpful for the teacher to know them because delineating living and nonliving objects can be tricky. A teacher needs to know why fire, a dead grasshopper, and a robot are not alive, because these are common student misconceptions. Although a fire can grow, it does not have DNA. Although a dead grasshopper is made of cells and has DNA, it can't grow or reproduce. A robot doesn't have DNA and isn't made of cells, although it can react to its environment. Conversely, some students don't believe that plants are alive because they don't walk around. To illustrate that they are alive, simple experiments can be used to show that they can reproduce, develop, and grow, such as planting seeds and using light-boxes to show that plants grow toward light.

Teachers must be able to explain that not all organisms move. Plants are alive because they are made of cells, have DNA, grow independently, and meet all of the other characteristics of life. Tiny germs are alive for the same reasons.

These nuances are complicated, but young students should be able to explain that living things grow and nonliving things don't. They should be able to identify mushrooms, plants, and animals as living, and fire, desks, and robots as nonliving.

Cellular Organization

Prokaryotes contain ribosomes, DNA, cytoplasm, a cell membrane, a cytoskeleton, and a cell wall. Eukaryotes vary between kingdoms but contain all of these structures except a cell wall because animal cells require so much mobility. Large, land-dwelling animals typically compensate with an exoskeleton (like insects) or an endoskeleton (like humans and other mammals, reptiles, and birds) for structure.

All bacterial cells are unicellular (existing as just one cell). Almost all types of protist and some species in fungi kingdom are unicellular, but they still have the complicated organelles of eukaryotes. A few protists, almost all fungi, and all plants and animals are multicellular. Multicellularity leads to development of structures that are perfectly designed for their function.

Cells combine to form tissue. Tissue combines to form organs. Organs combine to form organ systems, and organ systems combine to form one organism. The structures of all of these combinations allow for the maximum functionality of an organism, as demonstrated by the nervous system.

A neuron is a cell in the nervous system designed to send and receive electrical impulses. Neurons have dendrites, which are sensors waiting to receive a message. Neurons also have an axon, a long arm that sends the message to the neighboring neuron. The axon also has insulation known as myelin that speeds the message along. Many neurons combine to form a nerve, the tissue of the nervous system, which is like a long wire. The structure of this nerve is perfect—it is a long cable whose function is to send signals to the brain so the brain can process the information and respond. Nerve tissue combines with other tissue to form the brain, a complex structure of many parts.

The brain also has glands (epithelial tissue) that release hormones to control processes in our body. The brain and spinal cord together form the central nervous system that controls the stimulus/response signaling in our body. The nervous system coordinates with the circulatory system to make our heart beat, the digestive system to control food digestion, the muscular system to move an arm, the respiratory system to facilitate breathing, and all other body systems to make the entire organism functional. Cells are the basic building block in our bodies, and their structure is critical for their function and the function of the tissues, organs, and systems that they comprise.

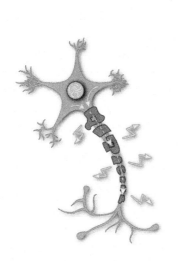 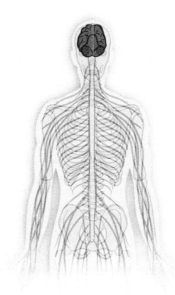

In the graphic above, the left depicts a neuron, and the right depicts the nervous system. A neuron is a nerve cell, and it is the basic building block of the nervous system. Cell, tissue, organ, and organ system structure are critical for function.

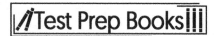

The following table lists organ systems in the human body:

Name	Function	Main organs
Nervous	Detect stimuli and direct response	Brain and spinal cord
Circulatory	Pump blood to deliver oxygen to cells so they can perform cellular respiration	Heart
Respiratory	Breathe in oxygen (reactant for cellular respiration) and release carbon dioxide waste	Lungs
Muscular	Movement	Heart and muscles
Digestive	Break down food so that glucose can be delivered to cells for energy	Stomach, small intestine, lots of others
Skeletal	Support and organ protection	All sorts of joints, skull, ribcage

Reproduction and the Mechanisms of Heredity

Cellular Reproduction

Unlike viruses, all living organisms can independently reproduce, but reproduction occurs differently between bacteria and the more complex kingdoms. Bacteria reproduce via binary fission, which is a simpler process than eukaryotic division because it doesn't involve splitting a nucleus and doesn't have a web of proteins to pull chromosomes apart. Prokaryotes have simpler DNA compared to cells that have a much larger number of individual chromosomes (humans have two sets of 23 chromosomes—one set from mom and one set from dad, for a total of 46 chromosomes). Think of going from class to class with two identical binders (like bacteria) versus going from class to class with 23 identical pairs of binders (humans); it would be much more difficult to organize the large set of binders than the smaller one.

Binary fission in bacteria is therefore relatively easy. Bacteria copy their DNA in a process called DNA replication, grow, and then the replicated DNA moves to either side, and two new cells are made.

Eukaryotic cell division is part of a well-defined cycle with the following phases:

- G1 phase: The cell is growing and working.

- S phase: The cell is getting too large, so it copies its DNA because it wants to make sure the two new cells have the full instruction manual that is DNA.

- G2 phase: The cell uses its workers to get ready for cell division.

- M phase: Chromosomes condense and line up in the middle of the cell. The copies are sent to either side.

- Cytokinesis: The moment when the cytoplasm is officially split in two, and then two identical daughter cells are produced and enter G1 phase.

The M phase has subdivisions because it quickly goes through a series of events. Each sub-phase of events is described and illustrated below.

PHASE	PHASE EVENTS	ANIMAL CELL DIAGRAM	PLANT CELL DIAGRAM
Interphase (G1, S, and G2)	DNA is loose and spread out and contained in nucleus. This is important because it is actively growing and needs access to its instructions to do chemical reactions correctly. Chromosomes are replicated (copied) in S phase so that they look like an X. Each side of the X has identical DNA.		
Prophase	Nucleus disappears and DNA condenses into chromosomes		
Metaphase	Chromosomes line up in center and proteins from either side of cell attach to them		
Anaphase	Proteins shorten and pull chromosomes apart so that one half (either left side of X or right side of X) of DNA goes to each new cell		
Telophase and Cytokinesis	Nuclei reform and chromosomes start to spread out **Animal cells**: cytoplasm to split in half **Plant cells**: cell plate (new cell wall) forms between daughter cells and extends (animal cells don't have a cell wall)		

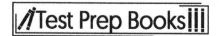

Organism Reproduction

For bacteria, cell reproduction is the same as organism reproduction; binary fission is an asexual process that produces two new cells that are clones of each other because they have identical DNA.

Eukaryotes are more complex than prokaryotes and can go through sexual reproduction. They produce gametes (sex cells). Females make eggs and males make sperm. The process of making gametes is called meiosis, which is similar to mitosis except for the following differences:

- There are two cellular divisions instead of one.

- Four genetically different haploid daughter cells (one set of chromosomes instead of two) are produced instead of two genetically identical diploid daughter cells.

- A process called crossing over (recombination) occurs, which makes the daughter cells genetically different. If chromosomes didn't cross over and rearrange genes, siblings could be identical clones. There would be no genetic variation, which is a critical factor in the theory of evolution of organisms.

In sexual reproduction, a sperm fertilizes an egg and creates the first cell of a new organism, called the zygote. The zygote will go through countless mitotic divisions over time to create the adult organism.

Heredity: Passing Genes Across Generations

All living things are a product of their DNA, specifically portions of their DNA called genes that code for different characteristics.

Learned behavior is not affected by DNA and is not hereditable. Changes in appearance like a woman painting her toenails, a bird whose feathers accidentally fall out due to a tornado, or a person getting a scar are also not heritable. Heritable characteristics are those coded by DNA like eye color, hair color, and height.

A man named Gregor Mendel is considered the father of genetics. He was a monk and a botanist, and through extensive experiments with pea plants, he figured out a great deal about heredity.

Our genetic code comes in pairs. Each chromosome contains many genes, and since we have one chromosome from our mom and one chromosome from our dad, we have two copies of each gene. Genes come in different forms called alleles. The two alleles work together, and when the cell reads them and follows their instructions, the way an organism looks or behaves is called a trait. For some traits, there are only two alleles: a dominant allele and a recessive allele. Even though eye color is a bit more complicated, pretend that brown eyes are dominant over blue eyes, and there are the only two alleles:

- B = Brown eyes
- b = blue eyes

A child inherits these alleles from his parents. There are three possible combinations a child can inherit, dependent on his parents' alleles:

- BB (homozygous dominant)
- Bb (heterozygous)
- bb (homozygous recessive)

The combination of genes above will determine the trait in the offspring. If the child gets any combination with a B, the more powerful allele, his eyes will be brown. Only the bb combination will give the child blue eyes. In this example, the combination of alleles is called a genotype, and the actual eye color the child has is called a phenotype.

Adaptations and Evolution

Change Over Time

The theory of natural selection is one of the fundamental tenets of evolution. It affects the phenotype, or visible characteristics, of individuals in a species, which ultimately affects the genotype, or genetic makeup, of those same individuals. Charles Darwin was the first to explain the theory of natural selection, and it is described by Herbert Spencer as favoring survival of the fittest. Natural selection encompasses three assumptions:

- A species has heritable traits: All traits have some likelihood of being propagated to offspring.

- The traits of a species vary: Some traits are more advantageous than others.

- Individuals of a species are subject to differing rates of reproduction: Some individuals of a species may not get the opportunity to reproduce while others reproduce frequently.

Over time, certain variations in traits may increase both the survival and reproduction of certain individuals within a species. The desirable heritable traits are passed on from generation to generation. Eventually, the desirable traits will become more common and permeate the entire species.

Adaptation

The theory of **adaptation** is defined as an alteration in a species that causes it to become more well-suited to its environment. It increases the probability of survival, thus increasing the rate of successful reproduction. As a result, an adaptation becomes more common within the population of that species.

For examples, bats use reflected sound waves (echolocation) to prey on insects, and chameleons change colors to blend in with their surroundings to evade detection by its prey and predators. Adaptations are brought about by natural selection.

Adaptive radiation refers to rapid diversification within a species into an array of unique forms. It may occur as a result of changes in a habitat creating new challenges, ecological niches, or natural resources.

Darwin's finches are often thought of as an example of the theory of adaptive radiation. Charles Darwin documented 13 varieties of finches on the Galapagos Islands. Each island in the chain presented a unique and changing environment, which was believed to cause rapid adaptive radiation among the finches. There was also diversity among finches inhabiting the same island. Darwin believed that as a result of natural selection, each variety of finch developed adaptations to fit into its native environment.

A major difference in Darwin's finches had to do with the size and shapes of beaks. The variation in beaks allowed the finches to access different foods and natural resources, which decreased competition and preserved resources. As a result, various finches of the same species were allowed to coexist, thrive, and diversify. Finches had:

- Short beaks, which were suited for foraging for seeds
- Thin, sharp beaks, which were suited for preying on insects
- Long beaks, which were suited for probing for food inside plants

Darwin believed that the finches on the Galapagos Islands resulted from chance mutations in genes transmitted from generation to generation.

Life Cycle
Here's a look at the life cycles of many animals.

Chicken	Hens are female chickens, and they lay about one egg per day. If there is no rooster (male chicken) around to fertilize the egg, the egg never turns into a chick and instead becomes an egg that we can eat. If a rooster is around, he mates with the female chicken and fertilizes the egg. Once the egg is fertilized, the tiny little embryo (future chicken) will start as a white dot adjacent to the yolk and albumen (egg white) and will develop for 21 days. The mother hen sits on her clutch of eggs (several fertilized eggs) to incubate them and keep them warm. She will turn the eggs to make sure the embryo doesn't stick to one side of the shell. The embryo continues to develop, using the egg white and yolk nutrients, and eventually develops an "egg tooth" on its beak that it uses to crack open the egg and hatch. Before it hatches, it even chirps to let the mom know of its imminent arrival!
Frog	Frogs mate similar to the way chickens do, and then lay eggs in a very wet area. Sometimes, the parents abandon the eggs and let them develop on their own. The eggs, like chickens', will hatch around 21 days later. Just like chickens, a frog develops from a yolk, but when it hatches, it continues to use the yolk for nutrients. A chicken hatches and looks like a cute little chick, but a baby frog is actually a tadpole that is barely developed. It can't even swim around right away, although eventually it will develop gills, a mouth, and a tail. After more time, it will develop teeth and tiny legs and continue to change into a fully grown frog! This type of development is called *metamorphosis*.
Fish	Most fish also lay eggs in the water, but unlike frogs, their swimming sperm externally fertilize the eggs. Like frogs, when fish hatch, they feed on a yolk sac and are called *larvae*. Once the larvae no longer feed on their yolk and can find their own nutrients, they are called fry, which are basically baby fish that grow into adulthood.

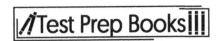

Butterfly	Like frogs, butterflies go through a process called *metamorphosis,* where they completely change into a different looking organism. After the process of mating and internal fertilization, the female finds the perfect spot to lay her eggs, usually a spot with lots of leaves. When the babies hatch from the eggs, they are in the larva form, which for butterflies is called a *caterpillar.* The larvae eat and eat and then go through a process like hibernation and form into a *pupa,* or a *cocoon.* When they hatch from the cocoon, the butterflies are in their adult form.
Bugs	After fertilization, other bugs go through incomplete metamorphosis, which involves three states: eggs that hatch, nymphs that look like little adults without wings and molt their exoskeleton over time, and adults.

All of these organisms depend on a proper environment for development, and that environment depends on their form. Frogs need water, caterpillars need leaves, and baby chicks need warmth in order to be born.

Regulation and Behavior

DNA is the instruction manual for every organism, including humans. It is identical in our cells (except for minor mutations); so why are neurons and heart muscles so different in function and appearance? The key is that in different cells, different parts of the DNA are read. Our DNA is an encyclopedia set with 46 volumes (chromosomes). The instructions for heart cells are different from instructions for neurons. And these instructions are scattered throughout the 46 volumes. It is still not completely understood how a cell chooses what parts of the encyclopedia to read, but it is known that different cells read different portions of our DNA.

Protein enzymes facilitate chemical reactions; they are the workers in the cell. Some unwind the DNA so that RNA can copy the genes in a process called transcription. RNA is similar to DNA except that it is single-stranded and has the base U, which stands for uracil, instead of the T in DNA. Another similarity between DNA and RNA is that they are both made of a base, a phosphate, and a sugar, though DNA is made of deoxyribose sugar and RNA is made of ribose sugar.

The final protein can have many destinations; it can become part of the cytoskeleton that holds the organelles in place, act as an enzyme, go to the cell membrane and act as a marker protein (a tag to identify the cell), act as a transport protein (allows materials to pass in and out of the cell), or as a receptor protein (can receive chemical messages like hormones and initiate reactions in the cell to respond), or leave the cell and become something else, like a person's hair and fingernails!

In the cell, processes are regulated at the DNA level because transcription and translation are tightly regulated. At the organism level, the entire nervous system controls activity. In humans, a stimulus is received by the sensory neuron, travels up the nerve to the brain, and a response travels down to whatever motor neuron is necessary for movement.

Sensory neurons detect environmental stimulus involving sight, sound, touch, taste, and smell.

Diversity of Life

Due to the speciation that has occurred over time, the variety of organisms is astronomical. Scientists have identified about 2 million species, and they suspect that there are at least 8 million others out there.

A man named Carolus Linnaeus developed a naming system to try to create some order in classifying all species. For example, the classification of humans through the seven levels, from all-inclusive to the most specific, looks like this:

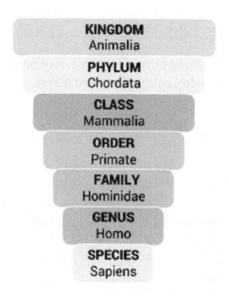

KINGDOM
Animalia

PHYLUM
Chordata

CLASS
Mammalia

ORDER
Primate

FAMILY
Hominidae

GENUS
Homo

SPECIES
Sapiens

One benefit of this universal naming system is that because some organisms have different common names, like the roly-poly and doodlebug, or the cougar and panther, it allows scientists to have a common language. Due to the sheer magnitude of species, scientists need the seven levels, but when referring to organisms, their official names are just the last two: genus and species. Humans are simply referred to as *Homo sapiens*. This two-name system is called binomial nomenclature.

There are currently six kingdoms, although the prokaryotes (simpler cells) used to be lumped together into one kingdom called Monera. Currently, there are two prokaryotic kingdoms, Archaebacteria and Eubacteria.

Archaebacteria
Prokaryotes that have a cell membrane made of fats. They live in harsh places including extremely hot areas (volcanic vents or hot springs) and extremely salty locations (Utah's Salt Lake). These are the rarest prokaryotes.

Eubacteria
Common bacteria that have a cell membrane made of a protein-carbohydrate blend. They make up the vast majority of existing prokaryotes. An example is staphylococcus.

Protista
This kingdom consists of eukaryotes. Most are unicellular. This kingdom is the most diverse and can be divided into three types: fungus-like (including slime-molds), plant-like (including algae), and animal-like

(including amoeba). Some scientists believe that there is so much diversity within the kingdom that they should be split into separate kingdoms, but so far they remain in one group.

Animal-like protists are heterotrophs (they do not make their own food), and plant-like protists are autotrophs (they make their own food). Fungus-like protists are heterotrophs. Like actual fungi, these organisms externally digest their food by acting as parasites and decomposers. Animal-like protists ingest their food via phagocytosis (cell eating) or by absorbing it.

Depending on the particular protists, some produce asexually via mitosis and others reproduce sexually.

Fungi

Fungi are eukaryotic heterotrophs that digest their food externally. Many of them, including common mushrooms and toadstools, act as decomposers by breaking down dead organisms then absorbing the broken down nutrients. Other fungi accomplish ingestion as parasites feeding off of living organisms, as in the case of a yeast infection. All fungi are multicellular with one exception—yeast. Fungi have cell walls made of a complex carbohydrate called chitin. Most fungi reproduce sexually and asexually.

Plantae

Plants are multicellular autotrophs like daisies, roses, and pine trees. They are closely related to the aquatic producer, algae, but different in that algae don't contain true roots, stems, or leaves. Plants are photosynthesizers, and their cells have surrounding cell walls made of the starch cellulose.

Animalia

Animals are multicellular heterotrophs, like fungi, except that animals move and internally ingest their food by consuming it. Animals are the only kingdom to not have cells with cell walls due to their flexibility and ability to move. The animal kingdom is very diverse and includes humans, jellyfish, and spiders, as well as all sorts of other organisms.

Organisms and the Environment

Interactions of Organisms and Their Environments

An **ecosystem** consists of all living (**community**) and nonliving components (abiotic factors) in an area. **Abiotic factors** include the atmosphere, soil, rocks, and water, which all have a role in sustaining life. The atmosphere provides the necessary gasses, soil contains nutrients for plants, rocks erode and affect topography, and water has many different roles.

An ecosystem not only involves living things interacting with nonliving things, but also involves the community interacting with each other. **Food chains** depict one type of community interaction, like the one shown here:

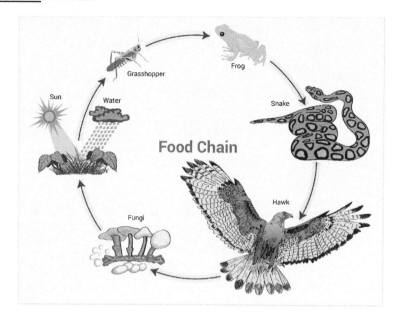

Food chains show the transfer of energy as one organism eats another. They also show an organism's eating habits. **Herbivores** eat plants and **carnivores** eat meat. A lion in grassland with no available animal prey will starve to death even though there is lots of grass because lions don't eat grass; that isn't their role in their habitat.

Food webs not only show predator-prey relationships, but they also show another relationship called **competition**.

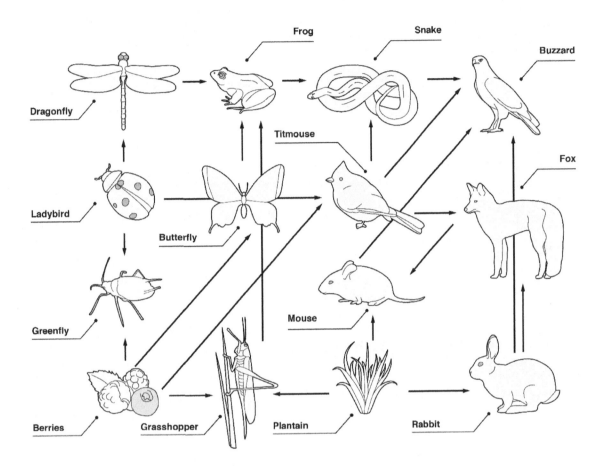

This food web shows that mice and frogs are competing for grasshoppers. If there is a scarcity of grasshoppers, the mouse and frog populations will decrease.

The final three types of community relationships all fall under the blanket term **symbiosis** and are described in the table below.

	Mutualism	Commensalism	Parasitism
Definition	Both organisms benefit from the relationship	One organism benefits from the relationship	One organism benefits from the relationship, and the other is harmed
Example	Birds and flowers	Whale and barnacle	Dog and flea
Explanation	Birds get nectar. Plants get pollinated.	Barnacle gets a free ride and access to food. Whale doesn't care because the barnacle is just latched on and isn't hurting anything.	Flea sucks dog's blood and gets nutrients. Dog is itchy and gets its blood drained.

The important knowledge for students to retain is:

- Plants need soil and sunlight to survive. This can be demonstrated by growing plants in the classroom.

- Animals in an area can have relationships other than predator-prey.

- Animals have niches in their environment. Some are herbivores (eat plants only), some are carnivores (eat meat only), and some are **omnivores** like humans (eat both plants and animals).

Inherited Traits, Learned Behaviors, and Organism Survival

Many characteristics are inherited from the DNA obtained from an individual's parents, including skin color, eye shape, hair color, and color-blindness, among others. Learned behavior isn't related to genetics and is a result of training. For example, a dog catching a stick is learned. The overall intelligence of the dog, however, has to do with its genes.

An organism's survival depends on its **fitness** relative to the environment, and any trait that helps it survive is called an **adaptation**. Whale blubber and shark teeth are examples of adaptations. Blubber keeps whales warm, and a shark's many teeth ensures it's better able to capture prey. Whales don't decide to grow blubber, and sharks don't decide to grow teeth. These characteristics have been inherited from their parents.

Discussion of adaptations can involve showing pictures of various organisms and identifying which of their characteristics would be helpful and why. See below for some ideas for discussion.

Organism	Adaptation to identify	Why it's helpful
Cactus	Spikes	Help protect from water thieves
Peacock	Feathers	Help scare off predators (look like eyes); also help attract mates
Elephant	Trunk	Helps suck up water
Skunk	Smelly secretions	Help protect from predators

Interdependence of Organisms

The biosphere has layers and layers of complexity:

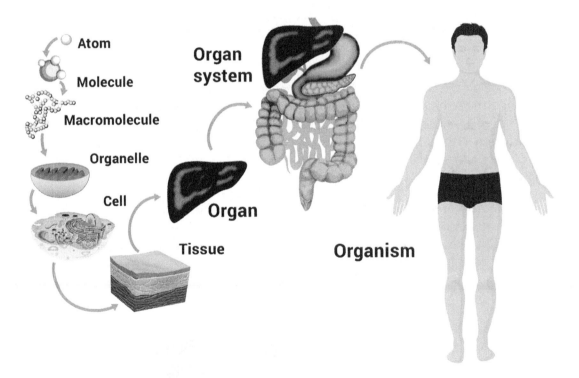

All organisms work together so that life can exist. An organism represents one of a species, like the fish below, and all organisms serve a particular function. The fish's niche is to eat aquatic producers and excrete waste that acts as fertilizer.

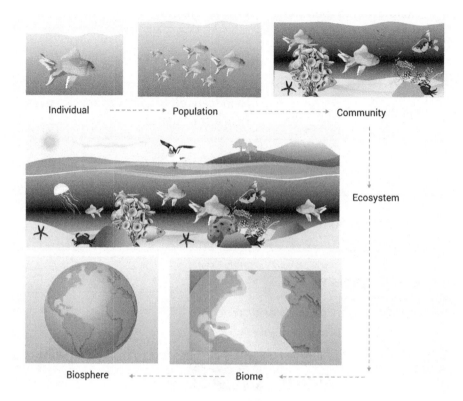

Individual --------→ Population --------→ Community

Ecosystem

Biosphere ←-------- Biome ←--------

This fish is just one organism within a population. A population represents multiple individuals living in the same habitat. The community includes every biotic factor (living organism) within an ecosystem, in this case, the fish, jellyfish, algae, crab, bacteria, etc. An ecosystem includes all the biotic factors as well as the abiotic, which includes anything non-living—for the fish, that's a rock, a shipwreck, and a nearby glacier. For biomes, add weather and climate into the mix. The biosphere is all of Earth, which is the combination of all biomes.

We already discussed that producers (plants, protists, and even some bacteria) photosynthesize and make the food that provides energy required for all chemical reactions to occur and therefore all life to exist. A non-photosynthesizer must find and eat food, and this feeding relationship can be visualized in food chains. Consider this food chain:

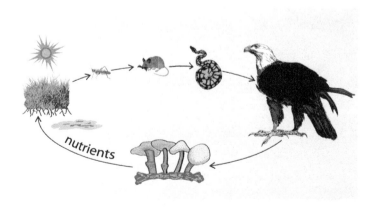

The true source of the energy for every living organism is the sun. Plants absorb the sun's energy to make glucose and are on the first trophic level (feeding level). The grasshopper on the second trophic level is an example of an herbivore and is a primary consumer, as he is the first eater in the food chain. Unfortunately, he receives only 10 percent of the energy that the plant absorbed (this is known as the 10 percent rule) because the other 90 percent of energy was either used by the plant to grow or will be lost as heat. The mouse on the third trophic level is the secondary consumer, or second eater. Food chains are not as inclusive as food webs, which show all feeding relationships in an ecosystem. Looking at this food chain suggests that mice are carnivores (eaters of animals), but mice also eat berries and plants, so they are actually considered omnivores (eaters of both plants and animals). The mouse only gets 10 percent of the energy from the grasshopper, which is actually only 1 percent of the original energy provided by the Sun. The snake on the fourth trophic level is a carnivore, as is the hawk on the highest trophic level.

The arrows in the food chain show the transfer of energy, and fungi as well as bacteria act as decomposers, which break down organic material. Decomposers act at every trophic level because they feed on all organisms; they are non-discriminating omnivores. Decomposers are critical for life, as they recycle the atoms and building blocks of organisms.

Feeding relationships and predator-prey relationships (hunter-hunted, like the hawk and the rabbit in the food web above) are not the only relationships in an ecosystem. There also can be competition within and between species. For example, in the food chain above, the rabbit and snail both eat grass, showing a relationship called competition, when two organisms want the same thing. Other relationships include symbiotic relationships, which represent two species living together.

Symbiosis comes in three varieties:

- Mutualism: an arrangement where both organisms help each other. An example is the relationship between birds and flowers. When birds consume the nectar that the flower produces, pollen rubs on the bird's body so that when it travels to a neighboring plant, it helps with fertilization. The plant helps the bird by providing food, and the bird helps the plant by helping it reproduce. This is a win-win.

- Parasitism: when one organism is hurt while the other is helped. Fleas and dogs are a prime example. Fleas suck the dog's blood, and dogs are itchy and lose blood. This is a win-lose.

- Commensalism: when one organism is helped and the other is neither harmed nor helped. For example, barnacles are crusty little creatures that attach themselves to whales. They don't feed on the whale like a parasite. Instead, they use the whale to give them a free ride so they have access to food. The whales don't care about the barnacles. This is a win-do not care.

Structure and Function of Earth Systems

Earth's Layers

Earth has three major layers: a thin solid outer surface or **crust**, a dense **core**, and a **mantle** between them that contains most of Earth's matter. This layout resembles an egg, where the eggshell is the crust, the mantle is the egg white, and the core is the yolk. The outer crust of Earth consists of igneous or sedimentary rocks over metamorphic rocks. Together with the upper portion of the mantle, it forms the **lithosphere**, which is broken into tectonic plates.

Major plates of the lithosphere

The mantle can be divided into three zones. The **upper mantle** is adjacent to the crust and composed of solid rock. Below the upper mantle is the **transition zone**. The **lower mantle** below the transition zone is

286

a layer of completely solid rock. Underneath the mantle is the molten **outer core** followed by the compact, solid **inner core**. The inner and outer cores contain the densest elements, consisting of mostly iron and nickel.

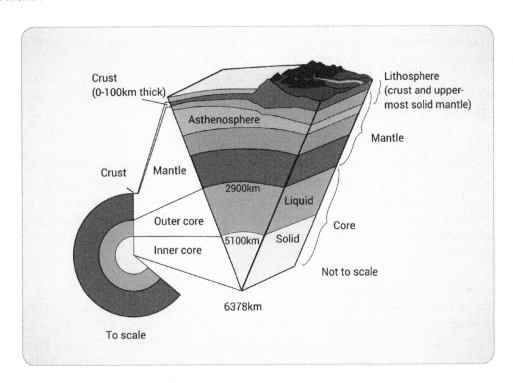

Shape and Size of Earth

Earth isn't a perfect sphere; it's slightly elliptical. From center to surface, its radius is almost 4,000 miles, and its circumference around the equator is about 24,902 miles. In comparison, the Sun's radius is 432,288 miles—over 1,000 times larger than Earth's—and the Moon's radius is about 1,000 miles.

Geographical Features

Earth's surface is dynamic and consists of various landforms. As tectonic plates are pushed together, **mountains** are formed. **Canyons** are deep trenches that are usually created by plates moving apart but can also be created by constant weathering and erosion from rivers and runoff. **Deltas** are flat, triangular stretches of land formed by rivers that deposit sediment and water into the ocean. **Sand dunes** are mountains of sand located in desert areas or the bottom of the ocean. They are formed by wind and water movement when there's an absence of plants or other features that would otherwise hold the sand in place.

Earth's Magnetic Field

Earth's **magnetic field** is created by the magnetic forces that extend from Earth's interior to outer space. It can be modeled as a magnetic dipole tilted about 10 degrees from Earth's rotational axis, as if a bar magnet was placed at an angle inside Earth's core. The **geomagnetic pole** located near Greenland in the northern hemisphere is actually the south pole of Earth's magnetic field, and vice versa for the southern geomagnetic pole. The **magnetosphere** is Earth's magnetic field, which extends tens of thousands of kilometers into space and protects Earth and the atmosphere from damaging solar wind and cosmic rays.

Plate Tectonics Theory and Evidence

The theory of **plate tectonics** hypothesizes that the continents weren't always separated like they are today but were once joined and slowly drifted apart. Evidence for this theory is based upon the fossil record. Fossils of one species were found in regions of the world now separated by an ocean. It's unlikely that a single species could have travelled across the ocean or that two separate species evolved into a single species.

Folding and Faulting

The exact number of tectonic plates is debatable, but scientists estimate there are around nine to fifteen major plates and almost 40 minor plates. The line where two plates meet is called a **fault**. The San Andreas Fault is where the Pacific and North American plates meet. Faults or boundaries are classified depending on the interaction between plates. Two plates collide at **convergent boundaries**. **Divergent boundaries** occur when two plates move away from each other. Tectonic plates can move vertically and horizontally.

Continental Drift, Seafloor Spreading, Magnetic Reversals

The movement of tectonic plates is similar to pieces of wood floating in a pool of water. They can bob up and down as well as bump, slide, and move away from each other. These different interactions create Earth's landscape. The collision of plates can create mountain ranges, while their separation can create canyons or underwater chasms. One plate can also slide atop another and push it down into Earth's hot mantle, creating magma and volcanoes, in a process called **subduction**.

Unlike a regular magnet, Earth's magnetic field changes over time because it's generated by the motion of molten iron alloys in the outer core. Although the magnetic poles can wander geographically, they do so at such a slow rate that they don't affect the use of compasses in navigation. However, at irregular intervals that are several hundred thousand years long, the fields can reverse, with the north and south magnetic poles switching places.

Characteristics of Volcanoes

Volcanoes are mountainous structures that act as vents to release pressure and magma from Earth's crust. During an **eruption**, the pressure and magma are released, and volcanoes smoke, rumble, and throw ash and **lava**, or molten rock, into the air. **Hot spots** are volcanic regions of the mantle that are hotter than surrounding regions.

Characteristics of Earthquakes

Earthquakes occur when tectonic plates slide or collide as a result of the crust suddenly releasing energy. Stress in Earth's outer layer pushes together two faults. The motion of the planes of the fault continues until something makes them stop. The **epicenter** of an earthquake is the point on the surface directly above where the fault is slipping. If the epicenter is located under a body of water, the earthquake may cause a **tsunami**, a series of large, forceful waves.

Seismic waves and Triangulation

Earthquakes cause **seismic waves**, which travel through Earth's layers and give out low-frequency acoustic energy. Triangulation of seismic waves helps scientists determine the origin of an earthquake.

Cycles in Earth Systems

Processes of Earth

The water cycle is the cycling of water between its three physical states: solid, liquid, and gas. The sun is a critical component of the water cycle because its thermal energy heats up surface liquid water so much that parts of it evaporate. Transpiration is a similar process that occurs when the sun evaporates water from plant pores called stomata. As water vapor rises into the atmosphere through evaporation and transpiration, it eventually condenses and forms clouds heavy with liquid water droplets. The liquid (or solid ice or snow) will precipitate back to Earth, collect on land, and either be absorbed by soil or run-off to the oceans and lakes where it will accumulate, circulate, and evaporate once again.

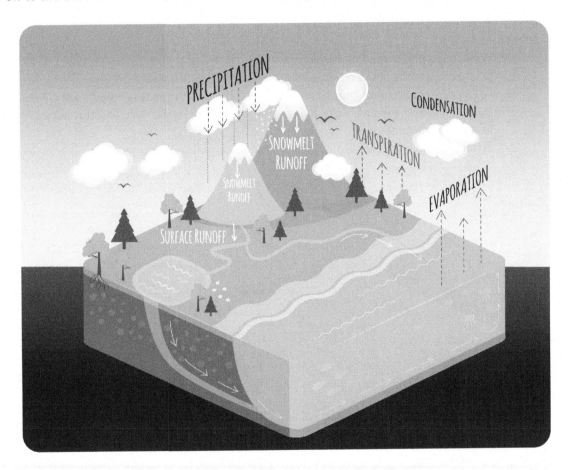

Clouds are condensed water vapor, which is water that has cooled from a gas to liquid, like the droplets on the outside of a glass of lemonade on a hot summer day. That water on the glass is water vapor that cooled enough to slow down the moving particles so that they become denser, forming a liquid. In the sky, water vapor combines in different ways so clouds appear in different forms.

Cloud height, shape, and behavior results in a variety of different types:

- **High-Clouds**
  - Cirrus: wispy and thread-like
  - Cirrostratus: like cirrus clouds, but wider and thicker sheets. They have a halo effect where sunlight and moonlight refract through.
  - Cirrocumulus: a cross between cirrus and cirrostratus clouds. These have rows of round puffs like a cotton-ball stretched out.
  - Contrails: clouds made by jets
- **Mid-Clouds**
  - Altostratus: thick, stretched clouds that block sunlight and are blue-grayish in color
  - Nimbostratus: a thick altostratus cloud accompanied by rain
  - Altocumulus: layered rolls of clouds
- **Low-Clouds**
  - Cumulus: white, round, puffy clouds
  - Stratus: wide, thick, stretched-out, gray clouds that may cause drizzle
  - Fog: lazy stratus clouds that have drooped so low that they reach Earth's surface
  - Cumulonimbus: the angry cloud that brings thunderstorms, hail, and tornadoes. It looks like a thick mountain.
  - Stratocumulus: stretched-out, grayish, puffy, cumulus clouds

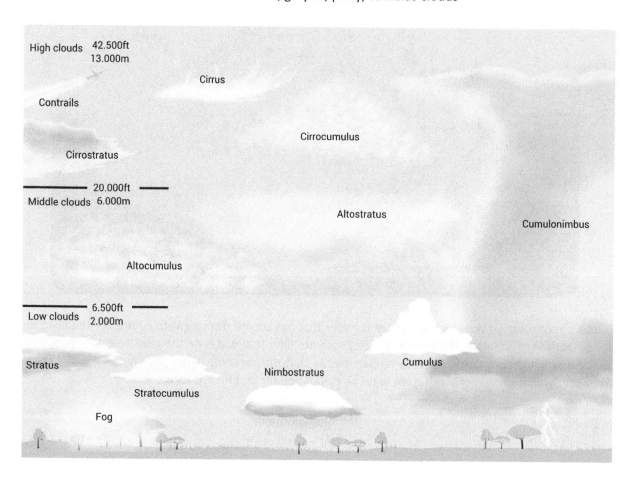

Precipitation comes in many different forms:

- **Rain** occurs due to water vapor condensing on dust particles in the troposphere. As more and more water condenses, the drops will eventually enlarge and accumulate mass, becoming so heavy that they fall to Earth.

- If the temperature is above the freezing point, rain remains liquid upon contact with the ground. However, when the temperature is below the freezing point and other conditions are right, rain can freeze upon contact with the ground or other surfaces, called **freezing rain**. This causes extremely dangerous driving conditions due to the slickness of the ice.

- **Sleet** freezes on its way down as opposed to freezing upon impact. Sleet starts as ice that melts as it falls through the atmosphere due to hitting spots of warmer temperature, and then it freezes again before hitting the ground.

- **Hail** is precipitation of balls of ice. Hail begins as ice at very cold temperatures in the atmosphere. Instead of precipitating sheets of ice like sleet storms, hailstorms precipitate ice that looks like rocks because hail is formed during thunderstorms. The massive winds throw hail up and down so more and more water vapor condenses and freezes on the original ice. Layer upon layer of ice combine, creating hail sometimes as large as golf balls.

- **Snow** forms as loosely packed ice crystals. Snow is less dangerous than the other frozen forms of precipitation and can produce beautiful snowflakes.

Even though seasons have predictable temperatures, there can be significant differences day to day. In the troposphere, the Sun's heat is trapped by the blanket of greenhouse gases and creates warm, low-pressure air. Because warm gas particles move faster and have less space between them, they are less dense than colder air, and they rise. Cool air moves below the warm air. This atmospheric movement is called general circulation and is the source of wind. Earth's spinning motion also causes wind.

Weather depends in a large part on temperature. Earth's equator is closest to the sun and receives more heat, so this area of earth is significantly warmer than the poles (Arctic and Antarctic). This warm air can form huge bubbles, as can the colder air at the poles. When warm air and cold air meet, the boundary is called a front. Fronts can be the site of extreme weather like thunderstorms, which are caused by water particles in clouds quickly rubbing against each other and transferring electrons, creating positive and negative regions. Lightning occurs when there is a massive electric spark due to the electrical current within a cloud, between two clouds, and even between a cloud and the ground.

While seasons are predictable trends in temperatures over a few months, climate describes the average weather and temperature patterns for a particular area over a long period of time, upwards of thirty years. While *fall* describes a season and *rain* describes weather, *rainforest* describes a climate. The climate of a rainforest, due to its proximity to the equator and oceans, consists of warm temperatures with humid air.

Even more extreme weather includes tornadoes and hurricanes. Tornadoes are spinning winds that can exceed 300 miles per hour and are caused by changing air pressure and quick winds. Hurricanes, typhoons, and tropical cyclones (the same phenomenon with different regional names) are storms with spinning winds that form over the ocean. Hurricanes are caused by warm ocean water quickly evaporating and rising to a colder, lower-pressure portion of the atmosphere. The fast movement of the warm air starts a cyclone around a central origination point (the eye of the storm). Blizzards are also caused by the clash of warm air and cold air. They occur when the cold Arctic air moves toward warmer air and involve massive amounts of snow.

Precipitation and run-off are constantly affecting the surface of Earth, as the run-off weathers rocks or breaks them down from the original bedrock into pieces called regolith. Regolith sizes range from microscopic to large and quickly form either soil or sediment. *Weathering* is the process of breaking rock while *erosion* is the process of moving rock. Weathering can be caused by both physical and chemical changes. Mechanical forces such as roots growing, animal contact, wind, and extreme weather cause weathering. Another cause is the water cycle, which includes flowing water, moving glaciers, and liquid ice seeping into rocks and cracking them as water freezes and expands. Chemical weathering actually transforms the regolith into clay and soft minerals. One consequence of chemical weathering is corrosive acid rain.

Rocks cover the surface of Earth. Igneous rock comes from the molten, hot, liquid magma circulating beneath Earth's surface in the upper mantle. Through vents called volcanoes, magma explodes or seeps onto Earth's surface. Magma is not uniform; it varies in its elemental composition, gas composition, and thickness or viscosity. There are three main types of volcanoes: shield, cinder, and composite.

Shield volcanoes are the widest because their thin magma flows out of a central crater calmly and quietly, like a gentle fountain. This flowing magma results in layers of solid lava. The slow flow results in a convex hill that spans a wide area.

Like shield volcanoes, *cinder volcanoes* typically have a central crater and thin lava. In contrast to shield volcanoes, they are small, cone-shaped hills with steep sides. They are made of volcanic debris, or cinders. They are often found as secondary volcanoes near shield and composite volcanoes. In cinder volcanoes, the central vent spews lava that shatters into rock and debris and settles around it, resulting in its characteristic cone shape. Cinder volcanoes are surrounded by ashy, loose, magma dust.

Composite volcanoes (also called stratovolcanoes) are the most common and the tallest type of volcano. Their thick magma gets stuck at the vent, and as more and more builds up, the volcano eventually explodes and removes the clog. These eruptions generate loose debris, and once the plug has been violently expelled, the thick lava oozes out like a fountain. These volcanoes are the most dangerous with their extremely violent behavior and huge height. Most volcanoes are located around cracks in Earth's lithosphere.

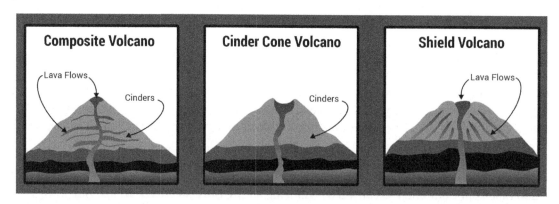

Once magma makes it to the surface, it is called lava. Once it cools, it solidifies into igneous rock. Common examples of igneous rock are obsidian, pumice, and granite. Weathering and erosion result in these rocks becoming soil or sediment and accumulating in layers mostly found in the ocean. These

loose sediments settle over time and compress to become a uniform rock in a process called lithification. Examples of sedimentary rock include shale, limestone, and sandstone. As layers are piled atop each other, the bottom rock experiences an intense amount of pressure and transforms into metamorphic rock. Examples of metamorphic rocks are marble and slate. After long periods of time, the metamorphic rock moves closer to the asthenosphere and becomes liquid hot magma

Magma's eventual fate is lava and igneous rock, and the cycle starts anew:

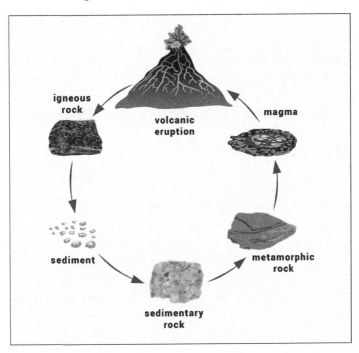

How does magma return to the surface if the lithosphere presses it down? Intense heat from Earth's core travels to the upper mantle via convection. Convection involves thermal energy (heat) that converts into kinetic energy (movement), resulting in rapidly circulating molecules. Convection moves heat energy through fluids. In a pot of boiling water, the water closest to the burner becomes hot, causing its particles to move faster. Faster-moving molecules have more space between them and become less dense, so they rise. Some will vaporize, and some hit the cool air and slow down, becoming dense and sinking. Likewise, Earth's interior particles undergo convection (the heat source being the nuclear fission from the core), and the rock in the upper mantle will acquire so much kinetic energy that magma will be expelled from underneath Earth to the surface.

There are seven or eight major plates in the lithosphere and several minor plates. These tectonic plates explain the changing topography, or shape, of earth.

There are three types of boundaries between plates: divergent, convergent, and transform. All boundaries can be sites of volcanic activity. A **divergent boundary** occurs when plates separate. Lava fills in the space the plates create and hardens into rock, which creates oceanic crust. In a **convergent boundary**, if one of the plates is in the ocean, that plate is denser due to the weight of water. The dense ocean plate will slip under the land plate, causing a subduction zone where the plate moves underneath. Where plates converge on land, the continental crusts are both lighter with a similar density, and as a result they will buckle together and create mountains.

In **transform boundaries**, adjacent plates sliding past each other create friction and pressure that destroy the edges of the boundary and cause earthquakes. Transform boundaries don't produce magma, as they involve lateral movement.

Just as plates pushing together cause mountains, **canyons** are deep trenches caused by plates moving apart. Weather and erosion from rivers and precipitation run-off also create canyons. *Deltas* form when rivers dump their sediments and water into oceans. They are triangular flat stretches of land that are kind of like a triangular spatula; the handle represents the river and the triangle represents the mouth of a delta.

Sand dunes are another landform caused by wind or waves in combination with the absence of plants to hold sand in place. These are found in sandy areas like the desert or the ocean.

Energy in Weather and Climate

Basic Concepts of Meteorology

Relative Humidity
Relative humidity is the ratio of the partial pressure of water vapor to water's equilibrium vapor pressure at a given temperature. At low temperatures, less water vapor is required to reach a high relative humidity. More water vapor is needed to reach a high relative humidity in warm air, which has a greater capacity for water vapor. At ground level or other areas of higher pressure, relative humidity increases as temperatures decrease because water vapor condenses as the temperature falls below the dew point. As relative humidity cannot be greater than 100%, the dew point temperature cannot be greater than the air temperature.

Dew Point
The **dew point** is the temperature at which the water vapor in air at constant barometric pressure condenses into liquid water due to saturation. At temperatures below the dew point, the rate of condensation will be greater than the rate of evaporation, forming more liquid water. When condensed water forms on a surface, it's called **dew**; when it forms in the air, it's called **fog** or **clouds**, depending on the altitude.

Wind
Wind is the movement of gas particles across Earth's surface. Winds are generated by differences in atmospheric pressure. Air inherently moves from areas of higher pressure to lower pressure, which is what causes wind to occur. Surface friction from geological features, such as mountains or man-made features can decrease wind speed. In meteorology, winds are classified based on their strength, duration, and direction. **Gusts** are short bursts of high-speed wind, **squalls** are strong winds of intermediate duration (around one minute), and winds with a long duration are given names based on their average strength. **Breezes** are the weakest, followed by **gales**, **storms**, and **hurricanes**.

Air Masses, Fronts, Storms, and Severe Weather
Air masses are volumes of air defined by their temperature and the amount of water vapor they contain. A **front** is where two air masses of different temperatures and water vapor content meet. Fronts can be the site of extreme weather, such as thunderstorms, which are caused by water particles rubbing against each other. When they do so, electrons are transferred and energy and electrical currents accumulate. When enough energy accumulates, thunder and lightning occur. **Lightning** is a

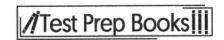

massive electric spark created by a cloud, and **thunder** is the sound created by an expansion of air caused by the sudden increase in pressure and temperature around lightning.

Extreme weather includes tornadoes and hurricanes. **Tornadoes** are created by changing air pressure and winds that can exceed 300 miles per hour. **Hurricanes** occur when warm ocean water quickly evaporates and rises to a colder, low-pressure portion of the atmosphere. Hurricanes, typhoons, and tropical cyclones are all created by the same phenomena but they occur in different regions. **Blizzards** are similar to hurricanes in that they're created by the clash of warm and cold air, but they only occur when cold Arctic air moves toward warmer air. They usually involve large amounts of snow.

Development and Movement of Weather Patterns

A **weather pattern** is weather that's consistent for a period of time. Weather patterns are created by fronts. A **cold front** is created when two air masses collide in a high-pressure system. A **warm front** is created when a low-pressure system results from the collision of two air masses; they are usually warmer and less dense than high-pressure systems. When a cold front enters an area, the air from the warm front is forced upwards. The temperature of the warm front's air decreases, condenses, and often creates clouds and precipitation. When a warm front moves into an area, the warm air moves slowly upwards at an angle. Clouds and precipitation form, but the precipitation generally lasts longer because of how slowly the air moves.

Major Factors that Affect Climate and Seasons

Effects of Latitude, Geographical Location, and Elevation

The climate and seasons of different geographical areas are primarily dictated by their sunlight exposure. Because Earth rotates on a tilted axis while travelling around the Sun, different latitudes get different amounts of direct sunlight throughout the year, creating different climates. Polar regions experience the greatest variation, with long periods of limited or no sunlight in the winter and up to 24 hours of daylight in the summer. Equatorial regions experience the least variance in direct sunlight exposure. Coastal areas experience breezes in the summer as cooler ocean air moves ashore, while areas southeast of the Great Lakes can get "lake effect" snow in the winter, as cold air travels over the warmer water and creates snow on land. Mountains are often seen with snow in the spring and fall. Their high elevation causes mountaintops to stay cold. The air around the mountaintop is also cold and holds less water vapor than air at sea level. As the water vapor condenses, it creates snow.

Effects of Atmospheric Circulation

Global winds are patterns of wind circulation and they have a major influence on global weather and climate. They help influence temperature and precipitation by carrying heat and water vapor around Earth. These winds are driven by the uneven heating between the polar and equatorial regions created by the Sun. Cold air from the polar regions sinks and moves toward the equator, while the warm air from the equator rises and moves toward the poles. The other factor driving global winds is the **Coriolis**

Effect. As air moves from the North Pole to the equator, Earth's rotation makes it seem as if the wind is also moving to the right, or westbound, and eastbound from South Pole to equator.

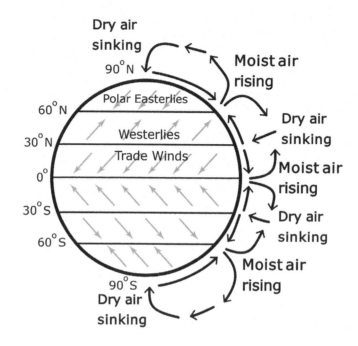

Global wind patterns are given names based on which direction they blow. There are three major wind patterns in each hemisphere. Notice the image above diagramming the movement of warm (dry) air and cold (moist) air.

Trade winds—easterly surface winds found in the troposphere near the equator—blow predominantly from the northeast in the Northern Hemisphere and from the southeast in the Southern Hemisphere. These winds direct the tropical storms that develop over the Atlantic, Pacific, and Indian Oceans and land in North America, Southeast Asia, and eastern Africa, respectively. **Jet streams** are westerly winds that follow a narrow, meandering path. The two strongest jet streams are the polar jets and the subtropical jets. In the Northern Hemisphere, the polar jet flows over the middle of North America, Europe, and Asia, while in the Southern Hemisphere, it circles Antarctica.

Effects of Ocean Circulation
Ocean currents are similar to global winds because winds influence how the oceans move. Ocean currents are created by warm water moving from the equator towards the poles while cold water travels from the poles to the equator. The warm water can increase precipitation in an area because it evaporates faster than the colder water.

Characteristics and Locations of Climate Zones
Climate zones are created by Earth's tilt as it travels around the Sun. These zones are delineated by the equator and four other special latitudinal lines: the Tropic of Cancer or Northern Tropic at 23.5° North; the Tropic of Capricorn or Southern Tropic at 23.5° South; the Arctic Circle at 66.5° North; and the Antarctic Circle at 66.5° South. The areas between these lines of latitude represent different climate zones. **Tropical climates** are hot and wet, like rainforests, and tend to have abundant plant and animal

life, while polar climates are cold and usually have little plant and animal life. **Temperate zones** can vary and experience the four seasons.

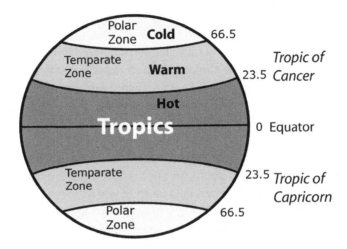

Effect of the Tilt of Earth's Axis on Seasons

In addition to the equator and the prime meridian, other major lines of latitude and longitude divide the world into regions relative to the direct rays of the Sun. These lines correspond with Earth's 23.5-degree tilt, and are responsible—along with Earth's revolution around the Sun—for the seasons. For example, the Northern Hemisphere is tilted directly toward the Sun from June 22 to September 23, which creates the summer. Conversely, the Southern Hemisphere is tilted away from the Sun and experiences winter during those months. The area between the Tropic of Cancer and the Tropic of Capricorn tends to be warmer and experiences fewer variations in seasonal temperatures because it's constantly subject to the direct rays of the Sun, no matter which direction Earth is tilted.

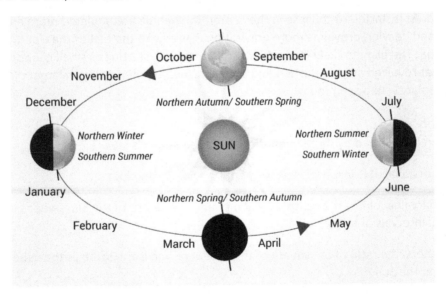

The area between the Tropic of Cancer and the Arctic Circle, which is at 66.5° North, and the Antarctic Circle, which is at 66.5° South, is where most of Earth's population resides and is called the **middle latitudes**. Here, the seasons are more pronounced, and milder temperatures generally prevail. When the Sun's direct rays are over the equator, it's known as an *equinox*, and day and night are almost equal throughout the world. Equinoxes occur twice a year: the fall, or autumnal equinox, occurs on September 22, while the spring equinox occurs on March 20.

Effects of Natural Phenomena

Natural phenomena can have a sizeable impact on climate and weather. Chemicals released from volcanic eruptions can fall back to Earth in acid rain. In addition, large amounts of carbon dioxide released into the atmosphere can warm the climate. Carbon dioxide creates the **greenhouse effect** by trapping solar energy from sunlight reflected off Earth's surface within the atmosphere. The amount of solar radiation emitted from the Sun varies and has recently been discovered to be cyclical.

El Niño and La Niña

El Niño and **La Niña** are terms for severe weather anomalies associated with torrential rainfall in the Pacific coastal regions, mainly in North and South America. These events occur irregularly every few years, usually around December, and are caused by a band of warm ocean water that accumulates in the central Pacific Ocean around the equator. The warm water changes the wind patterns over the Pacific and stops cold water from rising toward the American coastlines. The rise in ocean temperature also leads to increased evaporation and rain. These events are split into two phases—a warm, beginning phase called El Niño and a cool end phase called La Niña.

Solar System and the Universe

Major Features of the Solar System

Structure of the Solar System

The **solar system** is an elliptical planetary system with a large sun in the center that provides gravitational pull on the planets. It was formed 4.568 billion years ago from the gravitational collapse of a region within a giant molecular cloud that likely birthed other suns. This region of collapse is called a **pre-solar nebula**. As it started to collapse in the center, the nebula accumulated more energy and became hotter and heavier, providing more gravitational energy to the rest of the cloud, eventually becoming the Sun. The planets likely formed in a similar fashion, starting as small clumps called **protoplanets** that revolved around the Sun and then smashed together to form larger planets and, eventually, the solar system seen today.

Laws of Motion

Planetary motion is governed by three scientific laws called **Kepler's laws**:

1. The orbit of a planet is elliptical in shape, with the Sun as one focus.

2. An imaginary line joining the center of a planet and the center of the Sun sweeps out equal areas during equal intervals of time.

3. For all planets, the ratio of the square of the orbital period is the same as the cube of the average distance from the Sun.

The most relevant of these laws is the first. Planets move in elliptical paths because of gravity; when a planet is closer to the Sun, it moves faster because it has built up gravitational speed. As illustrated in

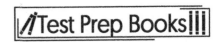

the diagram below, the second law states that it takes planet 1 the same time to travel along the A1 segment as the A2 segment, even though the A2 segment is shorter.

Kepler's Laws of Planetary Motion

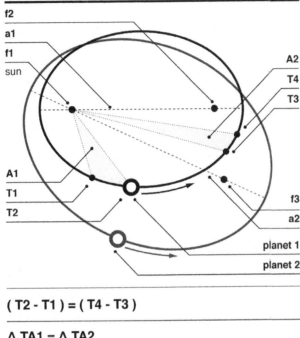

(T2 - T1) = (T4 - T3)

Δ TA1 = Δ TA2

Characteristics of the Sun, Moon, and Planets

The Sun is comprised mainly of hydrogen and helium. Metals make up only about 2% of its total mass. The Sun is 1.3 million kilometers wide, weighs 1.989×10^{30} kilograms, and has temperatures of 5,800 Kelvin (9980 °F) on the surface and 15,600,000 Kelvin (28 million °F) at the core. The Sun's enormous size and gravity give it the ability to provide sunlight. The gravity of the Sun compresses hydrogen and helium atoms together through nuclear fusion and releases energy and light.

The Moon has a distinct core, mantle, and crust. It has elevations and craters created by impacts with large objects in the solar system. The Moon makes a complete orbit around Earth every 27.3 days. It's relatively large compared to other moons in the solar system, with a diameter one-quarter of Earth and a mass 1/81 of Earth.

The eight planets of the solar system are divided into four inner (or **terrestrial**) planets and four outer (or **Jovian**) planets. In general, terrestrial planets are small, and Jovian planets are large and gaseous. The planets in the solar system are listed below from nearest to farthest from the Sun:

- Mercury: the smallest planet in the solar system; it only takes about 88 days to completely orbit the Sun

- Venus: around the same size, composition, and gravity as Earth and orbits the Sun every 225 days

- Earth: the only known planet with life

- Mars: called the Red Planet due to iron oxide on the surface; takes around 687 days to complete its orbit

- Jupiter: the largest planet in the system; made up of mainly hydrogen and helium

- Saturn: mainly composed of hydrogen and helium along with other trace elements; has 61 moons; has beautiful rings, which may be remnants of destroyed moons

- Uranus: the coldest planet in the system, with temperatures as low as -224.2 °Celsius (-371.56 °F)

- Neptune: the last and third-largest planet; also, the second-coldest planet

Asteroids, Meteoroids, Comets, and Dwarf/Minor Planets

Several other bodies travel through the universe. **Asteroids** are orbiting bodies composed of minerals and rock. They're also known as **minor planets**—a term given to any astronomical object in orbit around the Sun that doesn't resemble a planet or a comet. **Meteoroids** are mini-asteroids with no specific orbiting pattern. **Meteors** are meteoroids that have entered Earth's atmosphere and started melting from contact with greenhouse gases. **Meteorites** are meteors that have landed on Earth. **Comets** are composed of dust and ice and look like a comma with a tail from the melting ice as they streak across the sky.

Theories of Origin of the Solar System

One theory of the origins of the solar system is the **nebular hypothesis**, which posits that the solar system was formed by clouds of extremely hot gas called a **nebula**. As the nebula gases cooled, they became smaller and started rotating. Rings of the nebula left behind during rotation eventually condensed into planets and their satellites. The remaining nebula formed the Sun.

Another theory of the solar system's development is the **planetesimal hypothesis**. This theory proposes that planets formed from cosmic dust grains that collided and stuck together to form larger and larger bodies. The larger bodies attracted each other, growing into moon-sized protoplanets and eventually planets.

Interactions of the Earth-Moon-Sun System

Earth's Rotation and Orbital Revolution Around the Sun

Besides revolving around the Sun, Earth also spins like a top. It takes one day for Earth to complete a full spin, or rotation. The same is true for other planets, except that their "days" may be shorter or longer. One Earth day is about 24 hours, while one Jupiter day is only about nine Earth hours, and a Venus day is about 241 Earth days. Night occurs in areas that face away from the Sun, so one side of the planet experiences daylight and the other experiences night. This phenomenon is the reason that Earth is divided into time zones. The concept of time zones was created to provide people around the world with a uniform standard time, so the Sun would rise around 7:00 AM, regardless of location.

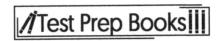

Effect on Seasons

Earth's tilted axis creates the seasons. When Earth is tilted toward the Sun, the Northern Hemisphere experiences summer while the Southern Hemisphere has winter—and vice versa. As Earth rotates, the distribution of direct sunlight slowly changes, explaining how the seasons gradually change.

Phases of the Moon

The Moon goes through two phases as it revolves around Earth: waxing and waning. Each phase lasts about two weeks:

- **Waxing**: the right side of the Moon is illuminated
  - **New moon** (dark): the Moon rises and sets with the Sun
  - **Crescent**: a tiny sliver of illumination on the right
  - **First quarter**: the right half of the Moon is illuminated
  - **Gibbous**: more than half of the Moon is illuminated
  - **Full moon**: the Moon rises at sunset and sets at sunrise
- **Waning**: the left side of the Moon is illuminated
  - **Gibbous**: more than half is illuminated, only here it is the left side that is illuminated
  - **Last quarter**: the left half of the Moon is illuminated
  - **Crescent**: a tiny sliver of illumination on the left
  - **New moon** (dark): the Moon rises and sets with the Sun

Effect on Tides

Although Earth is much larger, the Moon still has a significant gravitational force that pulls on Earth's oceans. At its closest to Earth, the Moon's gravitation pull is greatest and creates high tide. The opposite is true when the Moon is farthest from Earth: less pull creates low tide.

Solar and Lunar Eclipses

Eclipses occur when the Earth, the Sun, and the Moon are all in line. If the three bodies are perfectly aligned, a total eclipse occurs; otherwise, it's only a partial eclipse. A **solar eclipse** occurs when the Moon is between the Earth and the Sun, blocking sunlight from reaching Earth. A **lunar eclipse** occurs when the Earth interferes with the Sun's light reflecting off the full moon. The Earth casts a shadow on the Moon, but the particles of Earth's atmosphere refract the light, so some light reaches the Moon, causing it to look yellow, brown, or red.

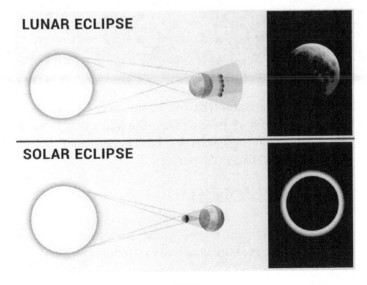

Time Zones

Longitudinal, or vertical, lines determine how far east or west different regions are from each other. These lines, also known as **meridians**, are the basis for time zones, which allocate different times to regions depending on their position eastward and westward of the prime meridian.

Effect of Solar Wind on Earth

Solar winds are streams of charged particles emitted by the Sun, consisting of mostly electrons, protons, and alpha particles. Earth is largely protected from solar winds by its magnetic field. However, the winds can still be observed, as they create phenomena like the beautiful Northern Lights (or **Aurora Borealis**).

Major Features of the Universe

Galaxies

Galaxies are clusters of stars, rocks, ice, and space dust. Like everything else in space, the exact number of galaxies is unknown, but there could be as many as a hundred billion. There are three types of galaxies: spiral, elliptical, and irregular. Most galaxies are **spiral galaxies**; they have a large, central galactic bulge made up of a cluster of older stars. They look like a disk with spinning arms. **Elliptical galaxies** are groups of stars with no pattern of rotation. They can be spherical or extremely elongated, and they don't have arms. **Irregular galaxies** vary significantly in size and shape.

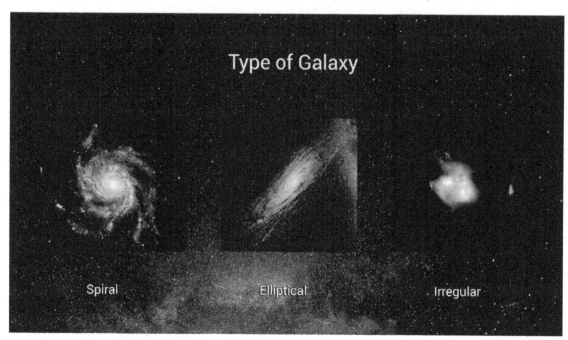

To say that galaxies are large is an understatement. Most galaxies are 1,000 to 100,000 parsecs in diameter, with one *parsec* equal to about 19 trillion miles. The Milky Way is the galaxy that contains Earth's solar system. It's one of the smaller galaxies that has been studied. The diameter of the Milky Way is estimated to be between 31,000 to 55,000 parsecs.

Characteristics of Stars and Their Life Cycles

Life Cycle of Stars

All stars are formed from **nebulae**. Depending on their mass, stars take different pathways during their life. Low- and medium-mass stars start as nebulae and then become red giants and white dwarfs. High-

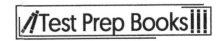

mass stars become red supergiants, supernovas, and then either neutron stars or black holes. Official stars are born as red dwarfs because they have plentiful amounts of gas—mainly hydrogen—to undergo nuclear fusion. Red dwarfs mature into white dwarfs before expending their hydrogen fuel source. When the fuel is spent, it creates a burst of energy that expands the star into a red giant. Red giants eventually condense to form white dwarfs, which is the final stage of a star's life.

Stars that undergo nuclear fusion and energy expenditure extremely quickly can burst in violent explosions called **supernovas**. These bursts can release as much energy in a few seconds as the Sun can release in its entire lifetime. The particles from the explosion then condense into the smallest type of star—a neutron star—and eventually form a **black hole**, which has such a high amount of gravity that not even light energy can escape. The Sun is currently a red dwarf, early in its life cycle.

Color, Temperature, Apparent Brightness, Absolute Brightness, and Luminosity

The color of a star depends on its surface temperature. Stars with cooler surfaces emit red light, while the hottest stars give off blue light. Stars with temperatures between these extremes, such as the Sun, emit white light. The **apparent brightness** of a star is a measure of how bright a star appears to an observer on Earth. The **absolute brightness** is a measure of the intrinsic brightness of a star and is measured at a distance of exactly 10 parsecs away. The **luminosity** of a star is the amount of light emitted from its surface.

Hertzsprung-Russell Diagrams

Hertzsprung-Russell diagrams are scatterplots that show the relationship of a star's brightness and temperature, or color. The general layout shows stars of greater luminosity toward the top of the diagram. Stars with higher surface temperatures appear toward the left side of the diagram. The diagonal area from the top-left of the diagram to the bottom-right is called the **main sequence**. Stars may or may not follow the main sequence during their life.

Dark Matter

Dark matter is an unidentified type of matter that comprises approximately 27% of the mass and energy in the observable universe. As the name suggests, dark matter is so dense and small that it doesn't emit or interact with electromagnetic radiation, such as light, making it electromagnetically invisible. Although dark matter has never been directly observed, its existence and properties can be inferred from its gravitational effects on visible objects as well as the cosmic microwave background. Patterns of movement have been observed in visible objects that would only be possible if dark matter exerted a gravitational pull.

Theory About the Origin of the Universe

The **Big Bang theory** is the most plausible cosmological model for the origin of the universe. It theorizes that the universe expanded from a high-density and high-temperature state. The theory offers comprehensive explanations for a wide range of astronomical phenomena, such as the cosmic microwave background and Hubble's Law. From detailed measurements of the expansion rate of the universe, it's estimated that the Big Bang occurred approximately 13.8 billion years ago, which is considered the age of the universe. The theory states that after the initial expansion, the universe cooled enough for subatomic particles and atoms to form and aggregate into giant clouds. These clouds coalesced through gravity and formed the stars and galaxies. If this theory holds true, it's predicted that the universe will reach a point where it will stop expanding and start to pull back toward the center due to gravity.

Practice Questions

1. At what point in its swing does a pendulum have the most mechanical energy?
   a. At the top of its swing, just before going into motion
   b. At the bottom of its swing, in full motion
   c. Halfway between the top of its swing and the bottom of its swing
   d. It has the same amount of mechanical energy throughout its path

2. What does the scientific method describe?
   a. How to review a scientific paper
   b. How to organize a science laboratory
   c. The steps utilized to conduct an inquiry into a scientific question
   d. How to use science to earn money in society

3. The energy of motion is also referred to as what?
   a. Potential energy
   b. Kinetic energy
   c. Solar energy
   d. Heat energy

4. Burning a piece of paper is what type of change?
   a. Chemical change
   b. Physical change
   c. Sedimentary change
   d. Potential change

5. A ramp leading up to a loading dock would be considered which type of simple machine?
   a. Screw
   b. Lever
   c. Inclined plane
   d. Pulley

6. Who is credited for simplifying the laws of motion?
   a. Einstein
   b. Hawking
   c. Copernicus
   d. Newton

7. The heat transfer due to the movement of gas molecules from an area of higher concentration to one of lower concentration is known as what?
   a. Conduction
   b. Convection
   c. Solarization
   d. Radiation

8. Which of the following is true of an object at rest on earth?
   a. It has no forces acting upon it.
   b. It has no gravity acting upon it.
   c. It is in transition.
   d. It is in equilibrium.

9. When researching a problem in science, what are the best sources to use?
   a. People you have seen on television
   b. Anyone with a Ph.D.
   c. Accredited laboratories and universities
   d. Any source with an internet webpage

10. What is a change in state from a solid to a gas called?
    a. Evaporation
    b. Melting
    c. Condensation
    d. Sublimation

11. The forces acting upon an object can be illustrated using what?
    a. A Venn diagram
    b. A periodic table
    c. A force diagram
    d. A stress-strain diagram

12. Which is not a form of Energy?
    a. Light
    b. Sound
    c. Heat
    d. Mass

13. A projectile at a point along its path has 30 Joules of potential energy and 20 Joules of kinetic energy. What is the total mechanical energy for the projectile?
    a. 50 Joules
    b. 30 Joules
    c. 20 Joules
    d. 10 Joules

14. What factors can prompt scientific inquiry and progress?
    a. Curiosity
    b. Competition
    c. Greed
    d. All of the above

15. Which of the following is considered a force?
    a. Weight
    b. Mass
    c. Acceleration
    d. Gravity

16. Why would a pencil appear to bend at the water line in a glass of water?
   a. The wood of the pencil becomes warped from being in the water.
   b. It appears to bend because of the refraction of light traveling from air to water.
   c. The pencil temporarily bends because of its immersion into separate mediums.
   d. The reflection of the light from water to a human's pupil creates the illusion of a warping object.

17. Which of the following is NOT one of Newton's three laws of motion?
   a. Inertia: an object at rest tends to stay at rest, and an object in motion tends to stay in motion
   b. $E = mc^2$
   c. For every action there is an equal and opposite reaction
   d. $F = ma$

18. The law of the conservation of energy states which of the following?
   a. Energy should be stored in power cells for future use.
   b. Energy will replenish itself once exhausted.
   c. Energy cannot be created or destroyed.
   d. Energy should be saved because it can run out.

19. Which of the following is true regarding magnets?
   a. Opposite charges attract
   b. Like charges attract
   c. Opposite charges repel
   d. Like charges do not repel or attract

20. Running electricity through a wire generates which of the following?
   a. A gravitational field
   b. A frictional field
   c. An acoustic field
   d. A magnetic field

21. When an ice skater spins on one skate in a circle, what happens if they extend their arms out like the letter "T"?
   a. They spin faster.
   b. They spin slower.
   c. They stop spinning.
   d. Nothing changes.

22. For circular motion, what is the name of the actual force pulling toward the axis of rotation?
   a. Centrifugal force
   b. Gravity
   c. Centripetal force
   d. No force is acting.

23. Which is not a method for transferring electrostatic charge?
   a. Polarization
   b. Touch
   c. Election
   d. Induction

24. What does the re-radiation of solar waves trapped in earth's atmosphere contribute to?
    a. Global warming
    b. Greenhouse effect
    c. Climate change
    d. All of the above

25. Velocity is a measure of which of the following?
    a. Speed with direction
    b. The change in position over the change in time
    c. Meters covered over seconds elapsed
    d. All of the above

26. Which of the following sources of energy are non-renewable?
    a. Wind energy
    b. Solar energy
    c. Fossil fuel energy
    d. Geothermal energy

Use the following image to answer question 27.

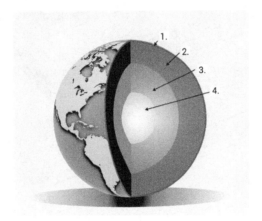

27. Which choice describes layer 4?
    a. Inner core: solid
    b. Inner core: liquid
    c. Outer core: solid
    d. Outer core: liquid

28. Which type of rock accumulates in layers at the bottom of the ocean due to run-off?
    a. Igneous
    b. Sedimentary
    c. Metamorphic
    d. Minerals

29. The water cycle involves phase changes. Which example below is evaporation?
    a. Clouds forming in the sky
    b. Rain, snow, or ice storms
    c. River water flowing to the ocean
    d. Sunlight's effect on morning dew

30. Which of the following is NOT directly caused by tectonic plate movement?
    a. Spreading of the ocean floor
    b. Earthquakes
    c. Mountain formation
    d. Precipitation

31. Which of the following statements is false?
    a. Magma circulates in the upper mantle.
    b. All volcanoes have explosive eruptions.
    b. Igneous rocks are formed by crystallized lava.
    c. Igneous rocks recycle and form magma.

Use the following image to answer questions 32 and 33.

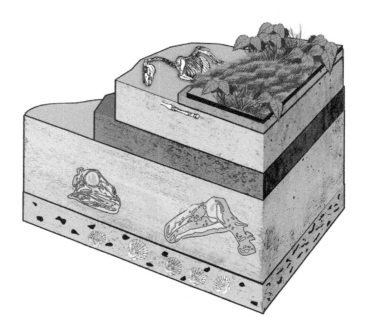

32. Which fossil is the oldest?
    a. Dinosaur head
    b. Seashell
    c. Skeleton
    d. Grass

33. The fossils in the figure are embedded in which type of rock?
    a. Metamorphic
    b. Igneous
    c. Sedimentary
    d. Magma

Use the following image to answer question 34.

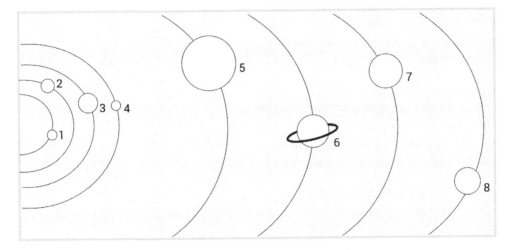

34. Where is the asteroid belt located in the figure above?
    a. Between structures #2 and #3
    b. Between structures #3 and #4
    c. Between structures #4 and #5
    d. Between each planet

35. Why is a year on Mars shorter than a year on Jupiter?
    a. Mars is much smaller than Jupiter.
    b. Mars is a rocky planet, while Jupiter is made of gas.
    c. Mars has a smaller orbit around the Sun.
    d. Mars is inside the asteroid belt.

Use the following image to answer question 36.

36. The figure above illustrates earth's orbit around the sun. What season is it where the dot is located?
    a. Summer
    b. Winter
    c. Fall
    d. Spring

37. Which statement(s) are true about the phases of the moon?
    a. Full moons are farther away from the sun than new moons.
    b. Crescent moons are smaller than half moons.
    c. Gibbous moons are larger than half moons.
    d. All of the above are true.

38. Why are greenhouse gases important?
    a. They allow UV rays to penetrate the troposphere.
    b. They insulate earth and keep it warm.
    c. They reflect light so that the sky looks blue.
    d. They form clouds and directly participate in the water cycle.

39. How is a theory different from a hypothesis?
    a. Theories are predictions based on previous research, and hypotheses are proven.
    b. Hypotheses can change, while theories cannot.
    c. Theories are accepted by scientists, while hypotheses remain to be proven.
    d. Hypotheses are always wrong, while theories are always true.

40. Which scientist is correctly paired with what he or she studies?
    a. Paleontologist: earth's crust
    b. Meteorologist: fossils
    c. Seismologist: earthquakes
    d. Geologist: weather

41. What part of most plants performs photosynthesis?
    a. Root
    b. Stem
    c. Leaf
    d. Flower

42. Which definition describes an ecosystem?
    a. One individual organism
    b. Rocks, soil, and atmosphere within an area
    c. All the organisms in a food web
    d. All living and nonliving things in an area

Use the following image to answer questions 43 and 44.

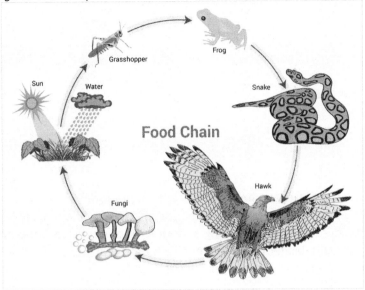

43. Which is the decomposer in the food chain above?
    a. Sun
    b. Grass
    c. Frog
    d. Fungi

44. Which is the herbivore in the food chain above?
    a. Grass
    b. Grasshopper
    c. Frog
    d. Fungi

45. What is a product of photosynthesis?
    a. Water
    b. Sunlight
    c. Oxygen
    d. Carbon Dioxide

46. What is cellular respiration?
    a. Making high-energy sugars
    b. Breathing
    c. Breaking down food to release energy
    d. Sweating

47. Which is true regarding DNA?
    a. It is the genetic code.
    b. It provides energy.
    c. It is single-stranded.
    d. All of the above.

48. Which one of the following can perform photosynthesis?
    a. Mold
    b. Ant
    c. Mushroom
    d. Algae

49. What happens at stomata?
    a. Carbon dioxide enters.
    b. Water exits due to transpiration.
    c. Oxygen exits.
    d. Glucose exits.

50. Which of the following represents a helpful inherited adaptation?
    a. A male elephant defending his territory by chasing another elephant away.
    b. A female dog that has a permanent strong odor that other male dogs tend to avoid.
    c. A male moose born with bigger horns that enable him to reduce competition for mating.
    d. A monkey learning to peel a banana after several tries.

Answer Explanations

1. D: It has the same amount of mechanical energy throughout its path. Mechanical energy is the total amount of energy in the situation; it is the sum of the potential energy and the kinetic energy. The amount of potential and kinetic energy both vary by the position of an object, but the mechanical energy remains constant.

2. C: The scientific method refers to how to conduct a proper scientific inquiry, including recognizing a question/problem, formulating a hypothesis, making a prediction of what will happen based on research, experimenting, and deciding whether the outcome confirmed or denied the hypothesis.

3. B: Kinetic energy is energy an object has while moving. Potential energy is energy an object has based on its position or height. Solar energy is energy that comes from the sun. Heat energy is the energy produced from moving atoms, molecules, or ions, and can transfer between substances.

4. A: A chemical change alters the chemical makeup of the original object. When a piece of paper burns it cannot be returned to its original chemical makeup because it has formed new materials. Physical change refers to changing a substance's form, but not the composition of that substance. In physical science, "sedimentary change" and "potential change" are not terms used to describe any particular process.

5. C: An inclined plane is a simple machine that can make it easier to raise or lower an object in height. Simple machines offer a mechanical advantage to performing tasks. While a screw, a level, and a pulley are also simple machines, they would be used to offer a mechanical advantage in other situations.

6. D: Sir Isaac Newton simplified the laws of motion into three basic rules, based upon his observations in experimentation and advanced mathematical calculations. Albert Einstein was known for his theories involving electricity and magnetism, relativity, energy, light, and gravitational waves. Stephen Hawking is known for his theories and studies of space, dark matter, black holes, and relativity. Copernicus was known for his observations and theories regarding the movements of the planets in our universe; specifically, that the sun was the center of our solar system, not earth.

7. B: Convection is the transfer of heat due to the movement of molecules from an area of higher concentration to that of lower concentration; this is also how heat can travel throughout a house to warm each room. Conduction is the transfer of energy from one molecule to another molecule through actually touching or making contact with each other. Radiation is how the sun warms Earth; no medium is needed for this type of transfer.

8. D: An object at rest has forces acting upon it, including gravitational, normal, and frictional forces. All of these forces are in balance with each other and cause no movement in the object's position. This is equilibrium. An object in constant motion is also considered to be in equilibrium or a state of balanced forces.

9. C: When conducting scientific research, it is best to rely on sources that are known for honest, ethical, and unbiased research and experimentation. Most laboratories and universities must have their work validated through independent means in order to publish or claim results. Anyone can publish things on the Internet—it does not mean their work has been validated, and therefore, their work may not be correct.

10. D: Sublimation is a change in state from a solid to a gas. Evaporation is a change in state from a liquid to a gas, melting is a change in state from a solid to a liquid, and condensation is a change in state from a gas to a liquid.

11. C: A force diagram shows all of the forces acting upon an object in a situation. The direction of arrows pointing around the object shows the direction of each force. A Venn diagram is used to show mathematical sets, a periodic table shows how the elements are categorized, and a stress-strain diagram is used in engineering.

12. D: Mass refers to the amount or quantity there is of an object. Light, sound, and heat are all forms of energy that can travel in waves.

13. A: The mechanical energy is the total (or sum) of the potential energy and the kinetic energy at any given point in a system.

$$ME = PE + KE; 50 \ Joules = 30 \ Joules + 20 \ Joules$$

14. D: Scientific inquiry can be prompted by simple curiosity as to how or why something works. As seen in the race to enter outer space, scientific progress can be driven by competition. Many inventors are motivated by the idea of finding a better, faster, or more economical way of doing or producing something so that they can prosper from their discovery.

15. A: Using Newton's equation for motion, $F = ma$, and substituting gravity in for acceleration (a), the weight, or force could be calculated for an object having mass (m). Weight is a force, mass is the amount of a substance, and acceleration and gravity are rate of speed over time.

16. B: It appears to bend because of the refraction of light traveling from air to water. When light travels from one material to another it can reflect, refract, and go through different materials. Choice *A* is incorrect, as the pencil does not actually become warped but only *appears* to be warped. Choice *C* is incorrect; although the pencil appears to bend because of its immersion into separate mediums where speed is different, the pencil does not become temporarily warped—it only appears to be warped. Choice *D* is incorrect; it is the refraction of light, not reflection. The latter happens within the same medium, which makes the answer choice incorrect.

17. B: While this is Einstein's application of Newton's theory to that of light, it is not one of Newton's original three laws of motion. Newton's three laws are $F = ma$, the law of inertia, and for every action there is an equal and opposite reaction.

18. C: This is a fundamental law of thermodynamics. Energy can only transfer, transform, or travel. The amount of energy in a system is always the same.

19. A: The ends (or poles) of a straight magnet are different charges. One end is positive and one end is negative. Therefore, the positive end of magnet #1 would attract the negative end of magnet #2 and repel magnet #2's positive end.

20. D: When electricity is run through a wire, it is carrying current and current has a charge. Therefore, there is a charge running down the wire, which creates a magnetic field that can attract and repel just like any magnet.

21. B: The ice skater is demonstrating the conservation of angular momentum. This means that the amount of momentum for the situation will remain the same. If the skater is redistributing the mass

(their arms), then the angular speed will compensate for that alteration. In this case, the mass is extended out away from the axis of rotation, so the rate of rotation is slowed down. If their arms were brought back in near their body, then the rate of rotation would increase, making the skater spin faster.

22. C: This is the actual force recognized in a rotational situation. The reactive force acting opposite of the centripetal force is named the centrifugal force, but it is not an actual force on its own. A common mistake is to interchange the two terms. But, the real force acting in a rotational situation is pulling in toward the axis of rotation and is called the centripetal force.

23. C: Electric charge can be transferred through touch of one physical object to another, induction by bringing a charged object near another object, and polarization, or the forcing of one charge to the end of an object in a centralized area.

24. D: The solar waves from the sun warm Earth. Many of the waves are meant to reflect back off of the atmosphere to keep Earth warm, and the rest of the waves are meant to reflect back out into space through the atmosphere. This is known as the greenhouse effect. However, when the atmosphere has become too dense (polluted by gases), the waves meant to escape are trapped and re-radiate in Earth's atmosphere, causing an overall warming of the climate, known as global warming.

25. D: Velocity is a measure of speed with direction. To calculate velocity, find the distance covered and the time it took to cover that distance; change in position over the change in time. A standard measurement for velocity is in meters per second (m/s).

26. C: Fossil fuel energy. Wind energy from turbines, solar energy from sun panels, and geothermal energy are all considered renewable and preferable alternatives to fossil fuel, of which there is a limited supply.

The following image is the answer to question 27.

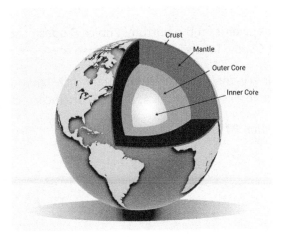

27. A: Inner core: solid. Layer 4 is the inner core; therefore, Choices *C* and *D* are incorrect. The inner core is solid due to the intense pressure upon it, making Choice *B* incorrect.

28. B: Sedimentary. Choice *A* (igneous) is incorrect, because that is crystallized magma found on land. Choice *C* (metamorphic) is incorrect, because that is unified, solid rock close to earth's mantle. Choice *D* (minerals) isn't a type of rock, but what composes rock.

//Test Prep Books📚

29. D: Sunlight evaporates dew from plants. Choice *A* is incorrect because cloud formation is condensation. Choice *B* is incorrect because rain, snow, and ice storms are different forms of precipitation. Choice *C* is incorrect because rivers flowing into the oceans are examples of run-off.

30. D: Precipitation. Precipitation has nothing to do with plate tectonic theory. Plate movement causes ocean floor spreading, mountain formation, and earthquakes; therefore, all other answer choices are correct.

31. B: All volcanoes have explosive eruptions. This isn't true; shield volcanoes have thin magma that oozes out gently. Choice *A* is correct because magma circulates in the upper mantle. Choice *C* is correct because igneous rock is cooled lava. Choice *D* is correct because igneous rock goes through the rock cycle and will eventually become magma again.

The following image is for questions 32 and 33.

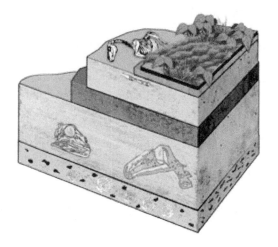

32. B: Seashells. The oldest rock layer is on the bottom. Choice *D* doesn't show a fossil—the grass is a living organism. Choices *A* and *C* show fossils in higher layers, so these are not the correct answers.

33. C: Sedimentary rock. Fossils are only found in sedimentary rock. Igneous rock, metamorphic rock, and liquid magma don't contain fossils, so Choices *A*, *B*, and *D* are incorrect.

The following image is for question 34.

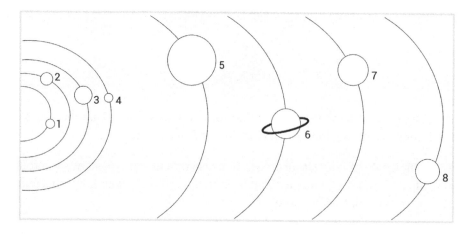

34. C: Between structures #4 and #5. The asteroid belt is rock orbiting between the inner, solid planets and the outer, gassy planets. More precisely, it is between Mars (planet #4) and Jupiter (planet #5). It is not Choice *A* (between Venus and Earth), nor is it Choice *B* (between Earth and Mars). Choice *D* is incorrect since it is not between every planet.

35. C: Mars has a smaller orbit around the Sun. This question requires critical thinking because every answer choice is true, but only one of them has to do with orbiting time. A year is the time it takes a planet to orbit the Sun, and because Mars is closer to the Sun and has a smaller orbit, its year is significantly shorter than a year on Jupiter.

The following image is for question 36.

36. B: Winter. Students must identify the lateral equator and know the difference between North and South. They should recognize that because the top hemisphere is tilted away from the Sun; it would be winter at that time. Spring and fall (Choices *D* and *C*) are incorrect because both hemispheres have the same exposure to the sun, and summer (Choice *A*) is incorrect since the top hemisphere is tilted toward the sun.

37. D: All of the above. All choices are correct. New moons are closest to the sun and full moons are farthest (Choice *A*). Crescent moons are smaller than half-moons (Choice *B*), and gibbous moons are larger than half-moons (Choice *C*).

38. B: They insulate earth and keep it warm. Greenhouse gases serve as a blanket and allow earth to exist at livable temperatures. Choice *D* is incorrect because greenhouse gases do not form clouds; clouds are formed by condensed water vapor. Choice *C* is incorrect because while it is true that particles in the atmosphere reflect light so that the sky appears blue, this isn't an important function of the particles in the troposphere. The blue appearance is just cosmetic. Choice *A* is incorrect because ozone in the stratosphere actually prevents UV rays from passing.

39. C: Theories are accepted by scientists, while hypotheses remain to be proven. Choice *A* is incorrect because theories are far more than predictions; they are actually highly supported and accepted as truth. Choice *B* is incorrect because theories can change with new technology and understanding. Choice *D* is also incorrect because theories may not always be true and can change. Also, hypotheses can be and often are supported.

40. C: Seismologist: earthquakes. All other choices have been mixed up. Paleontologists study fossils, meteorologists study weather, and geologists study Earth's crust.

41. C: Leaf. Leaves are the part of the plant that contain chloroplast (due to their green appearance), thus they are the parts that perform photosynthesis. Roots (Choice *A*) suck up water. Seeds and flowers are reproductive structures (Choices *B* and *D*).

42. D: All living and nonliving things in an area. Choice *C* (all the organisms in a food web) describes feeding relationships and not symbiosis. Choice *B* (rocks, soil, and atmosphere in an area) includes nonliving factors in an ecosystem. Choice *A*, one organism, is too small to be considered an ecosystem.

The following image is for questions 43 and 44.

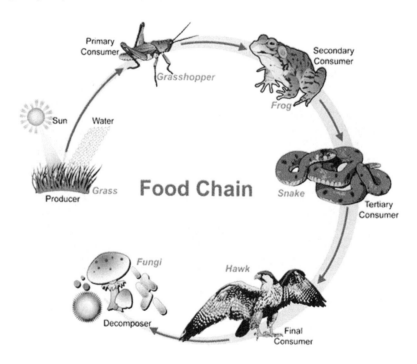

43. D: Fungi. Choice *A* (the sun) is not even a living thing. Grass (*B*) is a producer, and the frog (*C*) is a consumer. The fungi break down dead organisms and are the only decomposer shown.

44. B: Grasshopper. An herbivore is an organism that eats only plants, and that's the grasshopper's niche in this particular food chain. Grass (*A*) is a producer, the frog (*C*) is a consumer, and the fungi (*D*) is a decomposer.

45. C: Oxygen. Water (*A*) is a reactant that gets sucked up by the roots. Carbon dioxide (*D*) is a reactant that goes into the stomata, and sunlight (*B*) inputs energy into the reaction in order to create the high-energy sugar.

46. C: Breaking down food to release energy. Breathing (*B*) is not cellular respiration; breathing is an action that takes place at the organism level with the respiratory system. Making high-energy sugars (*A*) is photosynthesis, not cellular respiration. Perspiration (*D*) is sweating, and has nothing to do with cellular respiration.

47. A: It is the genetic code. Choice *B* is incorrect because DNA does not provide energy—that's the job of carbohydrates and glucose. Choice *C* is incorrect because DNA is double-stranded. Because Choices *B* and *C* are incorrect, Choice *D*, all of the above, is incorrect.

48. D: Algae can perform photosynthesis. One indicator that a plant is able to perform photosynthesis is the color green. Plants with the pigment chlorophyll are able to absorb the warmer colors of the light spectrum, but are unable to absorb green. That's why they appear green. Choices *A* and *C* are types of fungi, and are therefore not able to perform photosynthesis. Fungi obtain energy from food in their environment. Choice *B*, ant, is also unable to perform photosynthesis, since it is an animal.

49. D: Glucose exits. The stomata are pores at the bottom of the leaf, and carbon dioxide enters (it is a reactant for photosynthesis) and oxygen exits (it is a product for photosynthesis), so Choices *A* and *C* are correct. Water exits through the stomata in the process of transpiration, so Choice *B* is correct as well. Glucose is the sugar that is either broken down by the plant for its own energy usage or eaten by other organisms for energy.

50. C: A male moose with horns that enable him to reduce competition for mating. Choices *A* and *D* (elephant and monkey) are not caused by genes. These are learned behaviors from other animals. Choice *B* (smelly dog) is actually a detriment because the dog will be less likely to mate, so she will not pass on her smelly genes.

Fine Arts, Health, and Physical Education

Visual Arts and Music

Foundations of Art Education

The four general categories of **arts** are visual arts, dance, music, and theater arts. As children progress through elementary school, they should be exposed to the basic foundations, creative expression and production of each type of art, and the ability to critically analyze a work of art and make connections within a cultural and historical context. Art education should build progressively during childhood so that older children are able to eventually take on these more sophisticated and advanced applications.

There are a wide variety of visual and performing arts that can enhance a child's creativity and learning experience. It is optimal to expose young children to many different types of art – both as a creator and observer – for well-rounded cultural, creative, and comprehensive learning. Depending on the child's age, early childhood educators can tailor art assignments and activities to meet the child's interests, motor skills, attention, and needs.

Visual Arts

Visual arts include things like drawing, painting, sketching, collage, sculpture, etc. Before the age of three, most artwork is produced less in an artistic way and more in a scientific and sensory way. Children at these youngest ages are more interested in the textures, colors, and shapes of what they create rather than expressing any sort of emotion or symbol. There are a variety of crafting activities that young children enjoy and can benefit from including finger painting, pasting, modeling with Play-Doh and clay, folding paper for origami, tracing and making models, and using a variety of craft supplies in creative ways including pom-poms, googly eyes, glitter, pipe cleaners, felt, and yarn. Craft activities help small children develop fine motor skills as they use instruments such as scissors and try to make precise movements like stringing beads and coloring within boundaries. As children develop, they can focus for longer periods of time and can handle more precise movements with smaller materials and areas. For example, a three- to four-year-old child may make simple Play-Doh snakes or snowmen, while a six- to eight-year-old child can add spots, a tongue, and facial features to the snowman with smaller bits of material laid in more exact locations. Through arts and crafts, young children can learn about colors and observe colors in the world around them, recognizing things such as green grass and blue sky. Working on arts and crafts projects helps children develop skills in planning, attention and focusing, problem-solving, and originality. It also helps them learn how to observe the world around them, be appreciative

of other people's interpretations and ideas, deal with frustrations when things do not go as planned, and develop hand-eye coordination.

Early childhood educators should strive to expose children to a vast array of arts and craft materials and different types of arts. Activities should be age-appropriate. For example, four- to five-year-old children are likely unable to use small beads and fine pencils and markers, and do better with wider drawing utensils and larger beads that are easier to grasp and manipulate. Children who are ten to twelve are able to work with more intricate objects and may be bored with crayons and coloring books. There are a variety of other art forms that students may view or try to create such as jewelry, pottery, stained glass, wire art, sewing, quilting, knitting, and decoupage.

Music
Studies show that learning an instrument, especially at a young age, improves thinking, mathematical skills, attention, and brain activity. Children benefit from being exposed to a variety of instruments and musical genres including woodwinds, strings, brass, piano, vocals, jazz, blues, classical, folk, etc. Older children can learn basic music theory and how to read music, and may be able to take on more advanced instrument lessons and play or sing collaboratively in groups. As children mature, their attention spans, fine motor skills, ability to understand and maintain rhythm and pitch, and musical fluency improve. Activities and expectations should be age-appropriate. Smaller versions of some instruments are also manufactured and available to very young children to fit their small bodies and fingers.

For young children, learning to identify and maintain rhythm and beat is an important early skill and can be practiced by listening to music accompanied by physical movements such as clapping, stomping, dancing, or following the beat with percussive instruments like tambourines or small drums. They can learn to recognize **musical notes** and the position of the notes on a staff as well as the various characteristics of basic note types such as eighth notes, quarter notes, half notes, and whole notes. Singing and learning basic traditional and folk songs are simple ways to expose children to music as an easy, low-cost group activity. As children get older and more experienced, the group can be divided into sections to create harmonies and maintain separate singing roles within a varied group, which is a more advanced skill requiring concentration, attention, and group coordination.

Dance
Dance incorporates not only music, creativity, and arts, but also physical activity, which is very important to young children. Dance can help improve **kinesthetic sense** or awareness of one's body in space, rhythm and mathematical thinking, fluidity of motion, and coordination and balance. There are many varieties of dance, and educators should pick age-appropriate music and dances. The youngest children tend to do best with free movement to music or simple choreographed dances such as the hokey pokey, which are accompanied by easy sing-along songs.

Theater
Educators can expose young children to theater, both as participants and audience members. Young children may enjoy puppets, and older children can begin to take on roles and learn and memorize short lines. Memorization and recitation skills are transferable to educational activities in other subjects such as spelling words, learning history dates, and memorizing state capitals. Theater activities provide opportunities for imaginative play for children who enjoy dressing up, pretending to be various characters, imagining and acting out scenes, improvising lines, and mimicking jobs, characters, and roles in society. This is healthy and developmentally-appropriate.

Fundamental Concepts Related to the Arts

Artists, regardless of medium, typically rely on the following six main principles in art: emphasis, rhythm, balance, contrast, harmony, and movement.

Emphasis

Artists often want to make one part of their work stand out from the rest and guide viewers to pay attention to specific components of their piece. For example, lines and textures in paintings and sculptures may direct viewers to specific details or target features, and altering the texture of one area may make it stand out in contrast to the rest of the work.

Rhythm

Rhythm involves repeating elements within a work such as colors, shapes, lines, notes, or steps to create a pattern of visual or auditory motion.

Balance

Balance is positioning objects or using size, color, shape and lighting in the artwork so that all of the elements are equally present with no particular component overpowering the rest. Symmetrical balance is when two halves of an image create a mirror image, so that if the work is folded in half, each half is the same. Balance can also be **asymmetrical,** wherein the composition is balanced but the two halves are not the same. For example, a large central object is balanced by a smaller figure on one edge.

Contrast

Contrast exemplifies differences between two unlike things such as loud and soft music, major and minor tones, fast and slow dancing movements, and light and dark colors.

Harmony

Somewhat opposite of contrast, **harmony** highlights the similarities in separate but related parts of a composition. Rather than emphasizing their dissimilarities, harmony shows that different things can actually be related to each other and blend together.

Movement

Artwork that contains a sense of motion or action has **movement**. Even stationary art, like painting and sculpture, can imply movement based on the positioning of objects or the artist's use of lines, which draw the viewer's eye to different areas of the artwork.

Art Terminology

Each of the four forms of art have a vast list of terminology unique to that art form. Educators should be familiar with such terms to help effectively communicate with and educate students and, more importantly, to empower students to have intelligent and meaningful conversations about artwork with peers, artists, and community members. Listed below are some examples of common terms to introduce at age-appropriate levels with each of the various forms of art:

Visual Arts

Early learners can focus on the basic vocabulary of visual art like identifying colors and shapes. Older students can be exposed to more nuanced terms in the world of visual art. Some visual art is **representational** and depicts objects as they appear in the real world. One visual tool that heightens the realistic accuracy of visual art is **perspective**, an artistic technique that creates the illusion of depth through the use of line (for example, lines in the foreground converge in the background), size and

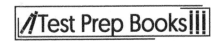

placement of objects (objects that are supposed to be closer to the viewer appear larger than objects that are further away), or color (for example, a hill that is close to the viewer is depicted in a vibrant green, while a distant mountain appears with a more muted, hazy color).

In contrast to representational art, other visual art is **abstract**. When artists use abstraction, they use line, color, and other elements to communicate the presence of objects and emotions rather than realistically portraying the objects. For example, a swirl of **warm colors** like red and orange might represent anger or anxiety; **cool colors** like blue and gray could communicate sadness or passivity. In this way, the artist's **palette**, or range of colors used in their work, can communicate a mood or emotion to the viewer. Some works are **monochromatic,** meaning that they only use one color (although the artist might use different shades of the same color—for example, dark blue and light blue). Different shades of color can also create the illusion of shape or represent different lighting.

Other tools of both abstract and representational visual art include **contrast** (the pairing of dissimilar elements to make each other stand out), **positive** and **negative space** (positive space refers to the areas of the artwork occupied by its subject, whereas negative space includes all the areas that do not contain any subject), **balance**, and **symmetry**. Some artistic techniques to introduce to students might include caricature, collage, painting, sculpture, portraiture, landscape, and still life. If educators are able to take students on museum field trips, students should know museum-related vocabulary terms like *gallery, exhibit,* and *curator.*

Music
Students should be familiar with terms related to **meter,** which is the repeating pattern of stressed and unstressed sounds in a piece of music. While meter is a somewhat complex concept, students can easily understand the idea of a musical beat, which is the audible result of meter. In written music, meter is noted by a **time signature**, which looks like a fraction with one number on the top and one number on the bottom, like ¾. The bottom number expresses the **beat** as a division of a whole note (for example, the number four means that it is a quarter note), while the top number shows how many beats make up a **bar** (so ¾ means that three quarter note beats make up one bar).

In addition to patterns of stress, music also contains an arrangement of sounds, known as its melody. **Melody** refers to the development of a single tone; when many tones are combined simultaneously in a way that sounds pleasing to the listener, it is referred to as **harmony**. Other sound elements related to tone include **chords** (the combination of musical tones), **keys** (the principal tone in a piece of music), and **scales** (a series of tones at fixed intervals, either ascending or descending, usually beginning at a certain note). These elements can be described as either major or minor.

Words to describe the **tempo,** or the speed of a piece of music, include, from slowest to fastest: *largo, adagio, andante, allegro, vivace,* and *presto.* In terms of the intensity of the sound, **piano** refers to music that is played softly whereas **forte** means played with force. Students should also be familiar with vocabulary terms that describe different instruments, different genres of music, and different musical periods.

Dance
In dance, a **step** is one isolated movement, and **choreography** refers to the arrangement of a series of steps. Even young students can learn simple choreography that they rehearse with an instructor and perform with classmates as a group. Older students can learn about different styles of dance such as the waltz, tap, jazz, and ballet, as well as more contemporary styles like **lyrical dance** (combining ballet and jazz) or **fusion dance** (a highly rhythmical dance form). Students of ballet should be familiar with terms

like **pirouette** (spinning on one foot or on the points of the toes), **arabesque** (standing on one leg while extending one arm in front and the other arm and leg behind), **plié** (bending at the knees while holding the back straight), **elevé** (rising up from flat foot to pointed feet), and **pivot** (turning the body without traveling to a new location; a pirouette is a type of pivot). Students can also learn about folk dances, partner dances, and line dances.

Basic Techniques, Tools, and Materials for Producing Art

Art has **personal** (self-expression, gratification, narrative functions), **social** (collective meaning for a group of people, such as symbolic art honoring a god or political art), and **physical** (such as a pottery mug for tea) functions that often overlap within a single piece of work. As children go through elementary school, they become familiar with an increasing variety and complexity of visual art forms beginning with things like drawing, painting, and sculpting, then adding printmaking, sponge painting, film animation, and graphics in third and fourth grades, and dabbling in environmental design and art based on personal experience and observation by the fifth grade. They may also try computer-generated art, photography, metalworking, textile arts, and ceramics. Materials include scissors, brushes, papers, glue, beads, clay, film, and computers.

Instruments used in the early education classroom typically fall into one of the following categories: **melodic instruments** (melody bells, xylophones, flutes, and recorders), **rhythmic instruments** (drums, triangles, tambourines, and blocks), or **harmonic instruments** (chording instruments such as the autoharp). The key elements of music include rhythm, melody, harmony, **form** (the structure or design of the music, usually referring to the music's different sections and their repetition, such as **binary** (AB), **ternary** (ABA), theme and variation and **rondo** (ABACA), and the musical phrases), and expression [**dynamics** (volumes) and timbre].

Self-Expression and Communication through Art

One of the fundamental benefits of the arts is their ability to be used as forms of self-expression, creativity, and self-identity, and a means to communicate emotions, culture, and personal and societal narratives. While the youngest students may not fully grasp the ability to express themselves through art, even fairly young children can use art to communicate ideas, stories, and feelings. Early childhood educators can encourage students to use all forms of art for self-expression and should engage children in active critical thinking and analysis to uncover the meanings and emotions behind artwork generated by others. For example, educators can play a variety of music clips with different tempos, moods, tones, and keys and ask students to explain how the music makes them feel and what they think the composer was trying to express. Compositions in minor keys, at slower largo and adagio tempos, and music with harmonic dissonance may evoke feelings of sadness, trepidation, anxiety, or fear, whereas lively, spirited songs in major keys at faster allegro tempos are likely expressing happier feelings. Students can begin to contrast different moods and types of music and talk about how the moods are conveyed by differences in the music.

Similarly, the students can look at visual artwork and analyze the artist's use of different colors, textures, brushstrokes, etc. to express the feelings behind the artwork. Students can also try to discern the narrative within art, particularly in theater, music, and dance. They can try to understand how stories can be told abstractly and recognize that not every story is told through concrete narrative writing. For example, operatic works and ballets often tell elaborate stories with few or no words. Yet, even when they are presented in foreign languages, operas and ballets can be universally understood by varying audiences due to the emotions and movements present on stage. While these abstract concepts are

likely too complex for young children, as students mature and develop, they will gradually become more aware of the nuances and arts' function as a vehicle of expression. Young children are able to understand how their pictorial drawings or paintings convey a narrative in their mind; from there, they can begin to understand how artwork generated by another person conveys his or her storyline. Educators can also encourage students to use art as a cathartic release when they are feeling sad, angry, frustrated, or nervous. Dance, visual arts, and music are constructive, safe, and appropriate ways to temper difficult emotions. Children can use dance choreography and improvisation to express feelings and ideas as well.

Strategies to Promote Critical Analysis and Understanding of the Arts

Early childhood educators should use techniques that foster their students' ability to critically analyze a variety of art forms. Students should develop a toolbox with the appropriate language and terminology to be able to intelligently discuss artwork from a critical standpoint with others. Each form of art has its own unique terms that are important for students to understand, both for their own appreciation and fluency in the arts and for their ability to communicate with others about arts. As students mature and develop their own interests, they will become increasingly able to effectively talk about why they may or may not enjoy a piece of artwork and how it makes them feel. Educators should emphasize that the artistic process is creative and subjective and that each person will have his or her own opinions about various art forms, but that in every case, the universal principles of respect, diversity, and acceptance apply.

Although generally there is no "right or wrong" in art, the ability to critique creative works is a skill that takes time, maturity, exposure, and intellectual understanding and appreciation of art. Early childhood educators can best help students improve these skills through a broad exposure to many arts, detailed explanations about the intricacies of various types of artwork, and discussions about self-expression through art. For example, a young student may inherently not enjoy a classical piece of music arranged in a quartet, but he or she can learn to critique it from an unbiased position based on that type of music. By understanding the details taking place in the piece (such as how the composer changes the key from major to minor halfway through to invoke sadness or mystery, or how the cello and violin feed off each other as if conversing), students can become more impartial and able to understand art for art's sake.

Educators should instruct students to evaluate questions such as: what was the artist's purpose in creating the work, and is the purpose achieved? Is the style the artist chose appropriate for the expressed purpose of the work? Does the artist have a unique idea in their work? The dialogue underlying these lessons should always focus on showing respect for artwork and creative ideas that are different from the student's own and celebrating diversity of preferences and art forms.

Arts in Various Cultures and Throughout History

It is imperative that early childhood educators focus on the fact that artwork has been used throughout history and in every culture as a means of expression and storytelling. Even seemingly new forms of art were not created out of nowhere, but rather, they have evolved from other previously existing forms of art. One of the best ways to discuss art is actually through embedding it in discussions of history and culture. The evolution of music can easily be discussed through various time periods. For example, the assassination of President John F. Kennedy, the Hippie movement, the Vietnam War, and the Beatles coexisted in the same time period, so students can find similarities and differences among these social and artistic ideals within their historical context.

Students can also study different time periods of art and architecture. In the **Classical period**, Greek artists focused on physical beauty and the human form, paying particular attention to Olympian gods and their idealized proportions in their works. The **Medieval period** that occurred in Europe from 500-1400 CE saw a flourish of Romanesque style art that shifted the emphasis from portraying realism to conveying a message, particularly symbolic Christian ideals. Students should also learn about the history of art in other countries such as China, with its jade, pottery, bronze, porcelain, and calligraphy. Educators should focus on how various influences over time affected the predominant artwork each period. For example, Buddhism in the early first century BCE increased calligraphy on silks, the Song dynasty created landscape paintings that were popular, and the Ming and Qing dynasties developed color painting and printing with an evolution towards individualism. As China became increasingly influenced by Western society in the nineteenth and early twentieth centuries, social realism predominated. In addition to covering other Asian nations, educators should expose students to traditional African art, which generally demonstrates moral values, focuses on human subjects, and seeks to please the viewer. Educators can also introduce art from the American Indians such as woodcarving, weaving, stitchery, and beading. Art in American Indian populations varies widely from tribe to tribe but tends to beautify everyday objects and create items of spiritual significance. Students should be exposed to music and theater from other cultures and observe the costumes, movements, instruments, and themes in performing arts from places like the Caribbean islands, Japan, Mexico, Australia, Africa, Italy, and Russia.

Health

Health Promotion and Disease Prevention

Early childhood educators should be able to incorporate health and physical education concepts into the classroom for the overall health, wellness, and growth of their students. Physical activity is especially important at young ages, and children need at least sixty minutes of moderate to vigorous physical activity daily according to the U.S. Surgeon General's Recommendations. There are five components of health-related **physical fitness**: cardiovascular fitness, muscular strength, muscular endurance, flexibility, and body composition. All five areas should be addressed in physical education classes. With cardiovascular training, as the heart enlarges, the volume of the chambers increase, allowing for a greater **stroke volume** (the volume of blood ejected in each heart beat) and cardiac output. This also enables the heart to be more efficient, with a resultant lowering of the resting and submaximal exercise heart rate and blood pressure, which increases the body's exercise duration and intensity tolerance. Blood volume—both in terms of plasma and hemoglobin—increases oxygen-carrying capacity and lactic acid metabolism improves, which allows the aerobic system to more effectively metabolize substrates

for usable energy. Muscle glycogen storage, another important form of energy storage in the body, also increases. Vasculature increases as well, improving the blood perfusion of muscles.

Other positive results of physical fitness include increased bone mineral density, improvements in body composition, and neural adaptations. Resistance training, even with body weight alone (such as squats and push-ups), affords strength, power, and coordination improvements and leads to greater efficiency of the anaerobic metabolic systems. Nervous system adaptations occur quickly with training as **motor units** (connections between the spine and other muscles throughout the body) become conditioned to activate more quickly and more often. As a greater number of motor units activate together and coordinate with each other, a higher percentage of fibers in a muscle contract simultaneously, increasing strength. Over time, muscle fibers increase in size and bone mineral density increases in load-bearing bones. Flexibility training increases elasticity and resting length of muscle and connective tissues and joint range of motion (ROM) before the stretch reflex is initiated (muscle spindle adaptation), reducing injury risk.

Health education – even beginning at preschool ages – has been shown to have a significant positive impact on an individual for maintaining healthy behaviors as an adolescent and adult. Preschool children who receive high-quality physical and health education may have improved nutrition and exercise habits and are more likely to receive routine medical and dental care as adults. Early childhood educators can start laying the groundwork for a lifetime of healthier behaviors and attitudes by fostering an environment of enjoyment of physical activity, an understanding of nutrition and hydration, and methods of disease and injury prevention.

Educators can talk with older children about the types, causes, and characteristics of chronic, degenerative, communicable, and non-communicable diseases, as well as ways to detect and prevent them. Students can learn about modifiable risk factors for various diseases and conditions such as diabetes, coronary artery disease, cardiovascular disease, and obesity.

The Relation Between Healthy Behaviors and a Healthy Person

Early childhood educators can introduce young children to a wide variety of healthy behaviors that will help improve overall health. An important concept to begin teaching students is that optimal health is brought about through routine practice of daily healthy behaviors and an overall commitment to a healthy lifestyle. For example, educators can discuss the importance of establishing regular physical activity and daily healthy eating habits and that, through these habits, students can control their body weight and help avoid obesity. Obesity is a modifiable risk factor for many diseases including insulin-resistant Type 2 diabetes mellitus and cardiovascular disease. It is important and empowering for children to start to understand their roles and responsibilities in healthy habits and disease prevention. By giving them the necessary knowledge and tools to put the information into practice in their lives, educators can increase the self-efficacy and behaviors of even young children. In this way, early childhood educators can be instrumental in bringing about a healthier generation of young children who have an awareness of their health and an understanding of their own influence on risk factors for certain diseases. The following are healthy behaviors that can lead to a healthy body and mind:

Nutrition

Children should be taught how to identify foods and the importance of consuming a daily variety of food within each healthy food group. The benefits of trying new foods, especially those from other cultures, can help students understand diversity and challenge their preconceived notions about different cultures and flavors. Older children can learn how to prepare simple foods, recognize the USDA recommended daily allowances of each food group in order to keep the body healthy, and classify foods based on their group and health benefits. Older students can also learn about the role of various nutrients in the body such as fat, fiber, and protein, and how to select nutrient-dense foods from a given list. Children benefit from understanding what makes a food healthy and knowing options for healthy meals and snacks. By the third grade, students can start learning how to read nutrition labels, how to compare foods based on nutrition labels, and how to modify food choices to improve healthfulness, such as replacing low-fiber foods with higher fiber choices, like opting for apples instead of applesauce. When students are in the fourth grade, educators can start talking about portion sizes and the relationship between food consumption and physical activity on energy balance and weight control. In the context of introducing the basics about calories, prevention of obesity and the ramifications of an unhealthy diet can also be discussed. Children in the fifth and sixth grades can learn about the differences in types of fats, examples of common vitamins and minerals and food sources of these nutrients, the disadvantages of "empty-calories," and how to recognize misleading nutrition information.

Physical Activity

In childhood, regular physical activity improves strength and endurance, helps build healthy bones and muscles, controls weight, reduces anxiety and stress, increases self-esteem, and may improve blood pressure and cholesterol. Children should get at least sixty minutes of physical activity daily. Typically, young children are less concerned about their physical fitness and more concerned about having fun; therefore, physical education should center on fun and play as a means to engage the body in activity. Play-centered physical education programs are an effective means to promote children's movement development and meet their requisite activity needs for health. Early childhood educators should develop physical education programs that focus on the enjoyment of movement rather than sport-specific skill mastery for two reasons. Firstly, play-centered activity will help the child be more engaged and likely to adopt a positive attitude towards exercise; and secondly, in early childhood, basic general fitness and movement skills are more important than mastery of highly specialized skills unique to certain sports. Young children also tend to lack the gross and fine motor skills and perceptual abilities needed for such highly specialized skills, which can lead to frustration or simply an inability to perform the activity.

For optimal results, it is best for early childhood educators to establish an environment of student-centered learning in regards to physical education. Because young children at any given age can have vastly different motor and physical abilities from each other, it is imperative that the educator simply set standards of enjoyment, movement, and physical discovery rather than specific mastery of skills. This prevents boredom in more physically advanced children and bewilderment and demotivation in less

skilled children. It is prudent for educators to provide a variety of options within every activity and game so that children can figure out what appeals and works for them at their own developmental level. This also starts children on the path to understanding themselves and evaluating choices at a young age within a fun, playful environment and begins to get their minds processing not just what to do but how to do it as well.

Educators should use simple instructions that are age-appropriate in terms of the steps and level of complexity, visual demonstrations of movements, and drills that help reinforce the skill. During practice and exploration of the new skill, educators should focus on positive feedback and evaluation to guide the children in learning. When teaching new skills, especially to toddlers and young children, instructions lasting longer than twenty seconds or that contain more than just a couple of steps will cause students to lose interest or get overwhelmed. It is typically advantageous to have very short instructional periods interspersed between longer breaks to play and try out the skills. To help manage a large group of small, active children, simple rules and expectations should be laid out with consequences for improper behavior.

Children should learn about the methods and benefits of a proper warm-up and cool-down, how to set goals to make exercise part of their daily routine, and the benefits of physical activity. Older children can learn about the effects of exercise on the heart and how to locate their pulse during and after exercise, how to stay physically active through more than just sports, and how to create a personal fitness plan.

Sleep
Early childhood educators should talk about the importance of sleep and why parents set a "bedtime," as well as healthy sleep hygiene and establishing a sleep schedule. Children can learn about how much sleep they need and ways to improve the quality of sleep, such as physical activity and avoiding screen time before bed. Young children who may experience nightmares can benefit from learning relaxation techniques as well as talking about their fears and feelings to trusted adults.

Stress Management
Students should be educated about stress management and exposed to techniques such as mental imagery, relaxation, deep breathing, aerobic exercise, and meditation. Children can be guided through progressive muscle relaxation and should be taught signs of excessive nervousness and stress, how to manage test and performance anxiety, and when and how to get help with excessive stress.

Healthy Relationships
Healthy family and social relationships are important to overall health and happiness. Studies have pointed to a negative impact of parental fighting on a child's wellbeing, including sleep and exercise habits, nutrition choices, stress, and social adjustment. Early childhood educators should talk about aspects of healthy relationships such as communication, emotional support, sharing, and respect. Younger children should learn skills that are helpful in making friends, cultivating relationships, and resolving conflict, especially as they relate to peers and siblings. Cooperation, taking turns, using words rather than physical means to communicate feelings, and exploring feelings are helpful concepts to instill. Older children should begin to be exposed to dating etiquette and forming healthy romantic relationships. Educators should work to create a classroom environment of inclusion where students have an awareness of peers who may feel left out and work to include everyone. Within discussions of healthy relationships, educators should talk about accepting and appreciating diversity, including differences in cultures, religions, families, physical appearance and abilities, interests, intellect,

emotions, lifestyle, and, in older children, sexual orientations. Life skills – such as having self-esteem, making decisions, calming oneself when angry or upset, and using listening skills – should be addressed.

Hydration

Early childhood educators should teach students about the importance of hydration and signs of dehydration as well as healthy choices for fluids, with a special emphasis on water. Children and their parents should be encouraged to send kids to school with a water bottle, and classrooms or hallways should be equipped with water fountains that children can access and use with limited supervision or assistance.

Safety Behaviors

Children should learn basic safety behaviors and the importance of following rules to prevent common injuries. Basic safety behaviors include wearing sunscreen and sunglasses when going outdoors; wearing protective gear in sports such as bicycle helmets, reflective vests, appropriate pads and cups, etc.; and using a car seat and/or always wearing a seat belt. Young children should learn about household safety such as not touching burners and not putting their fingers in electrical sockets nor opening the door to strangers. Educators should have children practice the "no, go, and tell" procedure for unsafe situations. For example, if a stranger offers the child an unknown substance, the child should know how to firmly refuse, carefully leave the situation, and tell a trusted adult. In this lesson, educators should also help children to identify trusted adults in their families and communities.

Educators can also discuss community safety measures such as using sidewalks, contacting city services (police, fire, and ambulance) in emergencies, and crossing the street safely by using crosswalks, holding hands, and looking both ways before crossing. Children should also learn about the health consequences of smoking, how to avoid secondhand smoke, and how to identify and avoid poisonous household substances. Fire safety such as "stop, drop, and roll" and emergency evacuation procedures should be rehearsed. Older children can learn about safety rules for various types of weather and how weather affects their personal safety, what different traffic signs mean, water/swim safety rules, and the importance of weighing consequences before taking risks.

Hygiene

Young children should learn about germs and the spread of infections. Older children can learn about bacteria and viruses. The importance of washing hands (including appropriate demonstration) cannot be overstated in elementary and preschool classrooms.

Other aspects of hygiene such as covering the mouth while coughing and covering the nose while sneezing, not sharing cups, practicing clean bathroom habits, showering and bathing, and, in older children, using deodorants, antiperspirants, and facial cleansers should be included in the curriculum.

Hygiene Stickers Remind Students to Use Healthy Practices

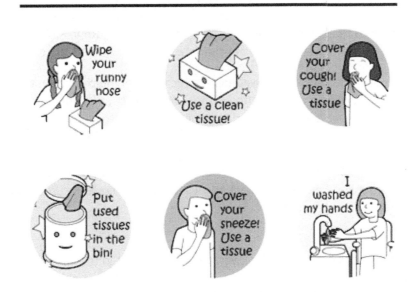

Learning to Seek Health Care

Early childhood educators can play an instrumental role in the lifelong practice of seeking routine medical and dental care as well as medical support during illness and injury by setting positive attitudes towards such care and explaining the benefits to young children. Not all children will necessarily have health insurance, so information regarding local free and affordable options should be made available to parents. It is important that children learn to identify signs of illness and injury such as sore throats, headaches, stomachaches that do not go away, swelling, etc.

Consistent Feelings of Sadness, Anxiety, Loneliness, and Stress

Just as it is important to get professional help for medical issues, it equally important to seek help with mental and emotional issues. Educators should talk about feelings and emotions and how it is normal to feel sad or anxious at various times, but that if such feelings persist, help may be necessary. Teachers can lead the class through stress management techniques to combat anxiety and talk about the role of physical activity, sound nutrition, and good sleep for mood stabilization. Young children should learn about identifying and communicating their emotions.

Lingering Pains or Aches

Children should be instructed to tell a trusted adult when they have pains, aches, or symptoms that persist for several days so that the adult can help determine if medical attention is needed. Children can also learn basic first-aid such as how to wash a cut and put on a Band-Aid or when and how to use **RICES** (Rest, Ice, Compression, Elevation, and Stabilization) after an injury.

Prevention of Common Injuries and Health Problems

One critically important component of health and safety education is the prevention of common injuries and illnesses. By practicing safety and exercising caution, many common injuries and illnesses can be avoided. For example, wearing helmets and seat belts can reduce the risk of injury during automobile or bicycle accidents. Washing hands thoroughly and frequently with antibacterial soap can help prevent the spread of germs, and thus safeguard against viral and bacterial infections. Even very young children should be encouraged to wash hands thoroughly before and after eating, after using the bathroom, after coming in from outdoor play, and when transitioning to a new activity. It is sometimes helpful to demonstrate how to wash in between each finger, under the fingernails, and up to the wrists, modeling not only how to wash hands but for how long. The common song "Row, Row, Row Your Boat" repeated three times is sometimes used to measure the appropriate length of time for hand washing.

By instilling an attitude of mindfulness and awareness, educators can help children to develop practices of safety, which will ultimately keep them healthy. Other longer-term behavioral and lifestyle principles – such as keeping a healthy weight through caloric balance and a healthy diet – will help prevent disease risk factors such as obesity, high triglycerides, hypercholesterolemia, and high blood sugar. Children should be informed about the dangers of smoking and the detrimental health consequences of tobacco products, including ingestion of secondhand smoke. Other simple safety practices include wearing proper footwear, practicing good hygiene, remaining alert when out in traffic, using sidewalks and pedestrian walkways, and wearing sunscreen.

Wearing Seat Belts and Helmets

Children should be informed that they should always wear a seat belt in the car. Children under eighty pounds should be in an appropriate car seat as well to maximize safety in moving vehicles. Many unfortunate traffic injuries and fatalities could have been prevented had the victim appropriately worn a seat belt. Riding bicycles, skateboarding, using scooters, and rollerblading are examples of excellent exercise and recreational pursuits; however, helmets and appropriate padding and protection on elbows and knees should always be worn. Children or their supervisors often neglect to fasten on a helmet when the child is simply trying out a skateboard or scooter around the driveway or park. This is quite dangerous because falls are inevitable in the learning process and even minor head bumps can be damaging. Helmets should fit snugly with the band clipped securely under the chin and the dome of the helmet should cover the entire forehead. Helmets should not move freely on the head and should be snug enough to stay in place. They should be sized appropriately to the child's head with use of additional padding if necessary. Kneepads and shoulder pads are great adjuncts to safety gear for rollerblading, skateboarding, and scooters. Children riding in bicycle trailers should also wear helmets, and children should never ride on the handlebars of a bicycle. Although more stable, tricycles and bicycles with training wheels still require helmets with their use.

Drugs, Alcohol, and Tobacco

Drugs, alcohol, and tobacco are unhealthy substances that early childhood educators should begin informing young children about. Exposure to drugs, cigarettes, and alcohol happens at increasingly younger ages, particularly when children have older siblings. By educating children about the risks and consequences of such substances at young ages, teachers can begin to thwart the risks of unhealthy behaviors. The Drug Abuse Resistance Education (D.A.R.E.) program is often helpful at introducing such substances, their health consequences, and how to navigate social situations involving peer pressure. The difference between alcohol abuse and alcohol in moderation should also be discussed.

Routine Preventative Medical and Dental Care

By practicing routine medical and dental care and adhering to recommended guidelines regarding the frequency of preventative healthcare, certain risks for various diseases and dental issues (such as cavities and gingivitis) can be reduced. It is typically recommended the children see their pediatrician and get dental cleanings at least once every six months. In between these appointments, healthy habits continue to safeguard against health issues. Examples include thoroughly brushing teeth at least twice a day and flossing daily, getting at least sixty minutes of moderate to vigorous exercise a day, meeting healthy sleep requirements (the National Sleep Foundation recommends ten to thirteen hours for preschoolers and nine to eleven hours for elementary school children), consuming an adequate amount of water, and following nutritional guidelines. By keeping children on a routine schedule of preventive care with consistency in providers of that care, the health and wellbeing of each child can be tracked during their growth to ensure health issues do not slip through the cracks.

Food Preparation Choices

Early childhood educators should devote instructional attention to the methods of food preparation and how various choices in preparation affect the nutritive value of the food. For example, baking and steaming are healthier than pan frying, deep frying, and sautéing. Eating whole foods is healthier than eating their processed counterparts because the whole foods retain a greater percentage of the inherent nutrients. For example, apples are healthier than applesauce because applesauce strips away much of the fiber and the vitamins in the apple skin. Similarly, whole grain bread is healthier than refined white breads, which remove the bran from the grain, thereby reducing the fiber, protein, and B vitamin content. Foods that are organic do not have the pesticides and chemicals used with certain **conventional** (non-organic) foods. This is an important consideration for thin-skinned fruits and vegetables such as spinach, tomatoes, and berries, which can absorb harmful chemicals.

Influence of Family, Peers, Culture, and Media on Health Behaviors

Health behaviors are heavily influenced by a child's environment, including family, friends, peers, media, and technology. These factors can shape the child's ideas of health, nutrition, and fitness, as well as influence subsequent health behaviors. It is important for educators to help children identify and cultivate positive influences while avoiding or modifying negative ones.

Educators should work with students to develop self-efficacy for healthy behaviors to help safeguard against any negative environmental influences. Children should learn about peer pressure, substance use, wearing seat belts, and how to make independent decisions and stick to them despite peer pressure or group dynamics. Discussed below are a few examples of potential environmental and situational influences.

Family

Family factors include health insurance status, safety and injury prevention education and care, nutritional meal planning and diet composition, family dynamics and stress, family culture during leisure time such as activity vs. inactivity, child care situation, and parental and sibling modeled behavior.

Peers

The peer group that surrounds a child can affect his or her health behaviors depending on those of the group. Example behaviors and influences include the use of helmets and seat belts, interests and activities, inclusion on sports teams or during recess and physical education, aggression and bullying or teasing.

School and Community

Factors in this domain include things such as the availability and choices of food in vending machines, school breakfast and lunch programs, health education and screenings, first aid and AED (automated external defibrillator) access, bike paths and walking trails, parks and community fitness and sports programs, crosswalks, and non-smoking zones.

Public Policy and Government

Tobacco and alcohol sales and policies, seat belt and helmet enforcement, child care laws, and other such regulations fall under the domain of public policy and governmental influences.

Media

Media use and exposure can have a significant impact on young minds. Children have not necessarily developed the critical thinking skills needed to evaluate the truthfulness of media claims. Television programming and commercials, PSAs, advertising, exposure to celebrities, knowledge of current events, and consumer skills all fall under this domain.

Technology

Technological factors including Internet access, handicap accessibility such as audio signals at crosswalks and wheelchair ramps and lifts, health technology apps, and pedometer availability can affect health behaviors.

Advocating for Personal, Family, and Community Health

Students have a lot to gain by cultivating advocacy skills, especially as they relate to promoting healthy behaviors. Students can learn how to advocate for personal, family, and community health resources and opportunities and establish health-enhancing messages that encourage others to also adopt and maintain a healthy lifestyle. Young children can work on how to advocate for healthy policies in their own schools and communities, such as ensuring easy access to drinking water and banning smoking on school grounds. They can also work on ways to encourage peers to make positive health choices, focusing on supporting one another and getting everyone to join the "team" of good health advocates. Older students can research and learn about various health issues and then make presentations to other students and family members to share accurate health information. The following are a few specific advocacy skills that educators should work to enhance in their students:

Locate Valid Health Resources in the Home, School, Community, and Media

One of the greatest challenges for children and adults alike is vetting various health resources in the home, school, community, and especially media for their validity and accuracy. Unfortunately, fad diets are popularized in the media daily. The weight loss industry is a multi-billion-dollar industry for a reason: people are desperate to lose weight and are often looking for the "quick fix" that many of these diets and exercise gadgets promise. However, many of these fad diets are dangerous, have not been developed by health professionals, or do not have sufficient scientific research to validate their safety or efficacy. For instance, fad diets often eliminate entire food groups or claim that the diet is some sort of health panacea. Other unhealthy methods promising rapid weight loss in popular culture include exercise in saunas or steam rooms to "sweat off pounds," starvation or liquid diets, cleanses, and mega doses of dietary supplements. These can cause dangerous dehydration, overdoses on certain micronutrients, and electrolyte imbalances leading to arrhythmias, and a reduced resting metabolic rate as the body senses starvation, which makes subsequent weight loss harder.

Educators should teach students how to critically evaluate information, particularly from the media, and judge its accuracy. School resources may include things such as the physical education department and health education resources, the Great Body Shop health curriculum, the infirmary or nurse's office, the D.A.R.E. program, and other health-informing programs. In the community, additional resources include S.A.D.D. (Students Against Destructive Decisions), the Red Cross, local medical and health offices, and WIC (Women, Infants, and Children) offices.

In the media, students should look for reliable sources of information such as myplate.gov and other government-sponsored health resources, peer-reviewed research journals, PBS or NOVA documentaries, TED Talks, course content from colleges and universities, etc. Students should not only be informed about correct and accurate information, but should also develop the skills to independently determine the validity of resources when they are faced with new information.

Develop Sound Opinions about Health Issues

A critical skill for children to develop is the ability to form informed opinions and back up their opinions with sound evidence. This need extends beyond the realms of health and fitness and can apply to all facets of life, but health information and behaviors are some of the more approachable and applicable topics for young children. Behaviors such as the choice not to smoke or consume drugs and alcohol, the practice of engaging in an active lifestyle over a sedentary one, the consumption of home-cooked or lower fat food choices over fried or fast foods, the intake of water over sodas and juices, and even safety behaviors such as wearing a helmet are all choices and issues that children can begin to consider and establish their own personal standards for.

Early childhood educators can help guide children to the healthful choices by presenting the information and facts about each choice and its consequences as well as engage children in brainstorming sessions to come up with ideas and tactics to support their choices for healthy behaviors. For example, if a family typically stops at the local fast food drive-through after soccer practice, children can talk to their parents about packing healthy snacks for the car ride home instead and even work with parents in the kitchen to make snacks such as vegetable sticks and hummus and cheese and apple slices. Children can even make posters or perform skits to defend their healthy opinions and share such information with younger grades.

The ability to not only form an opinion but also explain and support the reasoning behind it will serve students well throughout their education and lives in general. At the same time, educators should encourage students to keep an open mind and practice critical listening and analytical skills so that they remain open to other people's opinions and can modify their own with changes in research or situations. Particularly in the fields of health and nutrition, where research and science are constantly evolving, the "healthy option" does tend to change. Considering dietary recommendations alone, macronutrient (nutrients required in large amounts, like protein and carbohydrates) intake is constantly changing and the thinking about the healthfulness of saturated fats and carbohydrates shifts. The educated consumer is one who stays abreast of the research and also has the ability to alter his or her own opinions based on changes in the information.

Help Assist Others in Making Healthy Choices

One component of advocacy is supporting and assisting others in making healthy choices. Once students have formulated educated opinions about health-related topics like diet, exercise, safety habits, and substance use, they can become educators and advocates themselves. Students can then share their knowledge and reasoning with peers, family, friends, neighbors, and the community. For example, students can create posters with health information they have learned and hang them in their schools, homes, or other community areas. Students with younger siblings can help them develop good hygiene and safety habits.

Use Effective Communication Skills

Early childhood educators are instrumental in developing effective communication skills in their students. Verbal and nonverbal communication skills are important in setting a positive, educational, supportive environment to optimize learning. They are equally important for students to master for use in their own daily lives. When communicating with others, students should be mindful to be fully attentive, make eye contact, and use encouraging facial expressions and body language to augment positive verbal feedback. Postures including hands on hips or crossed over the chest may appear standoffish, while smiling and nodding enhance the comfort and satisfaction of the other party. **Active listening** is the process of trying to understand the underlying meaning in someone else's words, which builds empathy and trust. Asking open-ended questions and repeating or rephrasing in a reflective or clarifying manner is a form of active listening that builds a positive, trusting relationship.

In tandem with different communication styles, educators and students alike should be aware of different learning styles. **Auditory learners** learn through hearing, so the educator can use verbal descriptions and instructions. **Visual learners** learn through observation, so the educator can use demonstrations, provide written and pictorial instructional content, and show videos. **Kinesthetic learners** learn through movement, involvement, and experience, so the educator can prepare lessons with hands-on learning, labs, or games with a physical component.

An important skill for children is the ability to communicate effectively with adults, and developing this comfort from a young age will be helpful throughout life. Educators can facilitate this through providing experiences where children need to talk to adults in the community. For example, educators may take the class on a field trip to the local community library, where students must ask the librarian for help locating certain health resources. Students might also prepare a health fair and invite parents, community members, and those from senior centers to come learn from posters, demonstrations, and presentations. Children can also work on developing communication skills using an array of technologies such as telephone, written word, email, and face-to-face communication.

Physical Education

Motor Skills and Movement Patterns in Children

Educators should be familiar with physical and neurological development, especially in terms of motor skills and development, to provide developmentally appropriate motor movement tasks. As young children grow and mature, they develop the ability to handle increasingly complex motor skills. Children learn to move and move to learn and, for this reason, physical activity is especially important in the classroom for young children. As children grow, their physical abilities gradually increase, and educators can begin to modify lessons and activities to continue to challenge and improve new movement patterns and abilities. What looks like "play" actually consists of meaningful movement patterns that help the child move his or her body and use large muscle groups to develop physical competency. This is known as movement education. Children should learn basic movement patterns and skills for daily life so that they can maneuver safely and appropriately in their environment in relation to other people and objects. After basic skills are mastered, more specific sport-related skills can be achieved. Movement competency is the successful ability of the child to manage his or her body in both basic and specialized physical tasks despite obstacles in the environment, while perceptual motor competency includes

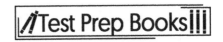

capabilities involving balance, coordination, lateral and backward movements, kinesthetic sense, and knowledge of one's own body and strength.

Educators should be able to assess the level at which students can control specific movements and identify patterns of physical activity that have been mastered. This information can be used to plan developmentally-appropriate movement tasks and activities. In addition, early childhood educators can be helpful in identifying students who seem to be lagging behind in age-appropriate motor abilities. In such cases, early intervention programming and resources may be beneficial.

There are three general categories of basic skills: locomotor, non-locomotor, and manipulative skills; more complex movement patterns combine skills from multiple categories. **Locomotor skills** – such as walking, running, jumping, and skipping – are the movement skills that children need to travel within a given space or get from one space to another. **Non-locomotor skills** are typically completed in a stationary position – such as kneeling, pushing, twisting, bouncing, or standing – and help control the body in relation to gravity. **Manipulative skills** usually involve using the hands and feet, although other body parts may be used. These skills help the child handle, move, or play with an object. Manipulating objects helps advance hand-eye and foot-eye coordination so that the child can more successfully participate in sports activities like throwing, batting, catching, and kicking.

Young children can begin to learn these skills with balls and beanbags at a less challenging level and progress to more difficult levels and activities with practice and development. Early stages usually involve individual practice first and then progress to involve partners and groups. Throwing and catching are actually quite complex skills that can be as challenging to teach as they are to learn. Early childhood educators should emphasize skill performance and principles such as opposition, following objects with the eyes, weight transfer, follow through, and, eventually, striking targets. **Motor planning** is the ability of the child to figure out how to complete a new motor task or action and depends on both the sensory motor development of the child as well as his or her thinking and reasoning skills.

Motor Development
Typical motor development milestones for various age groups are as follows:

Ages three to four: have mastered walking and standing and are now developing gross motor skills such as single foot hopping and balancing, unsupported ascent and descent of stairs, kicking a ball, overhand throwing, catching a ball off of a bounce, moving forward and backward with coordination, and riding a tricycle. Fine motor skills begin to progress including using scissors with one hand, copying capital letters and more complex shapes, and drawing basic shapes from memory.

Ages four to five: tackling increasingly complex gross motor skills that require some coordination and multiple movement patterns combined together such as doing somersaults, swinging, climbing, and skipping. They also can use utensils to eat independently, dress themselves with clothing containing zippers and buttons, and begin to tie shoelaces. Mastery of fine motor skills begins to progress more rapidly, including cutting and pasting, and drawing shapes, letters, and people with heads, bodies, and arms. They tend to engage in long periods of physical activity followed by a need for a significant amount of rest. Physically, bones are still developing. Girls tend to be more coordinated while boys are

stronger, but both sexes lack precise fine motor skills and the ability to focus on small objects for a long time.

Children Enjoy Exercise with Games Like Tag

Age six to eight: skating, biking, skipping with both feet, dribbling a ball. By the end of grade two, children should be able to make smoother transitions between different locomotor skills sequenced together. They can also accomplish more complicated manipulative skills such as dribbling a soccer ball with their feet and can better control their bodies during locomotion, weight-bearing, and balance. Students can begin to use feedback to hone motor skills from a cognitive perspective.

Ages nine to eleven: Children begin to get stronger, leaner, and taller as they enter the pre-adolescent stage and growth accelerates with the beginnings of secondary sex characteristics. Attention span and gross and fine motor skills improve. By the end of grade five, most children can achieve more performance-based outcomes such as hitting targets and can complete specialized sports skills such as fielding baseballs and serving tennis balls. They are also able to combine movements in a more dynamic environment such as moving rhythmically to music. From a cognitive perspective, they can begin to take concepts and feedback learned in other skills or sports and apply them to a new game. An example of this is increasing body stability by bending the knees to lower the center of gravity in basketball during a pick drill; this skill can also be reapplied on the ski slope. Additionally, children begin to observe peers more and can provide feedback to others.

Promoting Physical Fitness, Responsible Behavior, and Respect in Physical Activity Settings

The youngest students enjoy being physically active for the fun of movement itself, and they particularly enjoy non-structured activities in moderate and high intensities followed by sufficient rest. By the end of second grade, students will likely voluntarily incorporate activities from physical education class to leisure time activity and, although they are not typically concerned with structured exercise or activity recommendations for health, they do recognize the physical and mental benefits of activity and they self-select game-like play they enjoy. They are able to recognize the physiologic indicators of exercise such as elevated heart rate, sweating, and heavy breathing; they have a general understanding that

physical fitness improves health; and they know that there are five components of health-related fitness: cardiovascular endurance, muscular strength, muscular endurance, flexibility, and body composition.

By the end of fifth grade, students should be aware that participation in regular physical activity is a conscious decision, and they should choose activities based on both enjoyment and health benefits. At this age, they begin to develop an awareness of resources and opportunities in the school and community to support activity and may become more interested in healthy food choices, realizing that personal responsibility and their own choices can affect their health. They also become more aware of their body and voice in a complex dynamic environment with others, and have greater focus towards controlling parts of their body and their movements within an environment with others. Students should also begin to take an interest in improving aspects of fitness for better sports' performance or health indicators, and should apply the results of fitness assessments to gain a deeper understanding of their own personal fitness and health compared with peers and standards. Older students also understand that success comes with practice and effort, and they also enjoy broadening their skills and activities by learning new sports and skills based on prior mastery. They can engage in mutual physical activity with students of differing ability levels.

It is important that educators continually address the issues of personal and social behavior, especially as it relates to accepting and respecting differences in abilities, ideas, lifestyles, cultures, and choices. By the end of second grade, students should know how to follow the rules and safety procedures in physical education classes and during activities with little to no need for reinforcement. They also understand the social benefits of playing with others and how activities are more fun while interacting with other people. They should be able to effectively communicate during group activities in a respectful way, and enjoy working collaboratively with others to complete motor tasks or goals by combining movements and skills from many people together. By the end of fifth grade, students should be able to work independently or in small or large groups during physical activities in a cohesive and agreeable manner, understanding that the group can often achieve more than the individual alone. However, individually, the student should understand that he or she is also responsible for personal health behaviors and movements.

Theatre

Students can become familiar with a host of terms related to theater productions. In terms of people working in theater, there is the **director** leading the production and **actors** performing it. The **cast** is comprised of a group of actors, and an organization of actors and other theater workers is known as a **company**. During the casting process, actors usually need to **audition** for parts in a play, and they may get a **callback** if their audition goes well! In addition to a main performer, leading roles in a production might also have an **understudy**, an actor who can step into the role when the main performer is unable to appear in the show.

On the technical side, students can learn about props, sets, costumes and wardrobe, effects, and staging. Theater arts education also presents an opportunity to teach students about the literary aspects of a play, such as the narrator, act and scene divisions, and stage directions contained in the script. Students can also become familiar with different dramatic modes like comedy and tragedy. They can learn about the structure of classic drama as well as more open-ended structures like ad lib and improvisation.

The main skills of the theatrical arts are literary, technical, and performance elements. For theater, teachers can use a variety of techniques to incorporate dramatic arts into the classroom, including the following:

Theater-in-Education (TIE)

This is performed by teachers and students using curriculum material or social issues. Participants take on roles that enable them to explore and problem-solve in a flexible structure that is also educational. TIE productions are conducted with clear educational objectives, such as teaching facts or communicating a lesson to the audience.

Puppetry

Puppetry can be used for creative drama with either simple puppets and stages made of bags, cardboard, socks, or more elaborate, artistic materials. Using puppets in theater allows students to tell stories about a wide variety of characters and settings without requiring large and complex costumes, props, or sets. Telling stories with puppets also allows children to develop their motor skills.

More formal theater works for children are typically product-oriented and audience-centered, and children can be either participants or audience members. Such forms may include the following:

Traditional Theater

Actors use characters and storylines to communicate and the audience laughs, applauds, or provides other feedback. The performers and audience are separate entities and the acting takes place on a stage, supported by technical workers.

Participation Theater

Students can engage their voices or bodies in the work by contributing ideas, joining the actors, or contributing in other ways. This is more interactive than traditional theater.

Story Theater

Often told with simple sets, story theater can take place easily in the classroom with minimal scenery and costumes. Due to the sparse use of sets, props, and costumes, story theater often incorporates improvisational strategies to communicate character and setting to the audience. The actors function as characters and narrators and play multiple parts, often commenting on their own actions in their roles.

Readers' Theater

Readers perform a dramatic presentation while reading lines (typically from children's literature), enabling performance opportunities in the absence of elaborate staging or script memorization. This

allows students to focus on emotional expression and speaking skills while reading their lines. The students can sit or stand but no movement is needed.

Readers' Theater

Dance simultaneously incorporates a variety of elements, including the following:

Body: refers to *who*—the dancer—and may describe the whole body or its parts, the shape of the body (such as angular, twisted, symmetrical), the systems of the body and its anatomy, or inner aspects of the body such as emotions, intention, and identity.

Action: refers to *what*—the movement created in the dance such as the steps, facial changes, or actions with the body—and can occur in short bouts or long, continuous actions.

Time: refers to *when* and may be metered or free. Time may also refer to clock time or relationships of time such as before, after, in unison with, or faster than something else.

Space: refers to *where* through space, and how the dancer fills the space and interacts with it. For example, it can refer to whether the dancer's body is low to the ground or up high; moving or in place; going forward, backwards, or sideways; in a curved or random pattern; in front or behind others; or in a group or alone.

Energy: refers to *how*. It is with energy that a force or action causes movement. Dancers may play with flow, tension, and weight. Their energy may be powerful or it may be gentle and light.

Practice Questions

1. Which of the following is a primary reason to provide guidance and scaffolds for art activities for children?

    a. To create an unstructured framework so students are encouraged to experiment and improvise
    b. To give students a sense of direction and purpose
    c. To help students develop of sense of how to use art supplies appropriately
    d. To set expectations that push students to become the best artists they can be

2. Throwing a tennis ball at various targets is an effective and appropriate physical education activity for students in which grade level?

    a. Pre-K
    b. First grade
    c. Third grade
    d. Fifth grade

3. Which of the following is NOT one of the five components of health-related physical fitness?

    a. Body composition
    b. Cardiovascular fitness
    c. Agility
    d. Muscular strength

4. Which of the following is true regarding neural adaptations to fitness training?

    a. Neural adaptations to fitness training are slow because it takes a long time for the body to develop additional motor units and improve coordination of existing units.
    b. Increases in muscle fiber size are the primary cause of initial strength gains, and as training progresses, motor units become more coordinated.
    c. In the early stages of training, the body will experience increases in the ease of activation and coordination of motor units.
    d. Neural adaptations to fitness training are rapidly achieved because the elasticity and resting length of muscles and connective tissues decrease and shorten, respectively, in the early stages of training.

5. Which of the following is NOT an advantage of having a completed model of an art project to show prior to the students engaging in the project themselves?

    a. It helps give the student a frame of reference from which they can work for the activity.
    b. It helps the teacher determine an appropriate timeframe for the activity.
    c. It helps students visualize the step-by-step process that will go into the activity.
    d. It helps establish an enticing end-goal for students and can engage them in the activity.

6. A teacher is developing an art activity to demonstrate the concept of unity. She uses Vincent van Gogh's *Starry Night* (1889) painting as an example and as launch pad to discuss his contributions to the art world. The design of this lesson can best be described as which of the following?

    a. An implicit activity
    b. An explicit activity
    c. An emphasis activity
    d. A balance activity

7. The analyzing part of the performance sequence of art is best described as which of the following?

    a. The process where the performer learns as much as possible about the chosen piece.
    b. The process where the artist engages in practice and self-criticism for improvement.
    c. The process where the artist makes the piece distinct and their own.
    d. The process where the artist uses their judgment to make meaning out of the work and make it their own.

8. Young students' skills regarding responding to art is thought to be augmented effectively by which of the following evaluation methods?

    a. Formative evaluations
    b. Summative evaluations
    c. Formal assessments
    d. Self-assessments

9. Which of the following would NOT be included on a list of nutrition recommendations for children?
    a. Replace higher fat foods with lower-fat alternatives
    b. Replace higher fiber foods with lower-fiber options
    c. Reduce intake of sugary beverages
    d. Replace refined foods with foods in their more natural form

10. The optimal physical education curriculum for five- to six-year-old children should focus on which of the following?
    a. Movement for enjoyment
    b. Sport-specific skills
    c. Hand-eye coordination
    d. Low intensity, endurance activities

11. Which of the following is true regarding classroom instruction of new movement skills for young children?
    a. It should occur in one long session at the beginning of the class, followed by time for children to play and attempt the skill.
    b. It should contain many small steps for the children to keep track of during play.
    c. It should be limited to short twenty-second stretches of instruction interspersed with long periods of play.
    d. It should be given in written form so children can read it at their leisure.

12. Which of the following is a healthy lifestyle habit for children?
    a. Getting eight hours of sleep every night
    b. Keeping their emotions to themselves
    c. Following safety procedures like wearing a seat belt
    d. Brushing their teeth once a day before bed

13. Educators should teach students about the importance of visiting a doctor for all EXCEPT which of the following reasons?
    a. Routine medical care and check-ups
    b. Consistent feelings of sadness, anxiety, loneliness, and stress
    c. Pains or aches that do not go away
    d. When insurance coverage changes

14. Health insurance status, safety and injury prevention education and care, nutritional meal planning and diet composition, social dynamics and stress, and culture around leisure time are all potential health behavior influences related to which factor?
    a. Family
    b. Peers
    c. School
    d. Media

15. Which of the following is true regarding motor skill development in children?
    a. Motor skill development shouldn't begin until after kindergarten.
    b. Sports skills are learned more readily than generalized body movements such as skipping.
    c. Gross motor skills are mastered before fine motor skills.
    d. Students benefit from formal movement training rather than free play.

16. Which of the following is NOT a general category of basic movement skills?
    a. Locomotor skills
    b. Sports-specific skills
    c. Non-locomotor skills
    d. Manipulative skills

17. In a kindergarten classroom, physical education should include a focus on all EXCEPT which of the following?
    a. Hitting targets
    b. Weight transfer
    c. Following objects with the eyes
    d. Running and stopping

18. Which of the following age groups is likely to be most interested in the health-based benefits of physical activity?
    a. Two- to four-year-old children
    b. Five- to seven-year-old children
    c. Seven- to nine-year-old children
    d. Nine- to twelve-year-old children

19. Which of the following are the major categories of the arts that educators should focus curricular activities on?
    a. Music, dance, theater, visual arts
    b. Music, performing arts, visual arts, sculpture
    c. Painting, drawing, woodworking, visual arts
    d. Language arts, music, theater, visual arts

20. The youngest children just beginning in art tend to create art with a focus on which of the following?
    a. Self-expression
    b. Narrative storytelling
    c. Scientific and sensory observations
    d. Creative and artistic ideas

21. Which of the following is true of art education for children?
    a. Children should focus on learning about art from their own culture and time-period.
    b. It is important for children to see professional art before creating their own works.
    c. It is important for children to study art theory before beginning their own projects.
    d. Children should experiment with a variety of methods and materials to create art.

22. Which of the following is a way for young students to easily learn rhythm in music class?
    a. Have students memorize each song on multiple instruments.
    b. Have students sit still and focus intently on the music.
    c. Have students read the lyrics before they listen to the music.
    d. Have students accompany music with simple instruments like tambourines.

23. Which of the following is performed by teachers and students using curriculum material or social issues?
    a. Puppetry
    b. Participation Theater
    c. Reader's Theater
    d. Theater-in-Education (TIE)

24. The main skills in theatrical arts for children include all EXCEPT which of the following?
    a. Staging
    b. Literary
    c. Technical
    d. Performance

25. A three- to four-year-old child would likely create a drawing emphasizing which of the following?
    a. The emotions expressed in their work.
    b. The figural accuracy of the drawing.
    c. The symbolic meaning of their work.
    d. The colors they use and how they look.

26. Which of the following is a technique used to make flat objects look as though they have depth?
    a. Balance
    b. Perspective
    c. Optical illusion
    d. Abstraction

27. Art serves all EXCEPT which of the following main functional categories?
    a. Religious functions
    b. Personal functions
    c. Social functions
    d. Physical functions

28. Which of the following is a principle in art that highlights the similarities in separate but related parts of a composition?
    a. Contrast
    b. Harmony
    c. Movement
    d. Balance

29. What has contemporary research found about breakfast and children?
    a. Breakfast is damaging to school attendance.
    b. Breakfast spikes blood sugar in students and causes behavioral problems.
    c. Breakfast helps students do well on tests.
    d. There is no link between breakfast and student academic achievement.

30. According to the literature, why are educators being encouraged to incorporate art into the curriculum?
    a. To develop students' fine motor skills, and facilitate metacognition and abstract thinking
    b. Because there are many career opportunities in art
    c. To expose students to other cultures
    d. To offer discipline and structure

31. When developing an art activity, instructors are encouraged to do what first?
    a. Develop a model of the finished artwork or project.
    b. Establish clear learning objectives.
    c. Get clear on the overriding concept or idea that is embedded in the lesson.
    d. Offer praise and constructive criticism to the students.

32. What are the four parts of creating art?
    a. Conceptualizing, making, evaluating, and refining
    b. Imagining, planning, making, and presenting
    c. Developing, assessing, sharing, recreation
    d. Creating, revising, producing, and entertaining

33. Which word is NOT a part of the four-part process of responding to art?
    a. Selection
    b. Analysis
    c. Evaluation
    d. Assessment

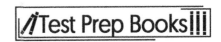

34. In visual media, how is a line typically looked at or understood?
    a. A framework that can be used to provoke emotions and paint mental pictures for the viewers
    b. As the outline of a three-dimensional object, the edge of a two-dimensional object, and the path of a moving point
    c. As the outline of a two-dimensional object, the side of a three-dimensional object, and the path of a static point
    d. A symbol that represents the continuation of time and the timelessness of art

35. What is the best way to create rhythm in visual art?
    a. By repeating visual movement
    b. By the manipulation of lines and figures
    c. Through the use of illusion
    d. None of the above

36. Which color is not a primary color?
    a. Yellow
    b. Blue
    c. Green
    d. Red

37. What helps to create unity in a piece of artwork?
    a. An artist's intention
    b. Shape, focus, and repetition
    c. Colors, theme, pattern, and texture
    d. The reader's perception

38. Which is an example of contrast in art?
    a. Large vs. small shapes
    b. Rough vs. smooth surfaces
    c. Black vs. white
    d. All of the above

39. The speed of music is best described as what?
    a. Pitch
    b. Tempo
    c. Rhythm
    d. Range

40. The psychological benefits of physical activity include which of the following?
    a. Relief of stress
    b. Better self-concept
    c. Improved capability to handle some stressors
    d. All of the above

41. Non-locomotor skills are best defined as what?
    a. Skills that move an individual from one point to another
    b. Skills used to propel or receive an object
    c. Skills of stability that require little or no movement
    d. Skills that include responding and moving with the beat, tempo, or pitch of music

42. Which of the following techniques is NOT proven to help maximize participation in physical education?
   a. Activity modification
   b. Multiactivity designs
   c. Punitive discipline measures
   d. Differentiated forms of grouping

43. Which of the following factors affect a student's development and fitness?
   a. Societal influences
   b. Psychological influences
   c. Cultural influences
   d. All of the above

44. What is the best definition of *expressive movement* in theater?
   a. Responding with your body to rhythm or using facial expressions to communicate
   b. Clothing and accessories worn by actors to portray a character
   c. Any articles used as part of a production
   d. Theatrical equipment, such as backdrops and platforms

45. Setting clear expectations is one way teachers can help foster healthy relationships with students and parents. Which of the following is NOT a strategy that teachers should employ to foster positive relationships?
   a. Consistent positive reinforcement
   b. Closed lines of communication
   c. Encouraging active listening
   d. Practicing empathetic listening

46. Which of the following is characterized by a persistent quest for a thin body?
   a. Bulimia nervosa
   b. Anorexia nervosa
   c. Scoliosis
   d. Autism spectrum disorder

47. Which of the following is characterized by repeated bouts of consuming and/or purging large amounts of food?
   a. Bulimia nervosa
   b. Anorexia nervosa
   c. Scoliosis
   d. Autism spectrum disorder

48. Which of the following qualifies as a type of child neglect?
   a. Medical neglect
   b. Emotional neglect
   c. Educational neglect
   d. All of the above

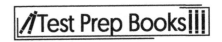

49. What is the difference between neglect and abuse?
    a. There is no difference—neglect is abuse.
    b. Abuse has to be violent.
    c. Abuse is only physical, not mental.
    d. Neglect is only mental, not physical.

50. Increased blood pressure and _____ are side effects of anabolic steroid use.
    a. Bloody cysts in the liver
    b. Decreased muscle mass
    c. Functional reproduction
    d. Heart strength

Answer Explanations

1. B: It is recommended that teachers offer clear, understandable guidance and scaffolds for art projects when working with children because it helps them gain a sense of direction and purpose in the activity. While some degree of flexibility and openness to the framework should be included so that children can experiment and engage their creativity, a structured environment helps define the goals and purpose of the activity. Choice *A* is incorrect because guidance and scaffolds create a structured, not unstructured, framework. Choice *C* may be a fringe benefit to guiding the activity, particularly if finished models are presented, but it is not the primary reason to provide guidance. Choice *D* is incorrect; the goal of art instruction at the early education levels is not to turn each student into the best student he or she can be, but rather to introduce the central concepts of art and its variety of functions, such as self-expression, communicating social ideas, exploring emotions, relating to the world, and creating usable pieces.

2. D: Throwing a tennis ball at various targets involves significant hand-eye coordination, fine-motor skills, and manipulative skills. It also is considered a performance-based skill, rather than a process-based skill. These criteria make it an inappropriate activity for young children because they have yet to develop these skills. Activities for younger children should focus on foundational movement patterns and developing a life-long love of moving. While children in the first and third grades do start to develop fine motor skills, the hand-eye coordination needed to hit targets is not typically present. To this end, process-based outcomes, such as the proper body position and follow through when throwing a ball, should take precedence over performance-based ones, like nailing a specific target with a pitch. However, by the end of fifth grade, most children's motor development is such that these skills are possible. Moreover, they are more developmentally ready to achieve some performance-based outcomes.

3. C: The five components of health-related physical fitness are cardiovascular fitness, muscular strength, muscular endurance, flexibility, and body composition. While agility is an important sports-specific, performance-based skill, one's agility does not significantly impact physical health.

4. C: Adaptations to the nervous system occur quickly with fitness training. The initial increases in strength are due to the conditioning of motor units to activate more quickly and more frequently. The number of motor units that activate in unison results in a higher percentage of muscle fibers in a muscle that contract with one neural impulse. As training continues over weeks and months, the size of muscle fibers increases, furthering improving strength. Choice *A* is incorrect because neural adaptations usually occur quickly after a fitness training program has been started. Choice *B* reverses the order of primary adaptations to the nervous system. Lastly, Choice *D* states the elasticity and resting length of muscles and connective tissues decrease and shorten, respectively, in the early stages of training, when in truth, particularly with regular flexibility training, they increase. These changes help improve range of motion and can prepare the tissues to handle higher loads without inducing injury.

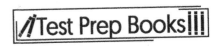

5. C: Having an on-hand model of the planned art activity that is fully completed offers a variety of benefits. It helps give the student a tangible frame of reference from which they can work for the activity. In this way, it can build excitement and interest in the activity because it gives students a concrete representation of what they can create. When the teacher goes through the process of making a model of the finished product, it allows them to figure out how much time is needed for the activity and to note any difficult steps that might require additional explanation. Because the model represents a finished product, it does not readily demonstrate the individual steps of the activity; therefore, Choice C is not a primary function of a completed model.

6. B: Art activities can be either explicit, implicit, or both. For example, an art activity that is explicitly designed may help students understand the biography and work of a particular artist, such as in the activity described in the question. To add an implicit component to the activity, teachers can educate students about the history of the period during which the artist worked and the social world that the artist lived in. Choices C and D are not defined types of art activities. The balance and emphasis are concepts of artwork, which can be explored through various art activities, either in isolation or in combination with other concepts like unity (the focus of the teacher's lesson in the question), texture, rhythm, color, movement, and contrast.

7. A: The performance sequence of art has five parts: selecting, analyzing, interpreting, rehearsing/evaluating/refining, and presenting. In the analyzing stage, the performer does research on the chosen piece, so that he or she can learn as much as possible about it. Doing so can enable the artist to become more immersed in the work, which can further enhance the interpretation. Choice B describes the rehearsing/evaluating/refining stage. This is also the stage where the artist hones their skills and perfects the piece for its eventual performance. Choices C and D both describe the interpreting stage, which follows the analyzing stage.

8. D: While formative, summative, and formal evaluations all have merit in the learning process, they are typically not the ideal assessments for art education at the early elementary levels. Art is highly subjective, and thus these more objective evaluations lack the same utility they carry for subjects like math or history. One of the primary objectives of art education for young children is to develop their sense of how to assess, interpret, and respond to art. The artistic process, particularly the aspects revolving around artistic interpretation and responding to art, can aid deep learning, including learning about society, the world, and oneself. Self-assessment, or the process of evaluating one's own art, is an effective means by which young students can learn to better assess art created by others.

9. B: Nutrition recommendations for children include replacing higher fat foods with lower-fat alternatives, reducing the intake of sugary beverages, and replacing more refined foods like applesauce with foods in their natural form, such as a fresh, whole apple. Answer Choice B is incorrect because fiber is beneficial in the diet because it increases the feeling of satiety, which can lower caloric intake, and fiber can also reduce LDL cholesterol by binding to it and helping the body excrete it. Lower fiber refined grains have the bran stripped away and should be replaced by higher fiber options.

10. A: The optimal physical education curriculum for five- to six-year-old children should focus on movement for enjoyment. Children at this age are motivated by fun and playing and will be active if it is fun. They are not necessarily ready to focus on sports-specific skills requiring significant hand-eye coordination. They do best with moderate- and high-intensity activities with adequate rest.

11. C: When teaching new skills, especially to toddlers and young children, instructions lasting longer than twenty seconds or containing more than just a couple of steps or cues will lead students to losing interest or getting overwhelmed. It is typically advantageous to have very short instructional periods interspersed between longer breaks to play and try out the introduced skills. Reading material is likely not appropriate for this age group, many of whom do not yet know how to read.

12. C: Following safety procedures like wearing a seatbelt is the best choice. Experts recommend that children get over nine hours of sleep per night. Also, children should brush their teeth after every meal, not just before bed. Finally, it is important for children to learn how to express their emotions in a healthy way and let a trusted adult know if they are struggling with persistent feelings of sadness or anxiety.

13. D: Teachers should educate students on the importance of visiting doctors for routine medical care and check-ups (every six months or so); consistent feelings of sadness, anxiety, loneliness, and stress; and pains or aches that do not go away. Research has found that even at the preschool level, talking about the importance of visiting the doctor can positively impact health behaviors in adulthood.

14. A: Family influences on health behaviors include health insurance status, safety and injury prevention education and care, nutritional meal planning and diet composition, social dynamics and stress, and the family's culture around leisure time.

15. C: Gross motor skills are mastered before fine motor skills. Students begin developing basic motor skills like walking, balancing, and manipulating objects from a very early age. They master gross motor skills before they move on to fine motor skills. Sports skills are not learned more readily than generalized body movements, because sports skills require more fine motor skills, complex motions, and cognitive abilities (e.g. locating and aiming for targets). Also, what looks like play actually helps children develop movement patterns and abilities.

16. B: The general categories of basic movement skills include locomotor skills like walking, running, and skipping; non-locomotor skills such as squatting and twisting; and manipulative skills such as throwing and catching.

17. A: In a kindergarten classroom, hitting targets is not an appropriate focus for physical education because children at this age have not mastered the fine motor abilities and complex skills to aim and hit targets. Hitting targets is more appropriate for fifth grade students. In kindergarten, activities should focus on foundational skills such as weight transfer, balance, following objects with the eyes, and basic skills like jumping and skipping.

18. D: Of the listed age groups, nine- to twelve-year-old students are likely to be more interested in health-based benefits of physical activity than younger children, who are primarily interested in movement for fun and enjoyment. As children mature, they gain a deeper understanding of physiology and healthy lifestyle choices and they become more interested in the health benefits of exercise.

19. A: Educators should focus curricular activities on the major categories of arts: music, dance, theater, and visual arts (painting, drawing, sculpture, pottery, etc.).

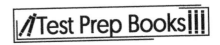

20. C: The youngest children tend to create art with a focus on the scientific and sensory aspects of the project rather than artistic creativity, self-expression, or conveying a narrative or story. They enjoy art more as a means to which explore the textures they make (for example, making texture rubbings with crayon on paper), the contrast of colors they use, and the various shapes they make as they move the drawing utensil around (although they are not making shapes for symbolic reasons, they are simply enjoying and exploring what they make when they use the supplies).

21. D: Children should experiment with a variety of methods and materials to create art. Educators should provide children with a wide range of materials like finger paint, glitter, and felt so that children experiment with different textures. *A* is not the best answer because art education should expose students to the historical and cultural context of art beyond that of their everyday experiences. Students can learn about famous artists and art history, but those lessons can be incorporated into creative coursework; they are not a prerequisite for student experimentation.

22. D: Have students accompany the music with simple instruments like tambourines. Students can easily beat along to simple songs using rhythmic instruments like tambourines, maracas, or small drums. Young children enjoy moving around more than sitting and focusing on one thing for an extended time, so learning rhythm through actions like shaking rhythmic instruments or stomping and clapping is more effective for students at this age. Also, *C* is not the best answer because many young children are not yet strong readers.

23. D: Theater-in-education (TIE) is performed by teachers and students using curriculum material or social issues. Participants take on roles, which enable them to explore and problem-solve in a flexible structure, yet in an educational theatrical way. In Readers' Theater, readers perform a dramatic presentation sitting on stools reading the lines typically from children's literature, enabling performance opportunities in the absence of elaborate staging or script memorization. Puppetry can be used for creative drama with either simple puppets and stages made of bags, cardboard, socks, or more elaborate, artistic materials.

24. A: The main skills in theatrical arts for children include literary (reading and writing the script and memorizing lines), technical (includes the staging, lighting, sound effects, etc.), and performance elements (such as the set design and the musical score). Staging is part of the technical elements.

25. D: A three- to four-year-old child's drawing usually emphasizes his or her color choices. At this young age, children typically do not use art for self-expression, symbolism, or realistic figural accuracy. These are all artistic skills that students develop when they are older. Young students tend to focus on sensory exploration involving color, shape, and texture.

26. B: Perspective is a technique used to make flat objects look as though they have depth. Balance is using size, position, color, shape and lighting in the artwork so that all of the elements are equally present with no particular component overpowering. Abstraction is unrealistic artwork that typically has geometric lines or patterns.

27. A: Art has personal (self-expression, gratification, narrative functions), social (collective meaning for a group of people such as symbolic art honoring a god or political art), and physical functions (such as a pottery mug for tea) that often overlap in a project. Religious functions fall under the realm of social functions.

28. B: Harmony is a principle in art that highlights the similarities in separate but related parts of a composition to show how different things can actually be similar and blend together. Balance is positioning objects or using size, color, shape and lighting in a way that makes all of the elements equally present. Contrast is exemplifying differences between two unlike things such as loud and soft music, major and minor tones, fast and slow dancing movements, and light and dark colors.

29. C: Breakfast helps students do well on tests. Choice *A* is incorrect; on the contrary, breakfast is *integral* to school attendance. Choice *B* is incorrect; eating a sufficient amount of nutrition in the morning helps students stay focused and awake. Choice *D* is incorrect because the link between breakfast and student academic achievement is that breakfast aids in academic achievement.

30. A: Educators are incorporating art into the curriculum to develop students' fine motor skills and facilitate metacognition and abstract thinking. Though there are many career opportunities for artists, Choice *B*, this is not cited as a driver for its incorporation into current curriculum. Exposing students to other cultures, Choice *C*, may be a second order consequence of art curriculum, though not a driver. Finally, Choice *D* is incorrect. Art offers as much, if not more, freedom and creativity than it does discipline and structure.

31. C: Educators are encouraged to get clear on the overriding concept or idea that is embedded in the lesson. Developing a model project, Choice *A*, has value because it gives students an example of the finished expectations. Yet, it is not the first order of business when designing a lesson for children. Establishing learning objectives, Choice *B*, is imperative, but it is not the first step when developing an art activity. Choice *D*, offering praise and constructive criticism, should happen after the activity is done, not before.

32. B: There is a four-step process to making art that includes imagining, planning, making and presenting. The third step, *making*, also includes *evaluating* and *refining*, both of which aren't mentioned in the question. Choices *A*, *C*, and *D* may be synonymous to the process of creating, but they are not listed specifically in the guide.

33. D: Assessment is a word that is not a part of the four-part process reviewed in the literature. Choice *A*, Selection, is the process where the person viewing the art chooses the type of art that they want to experience. Choice *B*, Analysis, is the process where the viewer assesses or makes meaning or judgments about the work, what they liked about it, what they did not like about it. Choice *C*, Evaluation, is where the consumer is capable of expressing a judgment about the quality of the work/performance. Interpretation is the fourth part, which involves the process of formulating a judgment or interpretation about the work, in part or whole.

34. B: A line can be best looked at as the outline of a three-dimensional object, the edge of a two-dimensional object, and the path of a moving point as found in the literature. In Choice *A*, art can be described as a framework that can be used to provoke emotions and paint mental pictures for the viewers. However, the best answer is *B* when it comes to how a line is looked at or viewed. Choice *C* is incorrect; "three-dimensional object" should replace "*two*-dimensional object;" "the edge of a two-dimensional object" should replace "the *side* of a *three*-dimensional object;" and "the path of a moving point" should replace "the path of a *static* point." Although Choice *D* is not absolutely incorrect, as a line could be viewed as representing the continuation of time, it is not the best answer for this question.

35. A: The best way to create rhythm in visual art is via repeating visual movement. Manipulating lines and figures, Choice *B*, can effectively create the appearance of rhythm in visual art; yet, repetition needs to be included into the process. Illusion, Choice *C*, is created in this form of artistic impression, but it is an effect of the process rather than the means to achieve it. Choice *D*, none of the above, is incorrect.

36. C: Green is not a primary color. The three primary colors are Choices *A*, *B*, and *D*: yellow, blue, and red.

37. C: Colors, theme, pattern, and texture help an artist create unity in their work. Intention, Choice *A*, can be the starting point, but to actually achieve unity, the answers in Choice *C* must be applied. Choice *B*, shape, focus, and repetition, are not wholly relevant to the answer. Choice *D* is incorrect; the reader's perception can help to create unity after the fact, but the use of colors, theme, pattern, and texture are the best answer regarding creating the artwork.

38. D: Choice *A*, large vs. small shapes, Choice *B*, rough vs. smooth surfaces, and Choice *C*, black vs. white are all examples of the principle of contrast found in art. Thus, Choice *D* is the correct answer.

39. B: The speed of music is its tempo. Pitch, Choice *A*, is a frequency of sound in something like a musical note. Rhythm, Choice *C*, refers to the number of beats per measure and the differences between note lengths that generate patterns. Choice *D*, range, is the scope of notes that a voice or instrument can produce.

40. D: Exercise often leads to psychological benefits like relief of stress, better self-concept, and improved capability to handle stressors.

41. C: Non-locomotor skills do not require much movement. Locomotor skills (Choice *A*) move an individual from one point to another. Manipulative skills (Choice *B*) are used to propel or receive an object. And rhythmic skills (Choice *D*) include responding and moving with the beat, tempo, or pitch of music.

42. C: Punitive discipline measures can actually stunt any kind of educational growth. Choices *A* (activity modification), *B* (multiactivity designs), and *D* (differentiated forms of grouping) are all best practices in physical education.

43. D: Choices *A* (societal influences), *B* (psychological influences), and *C* (cultural influences) all affect a student's development and fitness.

44. A: Responding to your body with rhythm or using facial expressions to communicate is the definition of *expressive movement*. Choice *B* (clothing and accessories worn by actors to portray a character), Choice *C* (any articles used as part of a production), and Choice *D* (theatrical equipment, such as backdrops and platforms) are not examples of expressive movement.

45. B: Closed lines of communication can shut students and parents out. Choices *A* (consistent positive reinforcement), *C* (encouraging active listening), and *D* (practicing empathetic listening) can all help foster healthy relationships with students and parents.

46. B: Anorexia nervosa is characterized by a persistent quest for a thin body. Bulimia nervosa (Choice *A*) is characterized by repeated bouts of consuming and/or purging large amounts of food. Scoliosis (Choice *C*) is a disorder that affects a person's spine. Autism spectrum disorder (Choice *D*) is the name given to a range of disorders that affect a person's ability to communicate and/or interact with others.

47. A: Bulimia nervosa is characterized by repeated bouts of consuming and/or purging large amounts of food. Anorexia nervosa (Choice *B*) is characterized by a persistent quest for a thin body. Scoliosis (Choice *C*) is a disorder that affects a person's spine. Autism spectrum disorder (Choice *D*) is the name given to a range of disorders that affect a person's ability to communicate and/or interact with others.

48. D: There are several types of neglect, including medical neglect (Choice *A*), emotional neglect (Choice *B*), and educational neglect (Choice *C*).

49. A: Neglect is a subtle form of child abuse. Abuse does not have to be violent, so Choice *B* is incorrect. Abuse and neglect can be both physical and mental, so Choice *C* and Choice *D* are incorrect.

50. A: Bloody cysts in the liver is just one example of the negative effects of anabolic steroid use. Anabolic steroid use also increases muscle mass, so Choice *B*—decrease in muscle mass—is incorrect. Steroid use also causes dysfunctional reproduction and weakens one's heart, making both Choice *C* and Choice *D* false statements.

Dear TExES Core Subjects EC-6 Test Taker,

We would like to start by thanking you for purchasing this study guide for your exam. We hope that we exceeded your expectations.

Our goal in creating this study guide was to cover all of the topics that you will see on the test. We also strove to make our practice questions as similar as possible to what you will encounter on test day. With that being said, if you found something that you feel was not up to your standards, please send us an email and let us know.

We have study guides in a wide variety of fields. If you're interested in one, try searching for it on Amazon or send us an email.

Thanks Again and Happy Testing!
Product Development Team
info@studyguideteam.com

FREE Test Taking Tips DVD Offer

To help us better serve you, we have developed a Test Taking Tips DVD that we would like to give you for FREE. **This DVD covers world-class test taking tips that you can use to be even more successful when you are taking your test.**

All that we ask is that you email us your feedback about your study guide. Please let us know what you thought about it – whether that is good, bad or indifferent.

To get your **FREE Test Taking Tips DVD**, email freedvd@studyguideteam.com with "FREE DVD" in the subject line and the following information in the body of the email:

  a. The title of your study guide.

  b. Your product rating on a scale of 1-5, with 5 being the highest rating.

  c. Your feedback about the study guide. What did you think of it?

  d. Your full name and shipping address to send your free DVD.

If you have any questions or concerns, please don't hesitate to contact us at freedvd@studyguideteam.com.

Thanks again!

Made in the USA
Coppell, TX
08 September 2021